JESUS WINS THE SERIES

Bill Medley

JESUS WINS THE SERIES

THE BOOK OF REVELATION
EXPLAINED AND EXPLORED

VOLUME 2

Bill Medley

WHINE PRESS

Unless otherwise indicated, Scripture taken from the Holy Bible, NEW INTERNATIONAL VERSION®, NIV® Copyright © 1973, 1978, 1984, 2011 by Biblica, Inc.® Used by permission. All rights reserved worldwide.

© 2020 Bill Medley

ISBN 978-0-6484159-1-6

All rights reserved. No part of this publication may be reproduced, stored in a retrieval system, or transmitted, in any form, by any means, electronic, mechanical, photocopying, recording or otherwise without the prior permission of the publisher.

Cover Design by Andrew Clarke Studios

Published by Whine Press, Melbourne, Australia

Printed by Ingram Spark, Melbourne, Australia

Reprinted 2023

ACKNOWLEDGEMENTS

Thanks to those who took part in proof reading. Special thanks to Jayni Manners for countless hours of proof reading, corrections and transposing the sermons into text, but also for providing the inspiration to tackle this work in the first place.

To my beloved Diana
my best friend always

Contents

1.	The Temple is Measured	(Revelation 11:1)	11
2.	The Outer Court Trampled	(Revelation 11:2)	23
3.	The Two Witnesses	(Revelation 11:3-4)	33
4.	The Witnesses' Power	(Revelation 11:5-6)	43
5.	Death of the Witnesses	(Revelation 11:7-10)	53
6.	The Witnesses Rise	(Revelation 11:11-14)	63
7.	The Time Machine	(Revelation 11:15-17)	73
8.	The Answer to Evil	(Revelation 11:18-19)	83
9.	The Woman	(Revelation 12:1-6pt.1)	95
10.	The Dragon	(Revelation 12:1-6pt.2)	105
11.	War in Heaven	(Revelation 12:7-8)	115
12.	Triumph Over the Accuser	(Revelation 12:9-11)	125
13.	The Fury of the Dragon	(Revelation 12:12-14)	135
14.	The Deceitful Mouth	(Revelation 12:15-17)	147
15.	The Beast	(Revelation 13:1-2)	157
16.	The Beast that Rises	(Revelation 13:3-4)	167
17.	The Beast is Worshiped	(Revelation 13:5-10)	175
18.	The Second Beast	(Revelation 13:11-14)	187
19.	The Mark of the Beast	(Revelation 13:15-17)	199
20.	666	(Revelation 13:18)	211
21.	The Lamb with 144,000	(Revelation 14:1)	221
22.	They did not Defile Themselves	(Revelation 14:2-5)	233
23.	Babylon	(Revelation 14:6-10)	243
24.	Day and Night Forever	(Revelation 14:11-13)	253
25.	Blood up to the Horses' Bridles	(Revelation 14:14-20)	263
26.	The Song	(Revelation 15:1-3a)	273
27.	Why They are Singing	(Revelation 15:3b-4)	283
28.	The Ten Commandments	(Revelation 15:5-8)	291
29.	The First Two Bowls	(Revelation 16:1-3)	301
30.	The Third and Fourth Bowls	(Revelation 16:4-9)	311
31.	The Fifth Bowl	(Revelation 16:10-11)	321
32.	The Sixth Bowl	(Revelation 16:12-14)	331
33.	Like a Thief	(Revelation 16:15)	341
34.	Armageddon	(Revelation 16:16)	353
35.	The Seventh Bowl	(Revelation 16:17-21)	363

1
The Temple is Measured
(Revelation 11:1)

At the end of Volume 1, Rev. 10 left us with the apostle John re-commissioned as a prophet. John is to proclaim the message to *many peoples, nations, languages and kings*. John couldn't do that until he had internalized the message, literally. He was told to eat the scroll! This image was straight out of Ezekiel, who had also been told to eat a scroll. Now something else parallels with Ezekiel. Get out the measuring rod and measure the temple. Is there a connection between the great temple plan detailed in Ezekiel 40-48 and the temple mentioned at the beginning of Rev. 11?

In fact, we've come to one of the most crucial verses in the book of Revelation. Depending how you understand 11:1, it will drive how you understand the entire book of Revelation and the end times unfolding. This is big. It's the future. It's all here.

> I was given a reed like a measuring rod and was told, 'Go and measure the temple of God and the altar, with its worshipers. But exclude the outer court; do not measure it, because it has been given to the Gentiles. They will trample on the holy city for 42 months' (11:1-2).

Which temple is being referred to here? The identity of this temple is one of the big issues in Christian circles. Is this temple referring to the hope of the rebuilding of the temple in Jerusalem at some future point? The hope that ethnic Israel will be restored to its former glory and that Jesus will reign from that temple in a future 1000-year millennial reign? It has been said the religious view of this temple has affected US foreign policy to Israel. I don't know if that can be proved, and no doubt US support for Israel has many factors and motives. But the theory is founded on the idea that if you believe the kingdom of God will be ushered in by ethnic Israel restored to their land and rebuilding their temple, then you have a vested interest in what is going on in Palestine now. That could be of significance if you are in a position of political influence. Either way, the issue of the temple being rebuilt is as hot as ever, at least in some Christian circles.

For the Futurist, surely here is the proof that this most popular view is intact! Here the temple is being measured out for that very purpose. The Jews are restored to their former glory in Jerusalem. The temple is rebuilt and the sacrificial system reintroduced, not as atoning sacrifices but as memorial sacrifices to remember what Jesus did. In fact, Jesus will oversee it all, because he will be there enthroned for his 1000-year, or millennial reign.

I hope I can approach this with some humility, as I don't believe we can judge faithfulness to the Bible from the different temple and millennial views, because, quite frankly, this is difficult! I can't rule out what God will do in the future. What concerns me most is how views on a difficult secondary issue like this become in some people's minds a test of whether or not you have a high view of Scripture. The gospel of Jesus should be the only test of our Christian fellowship with one another. Perhaps it's a good time to recall what the Lord told us and be careful not to judge one another in areas like this ...

> Accept the one whose faith is weak, without quarreling over disputable matters (Rom. 14:1).

Don't miss this. Maybe this is the most important thing I have to say in studying Revelation! There is such a thing as a *disputable matter* within the Christian church. So, if you don't like what I am saying, you have to at least accept me as the weaker brother on this disputable matter! But how do you know what is disputable (or secondary), and what is of first importance? Well, praise God for his word, because he has told us that too! Remember when we looked at the apostle Paul's list of things of *first importance* (1 Cor. 15:3-4), we noticed our view of the temple and the millennial reign was not on that list! So let's keep that perspective as we study this.

The writer of Revelation, the apostle John, would have immediately thought of Ezekiel 40-48 and the same measuring out of that temple when he was told, **I was given a reed like a measuring rod and was told, 'Go and measure the temple of**

God and the altar ...' But is this measuring signifying building surveying alone? Most of the different views on the temple agree that in some way the measuring signifies the security or protection of all within. 'Measuring off', as in setting apart the clean from the unclean. Inside is that which is measured by the Lord, protected and clean, but outside is unclean and unprotected, as it seems to be saying in 11:2 to '... **exclude the outer court; do not measure it, because it has been given to the Gentiles. They will trample on the holy city for 42 months.**' The outer court is *not* measured and is *not* under protection. It can be trampled on. It's like the measuring of the city later in Rev. 21, which concludes in 21:27 that *nothing unclean* can ever enter it. Same principle. Inside is measured, clean and protected. Outside not measured, unclean.

The Preterist is the one whose view is that all this occurred in the first century before the destruction of the temple in AD 70. So the Preterist sees this measuring as the measuring of the old Jerusalem temple before it was destroyed. This raises an immediate difficulty. The Jerusalem temple was not protected! The Preterist then responds that it's only the holy of holies that is protected, because the Greek word for 'temple' in 11:1 usually only refers to the holy of holies. But the trouble is that the Jerusalem temple was destroyed lock, stock and barrel, and none of it was protected! And if 11:1 was the first century temple, what are all those worshipers doing in the holy of holies where only the high priest can go?

So if this temple is not the old Jerusalem temple, then are these verses pointing to a future temple to be built in Jesus' millennial reign? Well they could be, but what have we learned so far in Revelation that should make us cautious? We were told right from the very first verse that Revelation was going to be revealed through signs and symbols.

> The revelation of Jesus Christ, which God gave him to show his servants what must soon take place. He <u>made it known</u> by sending his angel to his servant John, ... (1:1).

Remember the Greek word translated *made it known* is usually used in the context of *to make known by signs or symbols*. There is another common word in Greek that means *make known* that John chose not to use. Why? Because it wouldn't have conveyed that element of revealing by signs. The only other place where we have this combination of wording of *what must take place* and *made it known* is in Daniel 2, which is unashamedly filled with symbolic language.

Isn't this what we have seen in Revelation? Symbols! We are told up front to expect signs and symbols. Does anyone expect when the first four seals are opened that four literal horses will ride all over the earth to deliver death, plagues and famine? Does anyone expect that in heaven Jesus literally will look like a lamb slain with seven horns? Or with a sharp sword coming out of his mouth? We have seen throughout what we were told at the beginning. Symbolic language to describe literal truth just as Daniel did, because it's that kind of literature that we call apocalyptic.

Many people say Revelation should be taken literally unless otherwise stated, but if we took the genre of literature seriously, we should be looking at it as we do with the book of Daniel. We should expect symbolic language, images and numbers. Most importantly, we have been using the Bible to interpret those symbols rather than our imagination or the Internet or the newspaper. A slain lamb is not literal but a symbol of Jesus' perfect sacrifice as the Lamb of God.

There are more than a few hints that the vision of this temple measuring is pointing to something greater. Did you notice John the apostle was told to measure the temple along **with its worshipers**? In the original language, this is even clearer as it literally says John is to measure the temple, measure the altar and *measure the worshipers*. So this is already giving us a problem if we are talking about literal measuring. How do we measure worshipers? Are they tall enough, or too small? What does he mean by *measure the worshipers?* Why are they being measured along with the temple?

Are we getting a hint this vision is teaching us something more than just the architecture of a building when John is told to measure the worshipers? Is this heading the same way as that great city at the end of Rev. 21, where we are told specifically the heavenly building that is *measured* is *not* a literal building? In Rev. 21 we are told the temple in that city is God and Jesus, *not* a bricks and mortar building. And the names on the foundation of that building are from the 12 tribes of Israel and the 12 apostles. The people themselves in the presence of God make up the temple.

Weren't the first readers of Revelation prepared for this when Jesus told God's people in the letter to the church at Philadelphia *they* would become what? Pillars in the temple ... *The one who is victorious I will make <u>a pillar in the temple</u> of my God* ... (3:12). Did Jesus mean, 'I will make you to *stand next* to the pillars in the temple? Or lean on the pillars?' No. *You* are a pillar! You are part of the temple! Clearly it's symbolic. We noted when we looked at the letter to Philadelphia (vol. 1, ch. 9) that we don't expect to be literal pillars in heaven throughout eternity. 'Don't move for the next 50 billion years or otherwise the whole thing is gonna come down.' Rather, this is the way the temple is referred to in Revelation, which climaxes in Rev. 21 where it *specifically* says this Holy City, the New Jerusalem being *measured*, is not literal. We are told in no uncertain terms it is symbolic of the bride of Christ. Don't miss it! It doesn't say the people live *in* the New Jerusalem, but that they *are* the Holy City ...

> I saw the <u>Holy City, the new Jerusalem</u>, coming down out of heaven from God, prepared as <u>a bride</u> beautifully dressed for her husband (21:2).

We know who the bride is. Jesus' people. The Holy City, the New Jerusalem, *is* the bride! The Church. What does the Holy City, Jerusalem and the temple all point to? The presence of God!

> And I heard a loud voice from the throne saying, 'Look! God's <u>dwelling</u> place is now among the people, and he will dwell with them (21:3).

Dwelling in the original language is literally from the word *tabernacle*, the forerunner of the temple. So now the *tabernacling* of God is with men, and he will live with them. And then he identifies the people of God ...

> One of the seven angels who had the seven bowls full of the seven last plagues came and said to me, 'Come, I will <u>show you</u> the <u>bride</u>, the wife of the Lamb' (21:9).

Who is the bride? The church! Next verse tells us ...

> And he carried me away in the Spirit to a mountain great and high, and <u>showed me the Holy City</u>, <u>Jerusalem</u>, coming down out of heaven from God (21:10).

They are not *in* the Holy City, they *are* the Holy City. And note this

Holy City, the New Jerusalem, the people of God, *also* get measured!

> The angel who talked with me had a measuring rod of gold to <u>measure the city</u>, its gates and its walls … (21:15).

So the bride (the people of God) is measured. They *are the Holy City*. They *are the New Jerusalem*. The *tabernacling,* or the *templing* of God means *God with his people*. In 11:1 the worshipers are measured *with* the temple. So I am suggesting the temple fulfillment in Revelation *is* God with his people. Now, is this a new idea? And if so, is it only in Revelation? Let's have a look at some of the other places where the word of God speaks about this concept.

The deposit or foundation of God *dwelling* or *tabernacling* with his people began from the day of Pentecost and the outpouring of his Spirit. It's God coming down to dwell with his people in that new and special way. With Jesus offering the once for all sacrifice, the temple building has become redundant and now God is with his people by his Spirit. Look at what the NT says about the temple.

> Don't you know that <u>you</u> yourselves <u>are God's temple</u> and that <u>God's Spirit</u> dwells in your midst? (1 Cor. 3:16).

English fails us here. In Greek, as with most non-English languages, there is a distinction between *you* in the singular and plural. In modern English, there is no distinction. But in this verse the Greek *you* is not singular but plural. So he is not referring to individuals, but *you the church* are that temple. The gathered people are the temple. Why? Because Jesus' Spirit dwells in their midst. We've learnt that already in Revelation. He walks amongst his golden lampstands (his churches). In Matthew 18 he promises to be in our midst even if we are down to two or three elders, even in the difficulty of church discipline. He is there by his Spirit …

> What agreement is there between the temple of God and idols? <u>For we are the temple of the living God</u>. As God has said: 'I will live with them and walk among them, and I will be their God, and <u>they will be my people</u>' (2 Cor. 6:16).

Sound familiar? That is the end of Revelation (21:3-4). God's people are the temple. It's a theme in the NT …

> In him the whole building is joined together and rises to become <u>a holy temple</u> in the Lord. And in him you too are being built together to become a dwelling in which God lives by his Spirit (Eph. 2:21-22).

The context here is Jew and Gentile in Christ, joined to become a holy temple. What are the names of the foundations in the Holy City in Rev. 21? The 12 tribes of Israel and the 12 apostles joined together to become one holy temple. The NT deliberately uses the old covenant language of the OT temple to identify the fulfillment of God's people, Jew and Gentile in Christ, gathered with him …

> … you also, like living stones, are being built into <u>a spiritual house</u> to be a <u>holy priesthood</u>, offering <u>spiritual sacrifices</u> acceptable to God through Jesus Christ (1 Pet. 2:5).

So Peter says the offerings of this temple are spiritual, not literal sacrifices, because Christ has been sacrificed. As Hebrews says, we offer a sacrifice of praise for that which Christ has already done.

But isn't Ezekiel's temple in the OT a physical temple that is pointing to this temple in Rev. 11? Yes, Ezekiel's temple is pointing to *this* temple in Revelation. Read about Ezekiel's temple in Ezekiel 37:26-28 and 43:1-12 and notice the purpose of the temple is to teach about the presence of God in perfect worship, perfect sacrifices and the perfect presence of God — with his people *forever* (Ezek. 43:7). You will also see his presence is not for just 1000 years but forever! How will God's relationship and presence in this temple be forever? In the gospel of Jesus Christ! The temple to the OT believer represented the presence of God. God with us. Now we know Jesus is Immanuel, God with us. Jesus is the true and final temple to which all other temples/tabernacles were pointing. Wasn't that a theme of John from his gospel?

> The Word became flesh and made his dwelling among us (John 1:14).

Made his dwelling is literally *he tabernacled amongst us*. The forerunner for the temple, the tabernacle, is fulfilled in Jesus in the midst of his people. Isn't this the temple theology that Jesus gave us himself?

> Jesus answered them, 'Destroy this temple, and I will raise it again in three days.' They replied, 'It has taken forty-six years to build this temple, and you are going to raise it in three days?' But the temple he had spoken of was his body (John 2:19-21).

Jesus is the true temple! The fulfillment! So John is told, *Go and measure the temple of God and the altar, with its worshipers* (11:1). John has to measure the worshipers *and* the *altar* in the temple, which points to the ultimate altar, Christ and his cross. How did all this happen? What happened when Jesus died on the cross? The curtain of *the temple* was torn in two. The access into God's presence is no longer through the temple building but through Jesus! The true temple! Allowing the worshipers into God's presence!

I like to ask Jewish people why they don't offer sacrifices anymore. After all, it's in the Torah! The usual answer is, 'We don't have a temple'. 'Why not?' I ask. 'It was destroyed.' 'When?' 'AD 70.' 'Oh, you mean right within the generation that Jesus predicted the temple would come down. Jesus, who also predicted that *he* was the ransom, the true sacrifice and the true temple! You mean that time?' And it just happens from within a generation of Jesus' sacrifice there is no more physical temple. No more opportunity to offer the old sacrifices. The true temple has come!

If you want to know what Revelation is all about, it's like all of the Bible, it's *revealing Jesus! He* is the temple along with his people in his presence. This is the goal and eternal destination for those who love God. To be with God. This is the fulfillment of all things to which the OT was pointing, including the temple. It is *all* about Jesus.

How do you understand the OT including the temple? Jesus said how slow the disciples were to understand all that was written about him in the Law and Prophets. The OT was all about Jesus! The temple was about Jesus!

Now if everything in the OT was pointing towards Jesus, would that include Ezekiel's temple? I admit when I first read Ezekiel with its temple design and all that detail, I certainly could understand how someone would think it has to be built at some future point. But then think about when you first read Leviticus, with all its endless kinds of sacrifices — chapter after chapter. Are you really telling me that every one of those numerous sacrifices from every angle, every type, covering every detail of sin, are all pointing to Jesus? *All* that detail, just to point to Jesus? Absolutely! All the promises of God are 'yes' and 'Amen' in Jesus. All of the OT was pointing to him. Think about that in relation to Ezekiel's temple. Could all that detail really just be pointing to Jesus? We need to look at it more closely.

A detailed look at the dimensions of Ezekiel's temple from those who have tried to reconstruct its design show it's neither logical nor complete if you tried to literally build it. Despite this, the view that this is the temple from which Jesus will reign in a 1000-year millennial reign before the final judgment is very popular. This also includes the idea that the sacrificial system will be reintroduced (albeit memorial sacrifices, rather than atoning). But I must admit if nothing else, I find it really hard to accept the idea of sacrifices being reintroduced, memorial or otherwise. Surely that is offensive to the finished work of the cross. Jesus already gave us a memorial meal — the Lord's Supper. He said he would not eat it again until the new heaven and new earth. But to reintroduce sacrifices is also offensive to the writer to the Hebrews (10:1-12). Re-read the Hebrews letter! Hebrews is so big on *not* going back to the shadows of sacrifices. Why? The fullness of Christ's sacrifice *once for all* has come. What does *once* for all mean? The whole argument of the Hebrews writer is you can't go back to the OT ways. Jesus was sacrificed once for all!

In fairness, some Futurist scholars say the future sacrifices of the temple are not literal but symbolic. But that is exactly what I am saying! If we have opened the door to symbolic teaching in Ezekiel's temple sacrifices because they point to Jesus, why not all of it pointing to Jesus!

I sympathize with those who have read Ezekiel 40-48 and wonder if it's meant to be built. But is it possible we are just like the disciples when Jesus had to rebuke them for being slow to understand that the OT was *all* about him? We just haven't gone deep enough on the question of 'What is the Bible pointing to?' The OT points to Christ. All those detailed sacrifices in Leviticus; fulfilled in Christ. And Ezekiel's temple sacrifices? Fulfilled in Christ. Ezekiel's detailed description of the perfection of ritual worship? Fulfilled in Christ. Perfect temple where we enjoy God's presence. Fulfilled in Christ.
What did Ezekiel's temple mean to the readers in his day? It epitomized perfect worship, perfectly offered sacrifices *and* the perfect presence of God. That is how they understood all of that in shadows. But these are the very things now fulfilled in Christ, the once for all sacrifice, dwelling with his people in perfect worship.
To what then, is the measuring of the temple in 11:1 pointing us? The consummation of all things in Rev. 21! Jesus and his people secured and together forever. But the message of 11:1 is that for those of us still going through the tribulation, though you are not in

the final consummation yet, you are not forgotten. You are marked out. Though you are not at the end, you are measured as part of the temple of God already! So hold on. You *will* make it through the tribulation. Why? You have been *measured* and his presence is with you through it all and taking you on to the finality in Rev. 21 where Jesus (with his people) is the temple.

But some might say, 'I prefer to take the word of God literally and not spiritualize Revelation.' But we are not totally spiritualizing Ezekiel's prophetic temple or this temple in Rev. 11. It does have a physical fulfillment. Don't miss it. The physical fulfillment will be fully brought to light in Rev. 21-22 with the new heaven and the new earth, literally and physically, Jesus and the people of God! *They* are the New Jerusalem and the temple! Literal and physical!

In Hebrews 8:4 the heavenly sanctuary is the true tabernacle, the earthly is just a copy. It's ironic because that's just the opposite of the popular interpretation of Revelation today. Don't miss this. Hebrews says the literal temple in Jerusalem is *figurative* or symbolic of the *true* temple and the true temple is *not* a physical building, but the heavenly one above.

As someone who didn't grow up in the church, when I became a Christian I read the Bible through many times before I had even heard of the different millennial views, so without any preconceived ideas I never once saw any idea in the gospels or in the letters of Paul that the OT temple would be rebuilt in Jerusalem. Rather, I did see warnings of the destruction of the earthly temple, but not it's rebuilding. I saw warnings for the NT believer not to go back to the old shadows to their great detriment. It warned them that the temple has served its purpose. Why? Jesus is here! Jesus said it!

> I tell you that <u>something greater</u> than the temple is here (Matt. 12:6).

Everything is fulfilled in him! The theology of the temple is not about sacred architecture. It's about our destination. But if you are going through the tribulation, how can you know you will make it? Well, if you are a believer, you have been *measured* as part of the temple itself. It's God's guarantee.

Remember, Rev. 11 is an interlude before the final (seventh) trumpet to give believers the assurance that while they are God's people on earth going through the tribulation, God measures them as part of his temple. Just as the interlude in Rev. 7 (between the sixth and seventh seal), assured God's people going through the tribulation of their protection and being joined to Israel by the seal of the Holy Spirit; now believers in the tribulation are again assured they are one with God's chosen in the most profound Israelite way of all — the temple! Pillars in God's temple. They are the New Jerusalem and God will keep them through tribulation. How do they know? He is *measuring* them! The temple. His presence. Tabernacling with them. What is your hope for the future triumph of Jesus? An earthly victory and building of a temple? Or is it to be in the very presence of Jesus?

Depending on your view, when you look at 11:1 you are either seeing the surveying of building architecture or the great assurance that if you are a believer, the Lord has marked you out, measured you to keep you through the tribulation and be with him forever.

Study Questions

1. How could temple theology possibly have an influence on politics?

2. Explain what 'measuring' signifies in this text?

3. How does the Preterist understand this text and what difficulties might it have for that view?

4. What reasons are there for thinking this temple could be symbolic?

5. What reasons are there elsewhere in the NT for thinking this temple is symbolic?

6. What are three things the first readers of Ezekiel would have seen that temple as representing?

7. Give a reason from Leviticus as to why Ezekiel's temple (with all its great detail) is not to be built in the future.

8. Why would a fully functioning temple in the OT tradition work against NT teaching?

9. What is the primary teaching of this temple (11:1) to its first readers?

2
The Outer Court Trampled
(Revelation 11:2)

I acknowledge Christians have different views on this temple, but I wonder if this is what we need more than ever today? Understanding our goal. What is your hope in the end? What is your hope for Jewish believers in Jesus? Is your goal a temple of bricks and mortar? Or is it Jesus himself, and being with him face to face and with his people? The gospel is about the return to the Garden of Eden, God walking with his people again, rather than temple buildings. The temple was a shadow pointing to the way into God's presence. The substance was all about being with Jesus!

Today people get sidetracked on all sorts of issues, but the Bible can all be summed up like this, *everything* is all about Jesus! It's all pointing to him, including the temple. But now we are going to find out more about what the measuring of this temple means ...

> But exclude the <u>outer court</u>; do not measure it, because it has been given to the Gentiles. They will trample on the <u>holy city</u> for 42 months (11:2).

Remember, we are explicitly told what the Holy City is in 3:12 and 21:2, 9, 10. The Holy City is the bride of Christ. That is, the church *is* the Holy City. So this *outer court* is still a court of the temple, but it's *not* measured. Not all who claim to be part of the temple are true believers. In fact, the outer court is *trampling on the true church*, the Holy City. The **Gentiles** are *unbelievers*, as Rev. 11 continues using old covenant language to describe new covenant things. But why are unbelievers included as the outer court? Why are they part of the temple at all? Where could we see something like this?

Have a look at history! History, which may have previously confused you until now, that is, until Revelation explains it to you. Unbelievers have always had a strong presence in the outward visible church, and even great control. The outer court is actually the wider area of the temple. From there, the larger portion of the visible part of the temple, the unbelievers trample on the true church. We saw earlier in Revelation in the letters to the churches how many references there were to Satan infiltrating the church! False teachers in the church! Letting false teaching itself in the church! Warning after warning. And these people are visible in the church, but they are in the outer court. They don't really know the Lord, they are not measured, and they trample on the church. It's one of Satan's main ploys.

These people only get to the outer court. The history of the church is fascinating when you think of the powerbrokers. Unbelievers so often dominate it! Until about AD 300 there was great persecution against the church. But when the Roman Emperor Constantine stopped the persecution and granted legality to Christianity you would think Satan was thwarted in his attempt to eradicate the church, but instead he just came inside. The outer pagan society brought all kinds of pagan practices into the church, such as statues and superstition. How unchristian to have idols, images of Mary and Jesus in the church! But there they were. And on through the Middle Ages, centuries of darkness (about 1000 years), unbelievers in powerful positions calling the shots, even at the head of the church! The Crusades! Done in the name of Christ! The Bible forbidden! In the church! It remained prohibited for centuries. Praise God for the Reformation. But then …

What about the centuries of Protestant liberalism? Dominating. Theologians of the church who don't believe the Bible! Why do they bother calling themselves Christian then? It's almost as though someone is enticing them … *to trample on the true church.*

I find it embarrassing trying to explain to a new believer they shouldn't just go to any church. They should check them out first. But wait a minute the new believer says. Why can't I just go to any church? They are all Christian, aren't they? Well … they may not all believe the Bible. What! A church that doesn't believe the Bible? What is this Christianity? It's confusing to people, the idea that even the wider outer court, even the visible church may be filled with unbelievers in power positions. It's an embarrassment to the true church. But we should not be surprised. We should be reading Revelation. In fact, we should have been listening to Jesus warning us in the gospels about wolves in sheep's clothing. They are in the church! Sheep's clothing. But Rev. 11 is taking us a whole step further. It's wider than just a minority. It's the whole outer court!

The letters of Paul rebuke and warn what can happen inside the church with false teachers. And sure enough, much of what we see today is a Christ-less church. His word is not opened or is not believed. Liberalism. People are looking for a prosperity gospel, or for Jesus to fix-up their earthly woes, rather than finding their all in Christ himself.

So what are we going to do with this? Look at the mess! Why do you even bother with the church? Well, if you reject the church you are joining the hypocrites in the outer court who are not measured, who are trampling on the true church of Jesus. Jesus told his true followers not to give up on his church. He wouldn't himself. He said the gates of hell wouldn't prevail against his church. And if you are a true believer, you will not give up on his church either, lest you be one of those trampling on the church of Jesus by rejecting her. That is the message here. Don't be thrown by the state of the church — it has been predicted and is what 11:2 is teaching. The outer court is not measured. Many in the visible church are not part of the true church.

What's frustrating to us is when we hear the media exposing, for instance, Roman Catholic priests with all the pedophilia. The tragedy for the victims and their families is that it is all done in the name of the church. The headlines read ... 'The church does evil.' 'The church *covers up* the evil!' It's denigrating the name of Jesus. But it's not the true church. It's the outer court trampling on the Holy City, the true bride. People ask, 'Why would a priest in the name of Jesus do that?' Answer: Because they are unbelievers! Not measured. Outer court! Trampling on the church!

Of course pedophiles are predators who will try to work their way into any organization with children. So whether you are a Boy Scout group, a school, or a church, we are all targets for these predators. That doesn't mean the organization itself is inherently wrong. But there are anti-Christian doctrines in the RC church which have directly contributed to the abuses. Why is no one saying it plainly? Because it doesn't make for good copy to read that the reason for the evils is because the church rejects Jesus and the Bible as its sole authority. Why does the RC leadership fail to report and publicly expose and excommunicate pedophile priests? Because they reject the Scriptures as the only authority when it says ... *Publicly expose sinful elders* (1 Tim. 5:20) and *expel the wicked person from among you!* (1 Cor. 5:13). A church following God's word publicly deals with ministers caught in sexual immorality in what I call 'instant turf'. Instantly stood down, never to return to ministry. Can they be forgiven? Of course. All who are truly repentant and trust in Christ are forgiven. But they no longer *qualify for leadership* in the church according to 1 Timothy 3:1-7. And why the unnatural restriction of celibacy for RC priests? Again, because of a rejection of the Bible as supreme authority, which tells them the apostles were married. As the apostle Paul said ...

> Don't we have the right to take a <u>believing wife</u> along with us, as do the other apostles and the Lord's brothers and Cephas? (1 Cor. 9:5).

Cephas is Peter's name in Aramaic, so Peter, the so-called first Pope, was married! The celibacy of priests was only introduced as a man-made rule in AD 1079. A thousand years after the apostles. Where did it come from? Certainly not from the Bible ...

> The Spirit clearly says that in later times some will abandon the faith and follow deceiving spirits and things taught by demons. Such teachings come through hypocritical liars, whose consciences have been seared as with a hot iron. They <u>forbid people to marry</u> and order them to abstain from <u>certain foods,</u> ... (1 Tim. 4:1-3).

No meat on Fridays? Where is that in the Bible? We don't have to pass judgment on individual members of the RC church. They may or may not be clinging to the hope of the cross *in spite* of the teachings of their church. But what Christianity is left in the *teachings* of the church itself? We haven't even begun on Protestant deviations from the authority of the Bible, but the reason I am focusing on the RC church at this point is because it relates to our text. People are often very confused (and even use this as an excuse to reject Christianity), the fact that the *largest* part of the visible 'church' has all these issues. And it is not just today but throughout history. What about the Middle Ages? The RCs *were* 'the church', despite all the attempts of pre-Reformation Protestants. How could the RCs have such size and influence and yet all these problems? How can you say

Christianity remains credible? Well, Revelation is revealing to us again, and 11:2 is telling us we should not be surprised! The outer court *is* the *larger* part. Not all in the visible church are measured! So we don't have to be surprised that RCs reject Christ's way to heaven through believing exclusively in what he has done on the cross to save us from our sins. The official RC doctrine of salvation is that you also have to do enough good works. What does Jesus say are the works we require when asked that very question?

> Then they asked him, 'What must we do to do the works God requires?' Jesus answered, 'The work of God is this: to believe in the one he has sent' (John 6:28-29).

Believe in Jesus and what he was 'sent' for—the cross. Of course, good works will always follow true belief. The RC theologians respond quoting James 2:24, that we are justified by works. But James is speaking against hypocrisy, that is, people who claim to have faith but don't live it. They are in the outer court as well! Of course faith should produce good works, but that is a whole different ballpark from saying we are saved by doing enough of those good works. That is as far apart as heaven and hell! Our good works can never save us. They can never wash away our sin or erase our past record. Jesus alone must save us! The true measuring is what the Lord is doing here in 11:1. The Lord measures his people with that altar, the cross! He preserves them. He saves them! How? By grace through faith!

> It is by grace you have been saved, through faith—and this is not from yourselves, it is the gift of God—not by works so that no one can boast (Eph. 2:8-9).

If you are a believer, you are measured out because of faith in what the Lord has done, not based on what you have done. And the outer court is not measured. **But exclude the outer court; do not measure it, because it has been given to the <u>Gentiles</u>. They will trample on the holy city for 42 months (11:2).** *Gentiles* (again, old covenant language for *unbelievers*) are not a part of true Israel. This old covenant language will continue to be used for the new covenant people all the way to Rev. 21, describing the church in Revelation as the New Jerusalem.

So *Gentiles* representing unbelievers is natural to John's first readers.

Now, what about the 42 months? It's actually a commonly used length of time in Revelation and elsewhere. Sometimes it's called 42 months, sometimes 3½ years, and other times 1,260 days (30 days in a month x 42 = 1,260). Other times it's called a time (1), times (2) and a half a time (3½ years). All of these add up to the same 42 months. The OT book of Daniel speaks about this length of time in 7:25 and 9:27 when speaking of a future tribulation. That period was 42 months (time, times and half a time).

One possibility is this 3½ years is one half of the great seven-year tribulation, where Christians are raptured out before or in the middle of that tribulation. This is the popular Futurist view (with rapture). This means all of Rev. 4-19 has no instruction or comfort or exhortation for the church of the last 2000 years, because these 42 months will happen in some future period *after* the church is no longer on earth. I've argued that this is against the stated purpose of Revelation, which is to build up Christians *during* the tribulation.

So what else could the 42 months represent? There seems to be a real connection between the 42 months and Elijah's prophesy of Judgment, especially in 11:6. There, 42 months would remind the apostle John of the prophesy of Elijah and the rain, or lack of. In Elijah's time, there were 3½ years of drought and tribulation between Elijah's first appearance and the showdown with Baal on Mount Carmel (1 Kin. 17-18, cf. Jas. 5:17). This was how long? 42 months! But then there were 42 encampments during the Exodus wilderness wanderings. We have seen many Exodus references as types in Rev. 1-6, as here again in 11:6-8. Rev. 12 will also equate this period with the time of the wilderness wandering. Same length of time, that is, 1,260 days, which is 42 months. But the real wilderness wanderings were a lot longer than 42 months. So what is going on here? In fact, these 42 months come up more than once as a period of trial and tribulation in the life of Israel. The most famous is during the Inter-Testamental period, in the second century BC (between OT and NT times). Remember Daniel's prophesy about the Seleucid King, Antiochus Epiphanes, who desecrated the Jewish temple. But the Jewish rebels fought back with under-manned guerrilla warfare headed up by Judas Maccabee. This warfare lasted from 167 BC to 164 BC. The Israelites won and rededicated the temple 3½ years after it was desecrated. That is the Jewish celebration of Hanukah, or Feast of Dedication (John 10:22). And the period of that tribulation? 3½ years or 42 months. But we move on in history.

The Preterist (pre-AD 70), points out that Nero's persecution of Christians was 3½ years from November AD 64 to June AD 68. That is another possible 3½ years. But it doesn't stop there. There is the great tribulation when the Roman armies surrounded Jerusalem (Luke 21:20-24). That lasted how long? About 3½ years. Many of these tribulations concern the temple. So which one of them is the prototype? Or is it all of them? Is 42 months apocalyptic (Revelation) language for a time of tribulation?

Ancient Jewish texts took 42 months or 3½ years as representing a time of trial for believers. That's not so speculative when we see that 42 months in Rev. 11 has another parallel in Rev. 12 (12:6, 14), where there is a consensus among the different views that the 42 months culminates when Jesus returns. But 12:5-6 will also show that the 1,260 days *begins* from the time of Jesus' ascension. That would make the 1,260 days the length of the church age! Long days, but if the 42 months (1260 days) is like the rest of the numbers we have continually seen in Revelation, that is, *symbolic*, what would 42 months symbolize to the first readers who know the Jewish history of the many trials of this time period? It would represent a time of trial or tribulation. The numbers are teaching symbolic truth. What truth?

This period of 42 months gets repeated over and over through Revelation, symbolizing a time of tribulation. It's the time of the Beast's authority (13:5-17) and the time the witnesses prophesy (11:3). I hope to show you later in Rev. 11, the witness is throughout the church age. It's the time the woman will be kept in the wilderness (12:6). It's the whole church age! All of these are 42 months or 3½ years. Remember seven is the number of completion. But this seven is cut short (in half). It's a suffering and persecution that is limited by God from going on to completion. What did Jesus say about cutting those days short for the sake of the elect? That means the elect must be in the tribulation! The people of God are persecuted (as we will see in 11:3), because of their witness also lasting 42 months (1260 days). How long do God's people witness? The whole church age. We are told in 11:8 the opposition from Sodom and Egypt is figurative. So if we are told explicitly in Revelation that the Holy City means the church, and explicitly that Sodom and Egypt are figurative, is it really such a leap for the first readers to believe the 42 months are also figurative? Especially if the 42 months is patterned after Israel's past 'tribulations'. After John eats the *sweet scroll* of the gospel in Rev. 10, then follows the bitterness of persecution in the church age. And being trampled on even by the people in the outer court who claim to be Christians!

We have looked at various periods of 42-month tribulations that serve as types for this time of wilderness or great tribulation, but perhaps one of the most important is the time of Jesus' ministry, which lasted about 3½ years. Jesus' '42 months' of ministry and trial is a microcosm of what he would leave with his church. He was a faithful witness through tribulation. *They persecuted me, they will persecute you* (John 15:20). *Whoever serves me must follow me* (John 12:26). And the church has followed Jesus through its own period (or 42 months) of tribulation. There is no time *during* the church age when there will be no tribulation, until the *end* of the church age. Why? We are following our Lord. Just as Jesus fasted 40 days in the wilderness to symbolize the 40 years the Israelites wandered in the wilderness, so too Jesus' ministry of 3½ years symbolizes the ministry and trial to which the church has been commissioned. Tribulation.

Today, some of the most vehement opposition to the church comes from so-called liberal Christianity. Trampled on by those who claim to be part of the church, but they are the outer court. And it makes our witness to the world so much more difficult when we hear, 'Why is your Christianity so hateful? We know Christian churches that go along with same-sex marriage, sexual freedom and sex outside marriage. They also go along with abortion and euthanasia. There should be a law against people like you.' And laws are introduced that threaten to reach further to trample on the teachings of Jesus, and there are even churches which sign up to support them!

So while this was written to bring encouragement to persevere before the seventh and final trumpet, it also serves as a warning when it says to **exclude** the outer court. The original Greek word translated *exclude* comes from the root word to *cast out!* It's a strong word. It was used when Jesus *cast out* demons! It's stronger than our English word *exclude*. It's the same word at Matt. 22:13 … *tie him hand and foot and <u>throw</u> him outside into the darkness.* There is no protection in the visible church if you are not truly in Christ, in the inner court.

You are already *cast out*, already an object of God's wrath. Jesus said if you don't believe, you are already condemned. You might profess to be a Christian. You might be part of the visible church (the outer court), but if you don't have the seal of the Spirit who has convicted you of your sin and your desperate need of the Savior Jesus; if you haven't submitted to him as both Lord and Savior; then there is no protection for you. You are not measured. If you hold on to your idols, addictions, and look to the things of this world to deliver you, it doesn't matter if you have made it into the outer court. Coming to the church building won't save you. If you are not measured, you are already literally *cast out*. Many assume they are okay. They went to church after all. They took the Lord's Supper. They ate and drank with him. Remember those words from Jesus …

> Then you will say, 'We ate and drank with you, and you taught in our streets.' But he will reply, 'I don't know you or where you come from. Away from me, all you evildoers! There will be weeping there, and gnashing of teeth, when you see Abraham, Isaac and Jacob and all the prophets in the kingdom of God, but you yourselves <u>thrown out</u>' (Luke 13:26-28).

When Jesus says *thrown out*, it's the same root word in Greek as *exclude* in 11:2. That is the picture. You are so close, and yet so far. You are there in the outer court—but cast out! The 42 months was too much for you. Too much tribulation, trouble or persecution because of the word, so you just gave in to the temptations. The very prophecy that told you to persevere in the church (despite it being attacked from without and within), became your excuse to stop going to church. 'I gave up on the church because of a bad experience with bad people.' Or you gave in to the temptations of this world. You trampled on the cross with high-handed sin. You are part of the outer court.

God gave this book of Revelation to strengthen his people to keep going through those 42 months, through our tribulation. All Christians go through it, but also what a gracious God to warn those of us who are lukewarm, still in the outer court. The door is still open today. The door has not been closed—yet. Come in and be measured.

Study Questions

1. If the Holy City is the bride of Christ, what might the outer court of the temple represent?

2. How does this text give an important explanation of the history of the church that has otherwise confused people?

3. 'Outer court' and 'Gentiles' are terms used in the OT temple context. What might make us think this is referring to people in the new covenant time frame?

4. How might 11:2 help us understand some of the apostle Paul's warnings to churches?

5. In what context might 11:2 be helpful when speaking to non-Christians or new Christians?

6. Where else do you see the time of 42 months in Scripture and history?

7. Give reasons why the 42 months might be symbolic.

8. What period of time does the 42 months cover?

9. How is this text both an encouragement and a warning?

3
The Two Witnesses
(Revelation 11:3-4)

Now we come to a great question: 'If God's people, by the Spirit's presence, are already a part of the temple above, why not just take them to become part of the temple above now?' What is the point of God leaving Christians on earth to go through tribulation? The answer unfolds as we delve further into Rev. 11. First 11:1 says the worshipers are measured, that is, protected. Then 11:2 said unbelievers ('Gentiles') are trampling on the people of God in the outer court. But then he says …

> And I will appoint my two witnesses, and they will prophesy for 1,260 days, clothed in sackcloth (11:3).

Who are these two witnesses? The identity of the two witnesses is one of the most debated issues in the book of Revelation. And the book of Revelation is the most debated book in the Bible. And the Bible is the most debated book in the history of the world. Does this mean the identity of these two witnesses is one of the biggest debates in history? How can we ever understand it then?

Well, it's okay. You can trust me … No! I don't want you to trust me! I want you to wrestle with these things as we open the word of God. This is difficult!

There have been various opinions on the identity of these two witnesses. The most popular view (Futurist) is rather straightforward. Because it's future we don't know for sure who they are. Two people will be the last two standing for Jesus at some future point. Some say the two witnesses represent a return of Moses and Elijah, because they are alluded to later in this passage. Some Preterists (pre-AD 70) say it's Peter and Paul in the early church era. Others say the witnesses are Elijah and Enoch returning to earth, because they were the only people who went to heaven without dying. That sounds interesting.

The Greek word in the original language for *witness* is *martureo*, which is where we get the English word *martyr*. A martyr is one who gives their life for the faith. So that could be narrowing it down. But Revelation doesn't limit *martyrs* or *witnesses* to those who physically die for the faith, as even angels call themselves fellow witnesses (martyrs) in 19:10 and 22:9. And the word *witness* and our word *martyr* were not necessarily synonymous when John wrote Revelation. The meaning of the word developed as more witnesses *became* martyrs.

But which view of the witnesses is correct? We can eliminate a couple of them because the Bible is against reincarnation, so Moses coming back in bodily form before his own resurrection won't work. But these witnesses will come with that same prophetic power because we read here that they have some of the attributes of Elijah and Moses. In 11:6 they have the power to stop the rain (Elijah) and the power to turn the water to blood and bring plagues (Moses). Although it's important to note both witnesses have the power of Elijah and Moses, it's not one power per witness. So who are they? Let's try using our secret code, the Bible, to interpret—the Bible! And specifically, the book of Revelation.

> And I will appoint my two witnesses, and they will prophesy for 1,260 days, clothed in sackcloth. They are 'the two olive trees' and the two lampstands, and 'they stand before the Lord of the earth' (11:3-4).

The witnesses are olive trees. They stand before the Lord. They prophesy in sackcloth for 1,260 days. That doesn't immediately tell us much until we dig into the OT. But if we have been careful readers of the book of Revelation we should be able to see one piece of imagery we *can* build from. Foundational to the identity of the witnesses is something that has already been explained to us by Jesus. Rev. 11:4 says the witnesses are **two lampstands!** Jesus has already told us what the lampstands are …

> The mystery of the seven stars that you saw in my right hand and of the seven golden lampstands is this: The seven stars are the angels of the seven churches, and the seven lampstands are the seven churches (1:20).

The lampstand is one of the symbols in Revelation that has specifically been explained to us by Jesus. We don't have to wonder about this. *Lampstands are churches.* It would be totally illogical if such a conspicuous symbol as a lampstand could mean one thing in Rev. 1-2, and when we get to Rev. 11 it means something else. Two meanings for one symbol in the same book would defeat any purpose of using a symbol in the first place.

In the letters to the churches, one of the main themes was that the churches (lampstands) were a witness. They were to shine! The appearance of lampstands here in Rev. 11 is further evidence the church is going through the tribulation, when we see what these witnesses go through. And it ties Revelation together. The letters to the seven churches are not just a 'down to earth' introduction to Revelation with no relevance to the rest of the book. They are setting up all of Revelation. The number seven is the number for completion, so the whole church is being addressed. And these prophecies pertain to what the complete church will endure throughout the ages.

Still, we might have caught on sooner if 11:4 mentioned *seven* lampstands instead of *two*. If the lampstands here are the churches, why are there only two? Well, if we go back over those letters to the seven churches, we see there were only *two* churches which were faithful in their witness! All the others were rebuked for their flawed witness or lack of witness. So these two witnesses here could represent the faithful portion of the witness of the church. The wider church is not always a faithful witness.

What is another reason why the number of witnesses might be two? Without even looking up verses, you might know the minimum number of witnesses the Bible says are needed to have a matter established. Two! In fact, it is the OT (Deuteronomy or Numbers) that the apostle Paul and Jesus quote in relation to this ...

> But if they will not listen, take one or two others along, so that 'every matter may be established by the testimony of two or three witnesses' (Matt. 18:16).

At least two. It's also the number of witnesses central to Jesus' mission, when he sent out his witnesses in ... *twos*.

> After this the Lord appointed seventy-two others and sent them two by two ahead of him to every town and place where he was about to go (Luke 10:1).

Right from the outset of Revelation, Jesus says *he* is the *faithful witness* and the people of God are to represent him in a twofold way, kingdom and priests.

> ... and from Jesus Christ, who is the faithful witness, the firstborn from the dead, and the ruler of the kings of the earth. To him who loves us and has freed us from our sins by his blood, and has made us to be a kingdom and priests to serve his God and Father ... (1:5-6).

So the *faithful witness* (Jesus), addresses the seven churches that he identifies as lampstands, and says he makes them *to be a kingdom and priests to serve God*. A twofold witness to the world. Carry that identification over to 11:3-4 where these lampstands carry out priestly functions (lampstands belong in the temple), and like priests, they **stand before the Lord**. That is a priestly function.

Just as Jesus was the *faithful witness*, he calls us to serve him as a kingdom and priests — that is, to be witnesses. This is one of the themes of Revelation. It's the call of the lampstands to shine. Think of this each time you see the word *testimony* or *witness*. Remember, it's the same Greek root word from which we get martyr, and is important in Revelation.

> When he opened the fifth seal, I saw under the altar the souls of those who had been slain because of the word of God and the testimony they had maintained. They called out in a loud voice, 'How long, Sovereign Lord, holy and true, until you judge the inhabitants of the earth and avenge our blood?' Then each of them was given a white robe, and they were told to wait a little longer, until the number of their fellow servants, their brothers and sisters, were killed just as they had been (6:9-11).

Christian witness has to go on to the end! We will see the same root word for *witness* rendered *testimony* in 12:11, *They overcame him by the blood of the Lamb and by the word of their testimony*. In fact, this theme of the witness of the church goes through to 12:17, 19:10 and 20:4. Just as each lampstand in 1:20 symbolized *all the people* in each church, it also seems that these two witnesses here in Rev. 11 represent *all the people* in the church who are a *faithful witness* to the Lord, because as

John's vision unfolds, the unbelievers from all the world see them. Not a few, but ...

> For three and a half days some <u>from every people, tribe, language and nation will gaze on their bodies</u> and refuse them burial (11:9).

The whole world gets to see the dead witnesses. This is more than a hint that the witnesses are more than just two individuals. How can people from every nation gaze upon only two people at once? Some have explained this by saying that the two people can be seen by the whole world because they will be on TV. We can update that theory and include YouTube. All could be possible. But shouldn't we try following the explanation Revelation has already provided in those lampstands rather than imposing ideas from the outside?

There is another hint the witnesses (lampstands) are the church. What is the length of time for their witness? It just happens to be 42 months (11:2), or 42 x 30-day months = 1,260 days. *And I will appoint my two witnesses, and they will prophesy for 1,260 days, clothed in sackcloth.*

We have looked at this length of time and why it is symbolic of a time of tribulation. Remember there are many examples of tribulations of this timeframe that God's people have gone through in salvation history, even down to Jesus' faithful and true witness in his ministry and persecution of 3½ years. And his followers, his church, are to follow in his footsteps, through their trial and tribulation, through their 1,260 days.

It becomes even clearer when we get to Rev. 12 that this period of 1,260 days of tribulation is the entire church age. The witnesses must suffer tribulation. Also, the witnesses are ...**clothed in sackcloth**. Sackcloth is associated with mourning. John the Baptist was dressed in sackcloth preaching a gospel of repentance (Mark 1:6). And as we proclaim the message of salvation, we mourn over those who reject us. It tastes sweet in the mouth, but bitter in the stomach. You will be persecuted for your witness and it will cause mourning.

Why 1,260 days, instead of 42 months, if it's the same tribulation period symbolizing the church age? Why say it in days instead of months? I don't know for sure, but it could be simply that for the church, the time seems to drag out and hence seems longer. Is it that 1,260 days seems so long? Or maybe the days could be a way of saying a day-by-day continual witness from the true witnesses. We are not told, so it's difficult to say. But the witnesses also are 'the two <u>olive</u> trees' and the two <u>lampstands,</u> and 'they stand before the Lord of the earth.'

Olive trees! Lampstands! And they stand before the Lord of the earth. We know about the lampstands, but what about the olive trees? The apostle John, the aging Jewish man brought up under tutelage of the Rabbis, would have immediately recognized this temple furniture straight out of the OT book of Zechariah. In Zechariah's similar vision the olive trees provided oil for the lamps.

> I asked the angel who talked with me, 'What are these, my lord?' He answered, 'Do you not know what these are?' 'No, my lord,' I replied. So he said to me, 'This is the word of the LORD to Zerubbabel; Not by might nor by power, but by my Spirit,' says the LORD Almighty ... Then I asked the angel, 'What are these <u>two olive trees</u> on the right and on the left of the <u>lampstand</u>?' Again I asked him, 'What are these two <u>olive branches</u> beside the two gold pipes that pour out golden oil?' He replied, 'Do you not know what these are?' 'No, my lord,' I said. So he said, 'These are the <u>two who are anointed</u> to serve the Lord of all the earth' (Zech. 4:4-6, 11-14).

Two anointed. Two olive branches supplying the oil for the lamps, not by might nor power, but by my Spirit says the LORD. Despite opposition in Zechariah's day, the temple would be built by the power of the Holy Spirit. Now in Rev. 11, despite opposition through this long 1,260 days, through the power of God's Spirit (oil of the olive trees for the lamps), the temple of God (his people) will be built by the Holy Spirit. Remember what the apostle Paul said: *And in him you too are being built together to become a dwelling in which God lives by his Spirit* (Eph. 2:22).

You, the church, are the temple. Jew and Gentile believers! Now from the context of Zechariah there are 'two who are anointed' for this task. Most commentators agree that the two anointed olive trees (witnesses) in Zechariah are referring to the king and the priest. Zerubbabel the king and Joshua the high priest. They are the two witnesses under the old covenant. King and priest. What have we been saying all along? From the beginning of Revelation, Jesus commissioned his church with two functions (note two!), to carry out this witness. He ... *has made us to be <u>a kingdom and priests</u> to serve his God and Father...* (1:6, see also 5:10). The two functions under the old covenant are carried out by the faithful portion of the church. Twofold witness, *kingdom and priests* ...

> And I will appoint my two witnesses, and they will prophesy for 1,260 days, clothed in sackcloth. They are 'the two olive trees' and the two lampstands, and 'they stand before the Lord of the earth' (11:3-4).

The lampstands (church) live in this relationship (on earth) to the Lord that can never be broken because of the Holy Spirit. They are measured! (11:1) They are in his presence. *'They stand before the Lord of the earth.'* The lampstands were a vital inclusion with the furniture of the Jewish *temple*! And here they are, the believers, with Jesus in their midst, the temple measured out.

In 11:2 it all looked so ugly with the outer court being trampled on by unbelievers. We looked at the mess of the apostate church, of the many who claim to be followers of Christ but are actually hypocrites and instruments of the devil, wanting to destroy the church. There are great institutional church structures as well as cults like the Jehovah's Witnesses and Mormons, then there is liberalism, weak teaching and false teaching, prosperity gospels, anything but the simple gospel of Jesus. And they present themselves as true, or even the only true church. So you are overwhelmed and begin to wonder *Who can stand?* Or more to the point, *Who is standing for the truth?* The answer: *the Lord has his true witnesses in the church!* Not the whole visible church. A remnant of the complete number of seven. Down to two. The true church! *The two witnesses.*

As we will see with the references in 11:5-6, these witnesses have power to stop the rain from heaven and bringing plagues, and are modeled on Moses and Elijah, two faithful witnesses of the OT. Under the old covenant when Moses and Elijah stood up, they seemed to be outnumbered and opposed by their own people! The very people who should have been supporting them were often their fiercest opposition. But they were two true witnesses. And so also today, true witnesses are going to find that it will often be those who claim to be Christian who oppose them. Real biblical Christianity might seem outnumbered and marginalized, even in the wider church (the outer court!). But Jesus has his two lampstands fueled by the oil of the olive trees, the Spirit of God. His witnesses!

So who are these two witnesses? Brace yourself! *It's you!* The church of Jesus! You are a part of the body of Christ, aren't you? Do you belong to Jesus? Then why hasn't he just taken you to heaven? Have you ever said, 'Lord, I'm ready to go now?' The answer is, 'No you are not!' You have to be a *witness*, the practical outworking of how we are to glorify God on this earth!

Jesus said we are to be his *witnesses to the ends of the earth* (Acts 1:8)! A kingdom and priests. The priesthood of all believers. All are to be witnesses. You no longer have to wonder, 'What is the point of having to go through all this?' Yes, to be transformed into the likeness of Christ, to glorify him. But part of that is, you are here on this earth to be a *witness*. You are here for the full 1,260 days. Day after day. This life that drags on. But in the big scheme of things, even the church age will be shown to be a short, limited time. You are here for a purpose. God chose you for this purpose.

If you are a believer in Jesus, then you are one of the few. He set his love upon you from before the creation of the world. Why? To be a witness! According to Jesus' warning, the people around you are going to receive justice and fair judgment (weeping and gnashing of teeth). We don't want them to have that! We testify and witness that they might receive forgiveness and mercy. Do you see the urgency? Do you see the flames in front of their faces? This world is doomed. Jesus takes away our judgment in advance at the cross, but only for those who receive the witness!

Also, *you* are *the lampstand* to shine, to be a *witness* fueled by the Holy Spirit. It will seem like you are in such a minority, like Moses and Elijah. What did they do in the difficulty of witnessing? They prayed! We need to pray for more fuel. *Pray for more of the Holy Spirit* (Luke 11:13). You are not the whole lampstand on your own. You have a part to play in the body. Are you actually involved in this? It's time to join that prayer meeting! Join the evangelism spirit. We are called together to be a witness. Practically how? We need to get away from the idea of thinking of church worship services, Bible study, fellowship and prayer meetings are all about 'what I get out of it'. We need to start being Christians. To stand as a witness! It happens even when we meet together. *Let us not give up meeting together but encourage one another* (Heb. 10:25). Encourage one another! Are you an encouragement and witness in your support to your fellow Christians in your attendance at church, Bible Study, prayer meetings, as well as evangelism? Or a stumbling block to others because you don't stand in these?

What does *your* going to church and getting involved in church life have to do with the witnesses of Rev. 11? Everything! What did we learn in 11:2 about the outer court? We learned not everyone in the church is really part of the temple (the true church). There is a mission field right there in the church! Jesus spoke about the narrow path that leads to life and only a few find it. Only a few in the church! So being a witness begins within the church! You are either building up or tearing down those around you.

Why did God place you where you are? To be a witness! Why are you in your family? You are a witness to the people you live with. Husbands love your wives as Christ loved the church. Wives, submit to your husbands. Husbands and wives, you are a witness for the strengthening or tearing down of your spouse and children. Mums, the best teaching you can give your children is the witness you are in how you treat your husband. Husbands, the most influential witness you are to your children is how you treat your wife.

What has that got to do with Rev. 11? Everything! Are you a witness where God has placed you at work, at home and as a neighbor? People are judging Jesus by your conduct because you are his witness. Whatever they think about you, they think about Jesus. This is frustrating to us, but it's true.

Christianity is historically the inventor of aid organizations and care for the poor. What happened to our witness? We hold on to our wealth now instead of being a witness to the love of Jesus. And the witness of our good works is destroyed if we don't show the witness of the Holy Spirit. The fruit of the Spirit. Is your witness through that fruit evident with the people in your life? The list hasn't changed. Would others in your life describe you as having love, joy, peace, patience, kindness, goodness, faithfulness, gentleness and self-control? Our whole lives should be a witness.

The Lord is not looking for a silent witness. No matter how good the character of the witness, if you remain silent you are of no use. Do you grab the opportunity to share the gospel or a least invite people to read a tract or book, or come to a special service? Are you really a witness for Jesus? Why has God got you persevering through this tribulation? What is the point? This is why he appointed you …

And I will appoint my two witnesses, and they will prophesy for 1,260 days, clothed in sackcloth (11:3).

Study Questions

1. Why might the identity of the two witnesses be both controversial and crucial to the overall picture of Revelation?

2. What are the pros and cons of Moses and Elijah as being identified as the witnesses?

3. What or who are the witnesses? How can you support your answer?

4. Give reasons why there are only two witnesses.

5. What might the sackcloth and the oil from the olive trees represent?

6. The witnesses also 'stand before the Lord'. Where might this be drawn from and what is its significance in light of Revelation?

7. How does this text challenge you?

4
The Witnesses' Power
(Revelation 11:5-6)

There is so much drama going on in the movie we might have forgotten the Master film director Jesus, has been taking us through another movie interlude. There are seven trumpets leading up to the final judgment. Six have blasted, but before the seventh comes that same question might be asked, 'How can anyone stand in the face of judgment?' And this calm before the storm answers that. We saw the people measured in 11:1. They are the temple on earth. We know there is a temple above, but how do you know you will get there? The true worshipers are measured, protected, not like the outer court, professing believers but not true worshipers. They are not protected.

But the faithful ask, 'How long O Lord? Why do you keep us on earth through tribulation? Why not take us to join the temple (people of God above with Jesus)?' The answer we learned was in 11:3 … because you are to be his witnesses!

But when it comes to these next couple of verses, wouldn't it be a whole lot easier to explain these witnesses as two individuals from some futuristic time; two who have supernatural powers of fire coming out of their mouths; two who can also turn water into blood, bring plagues and shut up the heavens to stop the rain? How does that follow with the church as the witnesses? Herein lies the strength of the Futuristic view. It's all happening sometime in the future! No matter how amazing, weird and wonderful things might seem — anything is possible in the future. After all, how could these witnesses be the church, as we know it in history, based on this?

> If anyone tries to harm them, fire comes from their mouths and devours their enemies. This is how anyone who wants to harm them must die. They have power to shut up the heavens so that it will not rain during the time they are prophesying; and they have power to turn

the waters into blood and to strike the earth with every kind of plague as often as they want (11:5-6).

If you are part of the church, then what about the bit about fire coming out of your mouth and devouring your enemies? And those enemies must die that gruesome death. Surely it's easier to imagine this all happening in some future time when our imaginations can run wild with miraculous Star Wars type characters. There will be some flame-throwing, blowtorch breath coming from these two witnesses, with amazing powers on display. Anything could happen in the future. You can picture them like dragons breathing out fire and consuming enemies. Sounds good if you are an alien predator. But doesn't that create a problem? Does that imagery really work with what we know about the kind of witness Jesus wants his people to be on earth? It would certainly be a great way to ensure success in evangelism if this is to literally happen in the future. Forget about seeker-sensitive evangelism. This would be an absolute guarantee for conversion!

'Repent and be baptized!'
'No! I won't.'
'Poookkkk!' (Fire blasts out of your mouth and they die, which might not convert the first person you torch since they're charcoal by now, but it surely would be effective on the next one watching.)
'What about you, will you repent?'
'Hallelujah brother! Yes and Amen!'

So the future in evangelism methods is certainly not seeker-sensitive. In the future, we have the new (pardon the pun) sure-fire method! It brings a whole new meaning to the Christian being fired up. But is that the way of Jesus? Is that the way he wants his people to witness? Is that what this passage is teaching? Is taking the text literally being true to it? Is this really teaching there are two people walking around some time in the future, who when someone rejects the message of Jesus, the witnesses will smoke them with a flame-thrower like an oxy torch from their mouths and kill the unbelievers who dare to reject their message or persecute them? And is it being *unfaithful* to the text to take these as symbols literally when Jesus has already told us in plain language that lampstands are not literal lampstands but churches. In fact, if we take this text in the genre it's written (apocalyptic), and try to understand from other parts of Scripture what those symbols *mean,* the picture of fire coming out of the mouths of the witnesses devouring the enemies of God is *far more* terrifying than if you try to squeeze a literal meaning out of it.

The point of 11:1 with the measuring of the temple worshipers, the people of God, was that the Lord has measured them off for protection and Jesus wins! Unbelievers in the outer court are not measured and therefore not protected. The witnesses cannot be harmed (11:5). But how does that work when this text goes on to show they can be harmed physically, financially, socially and even to death? Before we get to the end of Rev. 11 we see that the witnesses, the people of God, are certainly not always safe from physical attack.

Surely the answer has to be that they are spiritually kept to the end. They are eternally secure in the Lord. They are part of his temple on earth and joined by the same Spirit of God to the temple above, where they will be kept forever. In that sense, they cannot be harmed. … *Do not be afraid of those who kill the body and after that can do no more* (Luke 12:4).

The same point was made in the interlude in Rev. 7 before the seventh *seal.* They cannot be harmed because they have the seal, the Holy Spirit. They are joined to Israel, the twelve tribes, as God's chosen. Now here in this interlude before the seventh *trumpet,* God secures and protects the believers by measuring them, but it has to be speaking eternally and spiritually, because they *can* be physically harmed (11:7). But if this speaks *spiritually* about *believers'* protection, what might it be saying about unbelievers? *If anyone tries to harm them* [the witnesses], *fire comes from their mouths and devours their enemies. This is how anyone who wants to harm them must die.* What happens to unbelievers who reject the message of the faithful witness? Are they devoured by fire? Isn't this where Revelation is headed?

> The lake of fire is the second death. Anyone whose name was not found written in the book of life was thrown into the lake of fire (20:14-15).

If we think eternal perspective, big picture, then all this makes sense. If the protection of the believers is spiritual and eternal, isn't it reasonable that the same thing applies with the enemies and how they must die. It's not just physically. It's worse. It's the *second* death.

The very fires of hell! Unbelievers who ultimately reject Christ will die this way. Especially those who persecute the church. So, with apologies to those who were hoping for 'onward Christian soldiers' with oxy torch flame-throwers coming out of their mouths, leaving anyone who rejects the gospel like a big stick of charcoal, I would say, look at this closely through the lens of the gospel. Because that is where the reality is far scarier than if you take these verses with an earthly literal fulfillment.

If the witnesses are you and me as part of the church, we can't be harmed eternally or spiritually. Though people may insult us, attack us in various ways and even kill the body, those who oppose and finally reject the message, this is how they *must die*. **If anyone tries to harm them** [if persecutors, rejecters of the message try to harm them], <u>**fire comes from their mouths**</u> [message of the fire of hell] **and devours their enemies. This is how anyone who wants to harm them must die.** That is how they must die! What fire comes out of believers' mouths? This idea can be found in the OT.

> Therefore this is what the LORD God Almighty says: 'Because the people have spoken these words, I will make <u>my words in your mouth a fire</u> and these people the wood it consumes' (Jer. 5:14).

So even in the OT we don't expect literal fire coming out of the prophet's mouth, but the message carries with it the very fire of God's judgment. The teaching of Jesus is a double-edged sword. The message of Jesus we carry to the world will be for one a sweet aroma, a saving message, but to the other, you are bringing the very judgment of the second death. This is why you could say 11:5-6 is literal, but not merely in an earthly sense. You who are witnesses for Jesus carry more power than you ever imagined. The message of the gospel that comes out of your mouth carries either the great hope or the very fire of hell.

> To the one we are an <u>aroma that brings death</u>; to the other, an aroma that brings life ... (2 Cor. 2:16).

And those who oppose it *must die* in that way! Now if this message can judge people, and is so terrifying, would we be better off not telling anyone? No. The gospel is their only hope! Is there any point in jumping from the sinking Titanic on to a safety lifeboat even if you might miss and end up in the water? Yes! Go for it. It's your only hope, because if you go down with the ship you are gone anyway! Jesus said we are not on neutral ground. We are already condemned until we believe in the Son of God (John 3:18). We are already sinners on our way to this fire. This is the only hope.

So we must witness! When people reject it to their death, they increase their guilt, but without it they are lost anyway. Those who try to harm believers in their witness will pay more dearly. Eternal fire. *If anyone tries to harm them, fire comes from their mouths and devours their enemies. This is how anyone who wants to harm them must die.*

This is looking specifically at those who persecute and attack the witnesses. Christians have always been under attack from every angle and every 'ism'. There was great persecution of Christians for the first 300 years until the Roman Empire made Christianity legal. But then the persecution starts again. It was that 'outer court' through the RC church that persecuted to death anyone who stood up for the Bible. Islam has played a role in persecuting the church throughout the centuries. And what about in the last century? Atheism and communism in the 20th century literally tried to stamp out Christianity, as did Fascism. But whoever it is, those who harm the witnesses will experience the fire of the message that will devour them and that is how they ... *must die* (11:5)! Eternally.

We carry a message that is either terrifying or exhilarating, depending on how it is received. Contrary to RC doctrine, Peter the apostle wasn't the only one given the keys of heaven to bind and loose heaven in Matthew 16. Later in Matthew 18:18, Jesus gives the same authority to the other disciples. All disciples of Jesus have the same message of Jesus, who has the keys of death and Hades (1:17). It's a message that can free you from hell, but to those who reject it, it is a message of fire coming from our mouths. Eternal fire.

And these witnesses in Rev. 11, the church, modeled on the ministries of Elijah and Moses, have the keys of *heaven*...

> They have power to shut up the heavens so that it will not rain during the time they are prophesying; and they have power to turn the waters into blood and to strike the earth with every kind of plague as often as they want (11:6).

We are to prophesy! **Prophesying** *can and does mean* forth-telling God's message, not just fore-telling. In fact, most of the OT prophets prophesied by speaking the word of God, forth-telling God's word, rather than predicting the future. So when you proclaim the gospel you are speaking God's word forth—prophesying this message of fire that opens up the heavens.

Moses and Elijah are two key OT prophets who did those things and are used as the great example. They also were two witnesses. Their great works and witness are what is taken up now as an illustration and model for the two lampstands, the church. Those miraculous powers of Moses and Elijah were inflicted on kings who persecuted God's people. Moses had the power to turn the water into blood and to bring plagues. *But now we've actually got greater power* (whoever is least in the kingdom is greater than the last OT prophet, John the Baptist). We have this greater spiritual power, the message the lampstands carry. It's even more devastating to those who persecute the church. This message doesn't just open or shut up the physical heavens of rain, but heaven itself! It doesn't just strike the earth with a plague. If it is rejected it takes a man all the way into the eternal plague (22:18), where there is weeping and gnashing of teeth forever. You hold those keys which can open the heavens or bring the plagues of hell.

The use here of Exodus imagery (Moses) as an analogy for the church is not without precedent or purpose. We are in the blasting of the seven trumpets. This is the interlude before the final one. And in the first six trumpets we saw *many* allusions to the Exodus. Remember the locusts and the sea turning into blood. This is following that pattern.

But if you disagree with me and believe this will happen in the future, and can picture Jesus' people using literal fire against opponents of the gospel in the future, you are in good company. There was a time when Jesus' own apostles thought that was the way to respond to enemies, but what did Jesus say in that context?

> ... but the people there did not welcome him, because he was heading for Jerusalem. When the disciples James and John saw this, they asked, 'Lord, do you want us to call fire down from heaven to destroy them?' But Jesus turned and rebuked them ... (Luke 9:53-55).

John, who is writing down this book of Revelation, was once a young brash follower of Jesus and was one of the two disciples who thought calling fire down on those who reject Jesus was a good idea. Jesus rebuked him. We are not the judges. We only carry the message of the Judge. We might rush to the idea of witnesses with blowtorches in their mouths because it tickles our sinful human nature to want to respond to enemies this way. 'Let's smoke 'em for their arrogance!' It's like Charlemagne in the Middle Ages ... he converted people by the sword. The apostle Peter picked up a sword to resist the opponents, but that's not Jesus' way. How does Jesus want his people to treat their enemies?

> But I tell you, love your enemies and pray for those who persecute you ... (Matt. 5:44).

Calling fire from heaven and the like are not the weapons Jesus would have us use. The weapons we fight with are *not* the weapons of the world. On the contrary, they have divine power to demolish strongholds (2 Cor. 10:4). More powerful than literal rain from heaven is the word of God ... the word of fire!

> As the rain and the snow come down from heaven, and do not return to it without watering the earth and making it bud and flourish, so that it yields seed for the sower and bread for the eater, so is my word that goes out from my mouth: It will not return to me empty, but will accomplish what I desire and achieve the purpose for which I sent it (Isa. 55:10-11).

This metaphor of rain coming down is about God's word coming down. We have the power to open heaven through this word. But only when it's accompanied by God's Spirit, the oil of the olive trees that powers this witness.

> Let my teaching fall like rain and my words descend like dew, like showers on new grass, like abundant rain on tender plants (Deut. 32:2).

So, like Elijah, we open the heavens with this message. In other words, this message has the very keys of heaven. But our witness should be characterized by love for our enemies because that is how we have been loved (Rom. 5:10).

Rev. 11 is a story of how the church should expect to be persecuted, and yet how it will be wonderfully kept, although not necessarily physically. God *will* keep you. You are in the Father's hand and you can never be snatched out. But, like John was told, you have to eat that little scroll and digest it thoroughly, because we have a message to proclaim through these dark times. And it's a consuming fire for those who reject it, especially those who persecute you. But it is also a message of hope for a dying world. So, if we have truly digested this scroll, how can we keep it in? It is the very hope of the world to escape the eternal fire. We proclaim a message with holy firepower!

> ... his word is in my heart like a fire, a fire shut up in my bones. I am weary of holding it in; indeed, I cannot (Jer. 20:9).

If you have believed this message and internalized it, you should be like Jeremiah. Can't keep it in! It's a message of fire, but also of hope. Revelation has taught me that we are living this reality. If you want literal—Revelation is happening before our eyes. It's alive. *We* are living this. *We* are the witnesses. *We* are to proclaim a literal message of the saving Jesus, but also the fire of hell. This is God-breathed, useful for teaching, rebuking, correcting and training us. It's alive and continues to unfold.

We don't know what literal hell will be like. We have Dante and other artists with graphic otherworldly ideas. Perhaps it's not as melodramatic, but just down to earth weeping, sorrow and torment in regret. What if just as Revelation is real and right before our eyes (rather than 'out there in some sci-fi kind of way'), hell is also real and relatable? Not nice, but not ethereal either. We know hell cannot be cruel, because God is love and he is fair and perfect in justice. Nor can it be anything less than what God has said in its severity. It's weeping and gnashing of teeth. It's an eternal fire. But what sort of burning? Burning of the soul, or torment of living with your own sin exposed to who you really are? Being isolated? Cut off? Cut off from God means cut off from all that is good. It's God giving humans up to what they asked for. 'I didn't want to live with God in this life, so I am cut off from him and all of his life-supporting goodness.' But for how long? You *never* wanted God, so you get him *never*. Weeping over your foolishness in your rejection of the greatest love of all ...

The unanswerable question is not why God would have such a place, when he is simply giving people what they wanted; the unanswerable question is, 'Who would even think of God going through the fire of eternal wrath himself, in the darkness of the cross for his enemies?' Incomprehensible love. And because our hearts are so hard, we still wouldn't believe, so God had to send his Spirit to quicken our hearts to believe. God had to do the rescue mission himself completely. And here is the amazing part. Even though it's all God's work, he actually uses those same pathetic sinners he saves to be witnesses to his love and to proclaim this message.

What a mercy and privilege to be a witness, to know God and be part of the rescue plan. I have been meditating on how undeserved I am to have Jesus take away my hell and sending his Spirit into my hard heart. How richly I deserve to be cut off from God too. Have you ever really thought about that? There are many people in that prison right now, and many still to come, and you could have been one of them. Cut off forever with no hope. Why do people get depressed and even commit suicide? They experience a feeling of darkness and no hope. They can't see a way out. No wonder there is weeping and gnashing of teeth! It doesn't have to look like Dante's fiction. Hell could be just as ordinary as some very dim looking holding cell. Who knows what it will be? But it may not have a dramatic gruesome look. Remember it is not cruel, but it's not 'fun with my mates' either. It's real existence, cut off from contact, with no hope forever.

Also, the fullness of hell will be experienced in the very real, down to earth resurrected bodies we lived in on earth. It will be weeping in darkness, gnashing of teeth in sorrow and regret at lost opportunity. 'Why didn't I take hold of the gospel? Now I'm cut off from God. This is what I wanted, to be apart from God. This is what I got. Not just for a year. Not a 20-year sentence, not a life-time sentence, but I got what I wanted, forever!' What is it like? One thing Dante got right is the entrance: 'Abandon hope all ye who enter here.' Do you get the point of this passage?

We are the witnesses who have the very power of the keys to open heaven. *We* have *hope*. The Titanic is sinking but there *is* a lifeboat, and today is the day we have a message of hope. It's Jesus! Everyone who crosses your path — see them in that prison. You have the power in that message. Greater than the power of Moses and Elijah who stopped the rain and turned water into blood … the message of 11:1-6 is God with us *in this witness*. You are surrounded by people who are headed to being cut off at any time. Think of people you know. A family member or friend? Picture them weeping, gnashing their teeth in frustration. Cut off with no hope.

So what are you worried about now? How am I going pay the bills and save for that holiday? Relationship problems? Lack of relationships? Wish that person at work wasn't so difficult? I have a lot of worries in my life. What worries! If you know Christ, what are you doing with this life? What is your life now? You are a witness! Are you part of it? Are you praying for it? You have the message that can open the heavens and close the fires of hell.

If anyone tries to harm them, fire comes from their mouths and devours their enemies. This is how anyone who wants to harm them must die (11:5).

Study Questions

1. What strength does the Futurist view have in a text like this?

2. What difficulties are encountered if this text is taken literally?

3. How can the witnesses be protected from harm and yet they are persecuted and killed?

4. How does the answer to question 3 help us interpret this text?

5. How do the witnesses breathe out fire and devour their enemies?

6. How does that relate to how the enemies 'must die'?

7. How does the ministry of Moses and Elijah relate to these witnesses?

8. What precedent can we find in the apostles literally wanting fire to consume enemies, and how should that affect interpreting this text?

9. How is the responsibility and urgency of this message being carried in your life?

5
Death of the Witnesses
(Revelation 11:7-10)

In the hotly debated topic of the identity of the *two witnesses* of Rev. 11, the Historicist view has some good things going for it. Remember the Historicist is looking for single events or people in history that fit the description of the text. The Reformers were big on this in the 1500s. It's understandable. After more than 1000 years of domination by the RC church, the Reformers thought *they* were the fulfillment of the ages. Every event could be applied to their age. So, the Historicist looks at 11:3 and interprets the witnesses testifying for 1,260 days as a day representing a year, hence 1,260 years. They see this as the time of the beginning of Papal rule to the Reformation, the Middle Ages. And when 11:7-10 says the Beast comes up and persecutes and kills the witnesses, then gloats, this fits well with the severe persecution of those who stood up for the Bible against Rome in the Middle Ages (before the Reformation), such as the Waldensians in the 12th century who were brutally put down, particularly by Pope Innocent III. The third and fourth Lateran councils of 1179 and 1215 decreed the denial of burial for heretics. And what have we got here for these witnesses?

> For three and a half days some from every people, tribe, language and nation will gaze on their bodies <u>and refuse them burial</u> (11:9).

We also have *two* great pre-Reformation reformers who were *witnesses*. John Wycliffe and Jan Huss. Instead of burial, Wycliffe's body was exhumed, and the ashes of his successor Jan Huss were cast into the Lake of Constance. All this was going on through the Middle Ages and the RC church seemed to have truly killed off the two witnesses who dared to stand for the gospel. They made declarations and rejoiced they had succeeded. The Lateran Council declared in 1514: 'There is an end of resistance to the Papal rule and religion, opposers there exist no more!' Pope Leo X and others then had a great festive celebration and the Pope granted plenary papal indulgence (giving gifts). What does 11:10 say when they put down the witnesses—they celebrated and gave gifts!

> The inhabitants of the earth will gloat over them and will <u>celebrate</u> by sending each other gifts ... (11:10).

How long were the witnesses *dead?* Remember the Historicist consistently translates days as representing years.

> But after the three and a half days a breath of life from God entered them, and they stood on their feet, and terror struck those who saw them (11:11).

What happened 3½ years after 1514 when the Lateran Council claimed victory and gloated over those witnesses being dead and gone? The witnesses came to life. In 1517, there arose the greatest witness in history since the time of Jesus and his apostles. *This* was the turning point in history when Martin Luther nailed his 95 theses to the church door in Wittenberg. To say the witnesses came alive is an understatement! The witnesses came alive in such a way it turned the world upside down and it has never been the same since. If 'rising from the dead' is not a fair description of the impact of the Reformation on the church, then I don't know what is. When the Diet of Nuremberg was held in 1523, Pope Hadrian declared, 'The heretics Huss and Jerome seem now to be alive again in the person of Luther.' The witnesses came back to life!

So the Historicists have quite an argument. Are they correct? Well, I would say yes, but are they going far enough? Revelation is addressed to the *servants of God*, and the *seven churches* (complete church). This book of Revelation should and does live for us just as much as it did for the Reformers, and is not confined to single events, but relates to the whole church in the whole church age. The church, the witnesses, will be under attack (tribulation), even killed. In fact, they will be attacked all the way to the end. But how does this part speak to the church through history?

> Now when they have finished their testimony, the Beast that comes up from the Abyss will attack them, and overpower and kill them (11:7).

Who is this Beast? At least we recognize where he comes from. The Abyss is where those other demonic beings (the locusts) were coming from (9:3). That is Satan's realm. Also, this Beast will **attack them**. The Greek word in the original language for *attack* is literally *makes war*. You don't *make war* against just two people. So there is another hint the two witnesses represent a greater number of people, the lampstands—the churches. But who is making war against the church? The Beast! He comes from the Abyss. We get to know much more about this Beast in Rev. 13, 17, 19, so stay tuned. Pray we live long enough to get to Rev. 13 to find out who is the Beast. But for now, with the power of this Beast, the witness of the church is killed. Does that mean every single believer is killed? Or does it mean the witness of the church is so decimated and beaten down, including many literally killed, that it could be said the church is dead? It looks like the bad guys are winning. They killed off the witnesses ...

> Their bodies will lie in the public square of the great city—which is figuratively called Sodom and Egypt—where also their Lord was crucified (11:8).

The witnesses are so cast down in their witness and attacked, physically yes, killed literally in many cases, but so beaten down as to appear completely defeated and dead in their witness. Their bodies will lie in public. They are refused burial. The ultimate stripping of dignity in the OT was that one would not have a burial. Jezebel was refused burial. It was the ultimate humiliation (1 Sam. 17:44,46; 2 Kings 9:10).

As well as martyrdom, there are other ways the witness is killed more subtly. On May 22nd, 2013, Pope Francis preached a sermon declaring you don't need faith in Jesus and his cross to be redeemed. It doesn't matter if you are a believer or atheist. It doesn't matter who you are, if you do good.[1] The Pope is the highest representative of 'the church' in the world. He effectively proclaimed to the world 'you don't need to believe in Jesus'. Unbelieving journalists actually wrote articles praising this development. The old Christian witness is dead. We should celebrate the death of the old Christianity and celebrate this new Christianity. But what kind of teaching says to you

---

[1] Vatican Mass sermon May 22nd, 2013

that you don't need to believe in Christ? It's anti-Christ.

When Jeff Kennett was Premier of the state of Victoria he is reported to have said the church is 'yesterday's people'. (Now he is yesterday's Premier.) But the church has declined even more since he said that about 20 years ago. Is he right? That's only a snippet of how the Beast has killed off the witnesses compared to some countries where they are literally killed. The rotting body of the church, whose witness is going, going …

> Their bodies will lie in the public square of <u>the great city</u>—which is figuratively called Sodom and Egypt—where also their Lord was crucified (11:8).

Many have said this **great city** has to be literal Jerusalem because it's **where their Lord was crucified**. But the problem is that Jerusalem is not mentioned in the text and Jesus was not crucified there, he was crucified *outside* the city. Actually, the *great city* is mentioned several other times in the rest of Revelation (16:19, 17:18, 18:10,16,18,19,21), always referring to the *great city* of *Babylon the great*, rather than Jerusalem. And why is this *great city* also called Sodom and Egypt? How can it be both? Egypt is not even a city. It's a country. So we are getting more than a hint we are not looking at a literal city. And then 11:8 spells it out for us when it says the cities are *meant* **figuratively**! So we are not stretching the boundaries of interpretation if we think of the witnesses being killed off as also figurative (although many may be literally killed).

So the *great city* from these descriptions is figuratively speaking of an area or sphere where Satan has a stronghold. Look at the three descriptions mentioned that we are meant to take figuratively. *Sodom*, which we know was depraved in its morals; *Egypt*, renowned for oppressing God's people; and the place where the *Lord was crucified* represents the rebellion of the so-called people of God, an apostate city of God.

When it says in 11:8 we are to take it *figuratively*, in the original Greek language it literally says *spiritualize*. That's interesting, because many criticize the approach that I (and others) have taken in Revelation by saying, 'You are just *spiritualizing* Revelation', as though spiritualizing is being unfaithful to the text. But isn't it being unfaithful when the text *tells you* to spiritualize it and you *don't* interpret it that way? Remember this book of Revelation told us right from the first verse (1:1) it was revealing in signs and symbols. So when we are told by the text to take this figuratively we are not surprised. *Their bodies will lie in the public square of the great city—which is figuratively called Sodom and Egypt—where also their Lord was crucified.*

It's a threefold characterization of the *great city*—Sodom, Egypt, and where they crucified the Lord. This is a characterization or character assassination on what the *great city* represents. We get more than a hint that this great city goes much wider than a literal Jerusalem or any particular city. It seems to be a worldwide thing ...

> For three and a half days some from every people, tribe, language and nation will gaze on their bodies and refuse them burial. The inhabitants of the earth will gloat over them ... (11:9-10).

The **inhabitants of the earth** can't gather in one literal city, let alone the whole earth to gaze upon just two people. So how do we understand it? The way 11:8 told us! Figuratively! Spiritualize it! The two witnesses, the lampstands (the church), are the worldwide church, not just two individuals in one location being gazed upon. This is describing the church and the decimation its witness suffers. The church's testimony is now cast down and defeated. Or it appears that way ... *For three and a half days* ... (We will look at this in our next installment, 11:11.)

So this *great city* epitomizes everything that opposes God. It is also personified with these descriptions mentioned. Sodom in its depravity; Egypt in its oppression of God's people; and an apostate 'city' who killed the Lord of glory. What did all this mean to the apostle John, who is writing this down? Remember he was writing to people in the first century. It's no good looking only at what it means to us, or the Reformers, or in the future. Our interpretation must make sense to those who first received it. What did it mean to John and those he wrote to in those seven churches? Well, there would be no question in John's mind what the *great city* represents. It would be Rome. Rome was immoral (Sodom), persecuted Christians (Egypt), and crucified Jesus.

Our Preterist friends who interpret Revelation as all occurring before AD 70 have something to offer here. They see this great city as Rome, which had all those features. So the Preterist must be correct! But are *they* going far enough? Does this not also speak to all *servants of God* (1:1) and the church through all the ages (all *seven* in completion)? There is a sense in which those first seven churches could feel as though Christianity was seen as dead and gone. The letters to the churches (Pergamum), talked about a faithful witness, Antipas, who was killed for the faith. In Smyrna the church was warned some of them would be killed. And there were martyrs as the *great city* gloats and celebrates. But then what happened? The blood of the martyrs became the seed of the church and it rises again.

Whether it's in the apostle John's day, where Rome is the *great city* and Nero and Domitian wreaked havoc and killed the witnesses, or whether it's during the Middle Ages with the RC church persecuting witnesses to death, celebrating, look what happened next. The witnesses rose again in the Reformation. History repeats itself.

French philosopher Voltaire boasted that within 100 years of his life, there would be no Bible on earth. Voltaire is dead, but the Bible is still the world's largest selling book. In the 1800s, Friedrich Nietzsche announced God is dead. But only Fred is dead. Christianity had revivals after that. In the 1900s, there was a pronouncement that went throughout the world from another *great city*, Shanghai. Mao Tse Tung's wife (Madam Mao), famously announced from that city that Christianity in China is dead and buried. She died in 1991, but not before seeing the start of one of the greatest Christian revivals of history in her own country.

In the 21st century there has been a surge of Christians being 'overpowered' and 'killed'. There have been nearly one million martyrs already this century.[2] Whether it's in modern day North Korea or closed Muslim countries where death and defeat is outward, or the subtler work of Christianity being killed off by being increasingly marginalized in the West, whether the city is Shanghai, China, or Melbourne, Australia, seeking to squeeze out Jesus and rejoicing with new laws and political correctness, the *city* is eliminating the witnesses. And it seems like they are winning, and Christ's church is defeated. The apostates and anti-Christian sentiment seem to have more witness than true Christianity. People are now more than ever saying, 'Christianity is dead. Your witness is dead.' People now celebrate the worldview of secular humanism. The

---

[2] www.ordonconwell.edu/ockenga/research/documents/1martyrdomsituations.pdf.

evangelical atheists are more aggressive than ever. It is the *worldview* of secular humanism that is now strict orthodoxy in our public education system. Christianity is a religious worldview and must be eliminated from the classroom, but the philosophical worldviews of humanism, secularism and evolution are *compulsory*. God as Creator is not allowed as an alternative view. They have managed to work it from, 'Let's be more open and tolerant' to, 'But we *cannot* tolerate Christ as an alternative.' And they celebrate! They **celebrate by sending each other gifts, because these two prophets had tormented those who live on the earth.**

When an international atheist convention was held in Melbourne, with Richard Dawkins headlining, it was called 'A *Celebration* of Reason'. Dawkins also supported the campaign in the UK which raised money (gifts) to fund an advertising campaign that was plastered all over London buses. 'There is probably no God, so stop worrying and start enjoying your life.' A 'church' in Melbourne also 'gifted' another $120,000 for their own advertising campaign called *The Ten Commandments: one of the Most Negative Documents Ever Written.* They are celebrating a 'new faith for the 21st century', beyond orthodox Christianity. [3] Celebration and gifts! The church (the witnesses) is dead. We have won, they say.

Why do they hate Christianity? Because they were *tormented* (11:10)! The witnesses preached against immorality and all the popular idols. They proclaimed the need to believe in the Savior to get to heaven, and the inhabitants of the earth hated it. They hated it so much that when the church is dying, they love it and celebrate. Now they cry, 'We no longer have the shackles of the old authorities. We are free now. Now we are in the new age. We want to do what we want, with sex and everything else. Just do it! Freedom! No more torment! They dared to say the only way to heaven was through Jesus. We had to stamp out that intolerance. And we did. In our *great city* we have other religions. We must protect them. We have religious vilification laws now so that they can't speak in that intolerant way. Anyone who dares to say they believe in the Bible will be laughed at now.'

Like a vaccination that immunizes the masses, they were able to immunize people from those witnesses. 'Now everyone knows they are just archaic bigots. There is no one left who really believes in the

---

[3] Barney Zwartz, Sydney Morning Herald, 16 September 2008

Bible anymore. Celebrate reason! We have won. And we rejoice because we have done a good thing. We had to eliminate hate speech when they spoke against us. They are violating our freedom to indulge in our pleasures. They were even against equality in marriage! How dare they? Bigots. Intolerant! Anti-love. No free love and sex. They *tormented* us, but we've broken down their nice little neat idea of the family. They said you need a mother and father. But now we've got same-sex marriage. We've got single parents by choice. We've got anything we want. And they said we had to honor our father and mother. But now we can divorce our father and mother! We are free now! *They have tormented us for long enough!* We just want to enjoy life and love and be free. They should not be allowed to speak that way and get away with it. They can no longer *torment* us. The church is gone and dead and irrelevant and we are here to do what we like and there is no one to stop us. Celebrate!'

So it seemed the *great city* had won. The Beast attacks the witnesses and this time it seems they are dead and gone for sure. And they gloated and celebrated …

Don't you feel it? We who have trusted in Jesus, the *great city* has attacked us so severely we truly look like we can't be any more 'dead'. Look at the population. What a pathetic, dead little outfit is the church. Look around you. How many people even go to church services anymore? You are surrounded by millions of people in your city right now who celebrate having thrown off the shackles of what your country once had as foundational. Don't you feel it when you stand up for Jesus? You believe in his resurrection and they say, 'Well you'll believe anything! You are dead! You had your day.'

We are like those men on the road to Emmaus when the stranger asked, why are you so upset? 'What? Are you only a visitor to this great city? Don't you know the things that have happened here? They have crucified our Lord and we had hoped he would be the one to save us, and now we are nothing. And it's been three days!'

We see it everywhere. If these witnesses (lampstands) are the churches, then people of the great city truly do gaze on their carcasses. Empty church buildings no longer attended. No people. Dead. The building shells are used for shops, restaurants, houses or torn down. If you are a believer in Jesus, your day is dead. The Beast and inhabitants of the earth have won… Or have they? Is there more to this story? You'll find out in the next installment …

Study Questions

1. What series of events might motivate the Reformers to take the Historicist view?

2. Why might the actions of the Beast make us think the witnesses are more than a literal two people?

3. Give examples of ways the Christian witness has been 'killed off'.

4. If Revelation is speaking to Christians through all ages, in what way might witnesses be dead and yet rising through all ages?

5. Why should we take this text as symbolic?

6. Give examples of how the city celebrates.

7. How is this city tormented?

8. How could this text be both a discouragement and encouragement in your faith?

6
The Witnesses Rise
(Revelation 11:11-14)

In our previous chapter, we began by looking at the Historicist interpretation of 11:7-10, which had some impressive points with events and dates that seemed to fit the text. However, without denying these facts, we asked if the Historicist approach was going far enough. The church has also appeared to be dead through other great periods, such as liberalism in the enlightenment, and other false teaching that seemed to have all but obliterated the true gospel church. The church seemed dead. When the likes of John Wesley and George Whitefield began preaching, the church and the general morality of society was said to be at its most depraved, but then came the Great Awakenings and there was a resurrection! This is the hope we have today. When it seems least likely.

The great OT analogy for this is found in the book of Ezekiel, when Israel seemed finished. They weren't even in Israel any longer. They had been exiled to Babylon. Then God, through the prophet Ezekiel, assured them they would rise again. The valley of the dry bones predicts Israel returning to life after their exile in Babylon.

> This is what the Sovereign LORD says to these bones: I will make breath enter you, and you will come to life… So I prophesied as I was commanded. And as I was prophesying, there was a noise, a rattling sound, and the bones came together, bone to bone… So I prophesied as he commanded me, and breath entered them; they came to life and stood up on their feet—a vast army (Ezek. 37:5,7,10).

So in the OT we have a great example of the people of God dead, then coming to life. Of course this wasn't the literal resurrection for Israel back then. It spoke figuratively. God returned Israel to their land in the time of Zerubbabel. Ezekiel was pointing to new life in Israel's return from exile. Likewise, in the NT, with the people of

God, we see that from the time of the apostles, the more the church was persecuted and killed, the more it grew. In Acts, one of the great turning points to the gospel spreading beyond Jerusalem stemmed from one of the lowest moments, the martyrdom of Stephen. While witness Stephen is taking his last breath, the Lord was breathing new life into an accessory to his murder. Young Saul was standing by, and though a killer of Christians, he never forgot the sight of that death. They gloated over Stephen's death, but the witness was raised up again in one of those very men who stood there. This witness (Paul), would reach to the ends of the known world, even Rome!

God can do it! God will continue to revive his dying church. But is that all this text is teaching? Aren't even Ezekiel's dry bones also ultimately pointing to and describing the final and literal resurrection? When we look at this text in 11:11-13, even where we can see it can be applied throughout the church age, the language of this text also seems to be pointing to a more complete finality. Earlier in 11:7 it says *Now when they have <u>finished their testimony</u>* ... When do the witnesses (lampstands) finish testifying?

Surely this is pointing to the end, when it seems like the world has won. Complete devastation just as it was for the disciples after their Lord had been killed. Heads down and shattered. It's all over. But what happened to the Lord after three days? The same thing that will happen to the church ...

> But after the three and a half days a breath of life from God entered them, and they stood on their feet, and terror struck those who saw them (11:11).

Remember the world was gloating over the demise of the church, just as they are doing today. The church is dead! It's irrelevant! But there is coming a time when all those who gloated and thought they had finished off the church will be struck with fear. Because there is a rising from the dead!

Here the rising from the dead is after 3½ days, just as Jesus was literally dead for three days before his resurrection. Now this is the final resurrection of the church. The Day of Judgment has arrived. Some say this resurrection only represents the times of survival and revival of the church, but not the end itself. For example, when we get to 11:13 we read of the earthquake, which is a *partial* judgment (tenth), and a rounded symbolic number of 7,000 people killed. But I think there is too much in this text which is clearly speaking of the last day. Yes, we have examined how this text speaks through history of 'revivals' of the church, so it has always been relevant in history and a blessing to all who have read it through the church age. But these are only historical 'types', because this text also points to the final death and resurrection of the witnesses. The end!

One piece of evidence for that is the parallel between the seven seals, seven trumpets and seven bowls. If we line them up as different camera angles leading up to the same thing, that can help our interpretation. The sixth seal unleashes the Day of Judgment and the seventh seal completes the judgment. The same thing is happening here. We have had the sixth trumpet (9:13). Again, we see the arrival of the Day of Judgment, which the seventh trumpet will complete. Rev. 11:7 told us the church has completed its witness, which surely points towards the end. Now 11:11 is also speaking in clear resurrection terms: **the breath of life from God entered them and they <u>stood</u> on their feet, and <u>terror struck</u> those who saw them.**

How will terror strike the hearts of unbelievers when they see Christians? Do you know of any unbelievers who are terrified of you now, apart from when you ask them to come to church? But they will be terrified on the Day of Judgment when the witnesses (Christians) are raised and taken up to heaven in a cloud ...

> Then they heard a loud voice from heaven saying to them, 'Come up here.' And they went up <u>to heaven in a cloud</u>, while their enemies looked on (11:12).

The original Greek language says 'in *the* cloud' not 'in *a* cloud'. The glory cloud of 1:7, when every eye will see him coming! This is it! The return of the Lord! This section then finishes with typical judgment language of earthquakes and devastation ...

> At that very hour there was a severe earthquake and a tenth of the city collapsed. Seven thousand people were killed in the earthquake, and the survivors were terrified and gave glory to the God of heaven (11:13).

When John saw this vision, he would have immediately seen the earthquake as a typical biblical announcement of judgment rather than focus on detail such as the 'tenth'. The tenth of the city falling and the 7000 losing their lives might simply be an introduction to judgment, just like when the tough guy bursts into the bar and rips off the doors and sends a couple of people flying. That's it, he's here! It's powerful! It's devastating! There is no escape! Or just as when Jesus blazes across the sky like lightning, that doesn't mean the fiery entrance alone will burn up the world, but it certainly introduces just that!

Also, look at the end of 11:13 ... *the survivors were terrified and gave glory to the God of heaven.* Why would unbelievers give glory to God for anything! Unless it is in line with ...

> ...that at the name of Jesus <u>every</u> knee should bow, in heaven and on earth and under the earth, and <u>every</u> tongue confess that Jesus Christ is Lord, <u>to the glory</u> of God the Father (Phil. 2:10-11).

The day is here. This is the day when unbelievers will give glory to God. All that the Bible has prophesied has led to this ...

> But after the <u>three and a half</u> days a breath of life from God entered them, and they stood on their feet, and terror struck those who saw them. Then they heard a loud voice from heaven saying to them, 'Come up here.' And they went up to heaven in a cloud, while their enemies looked on (11:11-12).

Two things to note: firstly, the **three and a half** could be related to the number seven, which we've seen many times in Revelation. It's half of seven. Could this be alluding to when Jesus said the tribulation Christians go through would be cut short for the sake of the elect? In other words, just when you think it's going on and on, and how much worse can this world get? Jesus' answer: it won't go on. It'll be cut short. When you least expect it, this will happen.

Secondly, **'Come up here.' And they went up to heaven in a cloud,** looks to me like a rapture! The most popular view of Revelation is the rapture of the church occurring *before* the tribulation, where the days are *not* cut short for the church because Christians have been raptured out already. They don't go through any of the tribulation. With that view, the rapture must occur sometime early in Revelation. I haven't been able to see the rapture so far in Revelation. But now we are up to Rev. 11 and towards the end of the tribulation, so what would the rapture be doing here?

Throughout Revelation we've seen the saints battling it out in the tribulation up to this point. I have not seen any place mentioning Christians being raptured, neither in 4:1 when John goes up (because he also comes down again in 10:1), nor anywhere else in Revelation. That is, until now! In Rev. 11 this is *real* rapture language. This is speaking well and truly of the people of God being taken up to be with the Lord, after they have been battling through tribulation raging throughout the ages.

This rapture happens on the Day of Judgment being described here. The witnesses of Jesus on the earth have finished their earthly witness and testimony. They were persecuted, even killed, and the dead in Christ shall rise and be taken up. Why? The Day of Judgment has arrived! And this seems to fit with that other passage of the saints being taken up on the Day of Judgment …

> For the Lord himself will come down from heaven, with a loud command, with the voice of the archangel and with the trumpet call of God, and the dead in Christ will rise first. After that, we who are still alive and are left will be caught up together with them in the clouds to meet the Lord in the air. And so we will be with the Lord forever (1 Thess. 4:16-17).

Christians taken up? Yes, indeed. But not in some secret way, or before the Lord comes back, or with the world continuing with those left behind given a second chance to come to faith. (How could they miss it, if all the Christians suddenly disappear?) John MacArthur says the reason those left behind won't believe is analogous to Luke 16:31, when people wouldn't believe even if someone rose from the dead. Hard hearts? But then MacArthur also says this will be a time when a greater number of people will be saved more than ever before and says of the very next verse that many Jews are coming to faith because 11:13 says they will give glory to God.[4] But that's hard to follow. Which is it? Is it people not believing, or mass conversions? It's all so confusing. Well no it's not, if this is the Day of Judgment! It's the resurrection. The dead rise. Jesus has returned from heaven! The people of God caught up with him and unbelievers on their knees giving him glory. Our text says all this …

---

[4] John MacArthur, *Because the Time is Near,* Moody Publishers, Chicago, 2007, p.187

> Then they heard a loud voice from heaven saying to them, 'Come up here.' And they went up to <u>heaven in a cloud, while their enemies looked on</u>. At that very hour there was a severe earthquake and a tenth of the city collapsed. Seven thousand people were killed in the earthquake, and the survivors <u>were terrified and gave glory to the God of heaven</u> (11:12-13).

The Day of Judgment and the earthquake is another great statement that the Day is here. A foot stamps on the earth. Judgment is here! It's the beginning of the end. First, a tenth of the city collapses and 7,000 people are killed. But then … **the survivors were terrified and gave glory to the God of heaven.** Every knee will bow and every tongue will confess that Jesus Christ is Lord to the glory of God the Father.

When we looked at 11:10 we saw those were the people who gloated over the demise of the church. They celebrated. Now in 11:13 they are terrified! You know who they are. They make fun of your belief in Jesus. They make light of your going to church. They say you are a dying passé group. They take God's name in vain and think nothing of it. They gloat over the demise of the church and they lump Jesus and his true followers in with the RC pedophiles and even Muslim extremists. 'You religious zealots are all the same.' You know them. You live with them and work with them. You see them in the media. But whatever you do, pray for them, because you wouldn't wish this on your worst enemy. There are no second chances. The idea of second chances is out of line with the rest of the Bible, and the shock and finality of that day is here on their faces—it's a look of terror! Once you 'look up', there is no more time to repent. It's over.

We have already seen the different camera angles of the last day. This is now the sixth trumpet. If we look back at the sixth seal, we have a parallel of what is going on here …

> They called to the mountains and the rocks, 'Fall on us and hide us from the face of him who sits on the throne and from the wrath of the Lamb! For the great day of their wrath has come, and who can withstand it?' (6:16-17).

The seals are parallel to the trumpets. This is a different camera angle of the same thing. The day has arrived and there is nothing about people being left behind for second chances, or unbelievers repenting at the last minute. The great day has come!

So what does this mean for us? It means *today is the day*. While the church can still be ridiculed, it can still be a witness. Today is the day. How do you feel about the people around you? Are we going to just wait this out and they will just have to find out the hard way? Or are we to pray and plead and invite and persuade? Or do what Jesus did when he wept over Jerusalem? Or like Paul pleading day and night with tears? Are you willing to put up with the persecution, Christian?

What are you worried about? Being a little bit embarrassed? You will see them again, when they are in terror! And you are worried about being embarrassed now? Would you want them saying on that day, 'Why didn't you warn me?' What would you say? 'Well I was a bit embarrassed and worried you might ridicule me.' The trumpets are a warning of what is to come on the unrepentant. But it is also a wake-up call for believers. What are you doing with your life that is so important right now that you couldn't be joining the prayer meetings and witness of your church? What is most important to you right now? Success? Is it getting the mortgage paid off? Or getting enough money to be comfortable? Or is it getting the right job? What are you thinking of right now, with this coming? It will come upon everyone on this earth, including the people who are in your life right now! What's most important to you? Where did your mind first go when you woke up this morning? What is your focus? The harvest is plentiful, but the workers are few. Today is the day! But there will be a time when the prayers and the witness of the church will come to an end. And once it's over, there will be no second chance.

This rapture is not in secret. And it will not happen before the Lord comes back. Everyone will be thinking life seems so normal ...

> As it was in the days of Noah, so it will be at the coming of the Son of Man. For in the days before the flood, people were eating and drinking, marrying and giving in marriage, up to the day Noah entered the ark; and they knew nothing about what would happen until the flood came and took them all away. That is how it will be at the coming of the Son of Man. Two men will be in the field; one will be taken and the other left. Two women will be grinding with a hand mill; one will be taken and the other left (Matt. 24:38-41).

Now that sounds like a rapture. 'One will be taken'. But what happens to the one left behind? In the same passage Jesus then explains where there is a servant who is ready and one who is not. What happens to the one who is 'left behind'? Jesus explains ...

> He will cut him to pieces and assign him a place with the hypocrites, where there will be weeping and gnashing of teeth (Matt. 24:50-51).

'Cut to pieces' and 'weeping and gnashing of teeth' does not sound like being left behind for another chance to change your mind over seven years or 1000 years. So too in Rev. 11, after they gloat over the church's demise, when Jesus returns, it's only terror!

> But after the three and a half days a breath of life from God entered them, and they stood on their feet, and <u>terror struck</u> those who saw them (11:11).

We get other hints in Scripture about the Day of Judgment, but nothing as vivid as this, with the unbelievers looking up and terror striking them. You can picture the very whites of their eyes as the unbelievers see the believers rise from the dead. The very people who were dead and gone and supposedly their beliefs buried with them. Those who killed the martyrs will see them raised, as God's people. There is Graham Staines, the Aussie missionary who was murdered for the faith in India in 2003. We know about him because he is an Aussie. But there are many from Muslim countries who have been killed for their faith. Multitudes from all over the world forgotten. Churches and people are burned. And the people who put them there gloated! But now terror strikes them. All of those who witnessed for Jesus are now coming out of their graves. How did Jesus describe it?

> Do not be amazed at this, for a time is coming when all who are in their graves will hear his voice and come out—those who have done good will rise to live, and those who have done evil will rise to be condemned (John 5:28-29).

No wonder it's terrifying for those who don't know him when they hear the voice of the Son of God! Terrifying indeed! It's like Ezekiel 37, with the tendons and sinews being renewed, the bones are rattling and forming. Have you ever been at a funeral where the coffin is open? Imagine being at a funeral of your enemy. The person is dead. It's all over. But then they sit up in that coffin? Terror! ... *a breath of life from God entered them, and they stood on their feet, and terror struck those who saw them.*

Resurrection of dead bodies seems so unreal to us because we haven't seen this happen before. There are many things we haven't seen, but that doesn't make them fanciful. Who was there to see this universe come into being? It had to have happened, no matter how you believe it happened. It's beyond comprehension. The world comes into being. It's beyond our reality, but it must have happened. And God who began this world is the same one who will raise humans at the resurrection. We know these bodies are so intricately made, there must have been an amazing designer-creator behind it. Obviously God made it. So why is it so incredible that he would re-create?

Dead bodies are coming alive. The breath of life comes into them. The graveyards are giving up their dead. They are kicking their dirt off. Look at them all. New bodies. Rotted coffins tossed aside. They are standing up. And those who persecuted them see them rising and are now in terror! They are left to face the wrath of the Lamb, as those they ridiculed are taken up before their very eyes ... *And they went up to heaven in a cloud, while their enemies looked on.*

The enemies look up and see this amazing phenomenon. This now parallels the sixth seal. Running and hiding. It's right at the very moment they realize all the ridicule, all the pathetic excuses, everything they were warned about is real. Their whole life flashes before their eyes. All that stuff about, 'You only need religion because you need a crutch!' All that self-righteousness. 'I'm a good person. Not as bad as some.' Now they realize they passed by the cross of Christ and said, 'Don't need you.' They took the name of God as an expletive and trampled on that name. And now they see the face of him who comes down in the cloud as the people of God are caught up to be with him, as he now comes down to judge ...

What are we to do? We've been called to be witnesses who give our lives for Christ! We just have to give up our embarrassment and be a witness. We only have a short time to be a witness! And if you reckon this is bad. You ain't seen nothin' yet ...

The second woe has passed; the third woe is coming soon (11:14).

Study Questions

1. How does Ezekiel 37 help us understand this text both in its application in history and the future?

2. Give reasons for and against this text speaking of the Day of Judgment.

3. How could an earthquake of a tenth and killing only 7000 be the Day of Judgment?

4. If the numbers are symbolic, to what could the 3½ days be referring?

5. Does this text support the idea of a 'rapture'? If so, in what way?

6. How do the seven seals help us understand this text?

7. How does this text challenge you?

7
The Time Machine
(Revelation 11:15-17)

Have you ever seen the old movie *The Time Machine*? If only we could go back in time, or into the future and change things, but of course it's only make-believe. We are at the seventh and final trumpet. If you are not right with God by the time this seventh trumpet blasts, it's too late. But this is the beauty of the book of Revelation. It's like a time machine. It is prophecy, so we can see what the future holds. Here you are, looking into the future, and you get this picture of what will happen, both the good and the bad. Right now you have this day of opportunity to put things right with God, so you will stand on the right side when this future comes to pass.

We are looking at the seventh trumpet. Some commentators have said these verses are just introducing the contents of the last trumpet and that it's not the real trumpet. They say the real content of the seventh trumpet unfolds in the next few chapters. But we have already been told previously that when the seventh trumpet sounds the end will most certainly be accomplished …

> But in the days when the seventh angel is about to sound his trumpet, the mystery of God will be accomplished, just as he announced to his servants the prophets (10:7).

It's all over. The reason people get confused is because they don't realize that the seals, trumpets and bowls are parallel. They are packages inside packages, rather than one after another. This is all a great replay leading up to the same end. Judgment Day. Remember my analogy of the film industry, where you can take all day to film a 15-second television commercial. Why? Because you have to film from all the different camera angles. This is what we have had with the Master film director, Jesus, giving us three different camera angles of the church age, which are the seals, the trumpets and the bowls, but with progressive close-ups. There is an increasing intensity. Here is a reminder of that pattern again …

> SEALS   1, 2, 3, 4, 5, 6 (interlude) 7 (final judgment, thunder, rumblings, lightning, earthquake)
> TRUMPETS 1, 2, 3, 4, 5, 6 (interlude) 7 (final judgment, thunder, rumblings, lightning, earthquake)
> BOWLS   1, 2, 3, 4, 5, 6 (interlude) 7 (final judgment, thunder, rumblings, lightning, earthquake)

Now we are at the end of the trumpets …

> Then God's temple in heaven was opened, and within his temple was seen the ark of his covenant. And there came flashes of lightning, rumblings, peals of thunder, an earthquake and a severe hailstorm (11:19).

This is Judgment Day language. It's the same ending we had at the seventh seal …

> Then the angel took the censer, filled it with fire from the altar, and hurled it on the earth; and there came peals of thunder, rumblings, flashes of lightning and an earthquake (8:5).

What happens when that day arrives? Judgment for those who didn't take this 'time machine' seriously. They didn't heed the warnings. But also, it will be a time of rejoicing and reward for those who have taken hold of the Savior in this life.

On that day, there is this great pronouncement …

> The seventh angel sounded his trumpet, and there were loud voices in heaven, which said: 'The kingdom of the world has become the kingdom of our Lord and of his Messiah, and he will reign <u>for ever and ever</u>' (11:15).

Some say this is a description of the beginning of the 1000-year (millennial) reign of Jesus on earth, after which there would be a final uprising followed by the Day of Judgment. One of the difficulties with that idea is that 11:15 just told us this reign of this kingdom is not for 1000 years, but how long? **… for ever and ever!**

So these songs they sing in this text, rather than just singing about some kind of future to come, are announcing the reality which has arrived! It's Judgment, where the kingdom has fully come. … **'The**

kingdom of the world has become the kingdom of our Lord and of his Messiah …' Jesus wins!

> And the twenty-four elders, who were seated on their thrones before God, <u>fell on their faces</u> and worshiped God, saying: 'We give thanks to you, Lord God Almighty, the One <u>who is and who was</u>, because you have taken your great power and have begun to reign' (11:16-17).

We see more evidence that this is the end of all things. The Lord is the One **who is and who was.** That would sound strange in John's ears—and to us too. Why? What is missing? Remember back at the introduction to Revelation.

> John, To the seven churches in the province of Asia: Grace and peace to you from him who is, and who was, and <u>who is to come</u>, … (1:4).

And…

> 'I am the Alpha and the Omega,' says the Lord God, 'who is, and who was, and <u>who is to come</u>, the Almighty' (1:8).

And again…

> 'Holy, holy, holy is the Lord God Almighty,' who was, and is, and <u>is to come</u> (4:8).

But in 11:17 what do we note? … *the One who is and who was*. He is no longer the *One who is to come*. We are so used to that last bit that ancient scribes copying the NT manuscripts must have thought it got left out, so a small number of late manuscripts added on the words 'who is to come' to this verse. You see it appear in the King James Version, but those words do not appear in the oldest manuscripts (or in other Bible translations), because they are not meant to be there. He has already arrived. He is no longer *to come!*

That's one of the reasons we have confidence in the accuracy of our Bible. The number of ancient manuscripts is so much more plentiful, and the age of them so much closer to the original than any other document in all of history prior to the invention of printing, that we can make these checks and balances. We can go back to the most ancient manuscripts and be assured we have God's word handed down accurately.

But back here in our text, the Lord is no longer praised as the *one to come*. This is it! This is finality! And there are the 24 elders we met back in Rev. 4. **And the <u>twenty-four elders</u>, who were seated on**

their thrones before God, fell on their faces and worshiped God. They are in the same location, before the throne. We noted back then the 24 elders represented the people of God under the new covenant that joined both Jew and Gentile together, the 12 tribes of Israel with the 12 apostles. We deduced this, not through a lucky guess, but noted in Rev. 21 the very foundation of the Holy City was built on the 12 tribes of Israel and the 12 apostles. So here we are again with the 24 elders representing the complete people of God. But notice their response. It is the same as back in Rev. 4 ... in spontaneous worship ... on their faces. And how is this for worship style? The contemporary thought on worship is that the more conservative style of worship lacks joy in the Lord, and perhaps there is some truth to that.

But if praising our God is not a time to be joyful, then when? Here we have an example of true heavenly worship, and however much we might imagine ourselves jumping, dancing, waving our arms and bouncing around, when we finally get to see the Lord in all his glory, the biblical evidence says you and I will be doing exactly what these elders are doing. Falling on our faces before him. Joy! Yes! But overcome with trembling that will express itself with such reverence and godly fear that we will not be jumping around, but on our faces in total awe! It's the same thing John did when he encountered Jesus back in 1:17, he fell on his face as though dead. This is the holy God! How great and awesome is our God!

The natural response of worship for those who are really in the presence of the Lord is indeed to sing praises and rejoice—but with godly fear. I suppose we will have trouble finding a balance between joy and reverence until we see him face to face. But I suspect today the church is following more of its surrounding culture than Spirit-led practice.

Nevertheless, however we might express our joy in worship, for those who are fully in the presence of the Lord, one thing is clear. Here they are at the height of all great moments—the victory cry of the Lord. And they are on their faces. Reverence and awe is the order of the day. They ... *fell on their faces and worshiped God.*

But why this spontaneous worship all of a sudden? Surely the elders already know the Lord is king. They have already been in his presence. What is it about this pronouncement that makes them react when they hear ... *The kingdom of the world has become the kingdom of our*

Lord and of his Messiah, and he will reign for ever and ever.'?

They know as well as we do, the Scriptures tell us one day the Lord will overthrow all the kings of the earth. Yet this spontaneous reaction tells us something we simply cannot grasp until we are face to face. No matter how much you think you know of the joy and awe and pleasure at seeing the glory and majesty of the Lord, when we have the full realization before us and see the Lord fully in his rightful position as King of kings, until then, you ain't seen nothin' yet!

I've tried to think of illustrations, but they all fall short. Is it like the love-struck teenybopper fainting in the sight of her heartthrob? No. Is it the football fan, in exhilaration at the final siren when their team wins the Grand Final? No. That doesn't work either. Is it like the most awe-inspiring sight in creation that makes you gasp and tremble like I imagine it might if you are standing at the edge of the Grand Canyon or one of the great wonders of the world? All of them rolled into one still don't work. No experience can capture this, because it's more than awe-inspiring. It's the pinnacle and destination of our existence. Right at this moment. It's the vindication of Jesus!

The One to whom all history and existence points to, this moment is *the* moment ... when *'The kingdom of the world has become the kingdom of our Lord and of his Messiah, and he will reign for ever and ever.'* The elders knew this would happen one day, but when it happens they ... <u>fell on their faces and worshiped God</u>, saying: *'We give thanks to you, Lord God Almighty, the One who is and who was, because you have taken your great power and have begun to reign.'*

This is our destiny. We should want to live here now. This is the answer to all your questions. What will become of my life? This! Jesus' vindication when ... *'The kingdom of the world has become the kingdom of our Lord and of his Messiah, and he will reign for ever and ever.'*

What is the meaning of my life, my struggles? What is the point of me keeping on going? Is it to get to that stage when I will achieve my goals? Or for my children to reach their hopes? When I get justice? Vindication? Security? Happiness? The time when I can feel like I can take it easy? No! It's this time. When the pronouncement comes that all of life was actually about Jesus and his victory. We are created for him and for this moment, to sing this song ... *'The kingdom of the world has become the kingdom of our Lord and of his Messiah, and he will reign for ever and ever.'* He will be the focus *forever and ever*. That's what we are destined for, if you know Jesus. And did you notice they give thanks because he has *begun to reign* (11:17). Begun to reign? Hasn't Jesus been reigning all this time? Here he has *begun* to reign. This is a good argument for the premillennial view that says Jesus does not begin his reign until the beginning of a future 1000-year reign on earth. But hasn't Revelation told us right from the beginning that Jesus has been reigning over the nations? He is already the ruler *… and from Jesus Christ … the ruler of kings on earth* (1:5). He rules those kings now! Isn't that the teaching elsewhere in the NT?

> For he <u>must reign</u> until he has put all his enemies under his feet. The last enemy to be destroyed is death. For he 'has put everything under his feet …' (1 Cor. 15:25-27).

From Jesus' ascension, when he rises on high, he begins to reign.

> … That power is the same as the mighty strength he exerted when he raised Christ from the dead and seated him at his right hand in the heavenly realms, far above all rule and authority, power and dominion, and every name that is invoked, <u>not only in the present age</u> but also in the one to come (Eph. 1:19-21).

Jesus reigns both in this age and the age to come. So why does 11:17 say he has *begun to reign* if he has already been reigning since his ascension? As one Jewish lady asked me 'if the Messiah has come, then why don't we have peace?' Where is his reign? And why is there war and violence everywhere? And why are governments making laws about morality and ethics, against Jesus … if Jesus reigns? Why do those movies always have to include excessive violence, or sexual immorality, or Jesus' name blasphemed? Is Jesus reigning when his people are persecuted? Why do you find yourself tempted to do the very thing you hate? Doesn't Jesus reign in your life? Why do you as a believer want to honor the Lord, yet find yourself putting *you* first?

The answer: because there is someone else who wants to reign! There is opposition! There is conflict in the ruling stakes. Yes, Jesus reigns, but not without resistance. What resistance? We read it before *… 'The kingdom of <u>the world</u> has become the kingdom of our Lord and of his Messiah …'* The kingdom of the world! Wasn't the world Jesus' kingdom? Well, yes, of course, but something happened. Something went terribly wrong. What did Satan tempt Jesus with?

> Again, the devil took him to a very high mountain and showed him all the kingdoms of the world and their splendor. 'All this I will give you,' he said, 'if you will bow down and worship me' (Matt. 4:8-9).

The kingdoms of the world! How did Satan get a hold of the kingdoms of the world that he can then offer them to Jesus?

> We know that we are children of God, and that the whole world is under the control of the evil one (1 John 5:19).

This is big. The most powerful being ever created, closer to God in power so he has more power than any to do good. But if he fell? More power to do harm. According to Genesis 3:1, he is also craftier than any other creature. What a scary thought! He used the enormous power given by God to try to take over God's sovereignty. He used one third of the angels, and he used humans, the creatures God had created as the pinnacle of creation, made in his own image. But Satan, this heinous powerful creature used them in his plan to take over the world. To try to assert *his* authority. And it worked! At least that is what it seemed like. Those made in God's image obeyed Satan rather than God. And look at the world now! Who does man follow? The devil. The world, flesh and the devil. Where did we get that saying?

> As for you, you were dead in your transgressions and sins, in which you used to live when you followed the ways of this world and of the ruler of the kingdom of the air, the spirit who is now at work in those who are disobedient. All of us also lived among them at one time, gratifying the cravings of our flesh and following its desires and thoughts. Like the rest, we were by nature deserving of wrath (Eph. 2:1-3).

There is your *world, flesh and devil*. Everyone outside of Christ is following this spirit at work in those who are disobedient. Everyone wants to be the Lord of their *own* life. Why is there so much havoc in the world? Everyone wants to have their own kingship, rather than have Jesus as their king. Look through the ages — violence and evil. Humans have all these amazing attributes and gifts, and there seems to be something about humans which says life should be good. There are such things as love and relationships and families and people who help each other. Humans are not like other creatures because they are made in the image of God. But why does it never fully come together? Families and relationships break down. Humans have these great abilities and yet they use them to hurt, even destroy each other. There is tension. They are in conflict. They lie. All the time. All of them. How does that work? Well, the father of all lies is *their* father. They are dedicated to worshiping anyone or anything except the true king. How does it all work? The spirit who is now at work in those who are disobedient, Satan, has had a field day, seemingly unopposed, until there came a rescue mission. Until the Creator infiltrated his own creation and came as an undercover boss, as a human and announced, 'Repent for the kingdom of God is near.' And, 'If I drive out demons by the Spirit of God, then the kingdom of God is *upon* you' (Matt. 12:28). He didn't say the kingdom would come in some future millennial. It is *upon* you *now!*

When Jesus came driving out demons and healing the sick, what was he doing? Trying to impress people? No! He was taking on the opposing kingdom. Look at the great level of demonic activity at the time of Jesus. Why that emphasis in Jesus' ministry with so many demons around Jesus? Why healing the sick and raising the dead? It was a kingdom issue. It was the clash of the two kingdoms! The devil brought in sickness and death and employed the help of many demons. Now Jesus was taking on Satan and taking back his kingdom. Casting out the demons was the beginning of the reign that will culminate in no more death or disease and no more demons!

But Satan still had humans under his rule, as long as men are lost sinners. This kingdom cannot be won until when? As Jesus said …

> 'Now is the time for judgment on this world; now the prince of this world will be driven out. And I, when I am lifted up from the earth, will draw all people to myself.' He said this to show the kind of death he was going to die (John 12:31-33).

The cross! Now the prince of this world is driven out. Without the cross, the lost cannot cross over from Satan's kingdom to Jesus' kingdom because they still have sin on their record, a record of rebellion against God. Sin separates man from God. The cross erases the record that separated them and reconciles forgiven sinners back to their God. But even after Jesus wins that victory, the mop-up continued. Jesus progresses his kingdom from the time he ascended, sending his Spirit forth through his people advancing to the ends of the earth. And although Satan is a defeated foe, he continues to resist. There is still opposition. The battle still rages. I always find helpful the well-known analogy of Hitler continuing to cause greater harm even after he knew he had lost the war. D-day had arrived, but V-day had not until he was completely eradicated. That is like Satan as a defeated foe.

So Jesus reigns from the time of his ascension and continues to advance the reign of his kingdom across the world and across the centuries until he reaches the ends of the earth with his gospel, until he finally reaches the last one who would believe. And then what?

The seventh angel sounded his trumpet, and there were loud voices in heaven, which said: 'The kingdom of the world has become the kingdom of our Lord and of his Messiah, and he will reign for ever and ever.' The *kingdom of the world* is fully overcome by the kingdom of our Lord and Messiah, and he will reign without any opposition from the world, flesh or the devil. That is what it means when it says *he will reign*. Yes, he is reigning now. Jesus is king. But he only *begins* to reign without *any* opposition from this point, when the kingdom of the world is fully overcome. No wonder the elders are singing this hymn! No wonder they fall on their faces *saying: 'We give thanks to you, Lord God Almighty, the One who is and who was, because you have taken your great power and have begun to reign'* (11:16-17).

Now Jesus begins the full reign without any resistance in sight. All judgment has taken place. Now is the fullness of eternal victory. No wonder we will all be on our faces! There are the redeemed in heaven finally seeing the complete victory and reward. And all those who rejected his rule will receive their deserved judgment. It has arrived and finally all who opposed the true king are brought into judgment (11:18). What is the significance here?

You've got a time machine. It looks forward and gives you the opportunity to play a part in the outcome of where you, and others, will stand when this takes place. You will either be judged or be rewarded. Now there is still time to turn from the things of the *world* that take away your focus from honoring the Lord. Now is the time to enter his kingdom by faith. There is still time to put your trust in Jesus and find your fulfillment in him, to live for him and his kingdom!

Study Questions

1. Why might some commentators think this text is only opening a part of the contents of the final trumpet?

2. What have we learned about the structure of Revelation that can help us understand where this event takes place in salvation history?

3. What are some specific points that show this is the final Day of Judgment?

4. How might this text be an argument for the Premillennial view?

5. How might this text work against the Premillennial view?

6. Does this text help our understanding of worship style?

7. When does Jesus begin his reign, and how does this text fit into that?

8. When does Satan's kingdom fall?

9. How does this view of Judgment Day affect the meaning of your life now?

8
The Answer to Evil
(Revelation 11:18-19)

In September 2012, Jill Meagher, a young woman who worked at the ABC in Melbourne, was brutally raped and murdered. It became worldwide news. The murderer, Adrian Bayley, had previously served about 11 years in prison for the rape and attempted rape of eight other women. He committed this crime while he was on parole. This time he received 20 years for the murder and 15 years for the rape. Tom Meagher, the victim's husband, was interviewed for the first time (ABC 7:30 Report) a year later (19th June, 2013). He was dumbfounded at the sentence. He was grieved. He felt it was inadequate. The maximum sentence for rape is 25 years and Bayley got 10 years less than the maximum. Tom Meagher's question was, 'If this is not a maximum sentence case, what would he have to do to receive the maximum?'

The judge who handed down the sentence spoke of the evil, callous nature of the crime, yet didn't deliver a maximum sentence. There was general outrage in society and people took to the streets to voice their fury. There was anger that the man who did this could ever see the light of day again.

It seems our society is struck with a dilemma and finds it difficult to put it into words. Judges, commentators and those affected, including Tom Meagher, all question and debate the sentencing criteria. They ask, 'What message does this send society? What is the deterrent value if someone can commit a crime such as this and not get a life sentence?' The legal academics bring up statistics and studies to argue that long sentences, even death sentences, are not a deterrent. So today we hear that after parole and time off for this or that, people who have murdered are out in 14 years, 10 years or even less! So, if harsh sentences cannot be proven to be a deterrent, then what grounds are there for more severe penalties?

Tom Meagher brought up the issue of rehabilitation. He questioned whether Bayley could be rehabilitated. He also questioned if rehabilitation should be an issue in sentencing. The experts say rehabilitation is another important criterion in determining the severity of a sentence. What hope is there that the criminal can be rehabilitated? So we go into more extended debate. Our society holds up these two elements as the great criteria for sentencing. The deterrence factor and the hope of rehabilitation. As long as defense lawyers can argue a good case to show a severe sentence will not contribute as a deterrent and/or there is hope of rehabilitation for the criminal, it seems as though judges and society's hands are tied from giving severe sentences. Tom Meagher was almost in tears. He knew it was wrong that this man did not get a more severe sentence. But he couldn't put his finger on *why* the sentence was not long enough.

Just what is the answer? Surely we don't want to be out for revenge or be vigilantes. So what is missing from all these discussions on the sentences for crime becoming more and more lenient? As we move further and further away from the Christian roots we have in our country, we are becoming more and more afraid to be found judging anyone. The most well-known verse in the Bible to the unbelieving world is no longer: *For God so loved the world that he gave his one and only Son* (John 3:16). Today the most well-known verse is *Do not judge* (Matt. 7:1). It's taken totally out of context, but that is the verse people know.

But the word and concept missing from the debate that Tom Meagher couldn't put his finger on, and yet inwardly he and the world were crying out for, is not 'deterrent' or 'rehabilitation' but this one ... *Justice*. Does the punishment fit the crime? Has *justice* been done? Why are people angry and almost afraid to admit it, lest they come across as though they are barbaric? Judgmental? It's because the thought of judgment and justice has been removed from society. Notice it next time you hear the so-called experts debating, pontificating about deterrent value, the hope of rehabilitation, but never mentioning that word ... *justice*.

That is why society seems to be constantly outraged at evil but unable to come to an answer. That is why lawyers win arguments and someone who kills another person is free to walk the streets again in just a few years. They have everyone tied up arguing about deterrence or rehabilitation, but they keep this one word out of the debate — *justice*.

But who can determine exactly what is justice? What about the different individual circumstances, motives, mental and emotional capacities or other influences our legal system should consider if true justice is to be applied? Even when judges have tried to operate with these factors and justice in mind, who really has the ability to judge the motives of someone's heart?

The answer is here in our text. There is a Day of Judgment where even the motives of men's hearts are exposed.

> 'The nations were angry, and your wrath has come. The time has come for judging the dead, and for rewarding your servants the prophets and your people who revere your name, both great and small — and for destroying those who destroy the earth' (11:18).

As we learned last time, there comes a time when Jesus will reign for the first time without opposition or other claimants to his rule. Yes, he is reigning now, but there is still opposition. There are still those who rage against him. Despite our best efforts, justice is not always served, and bad people often get away with things. What we need is a judge who can judge the motives of men's hearts and deliver perfect justice. And it's here. The apostle Paul described that time coming.

> Therefore judge nothing before the appointed time; wait until the Lord comes. He will bring to light what is hidden in darkness and will expose the motives of the heart … (1 Cor. 4:5).

What we have here in Revelation is a song of praise in heaven after Jesus' full victory. There was opposition to God. People opposed him and were even angry with him. **The nations were angry.** We saw them in action in 11:7-10. They were gloating over putting down the witnesses, the people of God. They loved to hate God's ways and opposed anyone who would stand in their way. Psalm 2 is so prophetic in this.

> Why do the nations conspire and the peoples plot in vain? The kings of the earth rise up and the rulers band together against the LORD and against his anointed, saying, 'Let us break their chains and throw off their shackles' (Ps. 2:1-3).

They want to *throw off the fetters.* Throw off the restrictions. They don't want God or his anointed (that means 'Christ'), telling them what to do or how to live. You can see their rage. When the ABC had their biggest Q&A program at the Sydney Opera House, Peter Hitchens was the lone voice for Christ. And they hated him. They want to break free from the restrictions God might place on them. They shook their fist at God. The nations were angry!

But there comes this time when it's God's turn to be angry. And if justice is ever to be served, it's not just those who did wrong who are brought to account. What about justice for victims? Those who suffered righteously, the innocent, the vulnerable and the downtrodden. This is where our text informs us it's also a time for the righteous who survived the tribulation to receive their reward. None of them have been forgotten ...

'The time has come for judging the dead, <u>and for rewarding your servants the prophets and your people</u> who revere your name, <u>both great and small</u> ...'

Did you notice it's not just the *great* names, the prophets, or Abraham or Moses, or the apostle Paul, or the great fathers of the Reformation who are rewarded. It's also the *small*, the tiny, the good and faithful servants persevering unseen in the home or in difficult places and times. Those who never did 'great things' for God, but also fought the good fight against temptation and inner battles. Those who endured a lonely or a suffering life, but also were faithful. Not just the *great*, but also the *small*. Now they are rewarded.

No wonder the elders have responded spontaneously by falling down and praising and thanking the Lord (11:16). It's the 'impossible'. It's the very thing the people said could never be done. Justice! Justice for evildoers. Reward for the righteous. It was one of the great excuses so many used to continue to defy God. 'I can't believe in a God who allows this evil to happen to little children, to innocent people. It's not as though he can reverse their suffering. You can't do it God! Abuse has taken place. Rape and murder. You can't undo what has been done.' They are angry with God. *The nations were angry ...*

What a terror it will be for those same people on that day when they see that justice and a full reversal of all evil is *exactly* what the Lord does. Not only judgment for evil, but glorious reward for righteous suffering. True justice!

At this point the Preterist says this text is describing all that happened to the Jews at the destruction of Jerusalem in AD 70 by translating the word *judge* as *vindicating*. Hence, they say this is not the Day of Judgment. The problem with this is that the word translated *judge* in 11:18 is always used in Revelation as *judging the unbelieving*. We will see that at the final judgment described at the end in Rev. 20. It's *never* used as vindication. No. This is *the* day!

The Futurist view also says this is not the full and final judgment. The Futurist has the resurrection of Christians *before* the millennial reign, with another resurrection and judgment of the wicked *at the end* of a 1000-year millennial reign of Jesus. But 11:18 seems to indicate the resurrection of all people at one time, rather than separated by 1000 years. The unbelieving dead are *judged* and the believers are rewarded at the same time …

> 'The nations were angry, and your wrath has come. The time has come for judging the dead, and for rewarding your servants …' (11:18).

In fairness to Futurists, they would respond by saying that 11:18 spans 1000 years. You need to insert 1000 years in between the words **judging of the dead** and **rewarding your servants …** That is one of the difficulties I have with this view. It seems to be always asking for special pleading to insert 1000 years where it is not mentioned and doesn't seem to fit. It's the same problem later in Revelation …

> And I saw the dead, great and small, standing before the throne, and books were opened. Another book was opened, which is the book of life. The dead were judged according to what they had done as recorded in the books. … Anyone whose name was not found written in the book of life was thrown into the lake of fire (20:12,15).

Some are found who have their names in that book and they have life, and the rest are judged, but the text seems to be saying the judgment is altogether, at one time. It would seem unnatural to insert 1000 years in between a judgment of the righteous and the wicked, as in the Futurist view. It's the same in other parts of the Bible. The resurrection of both the good and evil are not separated by 1000 years but are all in one final resurrection.

> Multitudes who sleep in the dust of the earth will awake: some to everlasting life, others to shame and everlasting contempt (Dan. 12:2).

With the Futurist (Pre-millennial) view you must read that as *some to everlasting life* [insert 1000 years], *others to shame and everlasting contempt.* Or again where Jesus spoke of the resurrection of both believers and unbelievers together …

> 'Do not be amazed at this, for a time is coming when all who are in their graves will hear his voice and come out—those who have done what is good will rise to live, [insert 1000 years] and those who have done what is evil will rise to be condemned' (John 5:28-29).

It's the same problem all through the teaching of Jesus' parables. Remember the wheat and the weeds? Jesus said they were to grow up together and be harvested together! But the Futurist view needs to insert 1000 years in between the two at the harvest. Then there is Jesus' parable of the net. Note only one net …

> 'Once again, the kingdom of heaven is like a net that was let down into the lake and caught all kinds of fish. When it was full, the fishermen pulled it up on the shore. Then they sat down and collected the good fish in baskets, but threw the bad away. This is how it will be at the end of the age. The angels will come and separate the wicked from the righteous' (Matt. 13:47-49).

If we take the Futurist position, then somewhere in that separation of the fish we need to insert 1000 years. If we study the parables closely, such as the parable of the ten virgins, the parable of the talents and most clearly the parable of the sheep and the goats in Matthew 25:31-46, both the wicked and righteous are all there together on the Day of Judgment. Both the sheep and the goats are to receive either punishment or eternal reward, with no 1000 years in between. And that is the issue in our text at 11:18. The believers and unbelievers are together; the dead are judged and the saints are rewarded at the same time, with no suggestion of 1000 years in between …

> 'The nations were angry, and your wrath has come. The <u>time</u> has come for judging the dead, <u>and</u> for rewarding your servants the prophets and your people who revere your name, both great and small—and for destroying those who destroy the earth.' Then God's temple in heaven was opened, and within his temple was seen the ark of his covenant. And there came flashes of lightning, rumblings, peals of thunder, an earthquake and a severe hailstorm (11:18-19).

We have already looked in our previous chapter at how this repetition at the end of both the seals and bowls—the flashes of lightning, rumblings, peals of thunder and earthquake—shows this is the final Day of Judgment. But there is something strange in this vision for John, the Jewish apostle. The *ark of his covenant* was seen. You are not supposed to *see* the ark! That is in the Holy of Holies for only the high priest to see. What is going on here? This is what Revelation has been building up to since the beginning in 1:5, *that God's people are a kingdom and priests* (alluding to Exodus 19:6 *You will be for me a Kingdom of priests*). It's the priesthood of all believers which has been unfolding throughout salvation history, now on display by the presence of the ark.

Now John gets a vision of the true temple and it has the ark open for everyone to see. Everyone has access to the mercy seat, to this merciful God, rather than just the high priest, who was the only one allowed to see the ark as he entered the Holy of Holies only once a year.

> But when Christ came as high priest of the good things that are already here, he went through the greater and more perfect tabernacle that is not made with human hands, that is to say, is not a part of this creation. ... For Christ did not enter a sanctuary made with human hands that was only a copy of the true one; he entered heaven itself, now to appear for us in God's presence (Heb. 9:11,24).

The earthly temple is not the true temple, says the Hebrews writer! It was only a copy! In this vision John sees the real thing. The true temple even has the Ark of the Covenant! The true temple is not a man-made temple. This is what Stephen the disciple saw when he was being stoned to death for supposedly speaking out against the temple. When he looks up and sees heaven open, what does he see? He gets a look at the true temple. He saw the Lord Jesus at the right hand of the Father. He saw heaven, the true temple. Not the shadow, the earthly temple they were arguing over, but the real deal.

So what is John seeing now? It's been building up all through 11:1-18. He has seen the suffering of God's people, the vindication of the witnesses and their resurrection. Now he sees a vision of the true temple—open! And there is God, reigning in full victory. This vision is given to John in the kind of symbolic imagery that John, as an aging Jew, would see as so rich in meaning. The Ark of the Covenant!

This was formerly hidden inside the exclusive Holy of Holies for only the high priest to see. It's now visible for all to see!

Let's not forget the presence of the ark also signals God's covenantal saving love with his people (Ex. 25:22). It's a picture of the intimate closeness of God in his mercy and now that ark is in full view. The mercy and holiness of God is fully revealed! The ark. This is the heavenly tabernacle of which the earthly was only a copy.

Judgment for unbelievers is terrifying, but it's a day of rejoicing in God's mercy and love for believers. *The nations were angry, and your wrath has come. The time has come for judging the dead, and for rewarding your servants* … (11:18). The nations were angry with God. What is fascinating about humans is their arrogance in that they think they have the right to be angry, as though *they* are the ones who are primarily offended. 'How could God have allowed this to happen?' It's not that humans don't have a right to be angry at evil. There is such a thing as righteous anger at evil. But what is missing is perspective. When Adrian Bayley (who murdered Jill Meagher) said in court he had some sort of remorse, he may well have been genuinely angry—angry at himself and angry at his life. Does he have a right to be angry? Yes, of course. But in light of the loved ones who lost this woman that he raped and murdered, who *really* should be angry? Get a perspective, Adrian!

We have a right to be angry at the sin in this world, but we have also played a part in the world being the way it is. Our part might be miniscule compared to a murderer. But Jesus says in God's sight, if you have been angry with your brother, you have sinned in the same category as murder and are worthy of judgment. We may not have raped, but Jesus said if you have ever looked lustfully you have committed adultery. We may not have committed deception leading to a major crime, but have you ever told a lie? The corruption of this world and the chaos it's in is because of human sin. That sin sent the world off its very axis. The creation is groaning because of human sin. Notice the end of this verse.

> 'The nations were angry, and your wrath has come. The time has come for judging the dead, and for rewarding your servants the prophets and your people who revere your name, both great and small—and for destroying those who destroy the earth' (11:18).

Humans are **destroying the earth** in many ways. Not caring for the environment is one way. We were commanded to care for the earth in the beginning (Gen. 2:15). But the primary reason the world is plunged into disaster (including the natural world), is because of human rebellion against God. So, if you have ever sinned, you have played a part in the very thing that caused this world to no longer be at peace. And you haven't always been the peacemaker either—in the home or at work. You haven't always had pure thoughts. You haven't always had a kind word or deed. Yes, you have a right to be angry at sin. But if you think you are angry at sin in this world, wait till you see what God thinks! God is infinitely *angrier*. In fact, his anger has been kindling for thousands of years. And the day we are looking at here is the day he finally lets it all go! You think you are angry with that rapist? God has also been angry with that rapist, but infinitely more! You think you are angry with that murderer? You don't know what anger is! On this day, God fully displays his justice and righteous anger and lets it go. And it keeps reverberating in hell forever. It's all perfectly measured justice and not one little bit of wrong is left out. God has also been angry at the one who told lies, who was selfish, who looked lustfully, who lacked love, who was materialistic, and so on. This is the day when he brings every deed into judgment, each one individually *according to the things they have done*. Now is the time for perfect justice.

But how can it be that in this same passage there are some who are being rewarded? Who is without sin? Who can stand? ... **The time has come for judging the dead, and for <u>rewarding</u> your servants the prophets and your <u>people who revere your name</u>, great and small ...** The original language says *those who fear your name*. The term *fear* is misunderstood as being afraid of God in the sense of dread. That is why translators highlight the reverence aspect, which is right to do, but the word is literally *godly fear*. It is displayed most clearly in the response we saw from the elders in 11:16. Their worship style wouldn't get a look in today's church. They fell. Not backwards out of control, but forwards on their faces in reverent worship. Godly fear.

But revering his name is not just the posture in worship. It means more than that. Worship means having a great awe for God *and* trembling at his word (Isa. 66:2). Those who revere his name are people who are going to believe what he says about their sin. So instead of the self-righteous anger at God, they realize *they too were an object of God's wrath* (Eph. 2:5), so they throw themselves on the mercy of Jesus and what he has done to take away their sin. They revered Jesus' words to *repent for the kingdom of heaven is near.* They revered his teaching that this world is passing and today is the day to live for him. And now they are rewarded forever. This is the Day of Judgment. The only question is, 'If God is so angry at sin, why did he allow it to go on so long?' We know the answer…

> The Lord is not slow in keeping his promise, as some understand slowness. He is patient with you, not wanting anyone to perish, but everyone to come to repentance (2 Pet. 3:9).

He has held back the Day of Judgment because there are those who are yet to come to repentance. There are those who if God brought about judgment today, would otherwise spend eternity in hell. So he has held it off. That is why he has held back his anger so long. He is waiting for the last one to come in. It might be one more missionary who needs to be sent out. It might be one who claims to know him but is yet to repent of a secret sin, or are lukewarm, or one who has yet to make a stand for Jesus, to revere his name. That is why he has held back. But his patience does eventually run out and that is this day described here.

The only unanswerable question about why God allows suffering is, 'Why did God allow the suffering and evil to be perpetrated against his own Son, for the very people who have the audacity to say they are the ones who have a right to be angry?' On this day, we will see there is only One who has the full right to be angry.

Study Questions

1. What are the two main criteria in our society that judges use to determine sentences?

2. What criteria is missing and why has society shifted in this regard?

3. Why are even the best attempts to bring just sentencing inadequate?

4. Why are people angry with God? Is there more to it than the state of the world?

5. What event does the Preterist say this text is describing? Evaluate.

6. How does the Futurist understand this text? Evaluate.

7. When does Jesus begin his reign and how does this text fit into that time?

8. What does the appearance of the Ark of the Covenant signify, and how does it help our understanding of temple theology?

9. Is human anger at sin right or wrong?

10. What is the unanswerable question about God allowing suffering and evil?

9
The Woman
(Revelation 12:1-6 Part 1)

When I was in the entertainment industry it always fascinated me how artists, singers, dancers and magicians would have this great persona, all smiles and glitter while on stage, but backstage, behind the curtains, you might see a totally different persona. Yelling, backbiting and everything from trying to calm nerves with cigarettes, to throwing up out of nervousness. The backstage crew is running around and it is chaos, all so this contrasting lovely presentation could go on in front of the curtain. Well, we have reached a turning point in the book of Revelation that divides the book into two halves in more ways than one and lifts the curtain to expose what is really going on behind the stage.

Revelation started out with the letters to the churches and revealed how the churches were under pressure to compromise with the world and to let false teaching inside the church. Then we had a change of camera angle from the Master film director. We had the heavenly perspective of who is on the throne, and the forces unleashed through the opening of the seven seals.

After the seals we got to the trumpets, and there was a serious unleashing of evil powers from the pit of hell, as it were, the Abyss. Locusts like demons. How would the Christians survive? Then we read they are sealed through this, and though they have trials, they are kept and the trials work for their good, whereas the locust-type creatures torment the unbelievers. So far, it has been a revelation of tribulation, destruction, death, attack on God's people, chaos in the world, plagues and havoc.

But what we get now from Rev. 12 onwards is a greater *revelation* of what (or more to the point, who), is behind the curtain and why evil comes into the world and Jesus' church. The curtain is suddenly *lifted*—to see all the ugliness behind it. And behind the curtain it is an ugly scene indeed. We see there *is* someone behind all this ugliness ... the originator and master of evil. It is revealed in these chapters how he is the instigator behind the Beast and the False Prophet.

There is a war going on. The spiritual warfare we have seen in Rev. 1-11 has been between the world and the church. But what we discover from Rev. 12 onwards is that it's not actually between the world and the church. It's a war between Satan and Jesus ... and guess who wins?

We have seen this spiritual war alluded to with signs and symbols of creatures coming up from the Abyss, which is the realm of the demons, 200 million troops at one point. But what is behind those ugly locust-type creatures? Where is all that power coming from? Who is driving it? Now the curtain is pulled back on what is behind it. We are even told who is behind it ... Satan.

In this revelation, the apostle John is getting the vision or the film version of Ephesians 6:12. Our struggle is not against flesh and blood (not what we see on the front of stage), but against what is behind the scenes in the heavenly realms. It is principalities and powers. Revelation is written for Christians to be strengthened going through the trial, and to know where the real battle lies, but more importantly, who is actually winning this battle. John told his readers from the outset what they should expect ... *I, John, your brother and companion in the suffering and kingdom and patient endurance that are ours in Jesus* ... John told the people to whom he was writing that they were fellow sufferers and patient endurance was needed. But now John is passing on to *you* Christian *why* you are suffering. Your true enemy is not impersonal random circumstances. Your enemy is *very* personal. But this turning point in Rev. 12 also shows the devil does not have the controls. The Lord reigns! Jesus wins. Everything the devil does is always playing into the hands of the one who is directing this film.

So, let's look at Rev. 12. What John is seeing in this chapter is the replay with the 'behind the scenes' camera angle. This is the classic 'making of' film. John is looking back over all he has seen in Rev. 1-11. I am going to argue John sees a sweep of the church age. The most popular view of this scene with the Dragon and the woman in the desert is that this is all confined to some future time that no Christian will be around to see.

So it will be important for us to identify two things. Who is this woman, and when is this period of time, the 1,260 days she spends in the desert? The first sight John sees is a beautiful one ...

> A great sign appeared in heaven: a woman clothed with the sun, with the moon under her feet and a crown of twelve stars on her head. She was pregnant and cried out in pain as she was about to give birth (12:1-2).

Let's start with the easier bit. We can figure out who the baby is. By the time we get through these first five verses we see it's Jesus, the Son of God ...

> She gave birth to a son, a male child, who 'will rule all the nations with an iron scepter.' And her child was snatched up to God and to his throne (12:5).

The one who would **rule all the nations with an iron scepter** is a quote straight out of Psalm 2:9. We saw how 11:18 was alluding to Psalm 2. Here also 12:5 is speaking of the Son of God being taken up to the throne of God, that is, Jesus' ascension. Not too many would argue with this interpretation. So if the son this woman gives birth to is Jesus, then the woman has to be ... Mary. Right? That is what the RCs claim. They love to have Mary up there, clothed in all her splendor. So is it Mary? You might think so, until you look more closely at the text. When we get to 12:6, we see this same woman is persecuted, flees into the wilderness, and by 12:17 we get the picture that this is referring in metaphor to something beyond a single woman, so it can't be Mary the mother of Jesus.

> Then the Dragon was enraged at the woman and went off to wage war against the rest of her offspring—those who keep God's commands and hold fast their testimony about Jesus (12:17).

RCs don't believe Mary had any other offspring (even though Matt. 13:55 says Jesus had brothers and sisters, they reject this because it destroys their doctrine of Mary's everlasting virginity). But the offspring of this woman are those who obey God and hold to Jesus. These surely are more than just Mary's other children. And this woman spends some days in the desert, and if this is some time in the future and reaches to the end, then Mary must still be alive today, which would make Mary kind of old by now.

The Preterist says all this happened before AD 70, so the woman fleeing represents the Christians fleeing the Roman siege and going to Pella in AD 66, which sounds reasonable. Those of the most popular Futurist view say this woman represents a remnant of Jews near the end of the world. They don't take this literally as a woman, but that she represents Israel. This interpretation has some merit. For it says at the end of 12:1 she wears ... *a crown of <u>twelve</u> stars on her head.* Twelve is the number of God's people. It could be 12 tribes of Israel (then it could be twelve apostles, or both). But it seems plausible this is referring to Israel, because it's definitely Israel who gave birth to the Messiah. But then what happens to the woman after that?

> She gave birth to a son, a male child, who will rule all the nations with an iron scepter. And her child was snatched up to God and to his throne. The woman fled into the wilderness to a place prepared for her by God, where she might be taken care of for 1,260 days (12:5-6).

After she gives birth it says her son ascends, snatched up to heaven; *then* in 12:6 the woman flees out to the wilderness. So how can this woman be ancient Israel who gives birth to the Messiah, and then flees to the desert for 1,260 days, if the wilderness episode is supposed to take place at some future end time as the Futurist understands this part of Revelation? In the text, the woman gives birth and then flees out into the wilderness, straight after Jesus has ascended, and then only for 1,260 days. There is no indication in the text of a delay. That would make it about 3½ years after Jesus ascended to heaven (AD 30s), not some future time. Futurist scholars vary on how to explain this. They tend to hover between either *inserting* an unspecified couple of 1000 years delay between 12:5 and 12:6, (so the woman represents Israel both at the time of Jesus' birth and Israel far into the future near the end). Others just ignore the elephant in the room altogether that a literal 1,260 days just doesn't fit between Jesus' ascension and the end of all things.

My question as always is: what would this text mean to those first readers of the book of Revelation? Isn't the plainest reading of the text that the woman gives birth to the son and then flees into the desert from the time Jesus ascends, rather than inserting or ignoring a great delay of time in between? The same woman is not separated from herself for thousands of years. The 1,260 days follows immediately after the ascension of Jesus.

But if we go back to inserting time, look how unnaturally it reads.

> She gave birth to a son, a male child, who will rule all the nations with an iron scepter. And her child was snatched up to God and to his throne. [Insert at least 2000 years of church age.] The woman fled into the wilderness to a place prepared for her by God, where she might be taken care of for 1,260 days (12:5-6).

I personally can't see the original readers understanding it that way. It would not be Revelation to them but hidden. It seems to be inserting something that is not natural. I do agree with the Futurist view that the woman is a metaphor for Israel when she gives birth to Jesus. The Futurist could point out that a 'woman' is a common OT metaphor that God uses to describe his people. God is the husband; his people are the wife, the 'woman'. I not only agree with that, but I don't think it's going far enough. Of course Israel is referred to as a woman, but what are the people of God referred to in the NT? Christ loved the church and gave himself up for *her*. The bride of Christ. What does this very book of Revelation call the people of God? She is the *bride*. The woman at the wedding banquet. This is where Revelation is heading. The woman is the great metaphor for all believers in the Messiah both OT *and* NT. The people of God!

So, if we take 12:5-6 in its most natural reading, this woman is the people of God who believe in the Messiah. That includes OT believers, Israel, who produced the Messiah, *and* the church *after* Jesus is snatched up to heaven. That explains how this same woman (believers) then goes into the wilderness. In other words, Rev. 12 is saying what Revelation has been hinting at all along, and what the NT teaches in Ephesians 2 and Romans 11, which is that the fulfillment of the woman (Israel) is the gospel of Jesus Christ, the mystery! Gentiles are joined to (*not replacing*) Israel. They are grafted into the citizenship of Israel (Eph. 2:12-13). If this is a new idea to you and you are operating on a preconceived concept of a separate salvation future for Jew and Gentile, then I would appeal to you to try looking at God's salvation plan through the lens of the *gospel of Jesus*. Through Jesus, this idea is neither novel nor new, if we believe that all the promises of God are 'yes' and 'Amen' in Jesus. And if Jesus has joined the two together in the gospel to break down that hostility (Eph. 2:14), it would seem strange to separate them again into two groups at some future time. What is the practical implication of this? Today is the day to evangelize the Jews! Go to the Jew today that many of those natural branches might believe in their Messiah!

In 11:19 Gentile believers could see the 'unseeable' Ark of the Covenant in the Holy of Holies. Why? The curtain of the temple was torn in two when Jesus died on the cross. One gospel. One Christ. One people of God. One woman!

This is the gospel and what it achieved. It made the two, one. We need to soak in these words again from the apostle Paul.

> Therefore, remember that formerly you who are Gentiles by birth and called 'uncircumcised' by those who call themselves 'the circumcision' (which is done in the body by human hands)—remember that at that time you were separate from Christ, <u>excluded from citizenship in Israel</u> and foreigners to the covenants of the promise, without hope and without God in the world. <u>But now</u> in Christ Jesus you who once were far away have been brought near by the blood of Christ. ... Consequently, you are no longer foreigners and aliens, but <u>fellow citizens</u> with God's people and members of God's household ... (Eph. 2:11-13,19).

So the Gentile believers in the Messiah are grafted into the natural branches, Israel. The woman. And we have in Rev. 12 one woman who *gives birth* to the Messiah *and* goes into the wilderness in the gospel era. One body, both Jew and Gentile. Here in Revelation we see the sweep of history and the people of the Messiah represented as one, covering all of salvation history. The woman represents the believers in the OT and NT because in the gospel ... *There is neither <u>Jew nor Gentile</u>, neither slave nor free, nor is there male and female, for you are <u>all one in Christ Jesus</u>* (Gal. 3:28).

You can understand why the apostle Paul also said later to the Galatians *you are the Israel of God* (Gal. 6:16). This thinking allows the continuity of this woman to be both Israel that gave birth to the Messiah, and Israel after, the true ethnic Israelites trusting in their Messiah along with Gentiles believing in the Jewish Messiah being grafted in. This is where Rev. 21 is taking us—the New Jerusalem. What is the New Jerusalem? It's a combination of the 12 tribes of Israel with the 12 apostles to build the city, as Ephesians 2:20-22 says: the *two* are being built into *one holy temple*. The Gentiles have been grafted into the natural branches and the church is a royal priesthood under the one great High Priest. This is why I reject the term 'replacement theology', because it gives the impression of Gentile believers replacing Israel. The woman (Israel) is not *replaced* with another woman. There is only one woman (from the time of those who gave birth to the Messiah, through to and beyond Jesus' ascension, and then into the wilderness). So Gentiles are *added* to the true Israel, the faithful remnant of Jewish believers—not replacing them. And the Lord continues to also call his ethnic chosen people in the gospel era as well. Today there are approximately 350,000 Messianic Jews[5], but when we consider that Israel remains a tiny nation of only about 14 million people, and that only a small percentage of those are religious or looking for *any* Messiah, that makes the number of Messianic Jews all the more impressive. It fits with OT history and Paul's argument that there was only ever a faithful *remnant* (Romans 11:1-5).

So here this woman has a crown of how many stars?

> A great sign appeared in heaven: a woman clothed with the sun, with the moon under her feet and a crown of <u>twelve stars</u> on her head (12:1).

The number 12 symbolizes the people of God and can apply to both the tribes and the apostles. Interestingly it's not 24 this time. A single number 12 covers all believers (one woman), joining both those who gave birth to the Messiah to those believers after Jesus ascended. In fact, as we noted, 12:17 seems to be describing God's people generally, not just Jewish believers.

> Then the Dragon was enraged at the woman and went off to wage war against the rest of her offspring--<u>those who keep God's commands and hold fast their testimony about Jesus</u> (12:17).

This doesn't seem like the way you would describe exclusively Israelite believers. This seems like the way you would expect any believers in Jesus to be described. *Those who obey God and hold to Jesus.* But we still have a problem. If we are not going to insert periods of time unnaturally in between 12:5-6, then what about the 1,260 days in the wilderness? The woman gives birth and then flees into the wilderness for 1,260 days. So after Jesus ascended, the church is in

---

[5] http://jewsforjudaism.org/knowledge/articles/many-messianic-jews/

the wilderness for about 3½ years. But we are not totally thrown here. We have already seen 1,260 days in 11:3. Remember the two witnesses? Based on them being lampstands, we said they were the faithful portion of the church. And sure enough, the length of their witness for Jesus to testify on earth went all the way through to the Day of Judgment. So the 1,260 days stretches right up to the end.

So we agree with the Futurist that these 1,260 days reaches right up to the end, and yet we see in 12:5 that the 1,260 days clearly *begins* from the time of Jesus' *ascension*. How can we put these two things together? The 1,260 days between the time of Jesus' ascension and the end? Mighty long days!

But we did look at this already. This period of time was called 42 months in 11:2; 42 x 30-day months = 1,260 days. We saw the same period of time referred to as 3½ years, or a time, times and half a time, 1 + 2 + ½ (3 ½ years). But as we said then, there are many forerunners of this timeframe that point to 1,260 days being the 'type' or model of tribulation.

Remember the several significant events in the life of God's people that all lasted for or about 1,260 days? There was Elijah's drought, the great persecution from Antiochus Epiphanes, Jerusalem sieged by the Roman armies, and Nero's persecution. And remember the most significant trial of all—the ministry of Jesus himself. Which trial is the type looking to the future? Or is it all of them? To an aging Jew like the apostle John, who is seeing this vision and is aware of the history of his people, 1,260 days is like code for a time of tribulation. We know by now it has become standard practice in Revelation to use numbers symbolically, as all the different views agree for instance that the number 12 (12:1) represents God's people in some form. So what would 1,260 days symbolize to John? A time of trial or tribulation.

We know this is symbolic because it tells us right in the text he is speaking in signs. What did John see in 12:1? A woman? No, he didn't! It says he saw a **sign**. *A great sign appeared in heaven: a woman clothed with the sun* ... He did not see a literal woman, but a sign or symbol. The word *sign* in 12:1 is the same root word in Greek that I keep referring to back at the start of Revelation, where in 1:1 it says the Revelation was given to 'make known', meaning *make known by signs*. He makes known (reveals) by signs. This woman is a sign or symbol, the number twelve is a symbol, and so it is only being consistent to take this period of 1,260 days as a sign or a symbol that John would recognize from Israel's history, that is, 1,260 days. A time of trial. So 1,260 days points to a time of trial. It's the time the woman spends in the wilderness, from Jesus' ascension to the end.

So what is this saying about the woman in the church age? Why have we spent so much time working out who this woman is and the time she wanders in the wilderness? *Because it's you!* If you are a believer, you are the woman (or at least part of the body that makes up the whole).

So what is this message to Christians from the time of Jesus' ascension through the ages? How is this part of Revelation useful (as all Scripture is to Christians)? It's telling you, believer … this is not your home! You are in the wilderness! You are wandering in the wilderness. Just like God's people of old. You are on your way to the Promised Land through a difficult wilderness trek.

If you are a believer in Jesus, a part of the bride of Christ (the woman), you and the rest of the believers go through the tribulation, this wilderness, in the church age. The woman who is pregnant in 12:1-2 represents 'believers in the Messiah'. After the birth of Jesus, they are taken into the wilderness, just like the people of old. This woman (as the people of Israel) spend their time in the wilderness and just as they were taken care of during that time, so too the gates of hell will not prevail against Jesus' church. They follow the example of their Lord, who went through his time of trial for about 3½ years.

> The woman fled into the wilderness to a <u>place prepared for her by God</u>, where she might be <u>taken care of</u> for 1,260 days (12:6).

In the Exodus wilderness, the Lord led his people. They were tested, refined, and yet miraculously **taken care of**! The wilderness this woman is going through is certainly a place of trial and a place where her people are refined and kept! So you people of Jesus are not only 'the woman', but you are also in the wilderness right now. A long trial, but a limited trial symbolized by 1,260 days. Do you feel it? Tested and tried. And yet the promise is this. You will be *taken care of*! Downtrodden and downcast, but not forsaken. Now do you understand what Paul meant?

> We are hard pressed on every side, but not crushed; perplexed, but not in despair; persecuted, but not abandoned; struck down, but not destroyed (2 Cor. 4:8-9).

This is what it is like to live as the woman in the wilderness. We are not home yet. But he will keep us. Just as Jesus himself went through his 1,260 days of intense trial and ministry, so his church must follow him. If you are one of his you must follow him. This is written to tell you—don't give up.

As we get further into this text, we see the reason the trial in the wilderness is so intense is that there is an enemy against Jesus and the woman. That is, there is an enemy against you! The curtain is pulled back, and we can see behind the scenes. We can see why this desert wilderness trial is so difficult. But to learn more about that enemy, we will have to wait until the next Act in *The Dragon*.

Study Questions

1. Why is this a turning point in the book of Revelation?

2. Who is this woman pregnant with? How can you support this?

3. Who is the woman? What makes it difficult to say the woman is simply ancient Israel?

4. When are the 1,260 days, and what is the difficulty if this time is taken literally?

5. How does the gospel of Jesus contribute overall to this text?

6. How might John see the 1,260 days and why might the text be telling us to take it symbolically?

7. How can this text apply practically to you?

8. How does this text give assurance to a believer?

10
The Dragon
(Revelation 12:1-6 Part 2)

The woman is *wandering in the wilderness*. We noted this alludes to the Exodus. Many times we've seen references to the Exodus in Revelation. Now we have the church's version of the wilderness wanderings. In the wilderness, the LORD took care of the Israelites. He miraculously kept them. They were tested and refined, but the LORD supplied their needs and kept them. Here, this woman is going through her own wilderness wandering (from the time of Jesus' ascension), and what does 12:6 say? *That she might be taken care of* in the wilderness. God prepares this journey and takes care of her in the wilderness.

We must never remove Jesus from any part of Scripture. Every part of Scripture is in some way pointing to Christ. Where does Jesus fit in all this? Well, Jesus had a wilderness testing. When he began his ministry where did he begin? He was taken into the wilderness! He was tested by the devil. What was going on there? Jesus is the Son of God that Israel never lived up to. Remember Israel was called the son of God? When Matthew 2:15 says *Out of Egypt I called my son*, Matthew is quoting Hosea 11:1, when God called Israel, the son of God, out of Egypt into the wilderness. But Israel was not the faithful son. So what was Jesus doing when he went into the wilderness? Look at all those temptations he resisted. Jesus was doing what Israel failed to do. Read Matthew 4:1-11 and see how all the references to Deuteronomy in Jesus' temptations are identical to Israel's tests which they failed, such as living not on bread alone but by the word of God (Deut. 8:3); not putting God to the test (Deut. 6:16); and worshiping the Lord only (Deut. 6:13). Jesus is the faithful Son of God that Israel failed to be. *Jesus* goes through the wilderness *without* giving in to temptation. In fact, Jesus' whole ministry was a trial leading up to the cross. About 3½ years or 1,260 days. And his followers must follow him. The church must follow him through *their* wilderness—their time of trial—their 1,260 days, that each generation of the church experiences all the way to the end. It's familiar typology looking back to Israel …

> He led you through the vast and dreadful wilderness, that thirsty and waterless land, with its venomous snakes and scorpions. He brought you water out of hard rock. He gave you manna to eat in the wilderness, something your ancestors had never known, to humble and <u>test you</u> so that in the end it might go well with you (Deut. 8:15-16).

What has that got to do with us? Everything. Just like Israel had to journey through tough times, *testing,* waiting, waiting for entrance into the Promised Land, so too the church is refined in this wilderness before she enters the Promised Land, heaven. But through the wilderness, the church is kept. *The woman fled into the wilderness to a place prepared for her by God, where she might be <u>taken care of</u> for 1,260 days* (12:6).

Even through the wilderness testing we know the church endures. The gates of hell will not prevail against her. She is *taken care of.* She is sealed (Holy Spirit in Rev. 7, 9). She is the temple which is measured (Rev. 11), that is, protected by God. And look at her splendor!

> A great sign appeared in heaven: a woman <u>clothed with the sun</u>, with <u>the moon</u> under her feet and <u>a crown</u> of twelve stars on her head (12:1).

Now this is the picture of the church. But wait a minute. Is that how you would describe the church? Arrayed in splendor and glory? We have seen the church going through the wilderness, with her frailty and clothes all tattered. We saw her in the seven churches, warts and all, with Jesus rebuking most of them. It's pathetic. She doesn't look like that here in splendor in 12:1. What's going on here?

This is exactly why John and his seven churches need this Revelation—*because* they are in such a mess. This is what we need when we begin to despair at the state of the church. On earth, she looks stained and corrupted, and we lament the state of the church. But the heavenly perspective is that she shines in beautiful array. She is *in Christ.* She has every spiritual blessing in the *heavenly realms* (Eph. 2:6). She is the woman who is the bride of Christ—righteous in him.

Through Revelation we will see the woman (the people of the Messiah) as one attacked, gasping for air in the wilderness, needing spiritual nourishment from the Lord. We have already seen in the seven letters to the seven churches she is fraught with difficulties, many of which are of her own making, compromising and allowing false teaching. But now, seven churches (including us), be encouraged, because this is the heavenly perspective of the woman. Clothed in splendor. This is her true identity. Who are we really? We are in Christ. We have a standing in heaven already. Where do you stand? Do you know Jesus? Have you put your trust in what Christ has done in his death and his resurrection to cleanse you from your sin? If so, then you are *in Christ* and heaven has declared you righteous and your place in splendor is already assured! Although for now you might be depressed or downcast or going through a serious trial, and things haven't worked out the way you hoped or planned in this life. Of course they haven't! You are not home yet! You are in the wilderness! But your standing in Christ is in splendor and glory in the heavenly realms.

We have seen from the letters to the seven churches that God's people will wear crowns. The victory, the vindication, they will reign with Christ (3:11). Where and when is that? It's already truth above! But it is not yet fully experienced. It's already secured in Christ. It's a done deal. The contract is already signed in the blood of God's own Son. But we don't always feel it. But look at this woman (believers) in her present splendor and glory!

You say, 'I don't feel like that. I don't feel like I am in splendor and glory or that my life is so good.' But that is why you need this. That is why Revelation is given ... when you are doing it tough through the wilderness. This is given so you can be built up, seeing who you really are in Christ.

The other reason those first readers (and we) need this perspective is so we can brace ourselves for what unfolds from here, as we see the woman is exposed to persecution and attack.

> She was pregnant and cried out in pain as she was about to give birth (12:2).

The birth pains are what believers went through leading up to the birth of Jesus. What did Israel go through up to the birth of Jesus?

They went through plenty—centuries of persecution and attack, even in the 400 years of silence between the OT and NT before the Messiah was born. There was massive persecution in the Inter-Testamental period, especially in the second century BC, with horrific persecution from the Seleucids under Antiochus Epiphanes, who desecrated the temple. It was with great pain the believing community brought forth the Messiah.

Now we see her splendor, but we also see that finally the curtain is pulled back on who is behind the attacks. Why did this woman go through so much pain to give birth to the Messiah? Another sign!

> Then another sign appeared in heaven: an enormous red Dragon with seven heads and ten horns and seven crowns on its heads (12:3).

The number seven represents God's number of fullness of *quality* in biblical imagery. The number ten contains the idea of a fullness of *quantity* (it's a decimal fullness). Back in 5:6 it was the Lamb who had *seven* horns, indicating completeness in strength and goodness. But here the Dragon has **seven heads**. Why does he have God's number? Because he is the counterfeit. The great fake and imitator. We know this Dragon is the devil (12:9). With the Lamb, the number seven indicated fullness in what is good. Here with the Dragon we have the fullness in evil, in counterfeit, and in mockery.

Also, he is a **red Dragon**, which shows that all those depictions of the devil in red pajamas and pitchfork were right after all. No. Actually, it's far more sinister than that. We are going to see later in 17:3-6 that the scarlet color of the prostitute woman is linked to her being drunk on the *blood* of God's holy people. The red indicates blood, as it did in Rev. 6 with the red horse indicating the *blood* of violence. So why is the Dragon red? Satan is covered in the blood of God's people. He is bloodstained, and he has a taste for the blood of Christians. He also has **seven crowns on its heads.** Crowns are what Kings wear. This is pointing to Satan as the great counterfeit king. By the time we get to 19:12 we see it is the Lord of lords and King of kings who has many crowns. But now the Dragon, the imitator, has his seven crowns. What else?

> Its tail swept a third of the stars out of the sky and flung them to the earth. The Dragon stood in front of the woman who was about to give birth, so that it might devour her child the moment he was born (12:4).

We know by now **stars** cannot literally fall on the earth or the earth would not exist. But we are not expecting a literal interpretation. We are expecting a symbolic interpretation. Many commentators see the stars as fallen angels.

> She gave birth to a son, a male child, who 'will rule all the nations with an iron scepter. And her child was snatched up to God and to his throne (12:5).

This is Jesus' entrance into the world, and then his ascension. It's a different picture from the world's view of Jesus. Yes, any serious historian will say Jesus walked the earth and was a good man. But this is cosmic. The Lord of glory was to first humble himself, born as a baby to save his people, before he is exalted to his rightful place from where he will **rule all the nations with an iron scepter**.

So what you have here is the Christmas story. I always struggle at Christmas time for another way to tell the same Christmas story. Well this is the Christmas story Revelation style. It's not just the baby in a manger. The baby will grow up to *rule the nations with an iron scepter*. But this isn't the Christmas story people actually want. People like the story of the baby in a manger. It's all so nice and cute. No challenge or threat there. But the baby in the manger as the focus doesn't make a lot of sense. Who celebrates a birthday and passes around photos of what you looked like as a baby? Baby photos at your birthday celebration? If you are going to celebrate a birthday, you celebrate your whole life! So what's going on here? It's the uncomfortable part of Christmas concerning what happens after the baby grows up. *He will rule the nations with an iron scepter.* He grows up to be the King of kings. And he is snatched up to heaven. It jumps straight to his victory in the ascension and assumes his ministry, his work on the cross and his resurrection. But if the kids acted out this version of the Christmas story it would be rated R. It's violent and scary. But it was always the plan for this woman to have this baby. It was always the plan for Israel to produce the Messiah. It was a plan from the beginning. Remember the first mention of the gospel in the Bible is when the LORD said to Satan ...

> And I will put enmity between you and the woman, and between your offspring and hers; he will crush your head, and you will strike his heel (Gen. 3:15).

Satan knew the deal back at the beginning of creation. He knew if this one (the offspring of the woman) arrived safely, he would grow up to crush his (the serpent's) head. He would slay the Dragon. This explains why this Dragon is stalking with murderous intent. This is the bloodthirsty version of the Christmas story... **The Dragon stood in front of the woman who was about to give birth, so that it might devour her child the moment he was born** (12:4).

As the Dragon waits, this moment is the culmination of an ancient, vicious pursuit to death. It is a death hunt that has been raging for thousands of years. The woman (God's people) can be traced throughout history. While this Dragon is looking so ugly here waiting for the baby, long, long before this moment, he has built up this rage. He is obsessed in his savagery, out to kill. Why? Because for thousands of years he has been thwarted, and it all comes down to this moment. This is what he has been trying to accomplish, for how long? The Dragon has existed since the beginning of creation and throughout all of history.

What a grotesque horror film John is seeing. *The Dragon stood in front of the woman who was about to give birth, so that it might devour her child the moment he was born.* If it wasn't in the Bible you wouldn't let your children see this. But John sees a woman about to have a baby, and this dragon, an evil slimy dragon, is lying in wait to kill and eat that baby. So as the baby is born, he tries to strike! Why? Because he knows that promise in Genesis 3:15, that *the offspring of the woman would crush his head.* He had to kill and stop him from ever being born. That's why this story covers the sweep of history. It began when the Dragon attempted to kill off this baby before it could be born, back in the time of Cain and Abel. The line of the Messiah, the godly line, Abel, and ... Cain murders Abel! Abel, the godly man who offered the right offering.

Who do you think was there, standing behind Cain? It was the Dragon! He was a murderer from the beginning! The line of the Messiah is exterminated. But Eve has another son and it begins *again* through Seth. You can trace it through the godly line of Seth and his descendants in Genesis 5. But again, in Genesis 6 the Dragon convinces the godly line of Seth, 'the sons of God', to marry the descendants of Cain and their ungodliness, so even the godly line becomes so corrupt that the LORD determined to destroy the whole earth in the flood. God's motive to destroy the earth is *because* of the sin of man (note his motive was not because of the sin of angels, Gen. 6:6-7). So, does the Dragon win when God floods the earth? No. The LORD spared Noah and his family. The line of the Messiah only just survived.

This is the most intense thriller, but it's real history. Then the people of God are born through Noah's line, through Abraham, Isaac and Jacob (Israel). Then Moses. Always under attack. Moses was only a baby when Pharaoh demanded all the baby boys be killed. Where have we heard that before? The king had all the babies killed in the little town of where? Bethlehem. That Christmas story was raging 1,500 years earlier when Moses was a baby under Pharaoh. Why? Who was behind Pharaoh, the serpent image of Egypt? All along it was the Dragon in the background. He wants to kill off the one who would free Israel, through whom the Messiah is to be born. The Messiah must come through the line of David. So who do you think was there in the great fight between Goliath vs. David? It is not just some kid's story. It's the Dragon trying to kill off the man through whom the Messiah must come. Even King Saul tried to pin David with a spear. And the kings that followed David's line are mostly failures, beaten down by either force or pleasure. Satan will use whatever it takes to bring them down. We read of failure after failure with the kings of Israel. In fact, Israel fails. But she is still kept through the wilderness, even through the exile.

Then in Esther's time, Haman tried to commit genocide to wipe out the whole Jewish race. But God raised up Esther and they were spared. Who was behind such an evil plan, when Haman tried to eliminate a whole race just because he has a tiff with Mordecai? The same Dragon. What labor pains Israel of old went through to bear the Messiah! Centuries of attacks. No wonder she cried out in pain. *She was pregnant and <u>cried out in pain</u> as she was about to give birth* (12:2). How much pain did Israel go through for this one? And when she gave birth, look who was waiting there …

> … The Dragon stood in front of the woman who was about to give birth, so that it might devour her child the moment he was born (12:4).

After all those centuries—now the Dragon makes his last strike at the baby. Just like he tried through Pharaoh 1,500 years earlier to kill off all the babies, the Dragon tries the same thing through King

Herod. He has all the babies in Bethlehem killed. Why? Who would do such a thing? The Dragon is trying to devour the child! He is running out of time and opportunity!

But again, he was outwitted! The baby is taken out of harm's way, out of Bethlehem. So when the baby grows up, the Dragon tries again. He tempted Jesus in the wilderness with the whole world. "Bow to me and I will give you the whole world." The Dragon knows if the Son of God gives in to temptation, the Messiah's mission to be faithful through his wilderness will be defeated. But the Dragon couldn't get him to give in, so it all came down to one last shot. The Dragon would have to kill him.

After centuries of trying to stop the woman giving birth, it all came down to a final showdown. This time he gave it his full force, infiltrating the very closest ranks at the eleventh hour. This time he will get him …

> …and the chief priests and the teachers of the law were looking for some way to get rid of Jesus, for they were afraid of the people. Then Satan entered Judas … (Luke 22:2-3).

Who entered Judas? The Dragon! Then Satan stirred up Herod, Pilate and the Jewish leaders and they crucified him. Got him! After thousands of years of history of trying to eliminate him, trying to prevent him from being born into the world and not being able to stop that, at the last possible moment, he got him. He killed the Messiah! So the one born of the woman cannot crush Satan. He got him. Dead! Buried! Finished! Final victory is to the Dragon. But then … Up from the grave he arose!

Jesus defeated even death! Jesus wins! He completed his ministry on earth and ascended on high … *And her child was snatched up to God and to his throne* (12:5). The deceiver was outwitted. Outsmarted by the King of kings! Can you imagine what a rage that Dragon was in? Satan couldn't devour the child. He has lost! Before he was a vicious, spiteful, cruel, vindictive predator. Now he is vicious, spiteful, cruel, vindictive, and he is also very angry! He has been defeated! He is furious! He has missed his intended victim, the child. Who is left? Where can this Dragon vent his anger? Who is this Dragon seeking out now? Answer: You!

> ...When the Dragon saw that he had been hurled to the earth, he pursued <u>the woman</u> who had given birth to the male child (12:13).

The woman, the people of the Messiah, Jews and Gentiles joined through Christ the Messiah. After the Son has ascended the Dragon is in a rage against the woman. If you are one of God's people, then the Dragon pursues you.

If you believe in Jesus, you have the most amazing privilege you can ever imagine. You are actually part of the salvation plan we are looking at here in this sweep of history. You have the privilege of being in the army of the King of kings and fighting on the winning side. All that John told us is ours in the kingdom from the start ... *ours is the suffering and patient endurance in the kingdom* (1:9).

It's a war. But it's not the church vs. the world. That's just the front stage façade. The curtain is drawn back and now we see behind the scenes. It's the Dragon vs. Jesus.

He has missed the child and is swishing his great body from side to side like a giant man-eating crocodile looking for the prey that has already ascended. But he missed him. So he asks who is left to devour? And he seeks out someone smaller to pick on—the remaining offspring of the woman. Who is that?

It's the church! And you wonder why things are tough! Why is the church so weak? So divided? So given to temptation and compromise? Lukewarm. Lost its first love. The church barely holds to the word of God, the very thing given to spiritually nourish it. You wonder why people don't get along. Why are there tensions in the church? Have you ever noticed why you sometimes think it's easier to get on with people outside the church? Have you wondered why you are having trouble with some particular temptation? It seems as though unbelievers don't struggle as much. And you hate it when you are taken down and fall back into that sin! Why does it happen? Why can't your marriage be like all those other perfectly sanctified families? (If only you knew what they go through!) Why do you have so much trouble with *your* children, when unbelievers don't even seem to have so much trouble? Why do you feel so lonely when you know the Lord should be sufficient for you? Why do you have these trials? Why do you have tension or conflict with others? Because the Dragon wants to devour you! **He pursued the woman.** A roaring lion seeking someone to devour! Worse. He is a dragon. But notice this. Firstly 12:6 says the woman flees into the wilderness where she is *taken care of!* The same one who outsmarted the Dragon all the way through thousands of years of history, all the way to the cross and resurrection, is the same one who outsmarts the devil now. And just as he did at the cross, he continually turns the worst tragedy into good for those who love him. He *takes care* of them.

Secondly, look at the state of the woman again from the heavenly perspective in 12:1. She is clothed in splendor, in the sun, moon and stars. She is victorious because she is *in Christ*. This is what we must remember as we head through this wilderness and as we go further into Revelation. Despite the attacks of the Dragon, Jesus wins. He has already won. We see the woman above in her heavenly standing.

Study Questions

1. What similarity is there between the life of Israel and the church?

2. What similarities are there between Jesus and Israel's life?

3. What is the point of Revelation depicting the people of God as a resplendent woman at this early point in the book?

4. Why is the Dragon depicted with seven crowns?

5. Why is he a 'red' Dragon?

6. Why don't Christmas stories usually include more of Jesus' life?

7. Who do you think this woman represents?

8. Give examples of how the woman gave birth through great pain.

9. How can this text help make sense of life in the church?

10. What assurance does this text give you?

11
War in Heaven
(Revelation 12:7-8)

A war in heaven? Is God the referee watching over some brutal violence in heaven? Heaven is the place where there is supposed to be peace, serenity and purity for Christians in the presence of the Lord. But now, all the Christians who have gone to heaven are like the spectators at Madison Square Garden watching a World Heavyweight title fight or at the Coliseum when the gladiators are fighting, and they are the most powerful gladiators of all. Have you read the descriptions of those angels in the OT with swords drawn? Colossal and powerful. According to the book of Daniel, Michael is a chief, so he is even more powerful. This text says Michael is fighting against the Dragon. It's the battle of the heavyweights. Is heaven filled with blood and severed angel limbs flying everywhere? All this with the Christians and God watching on? Is this what you think of when you read this verse? Is this heaven?

> Then war broke out in heaven. Michael and his angels fought against the dragon, and the dragon and his angels fought back (12:7).

The Historicist, looking for a single event in history, says this war in heaven is symbolic and represents the time when the Roman Empire had its final attempt to return to paganism during the reign of Emperor Julian the Apostate, who ruled from 361-363 AD. Julian symbolizes the Dragon cast out. Julian did fail, because after his reign, the empire had Christian rulers. Julian's dying words were: 'O Galilean, thou hast conquered'. In other words, Jesus, you win! Jesus conquers.

The trouble with this interpretation is this text says the war was going on *in* heaven! And Michael is not Julian. Even allowing for the fact that Revelation says it reveals by signs or symbols, it stretches the rules of interpretation to have *in heaven* meaning *on earth*.

Then there are the Jehovah's Witnesses who love this text, because they say Michael the archangel is Jesus. They want Jesus to be reduced to a mere created being, an angel. Michael means, 'Who is like God?' So Michael (Jesus), is *like God* but not God. Well, we agree Michael is not God, but we want to go further and say Michael is not Jesus either! But there are scholars from an orthodox Christian perspective who suggest Michael could be Jesus who fights the Dragon, so it's worth us taking a look at this central character to our text, Michael the archangel. Michael is mentioned in the OT …

> But the prince of the Persian kingdom resisted me twenty-one days. Then Michael, one of the chief princes, came to help me, because I was detained there with the king of Persia (Dan. 10:13).

Michael is *one of the chief princes*. So that rules him out as the unique Lord of glory, since he is only *one of* the chiefs. He is mentioned as an archangel in the NT …

> But even the archangel Michael, when he was disputing with the devil about the body of Moses, did not himself dare to condemn him for slander but said, 'The Lord rebuke you!' (Jude 9).

He is indeed an archangel, but Michael wouldn't even do what the Lord would do—rebuke Satan. We know Jesus rebuked Satan several times. So Michael, rather than being the Lord himself, is the equal opposite to Satan, who is also a chief archangel, though fallen. They are in the same category. In fact, if we look at 12:7, it shows Satan fights as the head of his fallen angels. In other words, it is chief angel and his angels vs. evil chief fallen angel and his evil angels. **Then war broke out in heaven. Michael and his angels fought against the Dragon, and the Dragon and his angels fought back.** The reason we have Michael vs. Satan and not Jesus vs. Satan is because Satan is not the equal opposite of Jesus. Michael is a chief angel as was Satan. Michael is Satan's appropriate rival and equal, though Michael is fighting for Jesus' cause. So no, we can't go with the view that Michael is Jesus. We need to remember Jesus is Lord and he does not fight against Satan as an equal.

The Futurist says this fierce warfare will occur in the tribulation, which happens at some time in the future. All things are possible, but how *can* we know for sure?

How can we tell when this will happen, or know if it is happening?

You might know the first three rules of Real Estate? Location, location, location. Well, the three rules for interpreting the Bible are similar. Context, context, context. So let's look at the context. In the first part of Rev. 12, there was this great drama surrounding the woman whom we identified as *the people of the Messiah*. And this people of God, as Israel, gave birth to a male child, Jesus, who will rule the nations. But there is an enemy waiting to devour him. Does he succeed? No. The enemy is outwitted, as the child is *snatched up to heaven* (12:5). There is a sweep across Jesus' story from his birth through to his triumphant ascension. Then there is an ongoing struggle for the people of God in the wilderness, or desert on earth (12:6). This is direction from the Master film director. Jesus has given us the camera angle changes from his life on earth to his ascension, and now we are given the heavenly perspective. This is the classic movie cliché, 'Meanwhile …'

So 12:1-6 gave us the overview of what went on earth. Now 12:7-12 gives us the 'meanwhile' in heaven. The context tells us this heavenly scene is going on and continuing from and even in response to what happened below in 12:1-6. So if this all happened with the woman and her son, that is, with the birth of Christ and his ascension, what would be going on in heaven at that time and why would there be a war over it?

What happened in the events of Jesus' life up to his ascension mentioned in 12:1-6? Does that give us a clue as to what this war is about and the nature of this war? The other clue to the nature and time of the war is the *response* of heaven when Satan is cast down.

> Then I heard a loud voice in heaven say: 'Now have come the salvation and the power and the kingdom of our God, and the authority of his Messiah. For the accuser of our brothers and sisters, who accuses them before our God day and night, has been hurled down' (12:10).

When does the salvation of God come? When does the authority of the Christ come? When did Jesus say, 'All authority in heaven and on earth is given to me'? What event would require a response from heaven that says, **'Now have come the salvation … of our God'**? What is the context? When is this salvation achieved? Surely it is at the cross, resurrection *and ascension* of Jesus. We have just read about the ascension of Jesus in 12:5! So while I accept all things are possible, including the popular view that these things could be happening at some time in the future, the context is that this is *heaven's response* to Jesus' victory on the cross, his resurrection *and ascension,* when it says in 12:10 *now have come the salvation ... of our God,* **and the authority of his Christ.** Also, as we read on in these verses, we see Satan is defeated as *the accuser.* He is *cast out* as the accuser. When is Satan defeated as the accuser as well as the time of the salvation of the Christ? The cross, resurrection and ascension!

Rev. 12 has unfolded for us the highlights reel of Jesus' ministry. First his humiliation (he is born of a woman), then his exaltation (12:5 with the death and resurrection assumed in that package), and then his ascension when he is *snatched up to heaven.* Victory! This is his salvation. This is the reason why the accuser is now powerless. And this is what 12:7-12 is now looking at. This is how heaven reacts to this victory.

But heaven has a war? How do we deal with that? Is 12:7 a blood and guts war with human weapons? No, this is a spiritual and legal war that has raged through the ages. If we are drawing on the context to drive our understanding, look at what caused Satan to be cast out.

> The great dragon was hurled down—that ancient serpent called the devil, or Satan, who leads the whole world astray. He was hurled to the earth, and his angels with him (12:9).

He is hurled out, but the next verse tells us why ...

> Then I heard a loud voice in heaven say: 'Now have come the salvation and the power and the kingdom of our God, and the authority of his Messiah. For the accuser of our brothers and sisters, who accuses them before our God day and night, has been hurled down' (12:10).

He is **the accuser**. That is the reason why he is thrown out. He can't accuse any more. *Accusation* is legal terminology. Since the fall of man and throughout the ages there has been conflict between God and humans. From Adam onwards, believers have been entering heaven and there has been a legal battle. There has been someone with every legal right to accuse them before God. Even Satan himself was allowed into heaven! He had full access to come into heaven and accuse. We see examples of Satan having this access in the OT.

> One day the angels came to present themselves before the LORD, and Satan also came with them. [Satan in heaven! He has a legal right as prosecutor/accuser.] ... 'Does Job fear God for nothing?' Satan replied. 'Have you not put a hedge around him and his household and everything he has? You have blessed the work of his hands, so that his flocks and herds are spread throughout the land. But now stretch out your hand and strike everything he has, and he will surely curse you to your face' (Job 1:6, 9-11).

Satan *accuses* Job of only being faithful to God because God gives him all the good stuff. Satan appears in heaven and accuses. Another OT example, Satan accuses the high priest Joshua in...

> Then he showed me Joshua the high priest standing before the angel of the LORD, and Satan standing at his right side <u>to accuse</u> him. The LORD said to Satan, 'The LORD rebuke you, Satan! The LORD, who has chosen Jerusalem, rebuke you! Is not this man a burning stick snatched from the fire?' Now Joshua was dressed in filthy clothes as he stood before the angel (Zech. 3:1-3).

Satan accuses Joshua of being unclean. Any OT saint who died in the Lord, though they went up to heaven, was open to accusation by Satan. Satan had the legal right to be in heaven as a prosecutor to bring accusations against those saints based on their lives, because they were sinners and could indeed be accused. 'Why should they be allowed in heaven? Why shouldn't I (Satan) be allowed into heaven if sinners whose sin has not been paid for are allowed? Where is the justice for their sin?' Satan was able to accuse, legally! He had the right to appear in heaven because sinners were allowed into heaven! So the issue of the battle of heaven is a legal one. It's over the right and ability of Satan to appear in heaven and accuse legally. Yes, Michael and his angels were fighting against Satan. Michael had fought Satan before. Even that occasion suggests the same kind of legal battle. We read it before in Jude 9: *But even the archangel Michael, when he was <u>disputing</u> with the devil about the body of Moses...* 'It was a legal 'dispute'! It was a legal fight over the body of Moses. It wasn't a punch up or 'swords out' fight, but a legal one. So in 12:7 Michael is having the same sort of fight, only on a greater cosmic scale. It's a war going on in heaven over the rights of souls to enter heaven. In other words, it's not a blood and guts war in heaven. How could we reconcile that? Rather, Michael is the chief defense barrister in the courts of heaven vs. Satan. Satan is the chief prosecutor, who has been presenting himself in the court of God through the ages making his accusations. But something happened which changes Satan's legal standing.

There the chief barrister for the defense appears in the court, Michael, along with his great array of legal staff, his angels, bringing a new challenge to Satan and his angels and it's a battle. A legal war! Rev. 12:7 says Michael initiates this attack. Why? Up until now Michael did not have the damning evidence he needed to make his move. But now 12:5 has told us the Christ has come, and after doing his work on the cross, he ascended. What happens next in the 'meanwhile'? **Then war broke out in heaven. Michael and his angels fought against the Dragon, and the Dragon and his angels fought back** (12:7). *Now* Michael has the firepower to *fight back!* He can produce the legal evidence to cast the accuser out of court, out of heaven. What evidence? When is this all happening? When does the NT say Satan is cast out of heaven? In the future? What did Jesus say?

> 'Now is the time for judgment on this world; now the prince of this world will be driven out. But I, when I am lifted up from the earth, will draw all people to myself.' He said this to show the kind of death he was going to die (John 12:31-33).

Jesus is saying Satan is being driven out *now*. It begins at the cross and ends with his resurrection and ascension. Those angels of Satan were defeated in public battle ...

> And having disarmed the powers and authorities, he made a public spectacle of them, triumphing over them by the cross (Col. 2:15).

When? At the cross! *Disarmed*. That's a military, but also a legal term. This changes the whole legal framework of what has been raging for centuries. Now Michael, the chief defense barrister, has new evidence. And this is what Jesus was anticipating when he said ...

> '... I saw Satan fall like lightning from heaven. I have given you authority to trample on snakes and scorpions and to overcome all the power of the enemy; nothing will harm you' (Luke 10:18-19).

Jesus said he saw *Satan fall from heaven*. He is anticipating what will happen as he completes his work at the cross, resurrection and ascension. Satan will be cast out and will no longer have any legal right to enter heaven.

There is one other parallel to Rev. 12 that many commentators have noted this legal battle seems to be following. If this legal war in heaven is in fact over Satan's accusations, as our text 12:10 says, then think of another classic text that uses those legal terms ...

> Who will bring any charge against those whom God has chosen? It is God who justifies. Who then is the one who condemns? No one. Christ Jesus, who died—more than that, who was raised to life—is at the right hand of God and is also interceding for us. [Who can accuse if Jesus has ascended? What about Satan or his demons?] ... For I am convinced that neither death nor life, neither angels nor demons, neither the present nor the future, nor any powers, neither height nor depth, nor anything else in all creation, will be able to separate us from the love of God that is in Christ Jesus our Lord (Rom. 8:33,34,38,39).

Neither angels nor demons can bring any charge or accusation! (Not even Satan or his demons!) There is the legal jargon again of bringing charges. Who can accuse now that Christ has completed his work and ascended? The answer is a resounding *no one!*

I know the popular view is to take Rev. 12 as some future distant war in heaven that will happen after Christians are already in heaven. But the gospel counterparts in Romans 8 and John 12:31, where Jesus says of the cross *now the devil is cast out*, allow the Bible to be its own interpreter instead of using our own speculations. This also makes sense of Revelation talking about the gospel written to strengthen Christians in their tribulation. So rather than some future time that has no relevance to Christians, it's written as the gospel story that we need to hear now to persevere through tribulation. It's the same story told in Romans 8:1 *There is now no condemnation for those who are in Christ Jesus*. It's the same story in John 12:31, *the prince of this world is now driven out!* It's the same story in Luke, *I saw Satan fall.* It's the glorious good news that Jesus won at the cross. Satan is cast out. He can't accuse us any longer. Jesus wins!

To further underline this, think about Michael and his angels fighting for a legal victory.

What do angels normally fight over? Is it angels vs. angels to see who gets the seats in heaven? No. The context of 12:1-6 tells us this war is not *about* angels. What do angels normally fight for?

> Are not all angels ministering spirits sent to serve <u>those who will inherit salvation</u>? (Heb. 1:14).

Think about this in the context of Rev. 12. The role and goal of angels is to *serve* (fight for) *those who will inherit salvation.* That is, the people of God! The saints! The *woman* of 12:1. Angels don't just have random violence against demons. Their fight is over and for the people of God, to defend God's people against the accusations of the accuser. But with this new reconvened courtroom battle, the chief barrister, Michael, and his legal team of angels can finally produce the evidence which enables them to deliver the crushing blow to have Satan thrown out of court! What is the evidence? It's the full and final payment for the sin of all of God's people, *including* for those who had gone to heaven from OT times. How did they get to be in heaven when their sin hasn't been paid for, before the cross? That is the very question Satan had asked. Now he can no longer ask that question. Why? Jesus ascends into the courtroom in person! In 12:5 *the son is snatched up to heaven!*

Jesus' entrance into heaven is the damning evidence against Satan! If this great battle is happening in the future, that would mean Satan still has access into heaven even right now. Too his credit, John MacArthur is consistent with his Futurist view confirming that Satan actually does still have access to heaven now.[6] This means any of us who go on to be with the Lord now could actually meet Satan in heaven! I don't know about you, but I don't find that a very comforting thought! I'm suggesting that view misses the very motive for the war, the type of war, and the reason for the victory. Otherwise you just have a random war in heaven and the imagination starts running wild, with even Satan running around in heaven!

No matter what your view is about this text, aren't you uncomfortable with the idea of a war going on in heaven? Heaven is that place of beauty and comfort in the presence of God. Should we try and picture the archangel with his Roman armor and swords and fighting Satan, who is tossed over the edge in the battle, or should

---

[6] John MacArthur, *The MacArthur Study Bible,* Word Bibles, 1997, p.2008

we see it as a great legal dispute that drives out Satan?

So this part of Rev. 12 is no small thing. I don't believe it has no relevance to Christians and is confined to the future. Rather it is alive for us now. It is a picture of heaven and heaven's view of reality. It's about our standing in heaven. It's about your name written in heaven. Jesus told his disciples not to worry about their power over demons on earth, but whether their name was written in heaven (Luke 10:20). Heaven is real and takes a real interest in salvation. Heaven even rejoices over one sinner who repents. Heaven is where the eternal perspective is fully understood. Heaven is where our real standing is known and counts. Heaven is this place we want to be eternally. But there was a time when your sins could be brought before God by Satan himself, with the accuser saying this person has *no* right to be allowed into heaven because heaven *knows* what you have done, even in your deepest thoughts. So what are you going to plead when you stand before God who knows everything and whose holiness cannot permit sin to enter heaven? You can have only one plea. 'I believe in the death, resurrection and ascension of Jesus! I know him as Lord and Savior. I trust in him! He took away my sin forever.' Our sins can no longer be presented in heaven. There can be *no* accusation any longer.

'Praise be to the God and Father of our Lord Jesus Christ, who has blessed us in the <u>heavenly</u> <u>realms</u> with every spiritual blessing in Christ' (Eph. 1:3).

Study Questions

1. What did you first think of when you read this text that says there is a war in heaven?

2. Who is Michael the archangel? How would you respond to the suggestion that he is Jesus?

3. What are the first three rules of Real Estate and how can that help us understand this text?

4. What is the strength of the view that this event occurs sometime in the Future? What is the weakness of that argument?

5. Who could Satan legally accuse and why?

6. Give NT texts outside Revelation that support a reason why Satan is cast out, and when.

7. What is the usual role of angels and how can that help understand our text?

8. Does the idea of meeting Satan in heaven fit with how you understand this text?

9. How can this text give strength in time of accusations against you?

12
Triumph over the Accuser
(Revelation 12:9-11)

Rev. 12 has brought us to this turning point. The curtain has been drawn back on the stage to reveal what is behind the scenes. The players are unmasked. Now we see *who* is behind the havoc and evil in the world. It's this great Dragon. He is none other than the same one who was there in the Garden of Eden. We are told that in three different ways in 12:9. He is the serpent, the devil, and Satan! The devil means slanderer, and Satan means accuser or adversary.

But we are so conditioned in the West into thinking of the devil as a children's story character. The devil is the boogie man, a bad guy in a red tights costume with horns and tail. And how Satan must *love* that caricature. He has a big grin all over his face every time he goes past the costume hire place. He thinks, 'They believe in God, and the world is falling apart, but they don't believe in me. Ha! Ha!' We are also conditioned to the dumbing down and ridiculing of the story of how he was there at the beginning with Adam and Eve. It is treated like a child's story, like Santa Claus.

But without a real and personal spiritual evil being behind this world, there are a lot of things unexplained. Not least of all, explaining how Jesus encountered him as a real opponent in the wilderness when he lived up to his names of slanderer and accuser. This is what this text is saying here. He is the ancient serpent, called the devil. Even back at the Garden of Eden he slandered God. He led Adam and Eve to question God's goodness, as if God was holding out on Adam and Eve by holding back wisdom and knowledge from them. But really, he was the adversary, the enemy of God. Jesus called him the father of all lies. He sold the greatest lie in the garden, and then continues that lie …

> The great dragon was hurled down—that ancient serpent called the

devil, or Satan, <u>who leads the whole world astray</u>. He was hurled to the earth, and his angels with him (12:9).

He entices the **whole world** to go after anything but the living God. But Rev. 12 showed the ascension of Jesus introduced a new dynamic into the equation of Satan's power to deceive and accuse. Before this time, Satan had access into heaven to accuse. We saw the OT evidence that Satan, though he roams the earth, also had access to legally bring before the throne of God accusations against the saints (Job). In the OT, the blood of bulls and goats could not take away sin, and Satan knew it.

But after Jesus ascended into heaven (12:5), after his cross and resurrection, the cry from above was: *now have come the salvation and the power and the kingdom of our God, and the authority of his Messiah* (12:10), and Satan and his accusations have been thrown out of heaven. But even though he is cast down, that doesn't mean the devil stops trying to accuse. The real point of Rev. 12 is that the dynamics have changed forever. He is operating in a limited and powerless way. The saints of God still get the accusations fired at them. The big difference now is Satan is firing blanks. And God's people have bulletproof vests that he can no longer penetrate, because they are clothed in the righteousness of Christ.

It still might be scary getting fired at by those accusations and feeling those bullets (or as it is, fiery darts) bouncing off your protective vest, but when you get to know he is firing blanks and that his live ammunition has been taken away, you realize he cannot finally get you. How do you know he can't hurt you? By reading this Revelation! That is why this book is written! To strengthen God's people and to remind them that though he still accuses, the war has been won. Satan and his accusations have been forever evicted from heaven when the Son of God drove him out through his cross, resurrection and ascension. And heaven responds this way …

> Then I heard a loud voice in heaven say: 'Now have come the salvation and the power and the kingdom of our God, and the authority of his Christ. For <u>the accuser</u> of our brothers and sisters, who accuses them before our God day and night, has been hurled down' (12:10).

Even though the accuser has been thrown out of heaven and his accusations hold no power any longer, he *continues* **day and night** to accuse on earth. He can't accuse in heaven anymore. But he can here on earth. And we feel it. Are you really measuring up? What if you have sinned really badly against God? Are you worthy? Have you got a particular sin in your past that troubles you? Where is that coming from? The accuser! Who *accuses day and night!*

These were once fair questions. What the devil is trying on you is the fact that God is holy. With all due respect to D. James Kennedy, the devil actually invented the classic *Evangelism Explosion* question: 'Why should God let you into a perfect heaven when no sin can ever enter?' What is your answer to that? Let me give you some wrong answers that will keep you *out* of heaven. First incorrect answer is: 'I haven't sinned that badly.' Or: 'I'm not a sinner.' Rather: *If we claim to be without sin, we deceive ourselves and the truth is not in us* (1 John 1:8).

If you don't confess sin you are a liar! Now most people will admit they have done wrong. Even many unbelievers will say, 'We are all sinners …', as though that somehow makes it not so bad after all. 'If we are all sinners, what's God gonna do, throw us all into hell? Ha! It's not as if he would do something like destroy the whole world like in some sort of flood or something.' But saying 'we are all sinners' is still lying in the sense that it's not really admitting *you* are the sinner, worthy of the weight of the law. It's kind of excusing your sin because everyone else does it. But the tax collector didn't say, 'God have mercy on *us* sinners' (Luke 18:13). The first step in the right direction is, 'God have mercy on *me*, the sinner. Even if no one else is deserving of punishment, I am.' It's honesty with who you are. No more self-righteousness such as, 'I'm not as bad as some.'

From God's point of view our sin is a personal attack on his character. It is our personal challenge to rival his Lordship and proclaim war against God as the only true Lord and God. The serpent's first lie back in the Garden of Eden was '*you* determine right and wrong'. *You* are the Lord of your own life, not God. But then that sin separates us from God. It kills us spiritually. It cuts us off from the true relationship with God as Lord and us as his children.

> As for you, you were <u>dead</u> in your transgressions and sins, in which you used to live when you followed the ways of this world and of the <u>ruler of the kingdom of the air</u> [the same ancient serpent], the spirit who is now at work in those who are disobedient … Like the rest, we were by nature deserving of wrath (Eph. 2:1-3).

We are objects of *God's holy wrath*. So admitting we are objects of wrath is honest, but even that doesn't get us into heaven. All that does is admit we should *not* be going there, and that is exactly what the accuser has been saying. You have a record against you that proves you are not worthy of heaven, and now you even admit it! I admit I am a sinner. Great! That is a start. But so far that only means you agree with the devil! Which is exactly the accusation of the accuser. God is holy and you are not worthy! Why should you be allowed into a perfect heaven? Let me give you another wrong answer: 'I have been a good Christian. I have tried my best. I have even read my Bible and do good… I, I, I, I…' You have trouble with your 'I's! It's all about you! This is called being *self*-righteous! You are right back to lying because you are not telling about the times you *haven't* been a good Christian. You have *not* always been nice to people. You have *not* done all that you should have. Self-righteousness before a holy God is no righteousness at all. It is just lying. Satan's accusations are correct.

In fact, Satan's accusations attack God as well as you. The devil is the slanderer, so he accuses God of being unjust if God lets you into heaven, and you have just given him the evidence to do that. If God forgives sinners just because he forgives, then he has not dealt justly with sin. He has swept it under the carpet or worse, he has swept it into heaven. Is God breaking his own law? The devil has a case in this courtroom. God stands accused if he lets you into heaven. The charges stand. Not only are you condemned, but so is God! Heaven forbid, but God is also on trial.

Satan is not accusing just to tie up the court to bide time. He knows this is a legitimate accusation. He is absolutely right! If God let's a single sin into his presence in heaven, his whole character would be corrupted. If there is an accusation of sin against you, God is *bound* by his own holy character and justice to throw you into hell. He *cannot* let a single transgression of the law go unpunished, and Satan knows it. He cannot legally forgive, and if you have sinned against God, you stand accused, and Satan is absolutely right. So how can we ever get into heaven? The answer is in our text …

> They triumphed over him by the <u>blood of the Lamb</u> and by the word of their testimony … (12:11).

They *testified of Christ* and what he has done. Not just, 'I believe in God.' Not just, 'I believe I am a sinner.' No. But, 'My sin is so bad I need the Savior to pay the penalty for my law breaking! The blood, signifying the death of Christ, is a substitute for me.' The great exchange. He takes my sin. I receive his righteousness through faith in what *he* has done. So I believe in *him*, not in myself. **They triumphed over him by the <u>blood of the Lamb</u>** …

This is the message Revelation has been trying to convey from the start. Though you go through tribulation, though you are accused, if you are in him you are free! … *To him who loves us and has <u>freed</u> us from our sins <u>by his blood</u>* (1:5). *Free* from accusation because of the blood of Jesus … *the Lamb*. Notice Jesus is called *the Lamb*. This signifies his sacrificial death in our place. This is the big one that we underestimate. The preciousness of the blood of the Lamb. For Satan's legal accusations to be defeated, Jesus' death has to equate to eternal hell, otherwise the full payment has not been made and the accuser still has a case. The cross must equate to paying for the *eternal* judgment of hell.

> He did not enter by means of the blood of goats and calves; but he entered the Most Holy Place once for all by his <u>own blood</u>, thus obtaining <u>eternal</u> redemption (Heb. 9:12).

How precious is that blood! It's not just any death. *Eternal redemption!* Do you know what that means? Jesus went through the equivalent of *eternal* hell. The cross is bigger than you think! Jesus had to become human to take human sins in his body, but only Jesus, the *eternal* Son of God, could pay an *eternal* redemption!

> How much more, then, will <u>the blood of Christ</u>, who through the <u>eternal</u> Spirit offered himself unblemished to God, cleanse our consciences … (Heb. 9:14).

This is how that blood can cleanse our conscience and free us from accusation. Thousands of people died on crosses in Jesus' day, but what Jesus did was take on an *eternal* redemption, and that is beyond comprehension. Imagine staring over into hell and having a choice of whether to go into it or not. Jesus did. The anguish was so great that even though he knew he would get out the other side of death, he was so stressed by the magnitude of going through that equivalent of hell and facing the wrath of God that his sweat was like drops of blood, and he asked his Father if there was any other way. *My Father, if it is at all possible let this cup pass from me* ... (Matt. 26:39).

What was going on in that garden? He saw *you* in that garden. It was a choice of either *your* eternal hell or *his*. Would he pay an eternal redemption through the eternal spirit? Would he become sin for you? To go through with it or not? It was either him or you. So how precious were those words of Jesus which followed his great anguish and agonizing as to whether to go through with it or not, when he said, '... *Yet, not as I will but as you will*' (Matt. 26:39). Your eternal destiny hung on those words. Oh, how precious is that blood.

Jesus knew you couldn't be punished twice for the same crime. The reason he frees us is not some benign fuzzy whim where God says, 'Don't worry about it, forgive and forget, we'll let that bit of your corruption slip through and hope it won't corrupt heaven too much.' Nor is it anything like our current legal system, when often sentences are given that don't fit the crime. In the blood of the Lamb the *full penalty* is paid! So ... they <u>triumphed over him</u> by the blood of the Lamb and by the word of their testimony ...

Though Satan might continue to accuse your conscience on earth, take a look at the heavenly verdict! Look at the *blood of the Lamb*. That is why this is written. It is for our benefit. Go to the blood of the Lamb! The hurling down of Satan we looked at last time was on the weight of forensic evidence. The DNA of the blood of the Lamb. Before that time the evidence for accusation was *there* in heaven already. All the OT believers in heaven were the evidence! The blood of bulls and goats can't take away their sin. How did God justify them? That is why Satan had access to heaven to accuse them and God. But now! *But now* as the apostle Paul says ...

> <u>But now</u> [after Jesus' death, resurrection and ascension] apart from the law the righteousness of God has been made known, to which the Law and the Prophets testify. [The Revelation equivalent says, 'but now, the accuser has been thrown down.'] This righteousness is given through faith in Jesus Christ to all who believe. There is no difference between Jew and Gentile, for all have sinned and fall short of the glory of God, and all are justified freely by his grace through <u>the redemption</u> that came by Christ Jesus. God presented Christ as a <u>sacrifice of atonement, through the shedding of his blood</u>—to be received by faith. He did this to demonstrate his righteousness, because in his forbearance

he had <u>left the sins committed beforehand unpunished</u> ... (Rom. 3:21-25).

There it is! Until Christ came, the sins of the OT saints were *left unpunished* and open to accusation by Satan. That's why in the OT you see these examples of Satan roaming on earth, but also able to appear in heaven. OT saints were saved. They trusted in the Messiah to come. They believed by shadows through OT sacrifices, but Jesus had not yet completed the payment.

Paul explains in Romans that God still had to deliver the righteousness through the blood of the one who could take away sins. Don't make the mistake of thinking God the Father has to be 'won over' before he can give you the pass into heaven. This righteousness comes 'from God'. It's God the Father, *who so loved the world that he gave his one and only Son.* In the book of Romans, Paul gave his great treatise on justification by faith. But here in Revelation we have it apocalyptic style. The accuser is thrown out! Why? Jesus has ascended. *They triumphed over him by the blood of the Lamb!*

The verdict is that Satan is a defeated foe and that is what the readers of Revelation need to see and take hold of. *Blessed are all who read this and take it to heart* (1:3). Why? Because Revelation is showing us that though it seems like Satan is winning, he has already lost. It can *seem* like he has an accusation. It can *seem* like your pain is too great as though you have lost, but Jesus wins! Have you ever failed badly and given in to temptation? Have you ever been so beaten down that you feel like you can't go on? Have you ever felt like your sin is too great? Your motives, your inner heart weighs you down and says, 'I'm not loving him enough.' Don't listen to the accuser!

It's not about you and where you are up to. Look to the *blood of the Lamb!* Satan wants you to look at yourself. Of course you won't find any relief in looking at yourself. Satan knows that. You are a sinner. He *wants you* to look at your life and how life *seems to you*. If you look at what things *seem* like, you might be tempted to think God can't possibly work all things together for good. It might *seem* like you can't overcome a particular sin. Don't believe Satan. Look at Jesus! *They triumphed over him by the blood of the Lamb and by the <u>word of their testimony</u>*.

Note that they didn't overcome him by working up enough 'positive thinking' and self-esteem. They overcame by the blood of the Lamb and their testimony of Jesus and what he has done. When you look to him and testify of *him*, that is, Jesus, not you—then you will have new strength. Satan's accusations are rendered powerless.

This is the great reversal. Accusations are emptied of their power, but secondly, this puts Satan in the courtroom dock because of his unjust murder of the Son of God. Satan is cast out of heaven for false accusations, but also now stands accused himself for his plot in the execution of the innocent man, the Son of God.

There you have it. If you believe in Jesus, even though you will feel the weight of accusations at times, they have no power. But what an interesting description of the believers in the second half of this verse.

> They triumphed over him by the blood of the Lamb and by the word of their testimony; they did not <u>love their lives so much as to shrink from death</u> (12:11).

They trusted in Christ, and yet that glorious freedom did not come without effect for true believers. **They did not love their lives so much as to shrink from death.** This must be the fine print on the contract. Just when we thought it was justification by faith alone, *then* you have to give up your life even to death? So is this is the fine print you only notice after you have signed up? Jesus did say it elsewhere.

> For whoever wants to save their life will lose it, but whoever loses their life for me will find it (Matt. 16:25).

There it is! You have to lose your life! And you thought it was just about having faith! Is this the undoing of justification by faith alone? You get the free gift, but the fine print says you have to give up your whole life! It's not free after all? Well, it's free all right. But only when you believe in the preciousness of that *blood of the Lamb*. Only if you've seen Jesus, by faith. If you knew the gift of God, says Jesus to the woman at the well ...

> Jesus answered her, '<u>If you knew the gift</u> of God and who it is that asks you for a drink, you would have asked him and he would have given you living water' (John 4:10).

What did that woman at the well do when she saw the gift? She forgot she was after earthly water. She *dropped* her water jar and ran to tell the great news to her hometown. She found the gift! Her whole focus changed!

If you know what it is to be headed to hell because of your sins and what you've done to God, and you discover what God has done for you ... If you have seen the blood ... If you have seen Jesus in that garden praying with sweat like drops of blood ... He knew why he had to go to that cross, into hell for you. It was those idols you thought were so important. It was those sins. And if you have truly believed in Jesus' gift of giving himself up for *your* sin ... If you have seen the darkness on the cross as equaling eternal hell—the hell you were headed for ... If you have really believed that you were separated from God, but instead of *you* being forsaken, *he* was forsaken, then you can't live in that sin any longer. Yes, you will still sin, but you will *hate* it, you will hate what put Jesus on that cross and will seek to put sin to death. You will see the dying Savior on the cross by faith. The treasure, the pearl of great price worth more than anything. *Nothing* will stand in the way ... <u>they did not love their lives so much as to shrink from death</u> (12:11).

Why? Because you have been given the gift. You are free! Free to serve the Lord even to death and beyond, knowing that even if you fall over, no accusation can stand because you have the Savior. Even though you walk through the valley of the shadow of death, across the Grand Canyon on a tight rope, there is a safety net right under you, even the arms of Jesus under you. You can't lose. Jesus wins.

You triumph by the blood of the Lamb. Jesus became the slaughtered lamb. If you have seen that blood, then this is not the fine print catch-clause of the contract but a joy ... *they did not love their lives so much as to shrink from death*. If you were offered the whole world, a fortune and success by the devil in exchange for your soul, would you take it? Would you curse Christ and renounce your faith to get those things? What if you were really given that choice? People this very day will be faced with that choice. Renounce Jesus and join Islam or you will die. What would you do? Become a Muslim? Some would. Would you give your life for Jesus?

If you *are* a believer in Jesus, you are one who *would* give your life for Jesus. He is probably not going to ask you to give your life for him. But he may be asking you to give up going near that addiction ever again. Like alcohol or pornography. Or are you struggling to forgive that fellow sinner? Die to it ... <u>they did not love their lives so much as to shrink from death</u>. Or maybe life has been a struggle and you think,

'I can't believe he really has my life planned for good.' But wait a minute. Don't believe that accuser. Jesus will come through. Jesus wins. The guarantee is in that blood. This is how much he loves you. He signed the guarantee in his own blood. Triumph by the blood of the Lamb. If you are a believer, you are one who would die for Jesus. Now, will you live for him?

Study Questions

1. What do the different names of Satan in Rev. 12:9 tell us about him?

2. How would you respond to someone who says they don't believe in the devil?

3. Satan no longer accuses. True or false?

4. Give examples of the way people might claim to believe but show they have not trusted in the blood of the Lamb.

5. Why is it important that Jesus paid an eternal redemption?

6. Why couldn't God just forgive without sending Jesus?

7. How is Paul in Rom. 3:21-26 effectively reflecting on the same accusations Satan makes?

8. What is a true Christian 'testimony'?

9. Is being prepared to give our life up for Jesus a 'work'? How can it be faith?

10. Are there areas of your life you still need to 'give up' for Jesus?

13
The Fury of the Dragon
(Revelation 12:12-14)

There is a choir in heaven singing. We don't know the tune, but we know the words. Many great songwriters have been inspired through other songs they have heard. Well, this great song in 12:10-12 seems to be influenced by what went before it. Remember Satan was cast out of heaven because he no longer had the legal right to accuse in heaven. There is another book of the Bible which has the same legal theme. So Rev. 12 has borrowed from, been influenced by, or perhaps more likely is similar because the Bible ultimately has one author and the word of God all fits together. It is the same gospel. We have noted this other book before which uses legal concepts to describe the gospel.

> Therefore, there is now no condemnation for those who are in Christ Jesus (Rom. 8:1).

Now we can see how even more of that Romans passage fits with Rev. 12 ...

> Who will bring any charge against those whom God has chosen? [In Rev.12 Satan the accuser.] It is God who justifies. Who then is the one who condemns? No one. [Satan tried but was thrown out after Jesus' death and resurrection.] Christ Jesus, who died—more than that, who was raised to life—is at the right hand of God and is also interceding for us. [Jesus' ascension in Rev. 12:5, He was snatched up. We have a legal advocate interceding for us!] Who shall separate us from the love of Christ? Shall trouble or hardship or persecution or famine or nakedness or danger or sword? [Rev. 12:11, They did not love their lives.] As it is written: 'For your sake we face death all day long; we are considered as sheep to be slaughtered.' [Rev 12:11 ... as to shrink even from death.] No, in all these things we are more than conquerors through him who loved us. [Rev. 12:11,

> They overcome by the blood of the Lamb! Then 12:12 says, Rejoice, the devil has been thrown down.] For I am convinced that neither death nor life, neither angels <u>nor demons</u>, neither the present nor the future, nor any powers, neither height nor depth, nor anything else in all creation, will be able to separate us from the love of God that is in Christ Jesus our Lord (Rom. 8:38-39).

Not demons nor even the devil himself. His power has been taken out. He has been cast down. So what does that mean for us now? The natural response to this news follows in our text ...

> 'Therefore <u>rejoice, you heavens</u> and you who dwell in them! [Good news in heaven, the devil is thrown out.] But woe to the earth and the sea, because the devil has gone down to you! He is filled with fury, because he knows that his time is short' (12:12).

Heaven rejoices! We can too as we are legally and spiritually sitting with Christ in the heavenly realms. But *woe to those left on earth*. Why woe to them if Satan is a defeated foe? The very fact that he is defeated makes him **filled with fury because his time is short.** Boy, you wouldn't want to be on his wrong side. So who exactly was he so angry at? We looked at this before ...

> When the dragon saw that he had been hurled to the earth, he pursued <u>the woman</u> who had given birth to the male child (12:13).

By now we know the woman represents the people of God in both OT *and* NT, just as *woman* and *bride* are used as a metaphor to describe believers both in the OT *and* the NT. So, who is it Satan is going to take out his fury on?

Remember it's *you!* If you are a believer, he is out to get you! You are the *offspring of the woman* (12:17). You who hold to the testimony of Jesus (12:11). The Dragon is furious at you! He hates you. And there is something else that fuels his ferocity, *because he knows that his time is short.*

The devil knows he is now doomed. It's no longer a case of who will win, Satan or Jesus. It's now just a matter of how long before Jesus throws his enemies into the eternal lake of fire.

And however near we are to the end of time, the time is getting a whole lot closer every year, every day. What a travesty that we live life as though we have time later to get serious in serving the Lord, when Satan knows the truth ... *he knows that his time is short.*

Satan has urgency about him *because* he knows his time is short. He is making the absolute most of his time, knowing that it is coming quickly. The devil knows if he can keep a soul in darkness just a little while longer this side, in this short life, then he has got you forever. So he is trying to make the most of the time.

There is an old joke which explains this. Satan was choosing which of his demons gets the front running for his work on earth. Whoever has the best proposal to deceive the world gets the prize. The first demon says, 'I will lie to them and tell them there is no heaven.' Satan says, 'No. They will never believe that. They know deep down heaven must triumph.' The second demon says, 'I will tell them there is no hell.' Satan says, 'That won't make any difference. Deep down they have a conscience which tells them there is justice.' Then the third demon comes forward and says, 'I will tell them there is *no hurry*.' Satan says, 'You get the job. Go for it!'

Satan knows his time is short. We know it, but we ignore it. Do you believe your time on this earth is short? If so, what are you doing about it? 'Oh, I have plenty of time to get closer walking with the Lord ... later. I've just got a few things to do first. Just got to get my life in order first. Just got to get life more stabilized, *then* I'll put more time and money and effort into the Lord's business. Later.' We are not in a hurry. Why is that? Why do we think life just goes on and on?

Because the one who *knows* his time is short is trying to convince us there is *no hurry!* Plenty of time! The opposite of what he knows to be true ... he *knows* that his time is short.

Satan is taking hold of reality and we are cruisin' through with excuses for worldliness like, 'Well...we still gotta live in this world.' We feel life is short when a friend or loved one dies. Was it Freud who said, 'A man doesn't become a man until his father dies'? I don't think any of us grows up until our parents die and we are confronted with that great issue. That era of life is over. Life is short. But then each time you have one of those moments, you go back to life as usual and forget how short life is, until the next tragedy and you are shocked at the next person's death, then back to business as usual ... never even *thinking* that one of those times it will be *you* who dies! How can we focus on what we know to be true? What Satan knows to be true? ... *He knows that his time is short.*

What does it take for us to hear what Peter said?

> ... set your <u>hope</u> on the grace to be brought to you when Jesus Christ is revealed at his coming (1 Pet. 1:13).

That is a most radical thought. Who of us has our *hope set on the grace to be given when Jesus returns?* We have our hope right here, firmly in this world! Only when this passing world is done and we *see forever* will we realize we had this short time that shapes our eternal destiny. What is eternal? It's not this *short time*. If only we could see the urgency to redeem the time and take every opportunity. How ironic that Satan sees it. But there is also something worse. Satan is not just more aware of the urgency because his time is short. He is *doing* something about it. Furiously! He is furious!

> Therefore rejoice, you heavens and you who dwell in them! But woe to the earth and the sea, because the devil has gone down to you! <u>He is filled with fury</u>, because he knows that his time is short (12:12).

He missed his lifelong goal to kill the male child. He had been vying to devour him. He tried to kill off the *woman*. He tried to eliminate Israel so the Messiah would never be born. But Jesus was not only born, he went on to crush Satan at the cross, resurrection and ascension. Jesus is snatched up to heaven (12:5) where Satan can no longer go. Satan has been thrown out. So Satan is furious! He is enraged! And he swings around like that giant Dragon whose prey has escaped him. He wheels around with his great jaws and teeth aimed in fury at whomever he can reach of those remaining on the earth. Especially at a particular people ...

> When the dragon saw that he had been hurled to the earth, he pursued <u>the woman</u> who had given birth to the male child (12:13).

After failing to defeat the male child, *the woman* was the next best thing and an easy target for the Dragon. Or so he thought. But ...

> The woman was given the two wings of a great eagle, so that she might fly to the place prepared for her in the <u>wilderness</u>, where she would be taken care of for a time, times and half a time, out of the serpent's reach (12:14).

Of all locations, it is *the wilderness* (the same Greek word is rendered *desert* in some translations). So the apostle John receiving this Revelation is taken aback when he sees the word *wilderness*. She will be taken care of for a time in the *wilderness*. That is what happened in Israel's famous journey through the wilderness escaping from Egypt. And John, who lived with Jesus, knows Jesus also spent 40 days *in the wilderness* to be tempted by the devil.

We established earlier in Rev. 12 that the time she spends in the wilderness is the time of trial for the church from Jesus' ascension (12:5 when he was snatched up), to the end—1,260 days in all. Those are pretty long days if they are literal days to stretch the whole church age. But we know by now that to John, 1,260 days is a well-known time symbolizing a trial for God's people, fitting with the genre of apocalyptic symbols and Rev. 12 in particular. The time the church has in the wilderness is called a time, times and half a time (12:14). It's the same amount of time as 3½ years, 42 months and 1,260 days, but it sounds like a short time when you put it like that. It is. The time is short! But when you are in the wilderness you feel every day of it. When those Israelites went through the wilderness, 40 years didn't seem short!

We all experience it. Every generation since John has lived through its own 1,260 days, when the accuser, filled with fury, targets Christians as they go through the wilderness. As if to underline that this time is symbolic ... **The woman was given the two wings of a great eagle** ... does the woman now have eagle's wings? Not literally of course, just as the 3½ years is not literal. No one expects a literal woman with wings of an eagle. But how do we understand what it is symbolizing? We use our secret code—the Bible. What would this imagery recall to John from the Bible? The Exodus! The wilderness. Just as God took his people into the wilderness and carried them through, as the LORD said to the ancient Israelites ...

> 'You yourselves have seen what I did to Egypt, and how I carried you on eagles' wings and brought you to myself' (Ex. 19:4).

God brought his people, *the woman*, through the wilderness on *eagles' wings,* and he is saying here he will do it again. God *kept* the Israelites in the wilderness of old. They had food and clothing. They were *taken care of.* What is 12:14 saying? The woman was given the two wings of a great eagle, **so that she might fly to the place prepared for her**

in the wilderness, where she would be <u>taken care of</u> for a time, times and half a time, <u>out of the serpent's reach</u>. God led his people into the wilderness to escape Egypt. He kept them from scorpions and snakes (Deut. 8:15). So too the Lord is doing it again with his people, taking them into this wilderness where the serpent's rage cannot devour them. They are *out of the serpent's reach*. Even though they are in the wilderness and the serpent is furious, the serpent cannot harm those who are in Christ. And what is their wilderness? Where is the wilderness of the church age where they are *'taken care of'*? It's this world! Jesus put it this way in his high priestly prayer …

> I have given them your word and the world has hated them, for they are not of the world any more than I am of the world. My prayer is <u>not</u> that you <u>take them out</u> of the world but that you protect them from the evil one. [Out of the serpent's reach!] They are not of the world, even as I am not of it (John 17:14-16).

The woman is in the world (the wilderness) but she is protected spiritually, and she (believers) is not *of* the world. God doesn't take us *out of the tribulation* of this world but protects us and nurtures us through the wilderness.

This wilderness has all the hallmarks of the Exodus wilderness both in trial and yet protection. It's a place where God's people need to be nourished along the way through their wilderness. It's a place where they will suffer. It's a place where they will be deprived of the comforts and glory of their true Promised Land. Like the saints of old … *the world was not worthy of them* (Heb. 11:38). Where is the wilderness? You are in it! This is not home! It's a *place God prepared* (12:14). You have to wander through it to complete the purposes for which God has *prepared*.

> For we are God's handiwork, created in Christ Jesus to do good works, which God <u>prepared in advance</u> for us to do (Eph. 2:10).

And they (the woman; the people of God) *will be* nourished in the wilderness. In the Exodus wilderness, the people were nourished by *manna*, bread from heaven. But what about now in the church age? What bread from heaven nourishes God's people in the church age?

> Then Jesus declared, 'I am the bread of life. Whoever comes to me will never go hungry, and whoever believes in me will never be thirsty' (John 6:35).

Now we have *the bread from heaven.* Jesus is the bread! The Word became flesh and tabernacled among us. He poured out his Spirit on his people from the day of Pentecost and he is with us always, to the very end of the age. He is the bread. He is the living water. He is the one who nourishes his people through the wilderness. In the first Exodus wilderness he provided manna. Now we have the living bread from heaven.

The Israelites failed in their wilderness wanderings, but the one who came after them was faithful. How? What was Jesus' first undertaking after his baptism? He went out into the wilderness for 40 days, which symbolically corresponds to Israel's 40 years in the wilderness. So we have already seen the desert, or wilderness, time used symbolically. Jesus went through the wilderness and now he calls on his people to follow him through the wilderness. Jesus is calling you! This is our wilderness wandering. The big question is, 'Will you be faithful?' Israel wasn't.

Revelation reveals. The curtain is drawn back on why *our* wilderness wandering is so difficult. Of course it's difficult! There is one who is *filled with fury* at you! But you are not being thrown into the lion's den without any protection. The end of 12:14 says *you are out of Satan's reach.* If you are in Christ, he can't touch you. He that is in you is greater than he that is in the world! We must not miss that. Rev. 12:14 says *the woman is taken care of,* which is a fair translation. But in the original language it is more specifically *nourished,* which reminds us even more of the wilderness wanderings. To be protected through the wilderness you need to be nourished. We have just learned that the Lord himself nourishes us, but how does that work practically? How were the Israelites to be nourished? What was Jesus' great response to the devil's temptation in *his* wilderness?

> ... 'Man shall not live on bread alone but on every word that comes from the mouth of God' (Matt. 4:4).

Where did Jesus get that idea? Jesus was quoting directly from Deuteronomy when Israel was where? In the desert, the wilderness! How did Israel struggle?

> He humbled you, causing you to hunger and then feeding you with manna, which neither you nor your ancestors had known, <u>to teach you</u> that man does not live on bread alone but on every <u>word</u> that comes from the mouth of <u>the LORD</u> (Deut. 8:3).

How does God nourish you as you are heading through that wilderness? By his word! What was Jesus' high priestly prayer as to how we would be taken care of in this world (wilderness)?

> They are not of the world, even as I am not of it. Sanctify them by the truth; your <u>word</u> is truth (John 17:16-17).

The word will sanctify you, set you apart. It's Christ and his word that will protect and nourish, take care of you. Nourished by his *word!* That is how you will be *taken care of* through the wilderness. Now it all makes sense! *In the beginning was the Word, and the Word was with God, and the Word was God.*

All this time you thought reading your Bible was some sort of Christian duty that good little Christians do if they want to get to heaven. Wrong! It is God's plan for how he prepared for you to get through the wilderness, to nourish you along the way to the Promised Land!

When you go to a church service and sit under the word, you are nourished … *faith comes through hearing* (Rom. 10:17). When you go to a Bible study, what is going on? Fellowship? Yes. But that is not the most important thing. You are being nourished. When you read the Bible at home, you are being taken care of! Nourished! You do read it, don't you? Are you struggling in the wilderness? I wonder why? Revelation is *revealing* how he planned to take care of you and keep you out of the serpent's reach. And you wonder why the wilderness is a bit tough if you don't read his word! You are being starved of nourishment!

This is why it's important that faithful lampstands (churches) have the preaching and teaching of God's word as the center of their worship service, above anything else. This is God's means of nourishment for his people … to sustain them through the wilderness all the way to the Promised Land. God planned it this way. He set aside a day, the Lord's Day, that we would come together and gather in worship around his word. The apostle Peter used that nourishment idea when he said we should … *crave the pure spiritual milk of the word of God* (1 Pet. 1:23-2:2). The apostle Paul says, *'Now I commit you to God and to the word of his grace, which can build you up and give you an inheritance among all those who are sanctified'* (Acts 20:32).

If you don't have that word in church and at home, you are not being built up. You are going to struggle. How could we have missed this! It was there all along when the apostle Paul told us directly the woman is to be prepared and made holy through that word!

> Husbands, love your wives, just as Christ loved the church and gave himself up for her to make her holy, cleansing her by the washing with water through the word ... (Eph. 5:25-26).

That was God's plan to take care of her all along ...

> All Scripture is God-breathed and is useful for teaching, rebuking, correcting and training in righteousness, so that the servant of God may be thoroughly equipped for every good work (2 Tim. 3:16-17).

How well are you being *equipped?* How much of the word of God are you reading and listening to? What is it that is missing in your life? Getting serious with the word of God? Take seriously what God has provided for you to be nourished with on your wilderness journey. Yes, there is a serpent who is furious. Yes, you will be buffeted even when you read the word of God. Yes, you will be tempted. Yes, to all of those things. The serpent remains furious! But if you are not being nourished, you had better believe you are more vulnerable when serious attack and struggles come.

The place in the wilderness is *prepared* for the woman. The Lord has not left us bereft in the wilderness without a plan. Think of the Israelites headed to the Promised Land. The wilderness was not home to them. Yet the wilderness was prepared for them to go through. During their wilderness wanderings, they grumbled (of course we would never do that!), but the LORD *took care of* them. All the Lord wanted from them was faithfulness. That is what he is looking for through our wilderness. No grumbling. Just be faithful. He will nourish you through that word.

But our heavenly home cannot be what God has prepared for us until this wilderness refining is complete. Don't miss it. It seems like our wilderness wandering is taking forever, just as it must have for the Israelites ... 40 years. But in the light of the big picture, it will be like nothing when we look back. The time is short!

Have you ever read the OT wilderness story and found it frustrating how foolish the Israelites were? Why don't they just trust the LORD and get on with it? But that is us! Do you realize you are going through the wilderness? It might explain a lot of things if you haven't realized this from Revelation. This whole world and the time we have in it is the wilderness which the Lord prepared for us to go through. Don't say, 'I just want to get straight to the Promised Land.' This desert wilderness has been **prepared** for you. The Promised Land cannot be all that it is meant to be for you unless you go through this preparation. There are rewards to be fulfilled (10:33-35), a transformation to take place (2 Cor. 3:18), and a refining of faith (1 Peter 1:6-7). The preparation he is giving you will all count in eternity.

Remember those sinless angels will rejoice with us in all eternity, but they will not be able to enjoy heaven in the same measure for two reasons: They never experienced being redeemed by Jesus *and* they have never gone through the wilderness! The wilderness is the path that has been *prepared* for us. Just like God's people of old, you have been wandering through the wilderness on the way to the Promised Land and you didn't even realize it! That's why you didn't realize how critical it is that you need to be nourished by his word. You need this *Revelation!*

Study Questions

1. Why is the devil furious, and whom is he targeting?

2. How can we learn to be more conscious of our time being short?

3. Give examples of the way this text is alluding to the Exodus.

4. In what ways do you see God has prepared works in your life?

5. In what ways has God 'taken care of' the woman through the desert?

6. How does this reflect in your life and church?

7. Have you considered the Christian walk as a wilderness wandering, and how will this affect your worldview?

14
The Deceitful Mouth
(Revelation 12:15-17)

'There is woe comin'! This section introduced us to a 'woe' at the end of 12:12. Not the kind of 'whoa' to slow horses down. In the last chapter we saw, *woe to you if you are on the earth*. Why? The devil is filled with fury! He is not happy. Look out. Make no mistake. The serpent, that ancient foe who knows his time is short, is in a rage and is now moving in for the express purpose of wanting to destroy the church. But this time we take note of *where* the enemy brings forth his woe. He doesn't throw buckets of water at the woman (who is the church). He doesn't just send a wave her way. There is a torrent he spews forth upon the woman and the key is to notice that it *comes out of his mouth!* He is the father of all lies. That's how he tries to sweep her away ...

> Then from <u>his mouth</u> the serpent spewed water like a river, to overtake the woman and sweep her away with the torrent (12:15).

Remember the woman is in a place where she will be *taken care of* (12:14). Literally, *nourished* in the desert wilderness by the word of God! In the wilderness, you learn that *man does not live on bread alone but every word that comes from the mouth of God!* The serpent wants to sweep her away with the torrent of lies from his mouth so she can drift into the world. How is he going to do that? He has to get her away from that word!

What we are seeing here is a sweep of history, and within that sweep we see all the problems that have come upon the church. There is opposition! The serpent is trying to deceive *with his* **mouth** to get the woman to leave her place of spiritual protection and nourishment with the word of God. He wants to deceive her to not just be in the world (wilderness), but to become part *of* the world, where there is no protection! He wants her to leave the word of God.

When we look at the sweep of history of the church, we see from the beginning there was persecution. In the first 300 years there was intense persecution. But when the church was accepted by the world, after the Roman Emperor Constantine declared Christianity legal, pagan concepts were brought into the Church. It looked good that there were more people coming to church. But they brought with them pagan idolatry. The world came in! Idols, statues, in the church! Worship of statues and Mary rather than the Lord! What happened to the word of God? The Church drifted from what the word says!

Then, when the church had the most power in the worldly sense during the Middle Ages, its focus became the world's affairs! It began getting involved in things like the Crusades, the holy wars. At one stage Islam had taken over two-thirds of the then Christian world, so there were genuine political, military and territorial concerns. But is that the church's role? Is that what the word says? The mouth of deceit had swept her up with two chains of command. One is the word that protects her, but two is the traditions and the Popes now having equal authority. The woman is being swept up like a torrent! Popes basically had more power than the word, and more power than civil Emperors by demanding holy wars. She is becoming *of* the world!

The church lost its nourishment from the word of God! What happened? The Bible teaches separation of church and state! That's not a secular concept. It's a Christian concept. It comes from teachings of Jesus in Matthew 22:17-21. Caesar and the church have their own mandates. The apostle Paul develops this in Romans 13:1-7, where he separates civil authority from church authority. We take the separation of church and state so much for granted we assume it is a part of life and liberty that every country wants. The modern secular Western society thinks the idea comes from them, as though countries would fare best if atheists ran them. But the great atheist experiment of the 20th century proved that given the power, atheists would not provide separation of church and state but try to eliminate the church. Communist Russia and China had no such separation. The church was eradicated and/or controlled completely by the state. Neither does separation of church and state exist in closed Muslim countries, nor even in Roman Catholic-controlled countries. Non-western countries have mostly suffered because they know little or nothing of separation of church and state. The idea of separation of church and state is a Christian concept that flowed out of the Protestant Reformation that returned the church to its nourishment while in the desert wilderness—the word of God. The Bible gives two authorities in society. Civil and religious. This allows Christians to enter politics as individuals and the church to testify as to its concerns in the political arena as a legitimate voice in a democracy. The state is not to rule the church and the church is not to rule the civil arena! It's not to rule the economy, civil law or declare war!

Jesus says the very protection of the woman is that she is separate. She is in a place of protection. She is in a place where she can be spiritually *taken care of* (12:14). A place where the word of God can keep her. She is in the world but not *of* it, so she can be salt and light to the world. The church doesn't allow the world to come into the church. Right? Or has that serpent been sweeping her away with a flood? **Then from his mouth the serpent spewed water like a river, to overtake the woman and sweep her away with the torrent.**

What about today? Is the church drifting? Is the world seeping into the church? Look how hard the serpent tries to flood her with that torrent of worldly pressure. We just said the church and individual Christians can and should speak out against moral evil and things which are wrong in society. But what happens today if you try to stand up against abortion or same-sex marriage? What if you stand for morality in general? What kind of pressure or ridicule do young Christian people encounter if they stand for sexual abstinence before marriage? The peer pressure is seeking to flood them away, to conform to the world. Many parts of the church (the outer court of Rev. 11), are succumbing to the pressure and side with the world on these things, as the serpent tries to sweep her away with the torrent.

The *serpent* image of the devil reminds us of his lies in the beginning when he deceived the woman. Now he tries to deceive *this* woman who bore the male child. We've looked at the metaphor of the mouth in Revelation before. For the serpent as the father of all lies, the mouth is the instrument of deception and lying. But here he has flooded her by it! People are deceived as to what is the true church.

How does the world view the church? You can read in the media right now about what the world says about the church. It is full of pedophiles, it's a cult, or a crutch. Who is the church to the unbeliever? It's those people who knock on the door. The Jehovah's

Witnesses. That's the church too, isn't it? The Mormons, aren't they Christians? They are very nice people, but are you saying they are not part of the Christian church? The 'mouth' has created great confusion so that unbelievers just throw their hands in the air.

And just when you think the lines are drawn, what are the evangelicals into? Anything but the word of God! New teachings that take us away from Jesus and his word. The *very* means God provided to take care of her, to be *nourished*, the place for her to find that spiritual protection, to be close to the Lord—the word of God, is laid aside. So the world floods in and now we have the prosperity gospel. That's what we need. Rich Christians. More of the world. Or the word we have is not enough, so we are flooded with 'those who have an *extra* word'. That's what we need. The word is not enough. We need experiences, and there has to be a personal word for you! A message from the Lord to you! But, in fact, he has already given us all a word. It's in our Bible but we don't read it! So we need all kinds of other things, but not the word of God. The Bible? That's archaic they say.

The Westminster Confession of Faith was written about 400 years ago in a context flowing out of the Middle Ages battle against RCs with all their traditions. What is the first chapter of the Confession about? The word of God! The full and complete sufficiency of the word of God. This Confession and its first chapter was written in the context of keeping leaders out of the church who espoused the RC doctrine of adding to the word of God. It's ironic, but those men who put the Confession together could never have known that 400 years later that first chapter of the Confession would be as relevant today as ever. The issue is still the same! It's the same serpent still trying to sweep away the church from the only source of her protection and nourishment, the sufficiency of the word of God.

It has been there all along over the last 2000 years. It just comes up in different forms. False teaching was one of the main subjects Jesus brought up in the seven letters to those seven churches of Revelation. Watch out for the synagogue of Satan. The *mouth!* Look at what those first readers where experiencing. False teaching. She is bombarded. Look at 2:14-16, 20-22 and 3:15-17. The devil keeps popping up in these contexts. In 2:9 and 3:9 it's the synagogue of Satan. It's where Satan has his throne in 2:13 and in 2:24 it's the deep things of Satan. The mouth. Trying to water down that means of nourishment in the word by adding to it or taking away.

That word was deliberately hidden in the Middle Ages. The serpent actually convinced the church to place it on the list of forbidden books in AD 1229. The RCs officially banned the Bible for centuries. The serpent would never get away with officially banning God's word in the church today. But he doesn't have to. We just don't open it. It's like Josiah's lost book in the temple. These days Christians tell me they think it's a novel idea that we preach consecutively through a book of the Bible. 'That's unusual, I've never heard of that before.' That used to be the most common practice of what Bible preachers did as a means of a thorough teaching of God's word. Now it's quaint. The contemporary tradition being built is one where the Bible is only used as a launching pad to bring in stories or self-help ideas rather than explaining the word itself. The 'mouth' doesn't even need to ban the Bible.

Even when the word is preached it is often selective in its message. Some teaching can be quite sound in general, but it's often not what is said but what is left out! 'We don't want to scare people off, so we leave out the hard stuff.' It's the word being squeezed out more subtly. The church is being flooded. The world is coming in. Following the culture around them, people think the church is there to entertain them. Music, lights, camera and action! The consumerism of the age has crept into the church, which is no longer focused on the glory of Jesus. The consumers think it's all about whether it suits me, whether it can lift my feelings, as opposed to going to church to worship God with his people and be nourished by his word. We are being flooded. But there is no use being critical of others. Are you reading the word and obeying it?

And we wonder; will the woman even be kept? Satan controls this world (1 John 5:19), but the Lord is still the Lord of all the earth, just as the *desert was a place prepared for the woman.* Prepared by whom? We know it's the Lord. It's implied. Just as God sovereignly prepared this desert wilderness (this earth) for his people to go through, he also uses his providential power to outsmart the deceit of the devil to keep his church through it.

> But the earth helped the woman by opening its mouth and swallowing the river that the dragon had spewed out if his mouth (12:16).

The Lord is sovereign over all the earth and helps the woman. There are a lot of references to the Exodus throughout the book of Revelation, but especially in Rev. 12. The woman, (the people of God), in the desert wilderness, is kept on eagles' wings just like the Israelites of old. But this is the uncut version. The water is looking to overtake the woman, like in the Exodus with the parting of the Red Sea, but here the source of the water is Satan and his mouth of deception and lies. So just like the Egyptians, Satan can't get her, and he is furious so ...

> Then the dragon was enraged at the woman and went off to wage war against the rest of her offspring—those who keep God's commands and hold fast their testimony about Jesus (12:17).

Satan can't destroy the whole church, so he targets individuals, the offspring of the woman. If you have been born again into the living hope then you are part of the church (the woman's offspring), and you are a target. He hates you. He is *enraged* (12:17)! Do you understand that? If you are struggling with temptation, feeling downcast or depressed, then look at this. Satan hated Jesus who defeated him, and now he can't beat Jesus, so his primary target is Jesus' people. Can you think of anyone who really hates you? Hates you enough to want to kill you? Hates you enough to want you in hell forever? There is one. If you are one of those ... **who keep God's commands and hold fast their testimony about Jesus,** then you are the woman's offspring. It's an interesting description of believers. Those who obey. Those who hold to the testimony of Jesus. Is that how you would describe yourself?

Is this salvation by works? Obey enough and do enough witnessing to be right with God? No! It's the living faith we learn about in James 2 (faith without works is dead). Yes, believers will still sin, but they have a hatred for sin, and when they sin they genuinely confess and repent. They go on seeking to obey and hold to the testimony of Jesus. These are those whom Satan cannot touch. But these are the ones he makes war against. And that is why it is so *hard* to obey. You have the serpent against you and he hates you!

You thought there were people in your life giving you a hard time. You thought the problem was that person at work, at home, or the one who has done wrong to you. But you are wrong. You've missed who the real enemy is. This is how the apostle Paul summarized it.

> <u>For our struggle is not against flesh and blood</u>, but against the rulers, against the authorities, against the powers of this dark world and against the spiritual forces of evil in the heavenly realms. Therefore put on the full armor of God, so that when the day of evil comes, you may be able to stand your ground, and after you have done everything, to stand. ... Take the helmet of salvation and the sword of the Spirit, which is the <u>word of God</u>. And pray in the Spirit on all occasions with all kinds of prayers and requests ... (Eph. 6:12,13,17,18).

The Word of God and prayer is our armor in this warfare we are in! It's a battle being raged not against flesh and blood (not against that person you thought was the problem). It's the forces of evil in the heavenly realms! This is the explanation of why it's so tough.

I was at a minister's conference years ago and the speaker said he once had a parishioner ask, 'Why are Christians so mean?' I was shocked how someone could say such a thing about Christians. But it can be the experience of some. And the parishioner missed the point. The struggle is not against flesh and blood. Now I know many Christians have been hurt by other Christians, but they haven't understood we have an enemy who is making war against us, to divide us. 'Oh, but this person sinned against me. This one is moody and doesn't speak to me. This one speaks too much. That one has a wrong attitude. And besides, they are responsible for their own sin.' Yes, they are. But they are also under attack, so that if the curtain were pulled back on what lies behind spiritually, then you would see this big fat mouth. If you could see that lying mouth you might be in sympathy a lot more towards your fellow sinners. If the apostle Peter can be sifted like wheat, can't Satan do that to other people? Or maybe it's *you* who is being sifted like wheat because you aren't forgiving and loving enough to persevere and bear with one another in love.

But the curtain is pulled back here in Rev. 12. We are told about the enemy's secret military information! We are given his names and his schemes! Why do real Christians get caught up arguing over such minor issues and can't agree so that the most important things are ignored? Why do we have so much division? Why do we say things like, 'Sometimes people in the world are easier to get on with?' Do you feel there is any negativity between you and another Christian?

How could that be if you are really a Christian? Answer: Satan is enraged. He is making war on you. He wants to divide Christians.

Satan is like a ferocious lion. He has the power to tear you to shreds. And he would, if not for the fact he is a ferocious lion *on a chain*. God sets the limits—like in the book of Job. Satan complained that though he was able to wreak havoc, God set a hedge around Job (Job 1:10). The ferocious lion is on his chain, but if you go into his territory … if you play with areas of temptation and leave the place of protection, he will tear you apart. So stay in the place of protection! Be nourished in the word. Pray for the Holy Spirit! Or this lion on a leash will consume you. Satan wants to stop the work of witness. He wants individual conflict to stop people getting on with the job together.

Then the Dragon was <u>enraged</u> at the woman … [those who] hold fast their <u>testimony about Jesus</u>. *Testimony* is the same root word in the original Greek language that means *witness*. Satan makes war against your *witness*. How? The same way he does with the word of God. He just entices you to not bother with it too much! Do you consciously try to develop relationships with non-Christians? Do you consciously think about your witness to the people in your life? Are you *pro-actively* going out of your way to testify to Jesus? Are you even praying daily for the people in your circle? And how is the testimony of your life going? Do the unbelievers around you see you as radically different? Do they know you as one to stand for Jesus? Would they describe you as loving, caring and generous? Do you give people the time of day? Is it a priority to develop relationships to testify? To be a witness for Jesus? Or is it all but forgotten. Are you too distracted? Are you too busy to read God's word or think about your witness to the people who cross your path? 'I'm not gifted in being a people person. It's so hard.' Yes, it is. Why? The Dragon is making war against you!

Will the woman make it against this torrent? Are you going to make it with this kind of opposition? Remember from the outset we were told this book of Revelation is written to comfort and strengthen believers going through *suffering and needing patient endurance* (1:9). Now the curtain is pulled back on who is behind that suffering and Revelation reveals to us the fury of the serpent. We are not unaware of his schemes! The church has been attacked! Persecution without and within. Always with the deceit and lying of that big mouth of Satan, seeking to sweep her away in a torrent. How can she combat against the deception of Satan's mouth? How are you going to survive? By holding to the word of truth! And holding to the testimony of Jesus. But how are you going to hold fast to the word if you are not reading it or if your church is not expounding it. Either of these two things leaves you open to be flooded by that water from the mouth of Satan.

I know the most popular view is that this is not speaking to Christians. The Futurist view is that 12:17 is speaking about Jews who have come to faith in some future time. But I'm suggesting this is *alive* for Christians to take hold of now. Tribulation. You are living it! This is *apocalypse now!* Satan wants you to deviate from the one thing that can keep you—the word of God—and sweep you away from your mission to witness!

I wonder if Revelation is a big disappointment for you. Many people think of Revelation as the book that is going to answer the very thing that Jesus said even he couldn't answer. He told us in no uncertain terms, 'No one knows the hour or time' (Matt. 24:36). When people learn I'm into the book of Revelation, the first thing they ask me is, 'Tell us, when is it all going to happen?' But Revelation *is not* revealing the time and hour. It *is*, however, revealing things even more important to us. How are we to survive until and through to that time and hour! It's not removed from us or out there for some other time. It's alive for us. It's now! Though Satan should buffet, look who wins! *They triumphed over him by the blood of the lamb* (12:11). Only one question remains: Are you the offspring of the woman? Are you *obeying the commandments of God and holding to the testimony of Jesus* (12:17)? Are you part of the testimony of your church?

Study Questions

1. What is the most significant metaphor in 12:15 that explains the attacks on the church?

2. Beginning in the seven churches, what are some of the shifts in church history where these attacks have been apparent?

3. What does the word of God say about separation of church and state, and how has that played a role in the history of the church?

4. How do the problems of the church in the Middle Ages differ from today and how are they similar?

5. In what ways do we need to take heed of this text in the church today?

6. Does the description of Christians in 12:17 characterize your life?

7. Does this text give insight into why the church struggles? How?

8. How could this text be of use to you in understanding your own struggles?

15
The Beast
(Revelation 13:1-2)

The apostle John has seen some amazing scenes so far in Revelation, but now he is shivering in his sandals as he sees this creature come up from the black lagoon. Actually 13:1 says it's coming out of the sea. It sounds like those evolution stories, the ones that always fascinate us and make us wonder whether some scientists are mixing happy juice in their test tubes or just secretly pulling our leg. You know the evolution story of the sea creature with fins that evolve into legs so it can make the transition on to dry land. And we are left wondering how it transforms its breathing respiratory system gradually from underwater to out of water without drowning, let alone how it transitions gradually over great periods of time from having fins to legs, so at some point it can neither swim nor walk properly because the fins have so slowly turned into legs that it's dead on arrival as it comes on to dry land. It can't walk properly with undeveloped legs and will be the first to die with survival of the fittest.

But that is not what John sees here. This creature John sees doesn't have any of that illogical nonsense. This Beast is *fully formed* as soon as it comes out of the water! John sees one ugly predator. He looks out to the sea, but it's not a pleasant walk on the beach, because look who is out waiting on the shore ...

> And the dragon stood on the shore of the sea ... (13:1).

We met the **Dragon** in Rev. 12. He is the devil. Here it's as though the Dragon is summoning someone up out of the sea. John is probably hoping that won't happen as he looks on, but he sees the ripples on the surface of the water and then up out of the water these horns appear. Ten of them! And sure enough, after the horns become visible, then up comes a head. No. There are several heads. In fact, seven heads! This Beast is grotesque. It is vicious and swift like a leopard (13:2), so John can't outrun it. The body comes out and John sees the water drip off it and it puts its first foot on dry land, so John sees its big hairy feet. They look like the feet of a bear! (13:2)! Worst of all, this ugly Beast has a mouth like a lion! The most feared king of the jungle and that is just its mouth. By the time we get to 13:5, this monster actually starts to speak!

Do you know those science fiction movies where the Terminator (or Mr. Bean) drops to earth from another dimension? Well, we know from Rev. 12 the Dragon and his minions were dropped out of heaven. Remember? They were hurled out. And remember the consequence? ... *woe to you on earth <u>and sea</u> because he has come down in great rage* (12:12). Well it's as though this Beast, along with Satan on the seashore, has been dropped down too, only the Beast landed in the sea! And now the Dragon is beckoning this Beast out from the sea, like the Terminator has arrived.

> And the dragon stood on the shore of the sea. And I saw a beast coming out of the sea. It had ten horns and seven heads, with ten crowns on its horns, and on each head a blasphemous name (13:1).

This Beast has **seven heads** (remember seven is God's number of completion). But wait, this Beast is not on God's side. It is the exact opposite. And we are reminded the Beast has characteristics of the Dragon. In 12:3 the Dragon has seven heads. This Beast has seven heads. The Dragon has ten horns. This Beast has ten horns. The Dragon has crowns on his head. So does the Beast. It's almost as though this Beast is a replica. Is the Beast trying to copy the Dragon? No, it's something more sinister than that. The Beast is the *image* of the Dragon!

What is going on here? Satan himself tried to take the place of God. He (the Dragon) is the ultimate *counterfeit*. The great mocker. So here, the Dragon has a son in his own image! The Beast! If we understand this, it will help us understand what is going on here, and much of Revelation from here on. It reveals Jesus and the opposition which tries to copycat him. The counterfeit!

Satan has been cast down and defeated (Rev. 12). He can't win, so he tries to replicate a counterfeit salvation in the world, just like the true salvation. He promises all sorts of things, but behind those promises are empty, hollow lies. It's a deception that leads to hell. In fact, the counterfeit is so effective it fools multitudes. It's enticing. Satan comes as an angel of light (2 Cor. 11:14). So seductive is this counterfeit that you wouldn't even know how to resist, if it was not for ... Revelation! The camera behind the scenes on the reality of the Dragon and the Beast!

We know the true, perfect image of God is Jesus the Son (Col. 1:15), and that is whom Satan and the Beast seek to counterfeit. The Beast has several things that copycat the true Son. He even has his own resurrection of sorts (13:3). After one of his heads is slain, he then appears as though the fatal wound is healed. He even has his own seal (13:16) that he puts on his followers' foreheads or right hand. That's the same thing God had for *his* people in 7:2-3 and again in 14:1. They have the seal of God, the Holy Spirit. In 13:11 the Beast has two horns like a lamb (imitating the Son of God who is the Lamb). The Beast has ten crowns; the Son of God has many crowns (19:12). The Beast has blasphemous names written on him (13:1), the Son of God has worthy names (19:12). In 13:2 the Dragon gives the Beast power, a throne and authority. In fact ... *he was given authority over every tribe, people, language and nation* (13:7). The salvation Jesus brings is in relation to every tribe, people, language and nation (5:9). And where else have we heard *all authority?* When was *all authority over every nation given?* In Jesus' giving the great commission ...

> ... 'All authority in heaven and on earth has been given to me. Therefore go and make disciples of <u>all nations</u> ...' (Matt. 28:18,19).

The Father has given all authority to the Son (Jesus), over all nations. But here in Rev. 13 the false father (the Dragon), the father of all lies, gives *authority* over every nation to *his* son, the Beast (13:2,7). God the Father has a plan through his Son to advance his kingdom to the ends of the earth (Acts 1:8) and everyone will worship him. In 13:8 we find this Beast has an identical plan where everyone throughout the world is to worship *him*, instead of the true Son of God.

So far the Father and Son are counterfeited. What about the Holy Spirit? Is he counterfeited to? We will see another Beast later in Rev. 13 and 16:13 (identified as the False Prophet), but here in 13:13 he performs *miraculous signs*, just as the Holy Spirit did in the book of

Acts. And the second Beast (the counterfeit of the Holy Spirit), points people to worship the first Beast (the counterfeit son in 13:12), just as the Holy Spirit points us to worship the Son of God. The Holy Spirit will guide you into all truth. The second Beast is a false prophet who leads you into all lies. What we have here with the Dragon, Beast One and Beast Two (B1 and B2), is not Bananas in Pajamas but the unholy Trinity!

But who are these ugly beasts? And do they literally look like this? This is where those who demand we take Revelation literally often desert the literal view. Surely consistency would mean this has to be a literal beast, but I can't find any commentators from any of the views (not even Hal Lindsey) taking the Beast literally. But instead of being thrown by these weird and wonderful images John receives, we can be consistent in our interpretation and should be expecting symbolism from these images. Otherwise it leaves you with a literal weird Beast coming out of the sea. But who decides when and if we take Revelation literally? Even commentators who demand we interpret Revelation literally, such as renowned Dispensational Futurist scholar John Walvoord, take this Beast symbolically.[7] So if it's agreed Revelation is symbolic in places, how many places and who decides which parts? Well, Revelation decided this for us in the opening verse, that we are to expect revelation in signs and symbols. So whom is this Beast symbolizing? We have already been introduced to the Beast or *a* beast ...

> Now when they have finished their testimony, the beast that comes up from the Abyss will attack them, and overpower and kill them (11:7).

This beast **comes up from the Abyss**, which is the realm of demons. But the Beast of 13:1 comes from the sea. That may be another way of saying the same thing. In the OT, the *sea* was often a metaphor for chaotic evil and all that opposes God, but specifically the *sea* could symbolize the unbelieving world ...

> Woe to the many nations that rage—they rage like the raging <u>sea</u>! Woe to the <u>peoples</u> who roar—they roar like the roaring of <u>great waters</u>! (Isa. 17:12).

---

[7] cited in Revelation Four Views, Ed. Steve Gregg, (Nashville: Thomas Nelson Publishers, 1997), p. 279

So the *sea* symbolizes the evil of unbelievers or unbelieving nations that oppose God.

In this text John **saw a Beast coming out of the sea. It had ten horns and seven heads, with ten crowns on its horns, and on each head a blasphemous name.** The crowns suggest some sort of kingly or political power. A ruler perhaps? But it's all a bit complex. How are we going to understand exactly who or what is this Beast? Should we start guessing? Or firstly ask, 'What would this Beast mean to the apostle John when he first saw this vision?' Remember John was brought up on the OT Scriptures. In the book of Daniel there are four Beasts.

> Four great beasts, each different from the others, came up out of the sea. 'The first was like a lion, and it had the wings of an eagle. I watched until its wings were torn off and it was lifted from the ground so that it stood on two feet like a human being, and the mind of a human was given to it.' And there before me was a second beast, which looked like a bear. It was raised up on one of its sides, and it had three ribs in its mouth between its teeth. It was told, 'Get up and eat your fill of flesh!' After that, I looked, and there before me was another beast, one that looked like a leopard. And on its back it had four wings like those of a bird. This beast had four heads, and it was given authority to rule. 'After that, in my vision at night I looked, and there before me was a fourth beast--terrifying and frightening and very powerful …' (Dan. 7:3-7).

These beasts are also from the *sea!* Each of the beasts represents four consecutive world powers from Daniel's day that oppressed God's people. The superpower, Babylon, then Medo/Persia, Greece and Rome. Four great earthly kingdoms that followed one another. And in our text in Rev. 13 we have features from *all four* Beasts represented in *one Beast*.

> The beast I saw resembled a leopard, but had feet like those of a bear and a mouth like that of a lion … (13:2).

It's terrifying, like the fourth beast in Daniel. The imagery is taken directly from the four beasts in Daniel. But in Daniel these four creatures are four separate kingdoms. A leopard, bear, lion and the fourth beast that has *ten horns* (Dan. 7:24)! The *terrifying Beast* (fourth) speaks against the most High and oppresses the saints (Dan. 7:25). But in Rev. 13 they are all one Beast, combining all these worldly powers in all their power and ugliness. The Beast in 13:1 has seven heads and ten horns. Remember seven is God's number of completion and ten represents numerical fullness. This Beast seems to be a composite of *all* the four beasts of Daniel 7, representing all the worldly power that oppresses God's people.

In John's day, the Roman Empire was the epitome of worldly power. The Beast to John would surely be the Roman Empire. That is exactly what the Preterist would say. This would make sense to John the apostle. This is alive for him in the first century! Are the Preterists correct? Absolutely! It would speak to John, as he sees the Beast in action persecuting God's people. But does the Preterist go far enough?

Those who hold the Futurist view often see the Beast as old pagan Imperial Rome being revived. I would agree that this Beast is a world power, but I'm suggesting the Futurist and the Preterist are both not going far enough. It's not just a future Rome or ancient Rome, but *all* worldly powers that oppress God's people. This Beast is the composite! He is all. He has seven heads (completion). The book of Revelation is written to seven churches as the complete church, and therefore speaks to all the church. So too this Beast reaches into all ages. The Beast of Rev. 13 is more complete than Daniel's individual Beasts. He represents all worldly power *including* the Roman Empire. This Beast has ten horns. Horns are associated with strength or power, as the Lamb had in 5:6. So it's complete power and domination in evil, *in contrast* to the seven horns the Lamb (5:6), which represents complete power for good.

So what we have in this Beast is the second person of the unholy-trinity. A counterfeit. The question Revelation brings is, who rules the world? Jesus or the counterfeit? The Beast represents the domination of worldly power, including political, institutional and governmental power of this world.

Let's have another look at this Beast. On each of the heads of the Beast is a **blasphemous name**, which could be blasphemous claims to authority. So if we are looking for a world power in John's day, it's the Roman Empire. Remember the Emperor Domitian at the time of John's writing blasphemously demands to be called lord and god. The Roman Empire fits the profile, but is that all ...? It has been alive to all readers of Revelation for the last 2000 years and it is alive for us (1:3)! The Beast is worldly powers in history which oppose the cause of Christ and oppress God's people. This is Scripture that is God-breathed and useful for teaching, correcting, rebuking and training for all Christians in *all* ages.

But we don't want to make the mistake of the JWs and think the Beast means Christians shouldn't enter government or law enforcement. Romans 13:1-7 reminds us God gave us the institution of government. Christians should be seeking to be salt and light in the nations and entering the spiritual warfare to take part in the true kingdom advancing.

Another important reason we can see the Beast exists throughout the last 2000 years is that this Beast is the image of the Dragon (12:3). No one denies the Dragon lives through *all* the ages and wreaks havoc throughout the entire church age, *and so* his Beast (the Dragon's image), crosses through generations. He represents worldly governmental and institutional power (just as those four Beasts did in Daniel), now existing through the church age.

So if you have always wondered about this Beast in Revelation and you were expecting some sort of literal, monstrous beast literally coming out of the sea, you might be disappointed (or relieved). After all, it's not a personal beast you have to face. What a relief! Or is it? The more I studied this I realized this is scarier than you first think. At first, it's a relief we aren't encountering a literal personal beast when we find out it simply refers to the earthly kingdoms and powers. But what are the implications of that? Behind the earthly institutional powers of this world, there is a very literal, personal being. The Dragon, the Devil, is the one who has the Beast at his beck and call, and summons him up out of the sea. And the Dragon is *very* personal! In the most evil way!

It's not some strange fluke that governmental and kingdom powers of this world always manage to either openly or subtly oppose Christ. Even in countries that start out with Christian heritages, there is always this strange leaning away from Christian values. The reason for this is there is someone very personal standing behind them, the father of the Beast! The Dragon. That's why this is so scary. There might be seasons when governments uphold Christian values, when Christians get involved in politics (and they need to). They seek to tame the Beast. But there is always this leaning away from Jesus and his values. The Beast rises from the sea.

What was one of the main temptations the devil tried with Jesus?

> The devil led him up to a high place and showed him in an instant all the kingdoms of the world. And he said to him, 'I will give you all their authority and splendor, for it has been given to me, and I can give it to anyone I want to' (Luke 4:5-6).

He's mine says the Dragon. The Beast is mine. The devil does have limited, delegated authority.

> We know that we are children of God, and that the whole world is under the control of the evil one (1 John 5:19).

So the Beast can take the form of any governmental power that opposes the authority of Christ or his ethics. We see obvious examples of this in the 20th century, like Mao Zedong, or Lenin and Stalin with their communist ideology/regimes that openly set themselves above the church to eradicate or oppress it. Hitler's fascism denied that humans were made equally in God's image. Today we have North Korea and closed Muslim countries which ban the gospel and where horrible things are happening to Christians, which remain largely unknown and unreported in the West.

The Beast also tries to stop Jesus advancing his message to the ends of the earth through more subtle forms by being the promoter of things like postmodernism, consumerism, relativism in ethics and religious vilification laws (which ban the exclusive claims of Christ), political correctness and every worldly power — all manifestations of the Beast who works against his opposition, the Christ.

So why the personal imagery? Because there is a real person behind the Beast. It is the devil himself who was standing on the sand of the sea and calling up the Beast. In one sense, the Beast is *very* personal! There is real personality behind him. The ancient serpent! Lord save our children from the Beast! Save *us* from the Beast! The Beast is promoting idols to take us away from the living God. And governments love to play God even on moral issues. They will determine what is acceptable for entertainment, the legality of prostitution, and gambling, as long as it brings in money for the state. They can tell you if you can change gender or marry someone of the same sex. So Jesus' concern for the little children is removed from everyone's thinking. The basic human rights of children are forgotten, that is, their biological right to be brought up where possible by their own mother and father. That's now masked by the

Beast promoting 'equality'. You won't win that one. The Beast will trample on you. The Beast will even tell us who can live and who can die with abortion laws and euthanasia laws.

Let's be clear, God gave the institution of government as a good thing. But like all things given by God, it can be abused. But by whom? The untamable Beast! So who is the Beast of Rev. 13? It's worldly state powers that opposes Jesus, throughout the ages.

But we have it easy in relation to this. In recent years in Sudan, the Beast has had multitudes of Christians either murdered or fleeing their homes. The Beast in Iran (and many other Muslim countries) and North Korea has all but eradicated the church. Iraq has seen 90% of its Christians killed or removed in recent years. When the Beast has freedom to move, he will bring the church under governmental control as he does today in China, where the government appoints Pastors.

But the Beast is subtler in the West. It's under the guise of tolerance and protection. You are breaking the law and hailed as a bigot if you dare to 'blaspheme' any religion such as Islam, or Buddhism. It's religious vilification! It's against the law! But what about Jesus? It's not against the law to blaspheme his name. People do it constantly. Jesus' name is a swear word throughout the nation! And yet if you blaspheme any other name you can be arrested! What's going on? The Beast is alive and well. He has the blasphemies on his heads (13:1). What hope do we have against the Beast?

And the Beast especially wants our children. The Beast knows if he can get to children through education and laws that promote anti-Christian behavior or beliefs, then he can gain momentum. The Beast invented the old adage: 'Get them while they are young.' So the young are bombarded with state-sanctioned values that even enter the home. Entertainment. Even disciplining children is under the control of the Beast. There are laws! What hope do we have against the Beast?

The book of Daniel told us from Daniel's day there were four Beasts, but in the middle of the reign of the fourth beast (the Roman Empire), a new kingdom would come with a new king. This king did come during the Roman Empire, just as Daniel predicted about 600 years earlier. This new king first arrived on planet earth about 2000 years ago and has been advancing his kingdom over these past 2000 years. The message of Rev. 13 is that the Beast will continue to attack and oppress the people of God, but don't give in to the Beast! He is the counterfeit. The true king is advancing across this earth. Right now, you are either living in allegiance to the kingdom of the Beast or the kingdom of Jesus. You will feel the pressure of the Beast. The Beast is telling you where to find your security and hope … it's in material things. That's what good government does. It provides prosperity! And the inhabitants of the earth expect that is what they are here for! So the Beast says if you lose material things then you've lost everything. You need more money. That is the answer. Or sexual freedom or pornography … look, it's free, it's accessible and the Beast made it legal … and everyone is doing it! The Beast says so.

This is why we need Revelation. Revelation reveals that everything is not what it seems. The Beast looks like he is winning and that you have to give in to get along. But the truth is Jesus wins! The message is this: Enter his kingdom by faith. Hold fast by faith. Don't worry about what you might miss out on, because in the end, Jesus wins.

Study Questions

1. Why does the Beast come up out of the sea?

2. Why does the Beast have so many characteristics of the Dragon?

3. What is the unholy trinity?

4. Is this Beast to be taken literally? Explain.

5. What Scriptures can we use to deduce whom this Beast represents?

6. Is the Beast personal? Explain.

7. Should Christians be involved in government?

8. At what time of history does the Beast manifest?

9. Give examples of the ways the Beast might challenge you.

10. How does Daniel's prophecy help us in light of the Beast's attacks?

16
The Beast that Rises
(Revelation 13:3-4)

Last time we discovered who the Beast was. He came up out of the sea riding on a surfboard! *And I saw a beast coming out of the sea ...* (13:1). This Beast represents not one, but *all* worldly powers which oppress God's people. We also noted the Dragon and the two Beasts are the great *counterfeit*. The unholy Trinity. This first Beast is the counterfeit of the true Son of God, who is the true image of God. This Beast is the second person of the *unholy* Trinity. He is the ultimate counterfeit of Jesus. We now see he even has his own death and resurrection ...

> One of the heads of the beast <u>seemed</u> to have had a fatal wound, but the fatal wound had been healed. The whole world was filled with wonder and followed the beast (13:3).

This is a direct parody of Jesus ...

> Then I saw a Lamb, <u>looking</u> as if it had been slain, standing in the center of the throne ... (5:6).

That sounds a little like this Beast, which **seemed to have a fatal wound**. It's a mockery of Jesus, the Lamb who *looked* as though he had been slain. How does the Beast have a head that *seemed* to have a fatal wound? Let's backtrack and examine his father, the Dragon, in whose image this Beast is made. Jesus defeated the Dragon through his death, resurrection and ascension (12:5). He crushed the head of the serpent (Gen. 3:15). Satan, the prince of this world, the Dragon, was defeated. He was *driven out* of heaven at the cross! *Hurled out*, as we saw in Rev. 12. No more accusations before God. But the trouble is that even though he was hurled out, when he hits the earth he is still alive! It's the great question we have as believers. If the devil is a defeated foe, how come he so often appears to be winning? In fact, the Dragon and the Beast seem to be alive and kicking more than ever. Does he really have the power to touch you?

This book of Revelation was written for you, Christian, to answer that question. Revelation tells us that despite appearances, Jesus is winning and Jesus wins. The devil has only delegated temporary authority. In reality, the Dragon *has* been defeated and there is judgment and a final end coming for the Beast and Dragon (see 17:14, 19:19-21; 20:10). But John the apostle says he is writing to God's servants as *fellow sufferers*. He seeks to encourage them to persevere in patient endurance in their suffering. Why? Because the Dragon is wreaking havoc. How can you say he is a defeated foe when he causes me so much grief, temptation and torment? Answer: This Revelation is given to look behind the curtain at the real picture. We need to know our foe is truly defeated. Jesus wins!

Just as John started this book in 1:9, calling on fellow Christians to persevere in *suffering and patient endurance,* so he continues this theme here in 13:10. *This calls for patient endurance and faithfulness on the part of God's people.* This book is written for Christians to encourage them to persevere. If you are part of God's kingdom you need to have *patient endurance*. Why? Because the Dragon is down on earth and in such a rage *because* of his defeat. We read in the NT in 1 John 5:19 the devil controls the whole world. But Revelation shows us it's in a limited way. Jesus is Lord even over the Dragon's delegated authority. Jesus wins! He told us at the start … *and from Jesus Christ, who is the faithful witness, the firstborn from the dead, and the ruler of the kings of the earth* (1:5). Jesus is the true ruler of kings and powers. But if you judge by appearances, it *looks like* the Beast is winning.

So how do we understand all this in relation to the Beast in this verse when it says **one of the heads of the beast seemed to have had a fatal wound, but the fatal wound had been healed?**

Preterists (pre-AD 70), have some strong arguments from this text. Preterists say the Beast is Nero, Emperor of the Roman Empire. He is head of the worldly power that oppresses God's people. This would make sense in the first century. The Roman Empire by any interpretation represents worldly power that oppresses God's people. Nero committed suicide in AD 68 and it slowed down the wave of persecution against Christians, but there were rumors at the time that Nero had risen and was hiding out. On top of those rumors there were imposters taking the name of Nero to keep the rumors going. So the Preterist says Nero is the Beast who was *as slain* but comes back.

This theory doesn't fully work though, because rather than a resurrection to be worshiped by the state, as described here in Rev. 13, Nero died as an *enemy* of Rome, a disgraced leader. And no, he didn't rise again.

But Nero can make sense as the Beast if we think of Nero not just as an individual, but instead as one head of the Roman Empire, the great superpower that persecuted God's people. Nero died, but another replaced him whose persecution was even more far reaching. By the time of John's writing it was Emperor Domitian demanding to be worshiped. And you thought the Beast in Nero was dead! Just when the worldly power, the Beast, is overthrown (dies), he resurrects again. And dotted throughout history we see this. Every time one worldly power which persecutes is overthrown, the Beast rises again. *One of the heads of the beast seemed to have had a fatal wound, but the fatal wound had been healed …*

Each time Christ, the true king, brings down one of these evil worldly powers or systems or figures, another persecuting power arises in its place. The Beast rises again! All evil worldly powers do not appear at once, nor fall at one time. Remember only *one* of the seven heads is brought down and rises. But this goes on throughout history.

This is the tension we highlighted when we noted that God gave the institution of government as a good thing, but Satan infiltrates and uses the Beast to try and thwart the advance of the gospel and the ethics of the Lord through worldly governments and institutions. This is what is unveiled in Revelation. Christ rules but the Beast mocks him. The counterfeit throughout history uses his limited delegated authority to take over and use what God instituted as good … governmental powers. But Revelation unveils that Christ still rules and in the end Christ's resurrection results in his final victory and glory, whereas the Beast rises to full defeat and destruction.

The book of Daniel predicted Jesus would come in the middle of the Roman Empire to inaugurate an eternal kingdom. But now the counterfeit tries at the same time to exalt his kingdom. We saw the coronation of the true King back in Rev. 5. The Father confers authority on the Son after his death and resurrection. Now the devil gives his authority to the Beast after his defeat when he was tossed out of heaven, after Jesus' victory at the cross and resurrection.

> People worshiped the dragon because he had <u>given authority to the beast</u> … (13:4).

Both Jesus and the Beast receive worship after their rising. But the Beast is so impressive in his counterfeiting, in his rising up, that the whole world marveled …

> One of the heads of the beast seemed to have had a fatal wound, but the fatal wound had been healed. <u>The whole world was filled with wonder and followed the beast</u>. People worshiped the dragon because he had given authority to the beast, and they also worshiped the beast and asked, '<u>Who is like the beast? Who can wage war against it?</u>' (13:3-4).

The Beast seems invincible. Remember the Beast is drawn from a composite of the four beasts of Daniel. What were they? Four worldly powers that oppressed God's people. Babylon, Medo/Persia, Greece and Rome. Each successive world power would fall badly, but another would replace that oppressive power. Well, now the Beast has characteristics of all four. He keeps coming up *in part* (at least one of his heads) again and again.

You can trace the Beast throughout church history from the time of the Roman Empire that persecuted Christianity in the first three centuries, to Constantine who effectively legalized corruption of the church by bringing paganism into her. But then the Roman Empire fell. The Beast died. But then it rose again. This time in the form of Islam in the seventh century that conquered some two-thirds of the Christian world. By the time you get into the heart of the Middle Ages, the Beast was almost indistinguishable from the power of the Roman Catholic church (we will have to take this up when we come to the second beast).

But there have always been worldly governmental powers persecuting or oppressing God's people. The Beast has been manifest and fatally wounded, most obviously in the states that have openly persecuted the saints. The unstoppable world superpower, Soviet Russia, sought to eradicate the church in the 20th century. How could a superpower be brought down? Jesus reigns over the kings of the earth! The Beast was slain, at least one of its heads died. But then the Beast resurrects again in horrible ways. We are only in the first part of the 21st century and already there have been nearly one million martyrs for the Christian faith.[8] There are extreme Muslim governments and even an Islamic State. Some survive but other heads are brought down only to be replaced again. The Beast was all but slain in the West, in so-called Christian countries, but is now rising again in far more subtler ways. In Western countries that were founded on Christian values, the Beast works more subtly.

Try and make sense of this and tell me there is no Beast. If you are like me and grew up outside the church, when you think of Adam and Eve you think *fairytale*. That's what the Beast (the state) taught us. Evolution is science. Adam and Eve are make-believe. But wait a minute! Try Google on how evolutionary theory explains the first humans. It says that we all evolved from—one woman! They even call her Eve! No joke. Somehow, it's *not* a fairytale when an evolutionist says it! When evolutionists say humanity begins with one woman (called Eve), no one imagines a patronizing child's storybook with pretty Eve in an evolutionary textbook. Mind you it has to be a fairytale to start off with Eve but no Adam. How did things get started?

Tell me this question of origins is just intellectual and there is no Beast. We have democracy in Australia. We have freedom of press and freedom of speech, yet it is *compulsory* (no alternative allowed!) to be educated in a theory which says this world popped out of nothing, and it's taught as fact! Then a finely tuned universe sprang into being from nothing! Then it proceeded to have the drive towards designing itself and inanimate cells that sprang from nothing naturally knew how to carry out a mentality of survival of the fittest.

But try that with any other school subject, such as history. For example, Australia's first European settlement. Captain Cook landed in Australia, then the First Fleet arrived in 1788 ... Or was it ... Some white people with Pommy accents started springing up out of nothing, amid the aborigines? You can't get away with the illogical nonsense of something popping out of nothing with no power or cause behind it in any other subject, let alone have it as compulsory study—unless there is a bigger motive behind it—unless you are trying to eliminate Christ. So it's not about intellectual debate. This is a battle between Christ and the Beast. Try asking for equal time in

---

[8] www.ordonconwell.edu/ockenga/research/documents/1martyrdomsituations.pdf.

public schools, or *any time* in public schools, to teach that this world didn't create itself, and you will see the power of the Beast. **Who is like the Beast?** The Beast is able to eliminate those religious crackpots. **Who can wage war against him?** If this was just an intellectual battle wouldn't a 'God hypothesis' at least get a hearing alongside the idea that this world popped out of nothing? And the Beast says we are the ones who are crazy and he gets away with it! How could that happen? *Who can wage war against the beast?*

We had a showing of the *Expelled* movie at our church one night. *Expelled* explores the situation in the US where scientists who dare to produce arguments for creation are more than marginalized, they are even expelled from universities. *Who can fight the beast?* Is it only in the US? When we showed the movie, we had a living example speak to us after the film. Our guest speaker was a science lecturer at a university in Melbourne at that time, but he asked that the name of the university not be mentioned in public when he wrote or spoke about creation for fear of reprisals from the Beast. There is no such thing as freedom of speech when it comes to the Beast. He won't allow it. Everyone worships the Beast. '*Who is like the beast? Who can wage war against the beast?*' Even that statement is a counterfeit. *Who is like the beast* is like a mockery of ...

> 'Who among the gods is like you, LORD? Who is like you—majestic in holiness, awesome in glory, working wonders ...?' (Ex. 15:11).

In the apostle John's day, the Beast had state-sponsored attacks against the church on the basis of religion. The Roman Empire had their pantheon of gods behind them. The Emperor was one. Worship the Emperor or die. Today closed Islamic states demand that anyone who renounces Islam to believe in Christ must die. But the Beast in the West works more subtly. He uses the media to promote the worldview of the Dragon. Your security is in this life—your health, wealth, beauty, fame and fortune, that is, the New Age view. The politically correct view. If a Christian gets into politics and dares to bring their own values to bear on their decisions, they are denounced. It's a downright affront to society and 'unethical' to have any belief in God which is strong enough to affect your decisions on ethics. It is against the law! But if your view is similar to that of the Beast, secular humanism, then it's quite all right. That is fair and unbiased. In fact, it is applauded! They *worship* the Beast (13:4).

The real question we need to ask is: How much has the Beast managed to sink his teeth into you? In closed Muslim or communist countries, he persecutes with violence. But in the West, he kills with kindness. The Beast promotes idols. Anything but Jesus and his ethics. The Beast makes it legal to exploit women (and men) in ways like prostitution, slavery, and in the world's largest legal business, pornography (many are trapped trying to feed drug-addictions by working in that industry).

But we would never fall for the Beast, would we? It's the followers of the Beast who worship him, not us. Right? Has the Beast managed to get into your life? Has the beast infiltrated the church? He is out to have you. He sets up every kind of idolatry that says you have a right to have whatever you want. It's freedom. It's your basic right. The Beast has made it law! He offers a salvation for your satisfaction. Security! The current Australian government was elected with the promise that it would cut $4.5 billion from overseas aid. Hardly a voice was raised against it. We need to take care of ourselves first. We poor people here in the 'lucky country'. We were said to be the only Western world country to survive the Global Financial Crisis. But now we can no longer afford to give to the poor. The 'global rich list' tells us the minimum wage in Australia makes us amongst the richest people in world. The Beast has convinced us we are struggling too much to give any more to the poor in the rest of the world. People this day will die of starvation and lack of basic medical needs. Jesus said whenever you didn't feed one of these you did it to him. Remember the poor. But the Beast tells you, 'No *you* don't have enough money!'

Look at the lobby groups leading up to any election. Everyone is hard done by. Everyone's cause is more important than the other. It's a frenzy. They call on and rely on the Beast! They worship the Beast and his values. They depend on him to provide. Our father Beast, give us this day *tomorrow's* bread. How much of that mentality has seeped into our lives? How much do we think 'we can barely get by', while millions are starving?

The Beast tells you that you need to store up. The Beast tells you your security is in your superannuation. You have to have more! Work towards that nest egg. That is what life is all about. Security is that time when you can take it easy and be secure through your superannuation and/or your pension that the Beast provides. The Beast says that is what security and life is all about. This life is short enough as it is, now the Beast has convinced us life is confined to an even smaller part, near the end of your life when you retire and are secure and can live it up, even though you are too old to do all the stuff you wanted to—and then you die anyway.

And then what? What will you do with all that stuff the Beast told you that you needed? The Beast said store it up. Live it up. It's all about you. Eat, drink and be merry for tomorrow we die. But what about the other side of death? What about the forever on the other side? The Beast was lying to you! He offered you a false salvation. It turns out Jesus is the true King. His kingdom is eternal. His is the true, forever security. He says don't worry about the things of this world. Don't worry about storing up treasures on earth. Don't worry about what you will eat or drink or wear. Don't worry about tomorrow. But *seek first his kingdom and his righteousness and he will take care of all those things you need.* The followers of the Beast run after those things (Matt. 6:31-34). But the Beast was lying! Which kingdom will you follow? The true King or the Beast?

Study Questions

1. How is the Beast shown to be a mockery of Christ in this text?

2. Evaluate the Preterist argument on this text.

3. Give examples of the 'resurrection' of the Beast from Daniel as a precursor and through church history?

4. Give examples of the institutions and political systems of the Beast?

5. In what ways are the values of the Beast seen today in the West?

6. What ways has the influence of the Beast crept into the life of the church and your life?

17

The Beast is Worshiped
(Revelation 13:5-10)

Father, Son and Holy Spirit? Not in Rev. 13. We have been introduced to the *unholy* trinity. The Dragon, the Beast and a second Beast we read about later in 13:11-17. We have learned this first Beast is not a single person or a literal beast, but drawing on its characteristics in 13:2 we found this Beast is a composite of the four beasts in Daniel 7 which represent worldly powers, governing authorities or institutions that persecute God's people. Now we learn more about the Beast ...

> The beast was given a mouth to utter proud words and blasphemies and to exercise its authority for forty-two months (13:5).

Why does 42 months get repeated here in Rev. 13? We have seen that period of time in Rev. 11-12 and in other places variously described as 1,260 days, or a time, times and half a time, adding up to 42 months. We established this period of time must be symbolic of a tribulation based on 'types' in Israel's history, rather than a literal amount of time, because it begins at Jesus' ascension (12:5) and goes through to the end. But 42 months is of interest here because it also covers the time of Jesus' work in the church age. Therefore, in this context it could be highlighting the Beast's activity in copycatting Jesus' work reigning on high during the church age.

Remember the Beast is the great counterfeit. While the true King is advancing his kingdom to the ends of the earth from every tribe, people, language and nation, the Beast seeks to advance his counterfeit kingdom, as 13:7 tells us, from every *tribe, people, language and nation*. The Beast is the imitator of Jesus. He is one who is made in the image of the devil. He is the second person of the unholy Trinity. And what else is the apostle John seeing?

> The beast was <u>given a mouth</u> to utter proud words and blasphemies and to exercise his authority for forty-two months. It opened his <u>mouth</u> to blaspheme God, and to slander his name and his dwelling place and those who live in heaven (13:5-6).

There is that **mouth** again. We were first introduced to it in 12:15 with the Dragon himself. It's that mouth which utters blasphemies and boasts. Remember the mouth flooding the church with false teaching and deception. And this is where it gets personal …

> It was given power to <u>wage war against God's holy people</u> and to conquer them. And it was given authority over every tribe, people, language and nation (13:7).

Wage war against God's holy people. We are declared holy by Jesus' death in our place. So *holy people*, refers to anyone who believes in Jesus and follows him as Lord and Savior. This means if you are a Christian the Beast makes war against you! Are you looking for a good church? If you want to find a good church, look for one that is under attack from the Beast. The Beast's goal is to **conquer** or to be *victorious* over God's holy people. The word *conquer* is the same word in the original Greek language we have also seen translated in Revelation as *victorious*. The Beast has this authority to conquer, or to be *victorious* over Christians.

What would the Christians in those seven churches be thinking when they see the Beast is to be *victorious* over them? Each one received a personal letter to their church in Rev. 2-3. How many times in those seven letters did Jesus exhort them, 'He who is *victorious* …'? 'He who is *victorious* will be in paradise.' 'He who is *victorious* will not see the second death.' 'He who is *victorious* will be dressed in white.' What was Jesus getting at?

Well, now those first readers in those seven churches all know! Now they get to Rev. 13 and see he was talking about being *victorious* over *the Beast*—lest he is *victorious* over you! And just as the letters to the seven churches talk to the whole of God's church, we don't have to look far to see the Beast … *waging war against God's holy people* throughout the 42 months. It's the whole wilderness period of the church age. Today we have the testimony of the blood of multitudes of Christians murdered, attacked, forced from their homes, and churches burned in Africa, India, Syria, Pakistan, and other Muslim countries. That is just in the last few years. Go back throughout the 20th century and we see communist Russia trying to eradicate the church and China persecuting believers. The Beast was there. What about Hitler's regime? The Beast was there. Iran or Iraq. African Muslim countries and North Korea. He is there.

But 13:7 says he has authority over *every* tribe, people, language and nation. So the Beast is not just in these obvious, 'persecuting'-type countries. But every *nation*! Even in countries with a Christian foundation the Beast fights and infiltrates to re-establish his authority. And *if one of his heads is brought down he rises again.* (13:3) And note this ...

<u>All</u> inhabitants of the earth will worship the beast ... (13:8).

Wow! Don't miss that! *All* the inhabitants of the earth (unbelievers), worship the Beast. The average inhabitant of Australia would say they don't worship *anyone*. But oh yes, they do. And what's more, they don't just worship anyone. I don't know whether you want to tell your unbelieving friends and family this because it might not be the most effective evangelism strategy, but they are actually Beast-worshipers! *Revelation* is *revealing* that everyone is worshiping. We were created to worship. If you don't worship the living God, you won't worship nothing. You *will* worship something or someone. So it's not a question of *whether* people are worshiping, but *whom* are you worshiping? If you are not worshiping the living God, you are worshiping the Beast (13:8), such as the values and things which governments promote as legal (but are against Christ), things where you find your security and satisfaction (they may be inanimate things but are still idols). You are actually worshiping the Beast! And he is made in the image of the Dragon! So you are actually worshiping the Dragon!

Rev. 13:7 says the Beast is *making war against God's holy people*, and before that in 13:6, he is slandering and attacking the dwelling place of God with his people. Wait a minute! Does this mean the Beast comes to church? Next time at church take a very close look at the person sitting next to you and see if their eyes look a little beady ... Watch out, the Beast goes to church! He wants to be worshiped, so he especially attacks our worship. First, he hates it when we worship God, so the Beast gives you good reasons why you are too busy to come to worship services. Too busy with what? Too busy following the Beast! Look at all the important things he gives you to do instead of going to church. And when you do go to church, he wants worship to be Beast-centered rather than Christ-centered. So when worship is focused primarily on the musicians or the worship leaders or self-help stories, rather than Jesus as revealed in his word, look out! The Beast is attacking!

Notice how even the definition of the word *worship* has changed in only a few years. Worship is something we can do in all of life (Rom. 12:1), but we are also commanded to have corporate worship (Heb. 10:25). Up until a generation ago the word *worship* in church life referred to the entire worship service including the reading and preaching of the word and prayers. Now the word *worship* in church culture is confined to just the entertaining music stuff. The Beast loves turning anything that is good into an idol. Even the means of worship. He is the great counterfeiter.

All inhabitants of the earth will worship the beast ... (13:8). This language seems to refer to all of history as a sweep of unbelievers across the ages and people groups. It is meant to be a contrast between those who are *saved* from every tribe and tongue across the ages (5:9), to those who worship the Beast from every tribe, people, language and nation (13:7). It's the sweep of history. This is another reason why I am suggesting the Beast is neither confined to only those living in the few years before AD 70 (Preterist), nor confined to a limited pocket of people just before the end of history (Futurist), having no relevance to any Christian of the church age. In contrast, this is alive for all the saints who live throughout *all* church history.

All this time you couldn't work out why your unbelieving family and friends don't listen to you. They worship the Beast! Beast worshipers are not just those heavy-metal guys who cut the heads off chickens and stuff like that. No! *All inhabitants of the earth!* They might be very nice people; they might be your loved ones. But they can't just suddenly change their own minds. It will take a radical re-birth. They would have to have their whole worship allegiance changed. Only God can do that. So you have to pray to God, who makes people alive.

And this explains to us what is going on in this world, and why you are under attack from every possible angle. Why is Revelation written? Remember John's visions are building on his opening statement that he is a *companion in the suffering* and *patient endurance that are ours in Jesus* ... (1:9). And this section winds up with what?

> If anyone is to go into captivity, into captivity they will go. If anyone is to be killed with the sword, with the sword they will be killed. This calls for patient endurance and faithfulness on the part of God's people (13:10).

Some will be imprisoned (**captivity**) for the faith. Some will have to give their lives (**killed**) for the faith. But all God's people will be attacked. Why? Because the Beast makes war against them! If you are going to worship the Lord, you will be attacked. And you need **patient endurance and faithfulness**. In fact, *everyone* who wants to live a godly life in Christ Jesus will be persecuted (2 Tim. 3:12). That is *everyone!* Not just some Christians in one pocket of church history. *All Christians*. How are you going to persevere and resist the worship of the Beast? The Beast has all the inhabitants of the earth on his side worshiping him. His work is more blatantly operating in the persecution and death of Christians and has intensified in the last one hundred years. **If anyone is to be killed with the sword, with the sword they will be killed.** So this is real and alive for multitudes, even today!

But in countries with a Christian heritage, he operates with more stealth. In the West today, God's people are marginalized as the 'intolerant, bigoted' ones. And even more subtly, the Beast has infiltrated the church. Now many in the church are openly worshiping the Beast; materialism, worship of sex, worship of self, worship of money and status. The Beast promotes them all. Governments promote prosperity and comfort as an end in itself. They get elected on promises to do just that. The inhabitants worship the Beast and if he doesn't deliver on those promises, they will vote out that government until they find one that will. That's where their security is, in what the Beast can deliver. That is where their hope is. And that same doctrine of the Beast comes into the church. Come to Jesus and have all you want. Jesus wants you to be rich. Worship is all about *you* and whether *you* feel lifted up. But *you* are following the Beast!

If you are finding life a bit tough now, the reason is here—*the beast is making war against you!* Haven't you noticed? The question Revelation now poses for us is this, 'Who are you worshiping?' The

Beast wants you to worship him! All this time you thought it strange that your mind wanders in worship services and in your prayer life. Life can be tough to stay worshiping the Lord. And you just can't find time for God. Busy. Busy. Busy. Busy with what? Strange that. You have an enemy! You are under attack. He makes *war* against the saints.

Why do you find this life to be such tribulation? Because you are going *through* the tribulation! The Beast wants you to fix your eyes on the here and now. He knows he can only persecute you in this world. He has only a limited authority for a limited time, 42 months.

So, what is the main way the Beast is trying to drag you down now? He wants you to think *'this is home'*. He offers you false promises of satisfaction and comfort, to find your rest in things to worship him here and now. And that is why the end of 13:10 says *this calls for patient endurance and faithfulness on the part of God's people*. Revelation exhorts us to finish the race and set our minds on things above. Things eternal. Just as the apostle Paul says …

> For while we are in this tent, we groan and are burdened, because we do not wish to be unclothed but to be clothed with our heavenly dwelling, so that what is mortal may be swallowed up by life (2 Cor. 5:4).

We groan! We are not home. This is not meant to feel like home. We are in tribulation. In the wilderness! This calls for perseverance! You feel as though there is something missing and this is not how it should be? Well, this is exactly how it's meant to be! You are meant to groan. But don't give up. Stop trying to look for the triumph in this life. That is what the Beast would sell you to get you to bow down to him. Joy in the Lord may not always mean you are feeling 'happy' all the time. It's deeper than that. Joy in him may come through even the most heartfelt suffering.

The attacks are obvious in countries where people are threatened with 'deny Christ or die'. *If anyone is to be killed with the sword, with the sword they will be killed*. But as one young Indonesian man told me, living as a Christian in Australia is easier physically than Indonesia (no physical persecution), but much more difficult spiritually. The Beast knows how to work his audience. It's interesting that Muslims from strict Muslim countries often say Christians are immoral, because they see all Westerners as 'Christians' and don't have the concept of separation of church and state. So they see the Western governments (the Beast), with laws that allow all kinds of sexual immorality even in entertainment and the way people dress, which they interpret to mean that Christians are immoral. Of course we object and say most of these people are not Christians, but it's ironic how much the church is no different because of the influence of the Beast. The Muslim criticism of 'Christians' may be closer to truth than we realize.

There is a song on the Beast's favorite playlist from his radio program (in fact he puts it in most of his songs). This is his message: You can only be satisfied in this life with your true love partner. He has many beautiful love songs. This is true satisfaction in this life. 'I groan in this life, so I can only be fulfilled with the right life partner.' So the Beast promotes this idea, and it's one of the biggest idols that creeps into the church. Half the people in churches think, 'Yes, I've got Jesus, but I can only really be fulfilled if I have the right marriage partner.' The other half complain because their marriage didn't turn out to be all about meeting *my* needs. They believe the worldview of the Beast which says 'marriage is all about *me*'. Worshiping the Beast! Marriage as God intended is about both partners giving themselves for the *other* (Eph. 5:22-33). Even the Beast passing legislation for same-sex marriage was on the basis of satisfying the desires of adults rather than what would be best for children. It's all about me.

The word of God tells us that true fulfillment can only be found in worshiping the true God. Being a God worshipper. Life was never meant to be about me. That is slavery and an idol that will never satisfy. But this is love. Not that we loved him, but that he loved us (1 John 4:10). Jesus, the God who gave himself up that I might live for him—not for me. That's the meaning of life. That's true worship. That is release! Life is about who God is and what God has done in his eternal plan, and what a wonder that he has included me in it! Wow! But until we are face to face ...

This calls for patient endurance <u>and faithfulness</u> on the part of God's people. The Beast teaches the inhabitants of the earth a theology that he has managed to get into the church. In Christian theology, it's called *triumphalism*. It is all about the complete victory now. I want it now. I should have my miracle now. I should have my prosperity now. I should have my healing now. I should have my power now. I should have my perfect relationships now. What are we saying? I want heaven on earth! I don't want to have patient endurance and faithfulness!

But the apostle John gave us this Revelation as a fellow *sufferer* in prison on the island of Patmos with this word to Christians. Not all now! This calls for *patient endurance and faithfulness*.

If you have felt discouraged, oppressed, even beaten down with temptation and trial, and think you are on your own—you aren't. Forget about coveting someone else's life, because you don't know what they are really going through. But we can see from John in Revelation that you are not strange, Christian. Some saints will suffer in captivity. Some will even be killed (13:10). So in the West we have it pretty tame compared to what the Beast has been doing against our brothers and sisters throughout the world and history. But it's *meant* to be this way.

We live in this tribulation and the weight of the attacks of the Beast come upon you. If you have fallen for the idols without realizing it, then you have been enticed into worship of whom? The Beast! (What a scary thought!) Have you fallen for the Beast? And even if you want to repent, have you repented enough? How do you know if you are saved? What can you do? That is what this part of Revelation is written for …

> Whoever has ears, let them hear … (13:9).

Remember that line? You can be sure those first readers in the seven churches remembered it. As if to underline that this is alive and written for all Christians through time, this is the same phrase that was repeated in those letters to the seven churches in Rev. 2-3. Now we are up to Rev. 13, well into the tribulation, and those same Christians (along with us), are being told the same thing! **Whoever has ears, let them hear.**

So Revelation is not for the church to tune out after Rev. 2-3. The whole book is written to the church. And this phrase is here to say to those Christians who were told in the letters, *Whoever has ears, let them hear* … now that you have seen all that has unfolded (Rev. 4-13), and what you have to go through, are you still listening now? Do you *still* have an ear to hear? This is for you Christian! It's hearing with the heart! It's for all Christians. Turn from Beast worship. Turn to the living God. But how can I be sure I am saved? He told us that too.

> All inhabitants of the earth will worship the beast—all whose <u>names have not been written in the Lamb's book of life, the Lamb who was slain from the creation of the world</u> (13:8).

If you are one of Jesus' people, your name is written in a book from the creation of the world! Who wrote it? This is remarkable, is it not? Picture a book. It was around before the creation of the world. Names are written in it. Whose names? Those who worship the Lord and not the Beast. If the names were written in it before the creation of the world, then who wrote it? It can only be the Lord himself. The Father with the Son together in glory before the world began.

> And now, Father, glorify me in your presence with the glory I had with you <u>before the world began</u> (John 17:5).

The Father and Son were in each other's presence before the creation, and there was an exchange of names. The names in this book.

> And this is the will of him who sent me, that I shall lose none of all those he has <u>given me</u>, but raise them up at the last day (John 6:39).

The Father *gave* names to the Son. They are written in a book! We will see this book mentioned again several times in Revelation. It is opened at the end of history. But here is something just as fascinating. The book was around before the creation ... **written in the Lamb's book of life, the Lamb who was slain from the creation of the world.**

But we still haven't answered the question: How do you know if your name is in that book? If you have been compromising with the Beast, then how do you know? This is why Revelation was written to the church. It's a warning, yes. Trumpets warn. It's also a wake-up call. Yes! *Whoever has ears, let them hear.* But it is also written to strengthen Christians and to give them assurance as they fight through the tribulation and wonder: Who can stand? 'Will I be able to make it? I have fallen for those idols. I have an ear to hear, but I've also fallen for the Beast's tricks. How do I know I can make it now?' And the answer is: If your name is there then you will hear *now!*

Whoever has ears, let them hear. If you are one of the Lord's, you will not be able to *go on* worshiping the Beast. The Beast won't win. You *will* hear. You *will* see the deception that Revelation is exposing and flee in repentance to the Savior. You will believe in what *Jesus has done!* Slain from the creation of the world to take away your sin. Yes, you will still sin, but you will hate it and flee from it. Yes, your mind will still wander, but you will desire to realign yourself to worship the Lord and not the Beast. Even though there were times when you covered your ears, if your name is in that book you *will* come to your senses and you *will* hear!

So the only question is: Can you hear now? Do you have an ear? If you can hear, then your name is already written in the book. If you are one of his, you *will* hear.

This is Revelation, written for Christians in tribulation to give them assurance. In Rev. 7 you read how you are marked with the seal of God. You will *be victorious*. You are part of the 144,000, the complete people of God, joined to Israel. Then in Rev. 11 you are *measured*. The complete people of God! Part of the true temple. You will *overcome*. In Rev. 12 you are taken care of in the wilderness. You will *be kept*. And now in Rev. 13 you have a written guarantee. Your name is written in a book. Written in the blood of the Son of God who was slain. It was in him that you were saved, and as you have an ear to hear, you repent and look to the Son to be forgiven, and it turns out your name is already written in that book!

One last thing from 13:8 … *the Lamb who was slain from the creation of the world.* This is a difficult sentence in the original Greek language because it can be translated a couple of ways. It could mean either the book is written from the creation, *or* the Lamb *is slain* from the creation. Both are possible and confirmed in other parts of Scripture. But if it's the later, *the Lamb who was slain before the creation of the world,* it highlights the eternal work of the cross. The cross is *from* the creation of the world! In other words, Jesus' death spans eternity. And we haven't even come close to understanding it. We have already examined how Jesus' death on the cross has to equate to eternal hell. He had to pay the price of eternal hell. It's an eternal redemption (Heb. 9:12). It can't be any other way if he is to save his people from eternal hell, otherwise the accounting does not add up and God is not just. So he is eternally slain — from the creation of the world. But how does that work? He was slain once for us *in time*, but he is also the eternal Son. It was an eternal work. I cannot comprehend the mystery of the cross and what Jesus has done to purchase my eternal soul. How glorious is this love? He paid eternal hell ... *the Lamb that was slain from the creation of the world.*

If you have an ear to hear this, if you are a believer, your name is written in his blood before God even created this world. Say your own name in your mind now. That name was spoken (given), from the Father to the Son from the creation of the world and written down. How would you feel if you could get a look at that name written in blood of God's own Son?

Well, it's written here in Revelation that there is such a book and your name is there if you are a worshiper of Jesus, ... if you have an ear to hear. This is why you can endure. It's already written. But this is not home yet. We are in tribulation. ... *This calls for patient endurance and faithfulness on the part of God's people.*

Study Questions

1. What does '42 months' represent and what new thing do we learn about this time in relation to the work of the Beast?

2. Who are 'God's holy people' and which of them does the Beast make war against?

3. If the word for *conquer* and *victorious* come from the same root in the original language, how is that significant for the first readers?

4. How does this help us to understand others and ourselves when we know that we were created to worship?

5. Rev. 13:6 gives us an interesting insight into the work of the Beast. How can this help us to be more diligent?

6. What does *worship* mean in the Bible?

7. What themes of Revelation are being specifically highlighted here?

8. In what ways does this text remind us that the whole of Revelation is written for Christians?

9. Give ways in which the Beast creeps into the Church.

10. How can you know your name is written in the book of life?

18
The Second Beast
(Revelation 13:11-14)

Just when you thought it was safe to go back into the water … This is sounding like those reports we get from the Northern Territory about an increase in crocodile numbers. Well, these crocodiles are not just in the water. Just when you think you are safe on the bank, there is one hiding behind the tree right near you! We have looked at the Beast who comes up out of the sea earlier in Rev.13. Now a second Beast is coming out of the earth. And they are buddies, working together.

> Then I saw a second beast, coming out of the earth. It had two horns like a lamb, … (13:11).

Immediately we notice more mockery of Jesus (the true Lamb of God), with this Beast described as having **horns like a lamb**. But how much cuter is this second Beast than the first Beast. The first Beast made war against God's people. But this beast is far more subdued and more subtle. He has a real interest in religion, particularly worship …

> It exercised all the authority of the first beast on its behalf, and made the earth and its inhabitants worship the first beast, whose fatal wound had been healed (13:12).

This Beast is religious! He is getting people to worship. Isn't that okay? After all, as long as you have faith—and don't other religions have some good ideas, aren't they devout and respectable and give good messages like peace, peace (even when there is no peace)? This Beast is much more persuasive and reasonable. He speaks. But underneath that speech we are told the secret. He might have the appearance of a lamb, but whom does he actually speak like?

> Then I saw a second beast, coming out of the earth. He had two horns like a lamb, but <u>it spoke like a dragon</u> (13:11).

We met the Dragon in Rev. 12, identified as none other than the devil himself. And this Beast speaks like the devil. So who is this second Beast? Is it Satan himself? Is it the Antichrist? Who or what is it? The book of Revelation has given us his 'Curriculum Vitae'. In 16:13 he is coupled again with the Dragon and the first Beast, but there he is referred to as the False Prophet. Also in 19:20, the False Prophet performs miracles and is associated with the Beast. In 20:10 he is again coupled with the Dragon. This is also what we read in Rev. 13 about this second Beast. He works miracles and performs signs. So this second Beast is *the* False Prophet.

This second Beast directs people to worship the first Beast (13:12), just as the Holy Spirit directs people to worship Jesus. This Beast performs miracles, just like the Holy Spirit does in Acts. This second Beast is the *third* member of the unholy trinity! It mimics the Holy Spirit. That's why it gets people to **worship the first Beast**. Remember the first Beast represents political and state power against Jesus. The second Beast represents false religion against Jesus. They are both mocking Jesus with power and religion.

The first Beast can promote good things. Technology and science give us many comforts and advances. But the second Beast gets us to worship those things as an end in themselves. These are the very things God gave us in the mandate to have dominion on the earth, such as science, technology and medicine, all good things. But the second Beast gets us to *worship* these things. So now 'in technology we trust'. Formerly, science was a wonderful way to explore God's world and discover its potential for our use. Now it's turned into a monster that is personal and even drives our ethics. We will use human beings for experiments for stem cell research. We will abort. We will euthanaze. We will even change our gender. And genetically modify humans. Science is the new god. If science can accomplish it, then we must do it. Worship it. Give praise to it! Where is that coming from? The second Beast! And this False Prophet Beast also comes inside the church ... in 13:11 the second Beast is dressed up *like a lamb!* Where have we heard that before? Jesus said ...

> 'Watch out for false prophets. They come to you in sheep's clothing,

but inwardly they are ferocious wolves' (Matt. 7:15). We are still looking for wolves in wolves' clothing. The false prophets we look for are like the Waco cult leader carrying a gun or religious terrorist jihadists. But they are not wolves in sheep's clothing. No sheep suits! They are wolves in wolves' clothing. We are looking in the wrong place for this Beast. False teachers might have some good, even biblical things to say. But we have been told in 13:11 this beast speaks like a Dragon. Just like Satan in the Garden of Eden who mixed the truth with lies. It sounded good, but behind it all was a lie.

So as the *False Prophet*, the second Beast, can do his finest work inside the church to make the ways of the first Beast sound credible. Not just his political correctness, but also his ethics. If the first Beast can make sexual immorality legal and acceptable (whether heterosexual or homosexual or same-sex marriage), then the second Beast wants to get that inside the church so you are really worshiping the first Beast. So rather than the teaching of Jesus, the church moves with the times. The first Beast makes divorce 'no fault', and so the second Beast gets divorce to be just as prevalent inside the church as outside. 'The church needs to come into the 21st century!' says the second Beast. But what he really means is, 'The church needs to worship the first Beast.' The church no longer has a united front when lobbying the government on ethical issues. That is one of the great arguments used against the church standing for moral issues. The government (first Beast) says, 'What about all the other churches who don't agree with you?' The second Beast wants the church to worship the laws implemented by the first Beast as well as its culture and sanctioned institutions.

What did this mean to the apostle John writing this down and the churches in Asia Minor in the first century to whom he was writing? How many of those letters were a challenge and a warning from Jesus about letting false teachers in the pulpit? Some of them had already compromised with the Nicolaitans and Jezebel (known for her teaching on sexual immorality).

What did this mean to those seven churches? The first Beast, to them, was the Roman Empire, which promoted these things as acceptable, even legitimate worship. There was temple prostitution. The second Beast was promoting it in the church through these false teachers, pointing them to the values of the first Beast. The False

Prophet was telling those churches these practices were all right because they were sanctioned by the state. Also in John's day, the pagan priests were already in co-operation with the state against the church. So this False Prophet was not just in the church but also in all false religions, philosophy and ideology.

In the last century with communism and strict Muslim countries, the first Beast (state power/government) oppressed the church, and the second Beast (false religion/philosophy) convinced the people of that nation to bow down to that philosophy/religion as the truth. Or in the West it might be more subtle, with the first Beast marginalizing the church, demanding political correctness and tolerance. Then the second Beast takes this way beyond just respect for what other people believe. He turns it into a new spirituality where everyone *must* acknowledge that all spirituality is valid and an alternative truth. You *must* bow down to that first Beast! In other words, it starts out with what seems like a good concept, that is, we should have respect for what other people believe and their right to believe it. But the second Beast *spiritualizes* this and gets people to *worship* the concept. They now say all religions are equally valid and you *must agree with them!*

This second Beast has power. It was scary enough when we discovered the first Beast has Satan behind him. Now this second Beast is the same. He speaks like his father, the Dragon (13:11). The JWs believe the Bible. So do the Mormons. And we get all excited evangelizing them because unlike other unbelievers, they believe in the Bible and open the Bible with you. They are at least open to discussion about the Bible … but you are falling for the second Beast! They are not 'half-Christians', or just a little off track. They deny Christ is supreme and the only Lord God of all. They are against Christ as the eternal Son of God. They are anti-Christ. They are no closer to meaningful discussion on the gospel than any other unbeliever. They are dead in sin and need to have the scales lifted from their eyes as much as anyone else. Their doctrine is all about worshiping the first Beast. Human pride and achievement. The second Beast turns that into religion. Salvation by works! The JWs will tell you why they believe they are the true Christians. They will say, 'By their fruit you will recognize them. And we are the ones who knock on the doors the most. We show the fruit! We do better and more works than everyone, so we must have the truth.'

Unbelievers become confused when they look at the vast number of religions and throw their hands up in the air and say, 'How could you know if you are right with all these alternative religions?' That was the exact plan of the *False Prophet* Beast. He has deliberately orchestrated this confusion with so many religions—so he can point people to the first Beast who says, 'Believe in *all* religions. There is truth in all—or none of them, but they are all equal.' Even the idea that there are 'many religions' is a deception in itself. There are not *many* religions. That is a lie of the second Beast. There are only two. The first religion is that of the *False Prophet* Beast. It is the religion of exalting mankind. The first Beast manifests in capitalist/materialism or communism, humanism, feminism, chauvinism, fascism, socialism or any other 'ism'. All have this in common; they all have human beings at the center. That is the heart of the first Beast.

But what does that have to do with the second religious Beast? He spiritualizes the 'isms'. All philosophies and religions of the world have this at their very heart. How do you get to heaven, or nirvana, or become enlightened, or reach paradise, or how do you become good, or how do you get rid of your sin? How do we advance society and get rid of inequality and racism? How do we progress as a society? The answer is always to be found in *you*, in *man*. That is the heart of every single philosophy *and religion* in the world ... Except one. Jesus' cross says you can't do it. There is nothing you can do to wipe away your sin. And you have no power to change your life. God has to do it for you! He has to give you a new heart. And you have to be emptied of all of your pride that says you could do it yourself and humble yourself before him. So while we might look at Buddhism and Islam and say they are so different from JWs or Hindus, all the second Beast false religion has at its very core is the exact same heart of the first Beast. What must I do to be saved? Exalt man. 'I may not be good enough now, but if I do all these things I will be good.' 'I may need more education or more programs or more religion. I may even really need God's help!' That is what the JWs or Muslims or Hindus would say. But whichever way you cut it, the bottom line is, 'I can be exalted through my own efforts.' Heaven, Nirvana, personal fulfillment. A good society.

So the motives for religious practice are what? This is the great divide of only two alternative religions in the world. Why does the Muslim pray five times a day? Why does the Buddhist meditate? It's not out of gratitude for what the exalted God has done to save them. It is the attempt to lift up self. It is the belief that I can achieve exaltation myself so that I will be good enough for God, or be worthy of enlightenment. Even if God has to help me, I can or will be good enough ...

But you never will be. And underlying all of this is what? 'I don't need Jesus. I am not so undone that I need a Savior to take away my sin. I can get rid of it myself by doing enough good. I don't need the cross!' You can say the word 'repent' in other religions, but that doesn't really mean I empty myself of all pride. It doesn't mean I see my sin as so bad that there is nothing I could ever do to get rid of it. 'I am not *that* bad. In fact, I am worthy of God forgiving me. Maybe I need some improvements, and with God's help *I* can be good enough. But I am not so bad that I need Jesus to fully take away my sin. I am against the need of the Savior.' Anti-Savior—Anti-Christ. But surely the second Beast couldn't get inside the Christian church with that? Look at church history. Salvation by works! Centuries that built up through the Middle Ages until the Reformation. The Reformation was started by devout Roman Catholics who protested that their church was not teaching what the Bible says, that is, we need faith in Jesus alone to take away our sin (not by works so no one can boast). The Reformers were mostly Historicists in their view of Revelation. They looked for individuals and events of history to explain Revelation. So they saw the Pope as the Beast and Antichrist (one who boasts, blasphemes and has authority throughout the world). The great blasphemy is making yourself equal to God. So the Historicist notes the Pope is called the Vicar of Christ. Vicar, 'vicarious', meaning 'in place of'. There have been many Popes who have *directly* boasted this blasphemy through the ages even up to more recent history. And the Pope does have 'authority throughout the world' as the Beast in 13:7. Official RC doctrine today still teaches salvation by works (plus Jesus). Be a good Catholic. Man *plus* Jesus.

We have noted before that the current Pope Francis has openly preached that you don't need to believe in Jesus to get to heaven. He denied the need for the Son of God when he said even atheists would be there with him if they do good.[9] I would think some older devout

---

[9] Vatican Mass sermon May 22nd, 2013

RCs would be shocked at this development, but it's actually a natural progression. If you let in 'exalting man', that you can be right with God through your good works plus Jesus' death on the cross, it only becomes a question of just how many good works do I need on my part to earn heaven? And if the Buddhist or atheist have *lots* of good works, who are we to judge? The cross is forgotten—man is exalted!

But should we only be picking on RCs? How much is going on in Protestant churches today that exalts man? Some say that to show you have real faith, you need to speak in tongues or heal people or be healed yourself. All works! The second Beast is in direct conflict with exalting the true King! The first Beast exalts man and the second Beast does it dressed in religious garb. *Man is good* or can be good enough. And this second Beast is so convincing …

> And it performed great signs, even causing fire to come down from heaven to earth in full view of the people (13:13).

If this second Beast is an imitator of the Holy Spirit and true religion, then we should have expected some fireworks of miraculous power. And we shouldn't be surprised at this. What did Jesus tell us? …

> For false Messiahs and false prophets will appear and perform great signs and wonders to deceive, if possible, even the elect (Matt. 24:24).

The second Beast is the False Prophet. It is false religion. And it performs miracles to back it up. So the deception must be great and the apparent power must be impressive, at least to many, maybe even many within the church! That's what makes it scary. The living God can do miracles or there wouldn't be anything to counterfeit. But how can you tell which is which? The scary part is not those Indian gurus who can appear to do miracles. But *within the church* some of the big names in miracle-working have another gospel. What is their primary motive? Getting you to worship the first Beast. These ones don't preach a gospel of repentance unto Jesus. It is Jesus plus. Jesus plus money. Jesus plus my worldly hopes and health and prosperity. All the stuff the first Beast promotes that worldly powers pursue.

RCs are also big on miracles. Again, is God able to do miracles? Of course! But how can you tell the source? RC miracles range from images coming down to light their own candles, and idols which have spoken and perspired, turned their eyes, and then there is stigmata. Mary has made many appearances, and many have been healed. Some of the RC miracles are quite extraordinary as Wikipedia reports.

> 'Joseph of Cupertino is an Italian saint. He was said to have been remarkably unclever, but prone to miraculous levitation, and intense ecstatic visions that left him gaping. In turn, he is recognized as the patron saint of air travelers.' [10]

I should have guessed. Air travel. Levitation! Then there is the Miracle of the Sun ...

> 'Miracle of the Sun is an alleged miraculous event witnessed by as many as 100,000 people on 13 October, 1917, in the Cova da Iria fields near Fátima, Portugal… after a downfall of rain, the dark clouds broke and the sun appeared as an opaque, spinning disk in the sky.'[11]

The sun was coming down as a disk and this was made officially a RC miracle in 1930. God can do that! Yes. But how can you tell it's from God? The second Beast has that power too **and it performed great signs, even causing fire to come down from heaven to earth in full view of the people.** This is scary. To think you can actually perform real miracles and do it in the name of Jesus and still be following the False Prophet. Jesus already told us that ...

> Many will say to me on that day, 'Lord, Lord, did we not prophesy in your name, and in your name drive out demons and perform many miracles?' Then I will tell them plainly, 'I never knew you. Away from me, you evildoers!' (Matt. 7:22-23).

So you *can* perform miracles and still be on your way to hell. Deceived by the False Prophet Beast. There are miracles going on, whether they are true or false, whether they are coming in the name of the Lord or not. We need to be careful. The text says this Beast can be *even causing fire to come down from heaven to earth in full view of the people.* A young man I met described to me how he saw tongues of fire from above come down on people in his church. I keep meaning

---

[10]https://en.wikipedia.org/wiki/Joseph_of_Cupertino#cite_note-Pastro-1
[11]https://ipfs.io/ipfs/QmXoypizjW3WknFiJnKLwHCnL72vedxjQkDDP1mXWo6uco/wiki/Miracle_of_the_Sun.html

to go there and check it out. But I have been busy. But how do you know the source of miracles if the False Prophet Beast has power to do this? Jesus said miracles would be used to deceive even the elect, if that were possible. How can we know which is which?

> Because of the signs it was given power to do on behalf of the first beast, it deceived the inhabitants of the earth. It ordered them to set up an <u>image in honor</u> of the beast who was wounded by the sword and yet lived (13:14).

Throughout history there have been worldly leaders **set up an image in honor of the Beast**. Some have even used these images to claim deity. Emperor Domitian had his own image *set up* in the temple at Ephesus. Before him, Caligula even tried to put his own image in the temple at Jerusalem. Tyrants through history have *set up* their images, down to the likes of Lenin and Stalin in 20th century Russia. There are great images of Mao in China. Hitler had his swastika. Saddam Hussein had his image erected in Bagdad. Even when they are torn down and appear to be dead, as in 13:3 (one of his heads is killed), the second Beast stirs the people of those nations to worship, to pay homage to those leaders and what they stand for. The first Beast comes to life again in another form to oppress God's people again.

If the False Prophet Beast sells what the first Beast promotes, such as prosperity, money, sex, power, health and living the good life as an end in itself, it's not hard to think of popular images (13:14) we associate with these things. They surround us! The advertising, mainstream media and social media images of who you should be, how you should look and what you should have.

So how does that second Beast (False Prophet), set up those images in the church? The Prosperity gospel. The self-fulfillment gospel. Sex appeal. Remember worship is the big thing this Beast is on about. Today, the secret that no one is letting out is that the Beast managed to get sex appeal into the church. And no, I don't mean the Pastor (at least not this one). I'm talking about the female worship leaders! That's a totally recent phenomenon in light of the last 2000 years of the history of the church. Women up front to do what? To be lovely to look at of course! Whoops. No. I mean they are just leading worship. Serving the Lord with their gifts. That's just my own paranoid thinking. But whatever you do, don't let the secret out men!

Well, I'm going to reveal the secret sins of men right here (one day I will expose the secret sins of women—just as soon as I find out what they are). But the secret is, men are wired differently when it comes to visual temptation. So when you have beautiful women dressed to look lovely, right up front in the worship service, men are either concentrating on making sure they don't look (that is, born again men), or they are being stumbled into sin. Either way, the focus is taken away from the worship of God to another image set up by the False Prophet.

But don't worry, the conspiracy will remain intact. Who is going to admit we snuck sex appeal into the church? No one. Women don't get it and men aren't telling! The secret of the second Beast is safe, and he is getting us to worship *the image* (13:14) of sex appeal—in the church!

I visited a large church along with a 20-year-old man who had aspirations for ministry. The worship was standard contemporary with big screens and close-ups on the beautiful female worship leader on the screen. I asked the young man afterwards how his concentration was in the worship and he confessed it was difficult while fighting the good fight to keep those images out of focus. But then he asked me, 'Do you think God may have called men to lead because he knew we would be more tempted visually?' I don't think that was the Lord's specific purpose, but it's a humbler approach to think it's better for men to be up front, not because of their superiority, but because of their *inferiority* when it comes to visual temptation. But we digress.

Perhaps the biggest image that has been set up in the West today is the image of the *self*. Woe to anyone who would dare to disparage that idol. It's part of the individualistic, Western-world age. Governments are expected to promote it and you dare not fail to give homage to that image. The image of *self* is the most important thing. *Your* rights and something for *you*.

And what does the second Beast do? He spiritualizes it! In the church today, everything is about *you*. The message is all about your felt needs, all couched in Christian terminology. Find yourself in Jesus. Self-realization in Jesus. It's all about *you!* But that's straight from the second Beast's mouth. He spoke like a dragon (13:11). He hasn't changed his tactics from the Garden. It's about you! 'You too can be like God!' And so we don't go to church to worship God. You are there to get something out of it—for *you!*

If you just 'believe', you can have anything you want. You are in the driver's seat. Power. Take up the power that is within you. Your health. You can have it all, never mind that pie in the sky when you die. It's all yours now! We are back to *triumphalism* again, but now we know how this worldly concept has been theologized. It's the False Prophet Beast.

The second Beast's teachings are all through the church. How do you know who is a teacher for the true and living God, and who is an apostle for the second Beast? They can come in the name of Jesus, even with the power to perform miracles. What hope do ordinary people like us have to discern the true from the False Prophet?

There is only one objective source God has given to test them all. He gave us his word! Now do you see how precious it is to read the word of God? 'But everyone says they follow the Bible.' Yes, but how many Christians actually read it regularly and test these teachers against it? This is our only hope in this deceptive world. His word must come first, even over miracles! As you go through this tribulation there is only one thing that can nourish you through this wilderness. Only one thing will last. Jesus said it. *Heaven and earth will pass away, but my words will never pass away* (Matt. 24:35).

Study Questions

1. Who or what is the second Beast?

2. In what ways does the second Beast imitate?

3. How does the second Beast get people to worship the first Beast?

4. How would the seven churches have seen the two Beasts operating in their day?

5. How would you respond to someone who is confused over the many religions?

6. What is the role of miracles in the church?

7. What are some images set up by the False Prophet Beast through history and today?

8. How do you know you are equipped to distinguish true from false prophets?

19

The Mark of the Beast
(Revelation 13:15-17)

It seems the apostle John has been having a series of dreams or nightmares because he has seen many strange images that have little or no connection (a bit like a dream). At least that is what is seems like to us. The reason the imagery seems so strange to us is that we don't know our Bibles well enough! In particular we don't know the OT as well as John did.

When *John* saw these images of the first Beast that everyone was to worship, he would immediately think of his favorite OT book, the book of Daniel. And when John saw the second Beast, the False Prophet with power such as this ...

> The second beast was given power to give breath to the image of the first beast, so that the image could speak and cause all who refused to worship the image to be killed (13:15).

John would have recalled in Daniel 3 the story of the statue of Nebuchadnezzar, when Daniel's three friends refused to bow down to the image, even though threatened with death. Remember the first Beast is state power that persecutes God's people. This was alive for John in his day. The Roman Empire demanded worship! All the seven churches John wrote to were in cities where temples were erected to the deity of the Emperor. Emperor Domitian demanded he be addressed as lord and god. To refuse could even cost you your life. The first church addressed in Revelation was the church at Ephesus. In their city, there was a great statue of Emperor Domitian. The inhabitants fervently worshiped it. His image was in their temple and that would have been in the minds of the first readers. It was the false pagan religion (the second Beast), that drove people to worship the first Beast, the Roman Empire. The normal cultural demand was to burn incense to Caesar for the compulsory festive events. Every industry had trade guilds (like unions) that required pagan Emperor worship or practices. If you worked in the military or officialdom, you had to partake in Emperor worship and increasingly this pressure was on Christians.

We know from the letter of Pliny the younger (a Roman official), written to Emperor Trajan in AD 112 (not long after John wrote Revelation), that those who refused to bow down were to face capital punishment.[12] The Beast had the power to kill. It had already happened at the church in Pergamum (2:13) with the martyrdom of Antipas. But even when capital punishment was not carried out, there were pressures with difficulty in getting work, social ostracizing and other ways Christians suffered. Just as not all were killed in Daniel's time, the power was still there to kill. There was life given to the first Beast driven by the false spirituality of the second Beast. **The second beast was given power to give breath to the image of the first beast, so that the image could speak and cause all who refused to worship the image to be killed.**

Throughout history there are examples of false spirituality that drives or *gives breath* to the state, the Beast, to enact the persecution. During the Middle Ages at the height of Papal power, there was a great working in tandem of the two Beasts. The Pope wielded as much strength as the state itself, and the two were almost indistinguishable. Popes gave the state authority (the breath), to execute people in the thousands for refusing to bow down to the Pope's beliefs. Read your church history and the stories of those who tried to stand up for Jesus and God's word long before the Reformation. Read of the Waldensians, Wycliffe, Jan Huss and their followers, along with many others. Many people were killed. The state power (first Beast) is given life to kill by the false religion (second Beast).

We see the two Beasts working together just as much today. False religion and state work together in many Muslim countries. The religion drives the state to enact blasphemy laws under which people can be executed for renouncing the Beast and believing in Jesus. We also see it in ideologies such as communism and fascism. Those ideologies give the state the power to kill God's people. People are being killed today because they refuse to worship the state.

---

[12] Pliny, *Letters* 10.96-97

The Futurist view is that sometime in the future, false religion stirs up state powers to persecute God's people. I am suggesting this is happening before our eyes and all throughout history. The only reason we miss it is because we have been living in a bubble in the West. The following is a quote from an article in *The Age* newspaper in Melbourne. It's not a broadsheet normally given to Christian sympathy, so for that reason it's worth quoting this lengthy section.

> Four of every five acts of religious discrimination in the world today are directed against Christians, according to the Germany-based International Society for Human Rights. The secular US think tank the Pew Forum says Christians face harassment or oppression in 139 nations, nearly three-quarters of all the countries on earth. …In Burma, Bhutan, Nepal and Sri Lanka, Buddhist militants have murdered Christians, Muslims and Hindus. In 2010 the Burmese military attacked Christian minorities from helicopters, reportedly killing thousands. These cases are horrific, certainly, but surely they are disconnected and accidental acts of cruelty and violence? Not so, rights observers say: they are all part of the biggest human rights challenge now facing the globe — religious intolerance — and also part of a largely unobserved global war on Christians. Things may be worse now for more Christians than at any time in history, including under the Roman Empire.[13]

Worse than under the Roman Empire! *The second beast was given power to give breath to the image of the first beast, so that the image could speak and cause all who refused to worship the image to be killed* (13:15). Millions have been killed for the faith over the past 2000 years, but it has intensified over the last 100 years. Rev. 13:10 told us *if anyone is to be killed with the sword, with the sword they will be killed.* It's right before our eyes, if you dare to look outside at what is going on in other countries.

I acknowledge the most popular view is that this is all to happen sometime in the future. But what are we waiting for? Waiting for a time when people will be killed for the faith? Are we to say, 'Okay, we admit the sword has killed millions, but they don't count? Just wait until people really get killed later.' Try telling the many in those 139 countries who have lost loved ones or suffer extreme persecution or torture for their faith. Are we supposed to comfort them by saying, 'Well, you may be tortured to death but be thankful the tribulation hasn't arrived yet'? 'Then you would really know what

---

[13] Barney Zwartz, *The Age Newspaper*, Fairfax Media, (Melbourne, Australia), November 2nd 2013.

suffering is.' This persecution has been happening to multitudes throughout the church age and continues in our time in greater numbers than ever before.

So how does this Beast *speak* (13:15)? The second Beast manages to get the first Beast to speak with authority, even put to death those who don't worship it. Look at the ethics in the West today. The description of the first Beast certainly fits the new ethics of the Western governments. There was a time when people acknowledged that the state couldn't take the place of God in determining ethical questions. Even atheists like Richard Dawkins admit that. Dawkins has said that it's pretty much impossible to determine ethics apart from religion.[14] Of course he is right! If there is no God, whose opinion is right? Who is to say who should live or die? But that was the old atheism. Now Dawkins, along with other atheists, are claiming ability to *speak*. They say science can *speak*. The state can and should *speak* and claim authority on issues of life and death. Science and the state can determine who should live and who should die, from the womb through to the nursing home. What's going on here? Science can't deduce ethical values. But now science and the political world do *speak*! The Beast in the West is becoming more open, like communist governments and closed Muslim countries where the state *speaks* authoritatively on ethics.

> It also forced all people, great and small, rich and poor, free and slave, to receive a mark on their right hands or on their foreheads, ... (13:16).

This is the moment we've all be waiting for! The mark of the Beast! This is the bit where the checkout lady insists on putting a stamp on your forehead, or you need surgical implants in your hand with your credit card so you can buy stuff at the supermarket. This is it! And I'm the first to admit that if it becomes compulsory to surgically implant my credit card into my hand or my forehead, I'll be humbling myself and re-checking my theology of Revelation! Or if the government demands I get a tattoo on my forehead or hand so I can buy or sell. This is the strength of the Futurist view—anything could happen in the future.

But as usual I start by asking, 'What did this text mean to the first readers?' What did it mean to those who were first told at the start

---

[14] Richard Dawkins, *The God Delusion* (London: Bantam Press, 2006), p.232

of this book that it was addressed to them (1:4)? What did it mean when they were told the time is near (1:3)? Was it near to them? Could they have taken this comment seriously? Was this *a blessing for everyone who has read it and taken it to heart* for the last 2000 years? Is it alive, especially for those first readers?

In the ancient world, the idea of people receiving marks on the hand or forehead would certainly be familiar. It would have immediate meaning to them. People were branded or tattooed for different reasons, but the common reason was that slaves were usually given tattoos, especially disobedient slaves, as well as soldiers and various devout religious people. But what was the point? With regard to slaves, it signified ownership. Who owns you? In the case of soldiers or religious enthusiasts, it signified devotion. To whom do you belong? So what does this mean when it says, it **also forced all people, great and small, rich and poor, free and slave, to receive a mark on their right hands or on their foreheads?** This is speaking of ownership, so the mark goes far deeper than an outer tattoo. We have already noted that God's people were given a *mark* on *their* forehead (7:3). It was called a *seal*. It wasn't hard for those first readers to deduce from Scripture what was the seal of the saints—the Holy Spirit. *When you believed, you were <u>marked</u> in him with <u>a seal</u>, the promised Holy Spirit* (Eph. 1:13). See also Eph. 4:30.

Christians are marked, not with an outward sign, but with the seal of the Holy Spirit. And yet this mark should be visible in their actions (the hand), and their ethics (the mind), what one believes in the head. They are marks of ownership. That is the question. Who owns you? *He anointed us, set his seal <u>of ownership</u> on us, and put <u>his Spirit</u> in our hearts as a deposit, guaranteeing what is to come* (2 Cor. 1:22). There is the ownership idea, the mark. The seal is the *ownership* of Christ. Are these marks visible? Yes, according to the Bible. The mark (or the fruit) of the Spirit is very visible in how we live, in what we believe (our heads), and what we do (our hands). The mark is obvious, even when there is no visible tattoo.

The most obvious mark of the Beast is seen in those who outwardly reject Christ and persecute the church and show it in their thinking and the action of their hands. It all comes down to this: 'Who owns you? Christ or the Beast?'

The idea of having a mark on your hands and foreheads would be familiar to the apostle John, who received this Revelation. He knew his Bible, particularly the OT. So John would remember …

> These commandments that I give you today are to be on your hearts. Impress them on your children. Talk about them when you sit at home and when you walk along the road, when you lie down and when you get up. Tie them as symbols on your <u>hands</u> and bind them on your <u>foreheads</u> (Deut. 6:6-8).

Did the LORD want the Israelites to literally tie these commands on their hands and foreheads? Some did, but sadly they missed the point. Jesus rebuked those who did as hypocrites for missing that point (Matt. 23:5)! They liked to wear the outward signs, but inside there was nothing. The mark of the true believer is that God's commands will be in your heart. You believe with your mind and you put your hands into action based on what you believe. So too the mark of the Beast. What you believe in your mind and put your hands to do will show whether you have the mark of the Beast …

> … so that they could not buy or sell unless they had the mark … (13:17).

If you don't have the mark of the Beast, if you don't believe in his ideology and don't put your hand to his practices, it will affect your livelihood, your ability to **buy or sell**. This spoke straight into the lives of the first readers. Their livelihoods were on the line. Remain faithful to Christ or join the trade guilds, which meant bow to the image of Caesar and worship him, or miss out on work and the ability to buy or sell your goods! In the church in Smyrna the Christians were *poor* (2:9). Why? They wouldn't bow down to the trade guild gods or Caesar's image. They didn't have the mark of the Beast. So the *mark will* affect people's living… *so that they could not buy or sell unless they had the mark* … (13:17).

This has been alive throughout church history and is really teaching that to be persecuted for Jesus' sake does not always mean death. One of the most common ways people suffer *will be economically … financially!* The application of this text is more obvious where the Beast can work more overtly, such as in closed Muslim countries or Communist countries where you cannot get work, or only certain types of work if you are a Christian. There are different pay rates and work opportunities, and Christians can be displaced or made homeless, and their businesses boycotted or attacked. For a great overview of how Islam has persecuted Christians economically over the past 1400 years, I highly recommend *The Third Choice* by Mark Durie. This still happens today in many parts of the world. Great numbers of Christians have been marginalized economically, displaced, made homeless and persecuted in other ways in recent years, affecting their ability to buy or sell.

I visited India a few years ago and went to a large city church in the state of Gujarat. The Pastor happened to be preaching through Revelation, so I asked him which view he took. He replied, 'The Idealist because Revelation is alive for my people. They are living it now.' In the state of Gujarat, Christian women traditionally gained jobs as nurses and teachers, however from around the time Narendra Modi was Chief Minister of the state (before he became Prime Minister of India), the employment prospects for these women changed dramatically, as these jobs were no longer given to Christian women. This is far subtler than in Muslim countries where pay rates and jobs are simply different for Christians. Of course, we are shielded from this in the West. Aren't we?

There are many other ways those with the mark of the Beast won't be challenged economically as believers are. Those with the mark of the Beast don't care *how* they make a living. They don't care what products they are associated with. But if you have the mark of the Spirit of Christ, you will not work for certain industries such as those whose primary product cuts across Jesus' ethics, like gambling or promoting sexual immorality, providing abortions, or a host of other things. If you work in the medical field and other fields associated with ethics, there are many challenges that could cost you. Will you stand for Jesus and maybe lose work opportunities, the ability to buy or sell? What if you run a business in an entirely ethical way, but your competition normally cuts corners? What if you stand up in the workplace against taking advantage of the system, cheating on time or sick days, or other expected unethical practices? Then you *will* lose money, perhaps an opportunity for promotion and even your job — *your ability to buy or sell.*

Remember where John is when he was writing this down. In a prison cave on Patmos. How did he describe receiving this vision? *On the Lord's Day I was in the Spirit* ... (1:10). The apostle John said he received these visions on the Lord's Day. Why did he mention that? Whatever the reason, John thought it was important enough to specifically point out that it was the Lord's Day. He was in the Spirit worshiping on a specific day he called the Lord's Day. The OT called the Sabbath the Lord's Day (Isaiah 58:13), but then it was celebrated on Saturday. But the Lord's Day John is referring to is Sunday, *the first day of the week*. Why the change? There is no direct pronouncement of the change. It just naturally appears in the life of Christians in the NT that they shifted from the Saturday Sabbath to worshiping on Sunday (Acts 20:7, 1 Cor. 16:1-2, when a collection is taken on this new worship day). What could be so earth-shattering that believers in the Messiah would change the Lord's Day? What could have possibly happened to make such a change occur so naturally? Well there was an earth-shattering event. The resurrection of Jesus! Clearly this event had such an impact on Jewish believers like John that it changed the day Christians worshiped to what John now calls the Lord's Day. It was a new beginning. A new day! Jesus rose from the dead on a Sunday and that new rest day points forward to the rest when we will all be resurrected (Heb. 4:9-10). Contrary to what our Seventh Day Adventist friends might say, this practice continued in the early church from the first century. Early church leaders who lived at the time of the apostles such as Ignatius of Antioch, AD 35-107.

> 'Let every friend of Christ keep the Lord's day as a festival, the resurrection day, the queen of all days.'[15]

The Epistle of Barnabas is one of the earliest Christian writings after the NT.

> 'Wherefore also we keep the eighth day with joyfulness, the day on which Jesus rose from the dead.'[16]

Tertullian (circa 160-220) says Christians laid aside daily business on Sunday. Jesus spoke more about the Sabbath than any of the other Ten Commandments to teach the correct use of that day. The Pharisees had added extra rules for the Sabbath not in the Bible or in the spirit of the Lord's Day. Jesus corrected them and taught that if you work in the area of mercy or necessity (which would include

---

[15] Ignatius, Epistle to the Magnesians, Ch. 9. Ante-Nicene Fathers, Vol. 1, pg. 62-63.
[16] The Epistle of Barnabas, AD 100, Ante-Nicene Fathers, Vol. 1, pg. 147

every kind of medical, fire brigade, police or other emergency fields), then your work is needed on the Lord's Day.

But otherwise the Lord set aside a day for us to meet, a day of sacred assembly (Lev. 23:3) as well as rest, and he called it the *Lord's Day*. The great French atheist philosopher Voltaire is alleged to have said, 'If you wish to destroy the Christian religion you must first destroy the Christian Sabbath.' And I would say Pastorally that one of the biggest issues in the spiritual decline of the church is simply getting God's people regularly spiritually nourished, strengthened, mobilized and unified as a people equipped for Jesus' mission, because today they no longer set aside that day for worship to be fed on God's word.

I accept not all Christians agree with the Lord's Day as having any connection to the Lord's Day in the OT. I accept some have genuinely thought it through Scripturally and decided that the fourth commandment is the one out of the ten we don't have to obey. I also accept this is an area of dispute among Christians (Rom. 14:1) and that each one should be convinced in his conscience and not for legalistic reasons (Rom. 14:23). Ironically, many of those who really love Jesus but disagree with the Sabbath are often just as diligent in church worshiping the Lord anyway (in my view because they have the law written on their hearts). But if you ask the average professing Christian why they can't worship next Sunday, it won't be anything to do with faith or theology. It will be some family party or pressing engagement or some work they are doing that is a veiled way of saying … 'The Beast says there is something more important than love for Jesus.'

The Beast changed all the laws in nations that formerly kept the Lord's Day aside for rest and worship to the extent that even unbelievers used to benefit (a day when families could be together). But now it's Sunday trading and everything else. So instead of worshiping the true King, the Christian feels the pressure to worship the Beast, pressure from the employer, pressure from an unbelieving family who tells you if you really love them you'll skip church and do their activity. And pressure from society that now puts 'my favorite things' on Sunday. Wow. Coincidence? Who put all this stuff on Sunday? Who introduced Sunday trading? The Beast!

The Beast has taken over the system. Jesus said the Sabbath was made for man. He didn't say the Sabbath was made only for Israel, *but for man*—for human beings. And unlike the other Ten Commandments, the Sabbath was given in creation to all humanity from the beginning. It's good for people to have one day set aside to stop, not just for our spiritual health, but also our physical and mental health. 'Sabbath' literally means to 'cease'.

All the Ten Commandments are given for our good. You would be surprised how good it is for society to not kill each other, or steal from each other, or lie to each other, or commit adultery in their marriages, etc. We still testify in society what Jesus said, that the Sabbath was made for man (not just for Israel). Nature testifies. Why do we have seven days in a week? Society is now filled with burnt out people working seven days a week. People are frazzled. There is no let up on the world being open for work and worldly domination. Even five-day international cricket test matches had a *rest day* on Sunday until recently. The last one was in 2001. It hasn't taken long. So what has happened?

The Beast changed the rules and now even unbelievers are worse off. No more family time, which leads to a breakdown of family. No more rest, so we are burning ourselves out and now have greater and greater needs for stress counseling. The pressure is on now. The Beast has taken over the one day a week that was for man to refresh physically, mentally and spiritually.

But what has all this to do with our text? Just this. If you believe there is a continuity between what John calls the Lord's Day (Sunday) and the OT Lord's day, and you are committed to keeping the Lord's Day, you *will* lose your ability to buy and sell. If you have a business, your competition will sell more. If you are an employee, you will lose work opportunities. You will *not* make as much money. You will miss jobs altogether. You will not be able to buy or sell as much.

However, unlike the Seventh Day Adventists, I am not suggesting the mark of the Beast is all about the fourth commandment. There is a principle in this text that lives for all of us today which goes way beyond your view of the Sabbath. There are all kinds of accepted things in work life that everyone with the mark of the Beast expects you to go along with, otherwise 'it could spoil it for the rest of us'. It will cut across your opportunity to buy or sell if you stand for Jesus and refuse to bow down to the image of the Beast.

When I was a younger Christian still in the entertainment industry, I was offered a television commercial for Oz Lotto. It was worth

$15,000 (30 years ago that was a lot of money). It was tempting because it was the most innocuous end of gambling. Lotto. The government (the Beast) had sanctioned it. It was legal. When I told the agent I wouldn't do it, she tried to entice me by telling me to do the commercial and give the money to the church! After 15 years in the industry, and more than 60 television commercials, within a year it went to zero after I started asking directors whether there were any sexual references, innuendo, or gambling in the proposed commercial. They don't like those kinds of questions. You get a name for yourself. Before, lots of buying and selling, lots of money—down to zero.

In my view, the mark of the Beast is not something that will happen in the future. You have either the mark of the Beast or you have the mark (seal) of the Lamb right now. It costs to follow Jesus! Even financially. Are you willing to miss out and trust him? *This calls for patient endurance and faithfulness on the part of God's people.* I don't think you have to wait for the implanting of the secret computer chip. That mark *is* visible in many ways.

Whose mark do you have? For whom will you stand? It's interesting that regarding unbelievers it's called a mark, but on believers it's called both a mark and a seal. The seal suggests a security that comes from a King.

But either mark will show up, whether you have the fruit of the Holy Spirit within you (Gal. 5:22), or whether you have the spirit who is now at work in those who are disobedient (Eph. 2:2). The mark *will* show in your life, most obviously by your allegiance. Who is your master? What do you believe (forehead) and what do you do (hands)? How do you use your money? The Beast promotes prosperity as the end in itself. He wants you to have all your money for you. Those with the mark of the Spirit will think of the poor and the mission of their king. The fruit of the Spirit includes self-control. The Beast in our country promotes the opposite. Money, buying or selling, is all about you. More and more the Beast puts pressure on us to make choices in the workplace or school or in public life. The choices we make are showing up the mark. Who do you stand for? Do you have the mark of Christ or the mark of the Beast? And what is his *name and number*? We will have to wait until next time to find that out.

Study Questions

1. How did the second Beast give breath to the first Beast in John's day?

2. How does this happen through history and in our own day?

3. What are the strengths and weaknesses of the Futurist view in light of persecution today?

4. What would a visible 'mark' have signified to John in his day?

5. What is the mark of the Beast? Is there Scripture to support that?

6. Give ways that refusing the mark would limit ability to buy or sell in John's day.

7. What about today in the wider world?

8. Does this affect the Western world? How?

9. Does this text bring a challenge as to which mark you carry?

20
'666'
(Revelation 13:18)

How do you interpret the Bible? There are different opinions and approaches, especially on the most difficult book in the Bible, the book of Revelation. In the Reformed tradition, the Bible is interpreted using what is called the historical-grammatical method. That is, seeking to understand what a text means in its original historical context, and using all the original grammar and syntax to try and determine what the author intended to say. That also includes taking into account the genre (the type of literature), whether it is a narrative, poetry, or in the case of Revelation, apocalyptic. This is surely the most faithful way to look at the text of the Bible, by taking seriously what the original author intended.

In the case of Revelation, we want to know important things like: who wrote it, to whom was it written, and for what intended purpose? We know the apostle John wrote this book, and he makes it clear he is writing to Christians in seven churches in Asia Minor in the first century during a time of suffering. He even says he is a *fellow sufferer* and he calls for *patient endurance for Christians* (1:9). So we firstly need to ask, 'What did this mean to the first readers?' It should at least have meaning to the Christians in those churches, because the book was addressed to them. So when we encounter the first Beast (state power that persecutes God's people), it should make sense to those first readers. And indeed, it would have been obvious to them the Beast in their day was the Roman Empire.

One of the four main views of Revelation, the Preterist, says *everything* is relevant to the first readers and *only* to them. So the Preterist can and does argue theirs is the most strictly faithful approach to interpreting Revelation. They interpret it simply as it's written and to whom it's written. There are some credible scholars, like R.C. Sproul, who hold this view. And I can understand a serious biblical scholar who wants to be faithful to the text finding this view attractive for those reasons. The Preterist is saying it's real and relevant to the people it is addressed to, and the text says it will unfold for them what must take place *soon*. (Of course, as always, I agree, but I want to go further and say it is addressed to *all* God's servants.)

I want to spend some time exploring this, because the central point on which the Preterist view stands or falls is the specific dating of when the book of Revelation was written. The Preterist depends completely on all the judgment and woes in the book of Revelation as describing what is happening up to the destruction of the temple in Jerusalem in AD 70. If Revelation was written at a later date, the whole Preterist view collapses because there are no other events that could describe such catastrophic events later in the first century.

None of the other three major views depend on the date Revelation was written. But if the pre-AD 70 date can be seen to be plausible, then there are lots of interesting facts that could support the Preterist view. For instance, when it comes to understanding our text …

> This calls for wisdom. Let the person who has insight calculate the number of the beast, for it is the number of a man. That number is 666 (13:18).

The number of the Beast is 666. The identity of who is represented by the number (666) is very controversial, but the Preterist has one of its strongest arguments right there from the first century before AD 70. Remember the Beast is state power which persecutes the church, so the Preterist has a candidate who not only fits the criteria, as a head of state who persecutes Christians, but his name can fit the number 666. He is the Roman Emperor Nero, who reigned from AD 58-64. In fact, in the ancient world Nero was referred to as a beast. Nero brutally persecuted Christians while he was Emperor. You can even read about it outside of Christian literature, such as in first century Roman historian Tacitus' *Annals of Imperial Rome*.[17]

How does Nero's name add up to the number 666? By using Gematria, which is an ancient method of applying numerical value

---

[17] Tacitus, Annals of Imperial Rome, Book XV, chapter 44

from languages, such as the Greek or Hebrew alphabets. This is not so cryptic as it first sounds, because with some ancient languages the letters of the alphabet were used for numerals. For instance, the first nine letters of the Greek alphabet represented the numbers 1-9. And when we add up Nero's name, what number do we get? One guess! 666!

The Preterist view takes seriously the historical context, but because the view rests entirely on a date of writing before AD 70, it's worth exploring just when Revelation was written. I have contended the book was not written before AD 70, but towards the end of the first century, during the reign of the Roman Emperor Domitian (AD 81-96). John the apostle, in his old age, was exiled to Patmos and is writing during Domitian's reign, and I am contending that John writes Revelation between AD 90-96. Which date is right?

Perhaps the strongest evidence outside the Bible comes from the testimony of the early church leader Irenaeus, born around AD 130. Irenaeus was a disciple of Polycarp, who was himself a disciple of the apostle John, the writer of this book of Revelation. Irenaeus says ...

> '... [John] beheld the apocalyptic vision, for that was seen not very long ago, almost in our own generation, at the close of the reign of Domitian.'[18]

That would seem to nail it. John saw the vision close to Irenaeus' day, and at the end of Domitian's reign, which ended in AD 96. But the Preterist scholars have questioned this statement saying maybe Irenaeus meant it was John who was seen at the end of Domitian's reign, not the Revelation. That seems to me to be stretching the grammar.

There are also other early witnesses. Clement of Alexandria (born AD 155 and died about AD 215), says John came back from the island of Patmos 'after the tyrant was dead.' Also, early church historian Eusebius identifies the 'tyrant' as none other than Domitian.[19] Again, this puts the date of Revelation as being written late in the first century.

The earliest commentary written on the book of Revelation is from the early 200s, by Victorinus. He wrote ...

---

[18] Irenaeus, *Against Heresies* 5:30.
[19] Eusebius, *Ecclesiastical History* III.23

> 'When John said these things, he was on the island of Patmos, condemned to the mines by Caesar Domitian. There he saw the Apocalypse; and when at length grown old, he thought that he should receive his release by suffering; but Domitian being killed, he was liberated.'[20]

Jerome (340-420) wrote:

> 'In the fourteenth then after Nero, Domitian having raised up a second persecution, he [John] was banished to the island of Patmos, and wrote the Apocalypse.'[21]

In fact, there is no record of anyone holding to that earlier date in the first century, or early church fathers in the first three centuries.

There are also other reasons in the book of Revelation itself why the later date is preferred. One of the strongest arguments for a later date is the way the letters to the churches read. For instance, it would be harder to believe the church at Ephesus would have had time to lose their *first love* if the earlier date was taken. Paul wrote to the church at Ephesus about AD 61 (Ephesians). If we go with the Preterist date of Revelation, that would mean they lost their first love within a couple of years. The church at Ephesus was given a grand uplifting letter (Ephesians) from Paul. Could they have lost their first love just after that? It's possible, but it's much easier to imagine that happening by the AD 90s.

There are other arguments the Preterists put forward. They point out there is no mention of the destruction of the temple in Revelation, so they say it must be written before AD 70 as the temple is still standing. But we might counter that by saying the destruction of the temple may not have had much relevance decades after (in the AD 90s).

Well, what about Nero as the 666? That is a strong point for the Preterist position. But I did fail to mention that Nero's name does not actually add up to 666, not in the Greek language in which John was writing. It only adds up to 666 when you take a Hebrew transliteration of Nero, so you have to translate Nero from Greek, which John is writing in, into Hebrew. And only then if you give him

---

[20] Victorinus, (*Commentary on Revelation* 10:11).
[21] Jerome (*Lives of Illustrious Men* 9).

the title Nero Caesar instead of just Nero. And only then if you include a questionable spelling of the Hebrew. This odd spelling appears only in one ancient Judean scroll as well as the Talmud.

So we have to ask, did John's first Greek readers all know Hebrew well enough, and think of making the transliteration into Hebrew from Greek, and with a particularly odd spelling?

The other problem is that the early church fathers were not aware of the idea of Nero as the 666. It was not something obvious to the people of the time. In fact, the first time it appears as an idea is in 1831 from four German scholars (Fritzsche, Benary, Hitzig, Reuss). Does that mean no one had 'wisdom' until then? So, while there are some arguments going for the Preterist position, it all hangs on a date that is highly questionable. So I will respectfully disagree with the Preterist position. But we still haven't solved our 666.

In fact, using Gematria you can also add up the number 666 from the name 'Hitler'. Surely he is a good example of the Beast (worldly power persecuting God's people). But then Hebrew transliterations of 'the Nicolaitans' mentioned in the seven letters also add up to 666. Others have used the number as years of the reign of a particular state rule, such as Islam, Papacy or some other world power. Historicists have noted Latanos adds up to 666, which means 'Latin-speaking man'. So the Pope is the Beast. Many Futurists have said 'www' represents 666 (the 'w' equivalent in Hebrew is the number 6). And I think we all knew deep down in our hearts the Futurist has to be right on this one—the Internet is the 666! Better still, surely we have nailed it when we discover that Prince Charles adds up to 666. When President Ronald Reagan moved into a new home and found his street number was 666, he had it changed to 668, which didn't help him as someone pointed out that only made him the *neighbor* of the Beast.

When using Gematria there seems to be *too many* options. One scholar (Salmon) pointed out that by using Gematria people have been able to fit almost any name to 666, by applying one of these three rules. First, when the person's name doesn't add up correctly, just add a title (as in Nero Caesar). Second, if Greek doesn't work, then try Hebrew or even Latin. And lastly, if everything else fails, tweak the spelling.[22]

---

[22] Salmon, *Historical Introduction to the Books of the new Testament*. London: Murray, 1904, 230-231

Obviously, the cleverness of these ideas becomes the problem. In 13:18 John was not asking his readers for mathematical genius. He is not calling for mathematical wisdom. Unbelievers can have that! Rather, John says, this calls for wisdom ... biblical wisdom. Godly wisdom.

We have to come back to the text and ask what it is saying to the original readers. We've seen Revelation has been consistently using numbers in symbolic fashion. Numbers have had symbolic significance, including the numbers four, seven, ten and 12 x 12 in the 1000s to make 144,000. Also, we have seen that each of these numbers had a rich symbolic meaning. It would be strange to come this far into Revelation if suddenly we were to find that a number was *not* symbolic, and we have to start using Gematria. In the next chapter, we see the number 144,000 again. But no one has suggested that 144,000 should be recalculated using Gematria, nor any other numbers elsewhere in Revelation. So why start here in 13:18?

If virtually any name can fit using Gematria, wouldn't John have narrowed it down if he wanted to do it that way? As G.K. Beale points out, John could have narrowed it down by saying that the number 666 was in Hebrew.[23] John did exactly that in 9:11 *whose name in Hebrew is Abaddon and in Greek is Apollyon*. And again in 16:16 *The name in Hebrew is Armageddon*. Why not in 13:18? Unless we are barking up the wrong tree!

So what did 666 mean to the first readers? They are told directly they should be able to figure it out if they have insight. **This calls for wisdom. Let <u>the person</u> who has insight calculate the number of the beast, for it is the number of a man. That number is 666.**

John says let *the person* who has insight! He doesn't qualify it. *Anyone* with insight! So it's not only for mathematical geniuses. It's a call to *anyone*. Anyone in the church in Ephesus, Smyrna or Pergamum or any of the seven churches in the first century with insight. And anyone in the church throughout any time because it is a call to *anyone*. If the Preterist is right, how come the people in the first century didn't calculate Nero? Maybe they just didn't have enough insight? And if this is for *any person* to calculate including those in the

---

[23] G.K. Beale, *The Book of Revelation*, NIGTC, (Grand Rapids: Eerdmans Publishing Co. 1999), p721

first century, it rules out Prince Charles being the answer. They had never heard of Prince Charles! So I am even rethinking my own theory about Oprah Winfrey. It can't be Prince Charles or Oprah because that would rule out *anyone* who has wisdom for most of the past 2000 years.

In fact, this brings into question the Historicist and the Futurist position because this verse says *anyone* from the first readers and over the past 2000 years who has wisdom can work it out. Both of those positions rule out *anyone* for most of history.

We have seen from the outset Rev. 13 is about the two beasts. Both mock and parody Christ and God. We have seen the Beast with seven heads. In 13:11 we saw this Beast has two horns like a lamb. Jesus is the true Lamb, but this one is the cheap counterfeit. So instead of looking 'out there' all over the world to work out 666, why not look in Revelation?

Look at how Revelation uses numbers, particularly God's number of completion. Seven churches are the complete church, all the churches. Seven spirits of God make up the complete Holy Spirit. There are seven stars, seven golden lampstands, seven seals, seven plagues, seven trumpets and seven bowls still to come. What is it talking about? The complete Judgment of God. Jesus the Lamb has seven horns and seven eyes, which are the seven spirits of God. Jesus is the complete Savior. There are the seven angels of God and God speaks with seven thunders. Seven is God's number of completion. It's used repeatedly! The reason I am highlighting this again is so we don't miss what is right before our eyes, that God's number is clearly seven! Don't miss the sevens!

When we encounter the Beast, who is the counterfeit god with seven heads, is he really complete? Is his number really seven? No. He really only adds up to man's number. In the original Greek language, in 13:18 the article is missing before *man*. A literal translation is, *for it is man's number*. It is not *the man* or *a man*, but man's number. So this is the number of humanity! What is man's number? Which day of the week was man created? The sixth day is the number of man! God's day of completion is the seventh. Man falls short of God. And in sin, man falls short of the glory of God. What does sin literally mean to the Hebrew? Sin literally means missing the mark or falling short. Like an arrow falling short of the mark. That's sin. That's man. He falls short of the glory of God. Man's number is not

God's seven. It's six. God is Father, Son and Holy Spirit. Holy, holy, holy is the Lord God Almighty, complete in holiness. He is 777. But man falls short, falls short, falls short. His number is ... 6—6—6.

The counterfeit is the *unholy* trinity. The Dragon, the first Beast and the second Beast. The threefold emphasis and humans who follow him have his number. Remember the beasts, worldly power and false religion are actually made up of people, made up of 'man'! So the Beast has man's number. Man falls short, six. He fails and sins. The incomplete number is repeated three times, 666. He is failure after failure after failure, 666. A complete failure.[24]

The counterfeit, the Beast, can entice you to think he is almost there, but look closely and see how he is always short of the truth. He looks good, but it's not quite right. A mere man's number. Man is a mere creature created on the sixth day. He is not God. He is still trying to lift himself up *to be like God*. This falling short infiltrates and permeates every area of culture, government, social and economic undertaking. Everything is corrupted and compromised. The corruption of man always ruins what God gave as good. Every human endeavor falls short of God's perfection of 777, so it is 666.

Therefore, based on these numbers, you either have the mark of the beast or the perfection of God. You are either in Christ or in the Beast. You are either in God's number, 777, or man's number, 666. So if the PIN on your credit card is 666, should you change it? No, 666 is an identification with the Beast and all the ways *man,* or *human beings,* align with the Beast.

This is a wake-up call for Christians. It's not a wake-up call to a math class. It's not a wake-up call to find the mystery man with a name that adds up to 666. The question is, 'Do you have the Beast's number?' He is offering it to you. The Beast made same-sex marriage legal. If you stand against him, you will be branded as unloving and bigoted, unchristian! Who will you stand for? We want to reach out to gay people and tell them they are no different from us. We all fall short and we all need to repent and find the Savior. But who is listening? They say you are restricting freedom. It seems like that. If you are following Christ you are not even allowed to marry *anyone* who is non-Christian (1 Cor. 7:39, 2 Cor. 6:14), let alone the same

---

[24] William Henriksen, *More Than Conquerors,* Baker Book House, Grand Rapids Michigan, 1967, p.182

gender. You might have to wait, or even stay single. You are not even allowed to look at anyone inappropriately! Do you really want to follow Jesus?

In contrast, look at all the Beast has to offer. You could be free to enter into any kind of relationship with whomever you want, whenever you want. And you get this number for free. That's the appeal of the Beast. Take a number! It's 666. But the promises always fall short. It only ends in heartache if you take up the mark of the Beast. It's the same as when we looked at how much more money you would have to *buy or sell* if you take the mark of the Beast, if you compromise in the workplace. And yet, in the end, it will not go well. It will fall short. The Beast promises, but it's a lie.

So what is 13:18 really saying? Watch out Christian! Don't fall for the counterfeit! Be wise! This calls for wisdom. Man falls short. Not 777, but 666. Missed it by that much! … But that means you missed it altogether.

We need to interpret this in the same way we interpret the whole Bible—through the lens of the gospel of Jesus. Do you see the cross in here? Not exactly, but the first half of the gospel certainly is. This is just a snippet of the great issue we all face. We fall short! No one has measured up. Man's number is 666. We need the cross! We need Jesus! And he calls us to follow him. Not yourself, or your will, or your idols, or the Beast. Follow Jesus!

Study Questions

1. What is the most faithful way to interpret the Bible?

2. What are the best arguments for the Preterist view in this text?

3. What date for Revelation do you prefer, pre-AD 70 or AD 90s? Give reasons.

4. What is Gematria? Why might it sound credible as a means of interpreting?

5. What are the arguments against using Gematria to interpret this text?

6. What is there about the use of numbers in Revelation that can help us interpret our text?

7. How does the fact that it is *man's* number, rather than *a* man's number help us understand the text?

8. Does this number of the Beast have any direct application to the life of a Christian? If so what?

21
The Lamb with 144,000
(Revelation 14:1)

What is the greatest division between human beings? For some it's the color of their skin. Black, white, yellow or brown. For others, their identity revolves around their race, especially those who have experienced racial prejudice. They live that reality and so their whole identity is defined by, or even dedicated to, seeking racial equality. What about the gender divide? Male vs. female. Again, if you are on the wrong side of prejudice, for some that is the all-consuming division of humans, and male vs. female defines who you are. There are also other distinctions between class, education, socio-economic status, political, and many more.

But none of these categories are the greatest division in humanity. Revelation has been giving us this great divide, contrasting back and forth a division that actually makes the petty distinctions humans try to make seem so superficial as to be embarrassing. The distinction that Revelation highlights more graphically than any other place in the Bible is an eternal distinction, and it's not just to which race or gender you belong, but whether you are in the kingdom of Christ or the kingdom of the Beast. It's not just a distinction for now, but a distinction that goes on forever. Right now, everyone, including you who are reading this, are in one kingdom or the other. Either Jesus' kingdom, which can start with suffering but goes on in victory forever, or Satan's kingdom, which appears to look good for a short time, but is a big lie and ends up losing—forever.

It's a difference that is as far apart as heaven and hell. It's a difference that is so stark, so colossal, yet as we live day by day, we can appear on the outside as if there is no difference at all. If only we could just get a glimpse of the reality of this great divide it would change us forever. If you could see that great eternal perspective of who you are and whose side you are on, it would charge you up. It would make you want to love Jesus and others so much more and make us realize what our true identity is. What really defines us as human beings? Black vs. white? Male vs. female? Successful? Gifted? Mediocre? Who are you really? What is your identity? If we could just see it! If we could just get a glimpse so that this reality would soak into our psyche and control our lives rather than the everyday stuff which drags us down.

Well, let me introduce you to Revelation. What is being revealed here sets a contrast between the great divide, which is this: People are either followers of Christ or followers of the Beast. The two previous visions John the apostle saw depicted the action in the earthly reality. The problem for believers is that the Beast was seeking to impose himself on God's people. Watch your step! Now this vision continues but from a different camera angle. Remember, the Master film director, Jesus himself, is delivering these visions to John, and now he switches scenes.

In Rev. 13, we were introduced to the counterfeit, the unholy trinity. The Dragon, the Beast and the False Prophet. The Beast had that number. Man's number, 666. It fell short of the glory of God. We were given that information to warn us: Don't fall for the counterfeit! Don't fall short. Don't fall for the Beast. Don't compromise. Which kingdom are you in? The great divide. It defines your whole life. There are only two kingdoms, and *most* come under the kingdom of the Beast. But we are not with them. We are for the Lamb. So everything will be fine for us, right? Oh really?

We have seen it's not so easy. Those who don't receive the mark of the Beast will be persecuted even as to what they can buy or sell. If you don't have the mark of the Beast, then you will be affected negatively, even your livelihood. The counterfeit offers so much more. Take the number 666 and you won't have persecution. Just accept the mark of the Beast. So, whose side are you on?

And what will keep you going when there is so much pressure from the Beast? It's this. Rev. 14 reveals … Jesus wins! This is what those first readers under persecution needed to see. It's what we need to see. This is pulling back the curtain on reality. This is what it is to be on the right side of the great divide. The Lord is the one who has the victory and the true glory. This is what it looks like. John sees what you look like if you are in Christ …

> Then I looked, and there before me was the Lamb, standing on Mount Zion, and with him 144,000 who had his name and his Father's name written on their foreheads (14:1).

But wait! What are the Jehovah's Witnesses doing there? There they are. The 144,000! So are the JWs right after all? Well, no. But there are differing views out there. The most popular view (Futurist) is that this is literally Mount Zion in Jerusalem, and these are literally 144,000 (Jews) who were saved during the tribulation and Jesus has returned to earth to begin his 1000-year millennial reign over them. I don't mean to keep throwing wet blankets on this, but this looks more like a scene of heaven to me. We will see from 14:3 that this is the director's 'cut shot' back to a continuation of Rev. 4 where the Lamb is on the throne, and this is the same crew in heaven that we met back then. There are the four living creatures and the same elders, but now the camera angle widens and we see all the people there as well.

It would be strange to suddenly have a literal Mount Zion when in the same verse no one thinks Jesus is literally a Lamb. It is symbolism. No one thinks that in Rev. 13 we have been dealing with a literal Beast crawling out of the sea, instead we recognize these as signs or symbols. So it would not be a consistent interpretation to suddenly change midstream to expect this to be literal. And yet like all symbols in Revelation, when it says he is standing on Mount Zion it must be teaching something significant, and it is. Mount Zion is used in other parts of Scripture to teach the great divide. Where do you stand? In 13:1 it was the Dragon *standing* (on the seashore). Now...

> Then I looked, and there before me was the <u>Lamb, standing</u> ... (14:1).

You are either before the Beast, or you are before the Lamb. This is the Lamb standing—in victory. He is standing on Mount Zion. John, the apostle seeing this vision, was familiar with Mount Zion (mentioned some 155 times in the OT). It's the place of God's people, so this could be looking to the end of times or simply the standing of those who are in Christ now *from the heavenly perspective.*

This interpretation goes against the popular view that Jesus must be standing at a literal Mount Zion. So am I stretching this interpretation? Mount Zion as a symbol? Is that a natural way of looking at it? Well, how does the rest of the NT refer to Mount Zion?

Let's look at the writer to the Hebrews who mentions Mount Zion, not as a literal mountain but as a symbol, and yet as the place of present reality of the relationship we have *in Christ*—not the literal location. Drawing on OT Scripture to describe a present spiritual reality, the writer to the Hebrews gives the contrast and compares Mount Sinai, which brought fear, to Mount Zion, our present reality in Christ. Not the physical location, but spiritual reality ...

> You have not come to a mountain that can be touched and that is burning with fire; to darkness, gloom and storm; ... <u>But you have come to Mount Zion</u>, to the city of the living God, the heavenly Jerusalem. You have come to thousands upon thousands of angels in joyful assembly, to the church of the firstborn, whose names are written in heaven ... (Heb. 12:18,22,23).

But wait. He is telling Christians they have already come to Mount Zion. Christian, do you feel like you have literally come to Mount Zion? Well, no. So what is he saying? He doesn't mean the literal location, but this is your standing as a believer. You have *already* come to Mount Zion. The Hebrews writer is not saying you will come to that location in the future, but you are already there in Christ! The kingdom of God is what we call 'already, but not yet'. It has already arrived, but is not yet here in fullness. The theologians call it 'inaugurated eschatology'. You *already* are in the kingdom by faith. The deposit of the kingdom is *already* yours, but it is *not yet* consummated. You have come to this mountain. *Not* the old one that can't be touched. Not a literal mountain. But Mount Zion is yet a present reality. It's 'not yet' in its final fulfillment. This is what the apostle Paul meant when he said you are *already* seated with Christ in the heavenly realms even while we are still on earth (Eph. 2:6). It's already a reality but ... it's 'not yet'. Not yet face to face.

The apostle John was well familiar with the Hebrews writer exhorting Christians that they are already at Mount Zion in Christ ... so it makes sense to John when he saw this ... **Then I looked, and there before me was the Lamb, standing on Mount Zion, and with him 144,000 who had his name and his Father's name written on their foreheads.** Jesus the Lamb is standing there. He is always there. This is the state of reality compared to the way things looked previously in Rev. 13. Is the Beast winning? This is the assurance that Jesus wins. He stands there on Mount Zion. He is *already* victorious, so he must overcome. And who is with him? The JWs? No!

This 144,000 is the people of God. We looked at this when we encountered the 144,000 in Rev. 7. The number for God's people is 12, that is, 12 apostles and 12 tribes of Israel. Remember where Revelation is taking us. The gospel of Jesus joins Jews and Gentiles together, personified at the end of Rev. 21 with the very foundations of the holy city. The New Jerusalem is made up with *both* the names of the tribes and the apostles, 12 x 12, but in a great number, in 1000s. And the wall is 144 cubits thick! It's a complete multiplication, 12 x 12 of all the people of God joined, but in 1000s. The number 1000 is a metaphor for a great indefinite number in the Scriptures. 'For every animal of the forest is mine, and the cattle on a thousand hills' (Ps.50); and 'a thousand years are like a day' (Ps.90). So 12 x 12 multiplied by the 1000 gives us 144,000, a symbolic, great, indefinite number. This is what we call a gross, 144 but in the 1000s, which is how we get 144,000. It's the number of believers as a whole.

Revelation has been telling Christians from the start how the gospel joins Jew and Gentile, drawing on the promises for Israel and applying them to Jew and Gentile Christians that make up the church. You are a *kingdom and priests* (1:5, 5:10). The promise of God to Israel (Exod. 19:6) now applies to all who believe in the Jewish Messiah. You are the New Jerusalem (3:12). Jew and Gentile joined in Christ. Again, if we remain consistent, just as we don't think Jesus is literally a Lamb, we look for the symbolic meaning of the 144,000. The 12 x 12 answers that it is the people of God. It is made clearer for us several times in this text that this is speaking about all Christians. What characterizes the 144,000?

> ... 144,000 who had been redeemed from the earth (14:3).

Who are those who have been **redeemed from the earth?** The people of God of course. That hardly sounds like a specific subsection of saved people. *The redeemed from the earth!* Those saved by the blood of the Lamb. These are all the people of God that were saved on this earthly sojourn. What else do we learn about them?

> ... They <u>follow the Lamb</u> wherever he goes. [What did Jesus say? 'My sheep hear my voice and follow me.' True believers.] They were <u>purchased</u> from among mankind and offered as firstfruits to God and the Lamb (14:4).

Again, who was **purchased**? Who are those that **follow the Lamb**? Believers! If you were reading this without any presuppositions, why would you think this was anything other than all those who believe in Jesus? Therefore, 144,000 is a symbolic number representing the fruit of the gospel of Jesus. Jews and Gentiles, 12 x 12, in great numbers, *purchased* by the blood of the Lamb, *purchased* from among the whole earth, *redeemed* from the earth. The 144,000 also symbolize a complete rounded number. Not one of his sheep will be lost. The complete people of God redeemed are now singing in the presence of the Lamb. And the ... *144,000 who <u>had his name and his Father's name written on their foreheads</u>*.

What did that mean to the first readers? To have the name of Jesus and his Father? I'll tell you what it meant if you were sitting in the church at Philadelphia in Asia Minor in the first century. You would recall Jesus' words in the letter to that church ...

> The one who is victorious I will make a pillar in the temple of my God. Never again will they leave it. I will write on them <u>the name of my God</u> and the name of the city of my God, the <u>new Jerusalem</u>, which is coming down out of heaven from my God; and I will also <u>write on them my new name</u> (3:12).

If you are there in Philadelphia and you have just read the personal letter addressed to your church in Rev. 3, you are told that *you* are the New Jerusalem and that *you* will be given the name of God the Father and Jesus' name! And then you keep reading through Revelation and you get to Rev. 14 and what do you read about this 144,000? They *had his name and his Father's name written on their foreheads.*

It's us! The Philadelphians can hardly contain themselves. There is the promise fulfilled! What Jesus promised to Christians is the same promise for the 144,000. So what did this mean to the average Christian in the first century in Philadelphia? You are part of the 144,000, redeemed from the earth and part of the new city, Mount Zion. The New Jerusalem! Remember Rev. 14 was written to you as much as was Rev. 3! The whole of Revelation was addressed to you (1:4).

This is giving us the great divide. The unbelievers following the Beast had the name of the Beast written on their foreheads (13:16-17). And here is the other side of the divide. The believers have the *name of God* and the mark of the Spirit. And we saw the seal the 144,000 believers receive in 7:2-3, the Holy Spirit, guaranteeing our inheritance.

So why are we getting this camera angle of the triumph of the Lamb and his followers here again? Zion is the place where God sat enthroned in the temple of Israel. So what is this saying about the Lamb? He is the true Son of God, the true heir to the throne in Zion. In this vision, John is getting the film version of Psalm 2. Psalm 2 is one of Revelation's favorites. We have seen it referred to many times.

> The One enthroned in heaven laughs; the Lord scoffs at them. He rebukes them in his anger and terrifies them in his wrath, saying, 'I have installed my King <u>on Zion</u>, my holy mountain' (Ps. 2:4-6).

When was Jesus installed as king? We saw his coronation in Rev. 5 when he ascended on high. What we are seeing is the heavenly standing of believers. It's also a message to the Christian reader of what their reality is in Christ. The apostle Paul put it this way: *And God raised us up with Christ and seated us <u>with him in the heavenly realms</u> in Christ Jesus, ...* (Eph. 2:6).

Literally? Yes, 'already'. But physically no, it's 'not yet' ... not yet face to face. This is a great pattern that has been going on in Revelation if we recall what we've learned so far. The Master film director has been shifting scenes for a purpose. Each time we are spent and our hearts faint from the terror and pain believers are going through, we get this revival boost through the big picture. We started off with the trials and pain going on in the churches in Rev. 2-3, and just when we get depressed with all the bad stuff going on in the churches—then the camera pans up to heaven in Rev. 4. We saw the big picture of the Lord on the throne! We are secure with the One who is in control of every creature and every action, with those living creatures with eyes in every direction. Nothing is out of his control. But then we go back into the trials below again. The seven seals are released and there is pain on earth. Who will survive? In fact, it leads up to the Day of Judgment and absolute terror. Indeed, who can stand? The great question left us hanging. But the answer came as the camera takes us to our standing in Rev. 7. The great reality of the 144,000 sealed, secured by God himself. But just when we get comfortable, we go back into the trials again. The seven trumpets. Again, we are caught up in the horror that is even more intense. Who can stand? Then in Rev. 10 we see the colossus of God at the end of all things. One foot on earth, one foot on the sea—in control of all things. You are secure if you believe!

Back and forth again. Rev. 11, the people of God, the worshipers, are measured as part of the temple. Secure. But then the witnesses, the church is cast down. But then see how she looks in her heavenly standing in Rev. 12! A beautiful woman. Taken care of through her wilderness wandering. But then on into Revelation switching scenes again, a new camera shot, and we see some of the most horrific scenes—ugly, grotesque Beasts coming from sea and land, with a Dragon as their head. Who can stand against this? Will the Beast overcome us? How do I know I won't fall for his number?

And that is why we get this next shot. Again, the camera pans up to the big picture and leads us to where we are now. Again, the assurance and security of those who have the seal of the Spirit of the Father, before you get downcast by the trial you undergo while under pressure from the beasts—take a look at your heavenly reality. This is your true identity! This is who you are! This is you, sojourner. This is you pilgrim. This is you Christian in the church at Philadelphia in Asia Minor. This is you Christian battling it out in the wilderness. This is you Christian living today reading Revelation. This is you, weak and beaten down believer in Christ. This is you who feels the pressure of temptation. This is you who is ready to give up … you who wonder if you can find your portion in the Lord under this pressure. Just when you doubt whether you will be able to withstand the pressure from Beast 1, Beast 2 and the Dragon …

> <u>Then I looked</u>, and there before me was the Lamb, standing on Mount Zion, and with him 144,000 who <u>had his name</u> and his <u>Father's name</u> written on their foreheads (14:1).

This is where you stand in Christ! Jesus is first showing us the trial we should expect. So don't be surprised when it happens! Then he gives us the assurance that we will be kept. Sealed. There is our heavenly reality. The believer's life is hidden with Christ on high. You are already there in Christ! You are already at Mount Zion—you can't physically touch it, but in your spiritual standing you are already there! By faith! That is why after each of the descriptions of tribulation, pain, persecution, and Beasts, there is this assurance. It's written to you to show you how you will be victorious in life with all its trials. It's written to you to persevere. This is why we keep remembering how John identified himself as one suffering and needing patient endurance (1:9). And why that same exhortation continues through this book to Christians through the tribulation. We saw it among the beasts in the last chapter. *This calls for <u>patient endurance</u> and faithfulness on the part of the saints* (13:10). And again, this theme of Revelation will continue even later here in this chapter.

> This calls for <u>patient endurance</u> on the part of the people of God who keep his commands and remain faithful to Jesus (14:12).

Patient endurance. Patient endurance. But how, in the midst of trouble? This is why this book of Revelation was written. It's written to you, Christian, in the church. Keep going. Don't give up. Patient endurance is required. But how can I keep going? Well, every now and then you need to get a look at this camera angle in the midst of these trials so you will take a look at your reality in Christ. Your true identity. Paul says it this way…

> Since, then, <u>you have been raised with Christ, set your hearts on things above, where Christ is</u>, seated at the right hand of God. Set your minds on things above, not on earthly things. For you died, and <u>your life is now hidden with Christ</u> in God. When Christ, who is your life, appears, then you also will appear with him in glory (Col. 3:1-4).

It's already, but not yet! And Revelation gives us the film version. John sees himself and all believers. Their ultimate reality is in Christ, the Lamb. They are already there at Mount Zion. Jesus wins! Revelation is one of the means the Lord has given to help us finish the race. That's why it's at the end of the Bible. The last thing God says to us before we see him face to face. Don't give up! Look at the finish line.

It's the same in the way he gives us his word to read, the sacraments, the means of prayer and the Lord's Day to worship together. You go off into the battlefield every week, but every week you need to come back to who you really are and where your life really stands because you are constantly in this battlefield. Why does the preacher go on each week about what God has done sending his Son to the cross to give you an eternal standing (at least I hope he does)? A living hope, despite the reality of the daily battle. Why do you take hold of the means, worship, and spend time putting on the armor each day in devotion time? You are being brought back to reality while you fight it out in the world. This will go on until the end. It's not going to stop. So you will constantly need to see this …

> Then I looked, and there before me was the Lamb, standing on Mount Zion, and with him 144,000 who had his name and his Father's name written on their foreheads (14:1).

Remember the OT story when the battle looks lost with Elisha and his servant surrounded by the Aramean army? The servant is panicking so Elisha prays …

> And Elisha prayed, 'Open his eyes, LORD, so that he may see.' Then the LORD opened the servant's eyes, and he looked and saw the hills full of horses and chariots of fire all around Elisha (2 Kin. 6:17).

Wow! Look at that. The LORD has the whole thing covered. The servant sees the spiritual reality behind the earthly battle. We are on the winning side! That is what 14:1 is doing! Take a look at the spiritual reality! You are the winners.

So yes, mankind tries to identify themselves as black vs. white, rich vs. poor, old vs. young, men vs. women, gay vs. straight and all kinds of other identities. But the true great divide is between those in the 144,000 and those outside his kingdom. However long this tribulation seems to be dragging on for you, it's nothing compared to how long the reality lasts on the other side. Every person born into this world will exist forever. You are on one side of that divide or the other now. If you are not one of his, enter his kingdom by faith now. *Then* you are already seated with him in the heavenly realms …

Then I looked, and there before me was the Lamb, standing on Mount Zion, and with him 144,000 who had his name and his Father's name written on their foreheads (14:1).

Study Questions

1. What defines who you are?

2. Where are these 144,000, on earth or in heaven? Explain.

3. Is Mount Zion in this text literal? Give reasons for your answer.

4. What Scriptural support can you provide to explain why the number is 144,000?

5. How would the church at Philadelphia have interpreted this text and why?

6. What other parts of Scripture speak of our heavenly standing that might be relevant to this text, and what is the context of those Scriptures?

7. Describe the overview pattern that Revelation has been giving in terms of trial vs. victory.

8. What is one theme of Revelation mentioned in Rev. 1, Rev. 13 and again in Rev. 14?

9. How has Revelation encouraged you in what you need to remain focused on through trial?

22
They did not Defile Themselves
(Revelation 14:2-5)

Have you ever been in a difficult job? Getting up early in the morning. Long days. Grinding away. Seems like the same old hard slog day after day. You get tempted to just chuck it in. What if you have to get up and go through that same toil, but you know that when you get to the end of the week, you have three months long-service leave? The leave has been approved. It's guaranteed. Your entitlement is already signed. Yes, you still have to go through a few more days of hard work. Nothing has changed in that regard. You still have to get out of bed for a few more days and work as you have for years, and *yet everything has changed* because you have a holiday entitlement which brings a whole new perspective and new motive because of where you stand in your rights.

We left off last time with the tribulation continuing, but we noted that interspersed in Revelation are these times which remind us of our status. The big picture. It's the perspective that helps us get up in the morning with enthusiasm. Yes, you have a long hard slog. Yes, you even have trouble and tribulation. Beasts without and beasts within. Dragons and pressure to compromise. What motivates you to keep going? It's something you already have. It's signed and guaranteed. It's your identity. It's who you are. You are someone who is 'in Christ'. It's *already*. Though you have *not yet* received the holiday, face to face with him.

John might be stuck in that cave on the island of Patmos, the first Christian readers might be under pressure from the Beast, and so might you! Life might be weighing in on you and then you look up and see, 'this is *who* I am' (14:1). I am with Christ in the heavenly realms. And then John *hears* something ...

> And I heard a sound from heaven like the roar of rushing waters and

> like a loud peal of thunder. The sound I heard was like that of harpists playing their harps (14:2).

How glorious this must have sounded to John! And we are meant to notice how big! Crescendos, *roars* of great **rushing waters**, even **thunder**, but this is only an attempt to try and describe its magnitude and power because it's actually really loud music ... **like that of harpists playing their harps**. So is this like Stratocaster guitars or something? There is a very popular idea of 'Rock-n-Roll heaven'. You've heard it referred to when some Rock star dies. 'They're up there playing away.' But those who say that miss the point, not because the music is not powerful in heaven. The sound from heaven would certainly be like the greatest, most powerful exhilarating music concert you've ever heard (*like the roar of rushing waters*), but what they miss is: The center is not the Rock musicians. The center is the Lamb on the throne! As 14:3 tells us, this song is before the *throne*. That is how this vision started out in 14:1. It was the Lamb at the center! The singing and musical instruments *accompany* a glorious song, but it's Jesus at the center, not the music as an end in itself. That is the difference between music for worship vs. music in entertainment. Worship is Jesus at the center, not the music itself.

> And they sang a new song before <u>the throne</u> and before the four living creatures and the elders. No one could learn the song except the 144,000 who had been redeemed from the earth (14:3).

No one else could learn the song except whom? Not only Jewish believers, but all those who had been **redeemed from the earth**. You have to have Christ! You have to be a believer. You have to have his seal, his mark, his name, and *only then* can you truly sing the song and learn it. Even the angels can't sing the new song. Why not? Couldn't the angels have just learned it from those singing? No. This is bigger than just learning the words. A sinless angel cannot sing of the Christ who died for me! 'When I Survey the Wondrous Cross.' 'How Deep the Father's Love for us?' These songs can't be truly sung by those who have not been *redeemed*. It's the same with all the songs we have already come across in Revelation. In 5:9 they are singing of the blood of the Lamb. 'Blessing and Honor and Glory to the Lamb.' This is a song of the new covenant that can *only* be truly sung by those who know what it is to have been redeemed from the earth …

> These are those who did not defile themselves with women, for they remained virgins. They follow the Lamb wherever he goes. They were purchased from among mankind and offered as firstfruits to God and the Lamb (14:4).

They did not defile themselves with women for they remained virgins. So if we take it literally, heaven is gonna be quiet. Only virgins, and only male virgins at that (*who weren't with women*). Well at least some people have thought that. Maybe the RCs could use this text to justify their celibacy of the priesthood. But then they would still have to explain why the apostles were all married. Jesus healed Peter's mother-in-law in Matthew 8:14-15. He must have had a wife. (It would be a bit rough if he had to have a mother-in-law without having a wife.) And all the other apostles were married …

> Don't we have the right to take a believing wife along with us, <u>as do the other apostles</u> and the Lord's brothers and Cephas? (1 Cor. 9:5).

Since the apostles were married, does that mean the apostles are not in heaven among the 144,000 because they were married and not virgins? Is it more holy to remain a virgin through your life? Revelation has been using symbolic language all through, and this is not the only place Revelation describes the people of God as pure or virgins. What is the great finish of Revelation? The Wedding banquet! The virgin bride will be presented to the bridegroom (19:7-9, 21:2). Who is this virgin bride in Revelation? It's the people of God! Does that mean they are all literally virgins? No! It is a symbol of purity. The bride is holy and blameless. It's the same symbol here. And this is not an idea foreign to the NT. The apostle Paul says …

> I am jealous for you with a godly jealousy. I promised you to one husband, to Christ, so that I might present you as a <u>pure virgin</u> to him (2 Cor. 11:2).

Literally a virgin? No. Christ gave himself up for his bride. Why?

> Husbands, love your wives, just as Christ loved the church and gave himself up for her to <u>make her holy</u>, cleansing her by the washing with water through the word, and to present her to himself as a radiant church, <u>without stain or wrinkle or any other blemish, but holy and</u>

<u>blameless</u> (Eph. 5:25-27).

Purity. That is what you are in Christ. In fact, this symbol of believers as pure virgins sets up a great contrast in 14:8. The epitome of the unbelieving world is Babylon, the great harlot! So for unbelievers, the metaphor is sexual immorality. And what is the antithesis? Believers described as virgins *abstaining* from sexual immorality …

So sexual purity is a metaphor to describe the people of God (14:4). It was familiar to John as an OT metaphor used when Israel fell into idolatry, they were said to be committing adultery. In contrast, the true believers, **they follow the Lamb wherever he goes**. Again, hinting that this 144,000 symbolizes *all* believers, not just Jews, because this is familiar territory for John who was the one who recorded the very thing that Jesus said of *all* believers … <u>*his sheep follow him*</u> *because they know his voice* (John 10:4). And what do we read of the 144,000? *They follow the Lamb!* But also, **they were purchased from among men.** All believers are purchased! It's the same word in the original language used at 5:9 referring to people 'purchased' *from* every nation, tribe and tongue. And here again it doesn't say Jesus purchased all men, but they were purchased *from* among men. You were bought at a price. A specific purchase price—for your specific personal sin. The personal love of God for us at the cross we cannot comprehend!

And 14:4 says they were purchased **and offered as firstfruits to God and the Lamb.** Firstfruits is the OT version of the harvest for offering. It can mean the whole people of God in the OT (Jer. 2:3), and in the NT *firstfruits* becomes the metaphor for the *whole* people of God, both Jew and Gentile.

> He chose to give us birth through the word of truth, that we might be a kind of firstfruits of all he created (Jas. 1:18).

Rev. 14:4 says they are *offered*. As Romans 12:1 says, we *offer* our bodies as living sacrifices. The other thing that characterizes the people of God, the 144,000 is …

> No lie was found in their mouths; they are blameless (14:5).

Again, we are in trouble. Who can say they have never told a lie and are blameless? And yet those who really 'follow the Lamb' also follow his character. He is the truth. He only speaks the truth. At the very least it means Christians should tell the truth. It's the mark of a true believer not to lie. But as usual these metaphors go beyond that. Our context is opposition from the Beast. Those who truly 'follow the Lamb' will testify to the truth of Jesus even in the face of the attacks from the Beast. It's not easy. You can lose friends and even family, standing for the truth, for following the Lamb. Pressure from the Beast can indeed be pressure to lie—in buying or selling. Pressure to lie about how hard you are really working for the boss. Pressure to lie about your taxes (never!). Pressure to avoid embarrassment. The lies of compromise. The lies of the easy believing gospel. The lies of the idols the Beast promotes. Paul Gardner points out the pressure from the Beast in closed Islamic countries where food aid is only made available to those who identify as Islamic. [25] The Beast pressures Christians, putting the *truth* of their faith on the line to buy or sell. The primary truth to be stood for is Jesus himself. Jesus is the truth!

So the metaphors are sexually pure for faithfulness and telling the truth for those who stand for the truth of Jesus, and yet they are metaphors where the symbol cuts through to the everyday life of faithful Christians. The symbol of *'no lie'* also means *we don't tell lies.* No half-truths. And sexually pure? *They kept themselves pure* ... A symbol yes, but these are carefully crafted symbols, considering the history of humanity and the terrible divider that will keep so many out of heaven. What an interesting choice of metaphor for those who are included in the 144,000 in contrast to those who are excluded. *These are those who did not defile themselves with women, for they remained virgins* ... (14:4).

It's a symbol that rings home with Israel's times of idolatry and unfaithfulness to their God, so often connected with literal sexual immorality. Just as the nations around them would engage in ritual temple prostitution and sexual immorality, so too Israel's idolatry was not devoid of literal sexual immorality. What a poignant and searching metaphor for the first Christians reading this book. What did we see in the letters (Rev. 2-3) as one of the main rebukes Jesus repeated to the churches? Sexual immorality! In Rev. 2 in the church at Pergamum, false teachers were teaching that sexual immorality was

---

[25] Paul Gardner, *Revelation*, (Great Britain: Christian Focus Publications, 2008), p.192

acceptable. And over at Thyatira, Jezebel was teaching the folks that sexual immorality was okay. And Jesus' message was that he is going to come and fight them with the *sword of his mouth!* That is, he is going to judge them! And Thyatira, if you don't repent, I will strike you dead. How serious is that?

Sexual immorality was a problem in the early church because they were surrounded by it in their culture. Good thing we don't have that problem! Back then did the Christians say … 'Oh well we are all sinners. You have your sin and I have mine.' Did they say, 'Well God makes more allowance for us because he understands the culture we are bombarded with, and at least we are not as bad as those unbelievers'? No! Jesus said he would strike dead those who said that and judge them with the sword of his mouth. It's the same message Paul told the Ephesians. How could you miss it? 'Do not be deceived, the sexually immoral will *not* inherit the kingdom of God.' He told the church at Corinth that it was a particularly evil sin …

> Flee from sexual immorality. <u>All other sins</u> a person commits are outside the body, but whoever sins sexually sins against their own body. Do you not know that your bodies are temples of the Holy Spirit, who is in you, whom you have received from God? You are not your own; you were <u>bought at a price</u>. Therefore honor God with your bodies (1 Cor. 6:18-20).

You were *bought* at a great price. That is the picture here in Revelation. Those who are really God's people do not defile themselves because they were bought *at a great price*. They are those who were *purchased from among men*.

Offer your body as a living sacrifice. Why? Because you were *purchased* at a great price, and we know how great that price was. That's why only believers can sing that new song of the Lamb. Revelation speaks with the direst warning, culminating in 21:8 where it reveals the fate of the sexually immoral: *their place will be in the fiery lake of burning sulfur*. And this is the great contrast. Those who follow Jesus are sexually pure and this (among other things) is a mark of faithfulness, and this is the great metaphor used here. Why that metaphor? Why doesn't 14:4 say, 'These are those who don't murder or don't steal'? Why this particular metaphor? Sexual purity distinguished the Christians from the culture around them and sexual immorality was among the great problems in the early church that brought into question where people really stood with Jesus.

Unfortunately, it seems things haven't changed much. What do you think is the secret killer today? However great a problem it was back then, and however many people it kept out of heaven, better multiply that many times today. It is downright frightening how many people are going to be exposed as hypocrites. We have in this day and age the perfect trick of Satan. Anonymous sexual immorality, easily accessible. And Satan says to you ... 'no one will know' ... Internet pornography. But according to Revelation, it is not anonymous at all. That is just the lie of the devil. Jesus told the sexually immoral at the church at Thyatira...

> ... I am he who searches hearts and minds, and I will repay each of you according to your deeds (2:23).

He sees everything! As a wider church, we really have to deal with this. Internet porn has become so common amongst professing Christians we are treating it is as though God has changed his mind on what is faithfulness. He describes his faithful people as ... *those who did not defile themselves* ... but it is unspoken in the church today. Secret shipwrecks of faith are going on. Marriages are hurt or broken. Heaven is missed! Over and again in the Scriptures, sexual immorality is one great contrast of the divide between heaven and hell, and this passage uses it as well. Who are the redeemed of God? *Those who did not defile themselves with women* ... (14:4).

The great excuse people use is the same one of Jezebel in the first century. Lots of 'Christians' are doing it. No, they're not! If they are real Christians, they will repent. Even if they have found themselves caught in this sin, they will see this picture in Rev. 14 of the purity of those who are really Christians, who were purchased at such a great price, and they will stop it! They will see the cost of what it is to be *redeemed* (14:3) and *purchased* (14:4). They will see the cross! Jesus hung there for sexual immorality—for those who repent—for those for whom the cross *means* something.

Does it mean anything to you? Jesus, my Savior, in the darkness on the cross, was soaking in the eternal wrath of God. Hell! He became the porn watcher. That is, he became sin to set you free! What a cost! What a purchase! All so that you could be included in the 144,000. Does that mean anything to you? If you really are one who was purchased it will. 'Oh, but we are all sinners.' Yes, but have you not seen the cross? Are you born again? Are you of the *firstfruits*? Ready to offer yourself as a living sacrifice to Jesus? To die for him? To follow him wherever he goes? ... *They follow the Lamb wherever he goes.*

Wherever he goes? What if he leads you through some sexual frustration? Will you follow him through that? *Wherever he goes.* If you are using the old excuse, 'I'm no worse than some,' or 'I am under more temptation than others', that won't cut it because true believers ... *follow the Lamb <u>wherever</u> he goes.* What if he leads you through life single? Will you follow him through that? ... *They follow the Lamb <u>wherever</u> he goes.*

> Then a teacher of the law came to him and said, 'Teacher, <u>I will follow you wherever you go</u>.' Jesus replied, 'Foxes have dens and birds have nests, but the Son of Man has no place to lay his head' (Matt. 8:19-20).

Will you follow Jesus wherever he goes? The 144,000 do. And if you are the satisfied Pharisee who is not tempted in sexual immorality, remember this 'purity' is a metaphor for *any* unfaithfulness. If you are caught up in the world in ways that are more 'respectable', you still have the same problem if you remain unrepentant. Will *you* follow Jesus wherever he goes? Take up your cross and follow me! Deny yourself and follow me. What does that mean? What does that really mean to you to deny yourself? He didn't offer that as an alternative. Ask yourself now, *how* will you deny yourself? What will it mean to you personally? Financially? Emotionally?

It means those who are really his ... *follow the Lamb <u>wherever</u> he goes.* They followed Jesus, his example, his *suffering* and his *teaching*. If you are not following Jesus' teaching, then how can you say you are following the Lamb? If you are not, then pray for the Spirit. That is the answer. Pray in times of temptation. Don't delay. Follow the Lamb wherever. Call on him wherever!

What is the point of the first readers seeing the 144,000, the firstfruits? Purchased for God. Do you remember why this was written? To the servants of God in times of *suffering and tribulation* (1:9). Take a look at yourself here in this text. See the attacks of the Dragon and his Beast and the False Prophet. But look at the victory here for those at the throne of the Lamb. The message is 'keep going!'. Finish the race. This is your certainty. This is your security. This is your future. Look and see, there *you* are standing in the midst of the 144,000. Jesus wins and the practical catch line of the book comes up again in this chapter: *this calls for patient endurance for the saints* (14:12). So follow the Lamb wherever he goes.

Study Questions

1. John hears a great sound of music in heaven. What is missing when people talk of musicians who have died as 'up there playing'?

2. Why could only certain people learn the song?

3. Are only virgins included in the 144,000? Support your answer from Scripture.

4. How is the personal love of God indicated in 14:4?

5. No lie was found in the mouths of the 144,000. Can anyone who has told a lie enter heaven? What does this refer to?

6. What do 'firstfruits' and 'offered' (14:4) mean and where do these concepts come from?

7. Why might the metaphor of sexual purity be chosen to describe believers?

8. What are some things a Christian can do to avoid sexual defilement?

9. What might be some of the challenges you have faced to 'follow the Lamb wherever he goes?'

23
Babylon
(Revelation 14:6-10)

Ever heard the saying, 'History repeats itself'? Well it's true more than you ever imagined. If you are a careful student of history, you can actually see what is going to come upon the world right here through Revelation. What we have seen in the progression of the seals and trumpets and all their devastation are warnings that come upon the earth, but these are only snippets of what is going to happen. Revelation also points to biblical history to show how history will repeat itself. In the OT, the great city of Babylon was brought down and ceased to exist, but this history is to be repeated. The great powers like Babylon, which humans put their hopes in, the idols they set up and place their security in will all come down, but in far greater devastation than Babylon of old. You ain't seen nothing yet!

We see snippets in a global financial crisis or stock market crashes. We see it with superpowers that get overthrown even in recent history. These events remind us there is no security in the things of this world. Rev. 14:1-5 laid out the security of those who are the Lord's, but 14:6-13 is the call to come to the only place you can find that security. In the gospel. And this is the call to follow it.

> Then I saw another angel flying in midair, and he had the eternal gospel to proclaim to those who live on the earth—to every nation, tribe, language and people (14:6).

Gospel means *good news*. But it's **the eternal gospel**. There is only one gospel. So I disagree with those who have one gospel for Jews (the gospel of the kingdom of Jesus in his millennial reign), and one for Gentiles during the church age. Many who hold the Futurist view believe the Jews are saved mostly separately from Gentiles. But we are looking in Rev. 14 at a single gospel, the eternal gospel. In

Romans 1:16 this gospel is the power of God for salvation of both Jew and Gentile. One Messiah. One gospel. Ephesians 2:11-22 explains the mystery of this gospel that joins Jew and Gentile together—all within one gospel—not separately. Well, here is an angel proclaiming the only one true *eternal* gospel to all people of **every nation,** including the Jews. It's not confined to particular dispensations. It stretches across all time *and* races.

An **angel** (which can also be translated *messenger*) proclaims it. This could be like the letters to the churches that were each addressed to an angel representing the church. It could be that this angel represents the church at large which proclaims the gospel. But then we also note that angels often pronounce judgment. And most of what follows is a warning of judgment. But gospel means *good news*. How is judgment good news? Well, it always starts with bad news, because you can't understand how good the good news is until you understand how bad the bad news is. Try telling someone who does not know Jesus that there is good news, there is a Savior, and they say, 'What do I need to be saved from?' They don't know why that would be good news, unless you tell them the bad news. I love the way Spurgeon is reported to have said, 'They don't feel the noose around their necks, so they don't weep for joy when the Savior cuts the rope.'

This gospel is like the scroll John saw in Rev. 10, the one he was told to eat. The scroll was both sweet to eat and yet bitter in his stomach. That is the gospel. It is good news, but when digested there is bitterness to it. There is often bitter rejection of it, even a bitter end to those who reject it. This message is foolishness to those who are perishing. It is not good news to them at all. But this offer of the eternal gospel must go to the ends of the earth before the end. The parallel is in Jesus' words ...

> And this gospel of the kingdom will be preached in the whole world as a testimony to all nations, and then the end will come (Matt. 24:14).

I think Jesus really means **the end**, not a delay of an extra 1000 years after he comes back *before* the end and judgment of unbelievers. The mercy of God is pronounced to the end! That is the message here. The double-edged sword. The gospel is as much a judgment for those who reject it as it is good news to those who are being saved.

Certainly for the saints it requires perseverance. Again, there is a parallel between 14:12 that says it requires perseverance for the people of God. See also Matthew 24:13… *but he who stands firm to the end will be saved.* And when the witnesses have finished their testimony the end will come (Matt. 24:14, Rev. 11). And here it is.

> He said in a loud voice, 'Fear God and give him glory, because the hour of his judgment has come. Worship him who made the heavens, the earth, the sea and the springs of water' (14:7).

Some have said this is the last-minute conversion of many Jews because at the arrival of the Judgment hour they give glory to God. I don't think that fits with the rest of Scripture, including the end of Rev. 6 when Judgment Day brings shock, terror and hiding for unbelievers, not last-minute conversions. The following context seems to indicate they were *punished*, not converted. But if 14:7 is judgment for *all* unbelievers, it's perfectly in line with Phil. 2:9-11, where every knee will bow and every tongue will confess to the glory of God the Father. On that day, everyone will give glory to God, whether they like it or not!

So if this warning has not convinced the unbelievers, and it's too late for them when this judgment arrives, then who or what is this written for? This whole book was addressed to those people in the seven churches (and by extension all the church), who had been warned in Rev. 2-3 about falling for idolatry and immorality. If you are a believer who is still lukewarm, clinging to an idol, then this is written to you, to say, 'This day is coming!' *Whoever has ears, let them hear what the Spirit is saying to the churches!* Listen! You have to do something drastic now. How many warnings do you want before it's too late? And then John gets a picture of, 'too late'…

> A second angel followed and said, 'Fallen! Fallen is Babylon the Great, which made all the nations drink the maddening wine of her adulteries' (14:8).

Some Futurists say Babylon is referring to a rebuilt literal Babylon or Rome. Some Historicists say Babylon is the ultimate false apostate religion. But how can we tell for sure? Again, we ask what would it mean to first century Christians in those seven churches? They know their Bibles. They know that in the OT, ancient Babylon was the great city of idolatry, immorality and self-glory, holding itself up against God. Babylon was the world superpower that ...

1. Oppressed God's people.
2. Was abundant in idolatry and immorality. And ...
3. The world power which destroyed the temple of God in 586BC (and exiled and held God's people in captivity).

The Christians in the first century knew the literal Babylon was destroyed. They also knew God said it would never exist again (Jer. 50:13, 51:37). In the first century, they weren't expecting ancient Babylon to be restored because the LORD had promised it would not! So, if Babylon is symbolic of something (like the rest of the images and OT references in Revelation), no prizes for guessing whom it would symbolize in the first century. Right before their eyes Rome fitted that description.

1. Rome oppressed God's people in the first century. Christians experienced their own exile. John is literally exiled on the island of Patmos as he wrote this Revelation.
2. Rome was the only superpower of the day and it was steeped in idolatry and immorality.
3. Just like Babylon (600 years earlier), the Roman Empire destroyed the temple!

In fact, some in Judaism in the first century even referred to Rome as Babylon because it destroyed the temple in Jerusalem and exiled Israel. But where is Babylon today? Haven't we been examining Revelation as addressed to the whole church? Aren't *all* blessed who read this book and take it to heart? Just as the Babylon symbol is clearly manifest in Rome in the first few centuries, the Babylon symbol should also make sense beyond that and into our day.

What city manifests Babylon in our day? Babylon is the city where you live! Worldly cities that lift themselves up and promote idolatry, immorality, the lights, lusts and luxuries, and yet they oppress God's people. But how do they destroy God's temple today? As Paul the apostle warned the Corinthians ...

> If anyone destroys God's temple, God will destroy that person; for God's temple is sacred, and <u>you together are that temple</u> (1 Cor. 3:17).

Paul says the temple is you, the church. And Jesus is in the midst of his lampstands. Jesus (together with his people) *is* the temple.

Anyone who destroys the church is destroying the temple. So speaking into our day, great cities, powers and world systems that oppress or even seek to destroy the church, manifest *Babylon*.

But the perspective John sees in this vision (14:8) is that this Babylon has already fallen. It is prophecy of what is yet to happen, and yet from the perspective the apostle John sees in this vision, it has already happened! Did you hear that, you who are placing your hopes in this world? Did you hear that, you who are planning your next holiday in that great city, or planning your career or work life as the plan and goal of your life? In God's sight, it's all over! The 'city' of the world has already been judged! Along with *all* who are aligned with her. Already gonners! So why would anyone want to be on the side of Babylon rather than Christ? Babylon is doomed! Answer: Because she is seductive. She entices with her maddening wine and her immorality…

> A second angel followed and said, 'Fallen! Fallen is Babylon the Great, which made all the nations drink the maddening wine of her adulteries' (14:8).

The **maddening wine of her adulteries** is all so alluring. Ever wondered why your favorite addictions are so tempting? It's meant to be like that. It's like maddening wine! But it's all coming to an end. Her judgment has come and she receives God's wrath. And it's that very immorality and idolatry which has ripened her judgment. This verse is recalling Isaiah …

> Look, here comes a man in a chariot with a team of horses. And he gives back the answer: 'Babylon has fallen, has fallen! All the images of its gods lie shattered on the ground!' (Isa. 21:9).

All shattered. Revelation is using this literal falling of ancient Babylon to say 'that was just a snippet pointing forward to the final judgment of *all* that is Babylon'. In John's day, if you wanted to survive and have financial and economic security, you had to drink in her *maddening wine*. You had to comply with the demands of the trade guilds and the idol worship to get your union ticket. You may have had to compromise with your faith in other ways just to *buy or sell* if you wanted economic security. Sexual immorality was part of the lifestyle in the city around you, and you are tempted to drink the maddening wine of her adulteries. But take a look at the final verdict.

'Fallen! Fallen is Babylon the Great ...' Today Babylon still leads us into much of our lifestyle in society. She is so connected to the first Beast she appears to be almost identical, but when we get to Rev. 17, we will examine more closely her connection with the Beast. There we see her riding the Beast! It's the political and state powers that are the Beast, but Babylon is all the cultural, economic, spiritual and ideological values — the *city* supported by the governments to carry out the *maddening wine of her adulteries*. Do we live for now, and indulge all of Babylon's maddening wine? Sometimes literally? More wine! We live in luxury compared to a generation or two ago. And we live in opulence compared to most of the world! Have we been caught up in the maddening wine of Babylon? What are we storing up for? Look at what happens here!

Those who lost everything in the last stock market crash are actually at an advantage. They have seen a small glimpse of what is coming on the whole world. A massive stock market crash that is coming on the great cities of the whole world and everyone will be devastated. All of what you saved up for. We are going to lose it all! All of your nice comfortable things. All of what you have put your hopes in. And you will cry, *'fallen, fallen, is Babylon the Great.'*

So what idols and self-glory do we need to clean out of the house lest we fall with her? While we drink her maddening wine, we are full and don't need a thing. Let us eat and drink and be merry. In fact, if you drink of this wine, 14:10 says you will also drink of the cup of God's wrath. Drink from one, drink from the other. Bit of a play on words for those who are heroes at drinking. Drink the wine in 14:8, and you get to drink even more in 14:10. But you won't enjoy that wine. Babylon is fallen! It's such a certainty it appears to John as though it has already happened! As Christians are more and more marginalized, we might feel like we are in a Babylonian captivity, but there are many countries which live out a real daily Babylonian captivity. And the message here is, 'Hold on, because the oppressor is coming down.'

Some say these verses refer to the time when those left behind from the rapture will be given a second chance, but when Babylon is judged, so are all those who followed her.

> A third angel followed them and said in a loud voice: 'If anyone worships

the beast and its image and receives its mark on their forehead or on their hand, they, too, will <u>drink of the wine of God's fury</u> ...' (14:9-10a).

Worship of the Beast is connected with Babylon, as we will see in Rev. 17. But worship of the Beast relates to what you believe (forehead) and what you do (hand). It's a rejection of God and finding your portion in things the Beast offers and provides. 'I don't need my Creator. I got here by myself and I can take care of myself. I love this city Babylon! I want its stuff. I want to be Lord of my own life.' And the message here is that this means you will get what you asked for. You don't want Jesus as Lord. Therefore, you don't want Jesus to take the cup of God's wrath for you, so God passes it to you!

> ... he, too, will <u>drink of the wine of God's fury</u>, which has been poured <u>full strength into the cup</u> of his wrath. They will be tormented with burning sulfur in the presence of the holy angels and of the Lamb (14:10).

You liked the wine of Babylon (14:8), so now you get another wine. The **wine of God's fury**. Babylon's wine is enticing, but not lasting. God's wine of fury lasts forever. And it's the full strength. Greeks would dilute their wine to half wine and half water, but this wine will be 'full strength'. And the burning sulfur reminds us of the judgment on Sodom, further enhanced by the smoke rising.

> And the smoke of their torment will rise for ever and ever ... (14:11).

Christians reading this in those seven churches in the first century would have seen this imagery speaking into their lives. It was a shocking reality that Christians were burned. Roman Emperor Nero, the 'Babylonian king' of the first century, used to burn Christians on stakes to light up his gardens in the evening.[26] If you were there in the first century, you knew what it was for your own brothers and sisters to ... *be tormented with burning* ... You knew what it was to have the *rising smoke of their very bodies*.

Indeed, many through the last 2000 years have known this literally. Those who stood for the faith during the Middle Ages were burned

---

[26] Tacitus, Annals of Imperial Rome, Chapter 15:44

at the stake. And many of the earthly powers in our own day, have killed multitudes in the 20th and now 21st century because of their Christian faith. But here is the great reversal. Now those onlookers receive the same.

God is not indifferent to evil. People say, 'Where is the justice?' But little do they realize it stores up and stores up. The cup fills up until this very time when it overflows. If you think you are angry with sinners, the Lord is furious! Did you notice what happens to the evildoer ... **they, too, will drink of the wine of God's <u>fury</u>** (14:10). It's God's fury! It's possibly the greatest terror that will come back on humans who dared ask, 'Why doesn't God do something about suffering and evil?' They will regret having questioned God's justice when they see that all the while he was holding back his fury, then they will see it poured out and how long it lasts ... **And the smoke of their torment will rise <u>for ever and ever</u>.**

We see evil perpetrated and get angry and wish it would be stopped and given the appropriate penalty, but what is appropriate? Who could ever know what is appropriate? God does. Penalty? Forever! And you say that is cruel. But did you notice the answer to that in this text? Just think of Jesus who came and opened his arms literally to the world to save all who would call on his name. We read things like, 'Jesus was filled with compassion.' 'Jesus loved them to the end.' 'Jesus looked at him and loved him.' We see love personified in Jesus, loving in the most awesome, sacrificial way at the cross. This is who Jesus is. This is who God is. Jesus is love. But look at this: **They will be tormented with burning sulfur <u>in the presence</u> of the holy angels <u>and of the Lamb</u>.** They are tormented in the presence of whom? The Lamb! We need to use this as our barometer to direct us as to how right and fair eternal punishment must be. It cannot be cruel or harsh, but it is so right that the loving Lamb of God, who once offered himself up for the world, now literally looks on at the justice, *in the presence ... of the Lamb.*

Note he is described as the Lamb. The one who was sacrificed. The same compassionate one sees that it is all so right. He does not flinch or waver. It is right to be this way as he looks on. I don't believe the Son of God, who went through torture and death on a cross for humans, could look upon this if it was in the slightest way cruel, or anything less than fair and right. There could be nothing unloving about it. How come we can't see that as we look at this picture? Because we just haven't seen how evil sin is. We are happy with Babylon and her maddening wine. Yet here in front of Jesus it will all seem so right and deserved. He drank the cup, but you didn't want him, you wanted your own Lordship and found your portion in what pleased you. You wanted to drink your own cup. So here it is ... *They will be tormented with burning sulfur in the presence of the holy angels and of the Lamb.*

How graphic! How ugly! But how much more warning do you want? This is the most amazing thing. This warning is not written to the world. It's written to the churches. Many in the church are not going to make it. Jesus said narrow is the road that leads to life and *only* a few find it. Read this book of Revelation through. Warning from the start! Who to? Unbelievers? No. Warning you! You who have lost your first love. You who are lukewarm. I am going to spit you out! Now it's the 'full strength' of the cup. There are no more chances by the time we get here. Only the fullness of righteous justice. No hope. No more day of grace. No end to it! Anyone who has the mark of the Beast will drink that cup. Anyone who clings to those idols. Anyone who practices immorality. Anyone showing the mark of the Beast in their lives, either in their beliefs (mark of the forehead), or in their actions (mark of the hand). They will have to drink the cup of God's fury. And who can stand? Who of us will stand on that day? What hope have you got?

Wait a minute. This is the same message of the *eternal gospel*. We had to feel the noose around our neck before we could weep for joy when the Savior cuts the rope. None of us want to drink the cup of God's fury. But we have one who drank the cup for us! The Lamb of God. He drank the cup reserved for you, if you will turn from the hopes you're placing in Babylon. He saves all who will turn to him in repentance and faith. If you have been lukewarm, this was written for you, not the world. It's the call to turn back from the idols and immorality. Turn to Jesus. Turn now. Join the mission. Get the message out there. Look at how long the alternative lasts. This text says this is the last warning before it's too late.

Study Questions

1. Does the saying 'history repeats itself' affect the way you read the OT and why?

2. How is this a 'gospel' when it is speaking about judgment?

3. How does your answer to Question 2 affect the way you present the gospel to unbelievers?

4. How can 14:7 be seen to be a last-minute conversion of many? Is that what it is teaching?

5. What are three characteristics of ancient Babylon that can be used to deduce 'Babylon' in the first century and beyond?

6. Where is Babylon today and what is the maddening wine of her adulteries?

7. Why should God be in fury?

8. What is there in this text that suggests God's eternal judgment cannot be cruel or unfair?

9. Who is this warning addressed to and what is it meant to elicit?

24
Day and Night Forever
(Revelation 14:11-13)

The story continues with what we have been looking at through Rev. 14. It's the story of the great divide of humanity. Not the worldly divides of black or white, male or female, rich or poor. But the big one. 'Who are you? What defines you?' There is an eternal divide. It lasts forever. Which kingdom do you belong to? Which mark do you have? The mark of the Beast or the seal of God? Depending on which one you have, it determines who you are. You are either in Christ or the Beast. It determines *whose* you are. Do you *belong* to Christ or the Beast? And it determines how you will exist, night and day, forever and ever. With Christ or with the Beast?

How many times have you heard people say when someone dies after a drawn-out illness, 'Well, it's good they are now released from suffering.'? I hope so. Because the alternative does not look good …

> And the smoke of their torment will rise for ever and ever. There is no rest day or night for those who worship the beast and its image, or for anyone who receives the mark of its name (14:11).

It's the forever-ness of it that takes us back. But this is the great divide. *Day or night* is continual. It's the same expression used in 4:8 and 7:15 to describe the blissful worship of the people in the presence of God *day and night*. Our lives are bigger than we imagine. This is just the beginning of eternity. Whose you are on this side determines the great divide that continues forever.

Therefore, we reject reincarnation, the belief that when you die you are born again as someone or something else. Jesus came back from the dead as himself, not someone else. And if reincarnation was true, then there is no justice. When you are reincarnated you receive suffering in this life because of the sins committed in a previous life, but you are *never conscious* you did anything wrong, and so even the rapist or murderer is *never conscious* of the punishment. The theory is there is a connection between the two, but in practice, someone else did it and you cop it, or vice-versa. The biblical view is that you are born once to face judgment and then exist forever in either one of two great divides. For now, you are going through this little phase we call *life* on earth, but this little phase exposes who you are and how you will exist forever. Serve and worship the Lamb now and you will serve and worship the Lamb in heaven forever. Serve and worship the Beast now and that's who you will be with forever. **There is <u>no rest day or night</u> for those who worship the beast and his image ...**

Those in the cults try to deny this and say the Bible teaches annihilation. Annihilation is the theory that when someone dies outside the Lord there is no punishment (or only temporary punishment), and they cease to consciously exist. All the cults go for it. It's one of the primary ways they get recruits. It's very enticing to people brought up with some traditional Christian understanding, but can't accept God's holiness (that is, they want to deny the existence of eternal hell). The cults are just waiting there beckoning like the Dragon himself saying, 'Come on over here, we have a god without any nasty hell.' Incredibly, some who otherwise hold to orthodox Christianity also believe in annihilation. But do they come to that conclusion through honest reading of Scripture, or do they come to the Bible with a presumption that an eternal hell must be cruel or harsh?

The Bible clearly states things like *torment forever* and *no rest day or night* (14:11). This is not one of those *disputable matters* that genuinely could be interpreted differently. This is an issue of the heart. It's one of trust in the Lord. People simply don't like the holiness of God, so they come up with schemes of interpretation trying to 'help God out' of the charge that he is cruel. We noted last time in 14:10 that this punishment occurs in the presence of the Lamb of God. How could Jesus look upon anything that is cruel and uncaring? And yet *torment forever* is so severe. How can you put those together? Well, the first thing is, don't try to change something God has said just because we don't grasp or understand or don't like it.

The annihilation view doesn't solve God's problems for him at all. It creates new ones. It believes the same lie of the serpent in the Garden. 'You will not surely die.' To die the second death is eternal hell, and the annihilationist says, 'You will *not* surely die.' And besides, annihilation is exactly what unbelievers hope for! (That should make us cautious.) The unbeliever says, 'I will do what I want. I will be Lord of my life and at the end there is no accountability. Nothing.' Or as some with the annihilationist view say, there is a quick temporary punishment and then off to sleep for eternity. But at the end, everyone gets away with whatever they did. And that means there is no justice for this world, ever. It is disturbing to think of someone in torment without rest day and night forever, but it is far more disturbing to think that there is no hell. Why do I say far *more* disturbing?

The evilest humans who ever lived, be it Hitler or willful child abusers or murderers, would receive at best some temporary penalty and then go to sleep, receiving the same escape and non-punishment as others who didn't commit such crimes. But by the time we get to the end of Revelation, we learn that the justice in hell is individual. Each one receives penalty *according to the things they have done* (20:12). This means that from the most evil people, down to the least offender, each one will receive a different measure of punishment in hell, because it is individual justice according to what they did (and how much they knew and responded to what they were given. Matt. 10:14-15; Luke 12:47-48).

Non-believers actually agree it is more disturbing to not have a hell. Well, they don't ever put it in those words, but what is the unbeliever's great reason for rejecting God? You know it! 'Why does God allow suffering and evil? ... Especially against the weak and vulnerable?' Without realizing it, they are saying it is a terrible thing if there is no hell (justice against evil). The trouble is that justice is far more thorough than they ever wanted. It turns out God not only cares about those who suffer, he also cares when people *commit* evil. And he cares far more than you could imagine—every detail, even down to bad thoughts. And look how the accounting adds up. For the righteous, those who suffered for good, *their deeds follow them* (14:13). There is reward. It is more explicit in other parts of Scripture that those who suffer righteously will be compensated. But even here there is a hint. You question how the torture of a child could be accounted for, considering what the child goes through. But it must add up in light of how rich the reward and how long it lasts, as 14:6 told us, it's an *eternal* gospel! It's good news forever! Look at how long the punishment for the abuser lasts. It's forever! It adds up all right!

When you really get to the bottom of why cults and others go for annihilation, especially if it includes some short burst of punishment just before they go to sleep, it's not because they don't agree with God punishing evil. They have just decided *they* know better than God as to the degree of punishment. For instance, most who believe God shouldn't punish people forever find this question difficult. 'Should Satan be punished forever?' Some say 'errr ... yes'. Revelation says he is (20:10). Why don't we have a problem with that? Because we think Satan deserves it! It's just our judgment or perspective on how bad sin is. What if God's perspective is far more holy than ours? Humans will last forever. The great divide is whether you have the mark of Christ or the mark of the Beast. The same texts that say hell is eternal also talk about heaven as eternal (Matt. 25:46). But no one ever complains that we should have a time limit on heaven. 'What? Joy and bliss *forever?* Man, don't we get a break from all that singing and harp playing. Couldn't we just die?' No one makes that complaint. The gospel is eternal, so is the alternative. *And the smoke of their torment rises for ever and ever.*

So what *do* those with the annihilation view do with this text? It's like any false teaching. If I debunked every way they try to twist it, it would not only take another book, but they would then come up with another way to twist the text anyway. But whatever they come up with, it will be anything but what the text simply says. So we have to deal with the real cause of why people want to change it. It's because they can never understand sin from God's point of view, and how guilty we truly are, how deserving. To us sin just happens and is forgotten, but to God it is defacing his image, attacking God as Lord. He sees sin *forever* and his holy character demands that he deals justly with sin, forever. Sin doesn't stop being sin and God can't change being holy, so he must deal with it justly—forever.

How do we manage this truth when we think of people we know and love that have gone on without the Lord? The answer is by keeping perspective on *who* the Lord is. He is the holy just judge, but never cruel or unfair. His justice is not anything *less* than what is described in this text, and yet there is nothing *unloving* in the Lord, even in his holy wrath. He is good and fair, not unkind. And it seems even the people in the pain of hell agree. When you look at the parable of the rich man and Lazarus that Jesus told in Luke 16, the response of the man in hell is not one of complaint about his treatment being unfair, and amazingly he does not even ask to be let out, even though he appeals for some relief from the pain in there. But he does appeal for someone to tell his brothers so they won't come to that horrible place. He assumes they too *deserve* to be there. The man in hell in Luke 16 is saying God was right and I was wrong. In this life, we don't see outwardly the great divide of who we are. The seal or mark is not an outward visible sign. But in the next life the curtain is drawn back on the evil of sin against God. It's shown up as to what people wanted. Those who wanted to be separated from God got what they asked for, to be on their own without God interfering. Their true nature is pride, selfishness, idolatry, and a complete lack of gratitude for everything God gave them. They even would rather credit nothing than God for their life. 'The world popped out of nothing. I popped out of nothing. I evolved by the hand of no one. I will not acknowledge God.' Or they claim they believed in God or Jesus, but where is the life of gratitude to the Lord? *And the smoke of their torment rises for ever and ever. There is no rest day or night for those who worship the beast and its image, or for anyone who receives the mark of its name.*

Remember to whom this was written. The unbelievers don't read this. It's to the church. Why? The next line says why ...

> This calls for patient endurance on the part of the people of God who keep his commands and remain faithful to Jesus (14:12).

What is this line doing repeated here again? Why is a description of hell followed by a **call for patient endurance** for Christians? I have suggested all along this book of Revelation is speaking to all Christians to exhort them to be faithful and to be wary of falling for the Beast, from those who first read it in the first century to God's people throughout the ages. This is alive for all Christians. And if you read this book without any preconceived ideas, doesn't this seem to be describing any believer of any specific time when it says: **the people of God who keep his commands and remain faithful to Jesus?**

A *call for patient endurance* is a theme of Revelation that speaks directly into the lives of all Christians throughout history. This formula has occurred from the beginning. It was first used in relation to the seven churches (1:9), then it was repeated in 13:10, and now the same phrase is used again in 14:12. *This calls for patient endurance.* Why is John saying the exact same thing to the seven churches at the start of Revelation as he does to God's people well into the tribulation in Rev. 13-14? Because they are the same people! The whole book is addressed to them! And John continues to address Christians throughout this book because we are all in need of patient endurance.

John is addressing all Christians here at 14:12, saying whatever *suffering* you may have to experience, whatever 'patient endurance' and faithfulness required, hold on! Because it is *nothing* compared to the suffering of those who have the mark of the Beast. Also note the interesting way Christians are described as those ... *who keep his commands and remain faithful to Jesus.* Doctrine and practice together. Living out faith in obedience. But the second part, remaining faithful to Jesus, is not just repeating *obedience* again. It is the same meaning in 2:13, that is, keeping the faith or not denying the faith. Standing on the truth of the gospel. This is classic Jude 3 stuff. Contending for the faith once delivered to the saints. True saints are those who obey God's commands. Obviously not perfectly or we wouldn't need a Savior, but those with the mark of the Beast don't hate their sin and what it did to the Savior. They take lightly the commandments of God. The world says God's commandments are old school. Now even the basics of the Ten Commandments like murder and adultery are not a given as to right and wrong. Pro-choice to what? To murder! Adultery, we are told by many experts, can be helpful for you and even your marriage. But it's the mark of the Beast. In contrast, Christians love God's commands and believe God's commands are good. They reflect God's very character.

> Then I heard a voice from heaven say, 'Write this: Blessed are the dead who die in the Lord from now on.' 'Yes,' says the Spirit, 'they will rest from their labor, for their deeds will follow them' (14:13).

Here is the great divide! God's people are more blessed if they die from now on. Does it mean they are more blessed from when they die? The grammar allows for it to mean a special blessing in heaven for those who die from this point, **from now on** (as opposed to those in heaven up to that point). Why would that be? People are more blessed to die from the time of the tribulation than before it? I'll offer a suggestion. What has happened *from now on*? We learned the ascension of Jesus (12:5) was followed by that great event when the Dragon was cast out of heaven (12:7). He was no longer able to accuse. The OT has Satan still with access to roam the earth, yes; but also to appear in heaven to accuse. But since the ascension of Jesus, Satan was permanently hurled out of heaven because of what Jesus accomplished in his death, resurrection and ascension. So *'from now on'* (14:13), from the completion of the gospel, Satan no longer has access to accuse in heaven, but more than that (that alone would make heaven a more blessed place), what else happens after the ascension? Jesus is there! Relating directly to us as the God/man! Oh, how blessed are those who die *from now on*. There is a new development in heaven that the OT saints hadn't been able to appreciate until then! **And 'they will rest from their labor, for their deeds will follow them.'**

No more toil in labor. Rest. We rest in Christ from the moment we believe, but that is not the rest we look forward to here. There is still this rest to come. *There remains, then, a Sabbath-rest for the people of God* … (Heb. 4:9). We need this Revelation. What is the real blessing? What is the final goal you look for? Have you ever really come to grips with this truth? …**Blessed are the dead who die in the Lord** … *Blessed!* Not just relieved after a tough one. Not just alleviated. Not just at ease. *Blessed!* Maybe you don't know what *blessed* really means. Look it up! The apostle Paul describes dying and being with Christ as better by far (Phil. 1:21, 23)! It's being with Jesus. This book of Revelation reveals snippets not found elsewhere. God himself with us—wiping away every tear. Everything that caused pain or loss is reversed! No more crying. No more pain. True blessedness. Joy. Face to face with Jesus. You have no idea what it will be like to see him! Exceeding joy (Jude 24)! Are you really a believer? Is this what you long for? The face of Jesus? Or are you still hoping for some final fulfillment in this life?

Blessed are many who had seemingly mundane or toilsome lives, lonely lives, persecuted lives, painful lives, or suffering lives, but *remained faithful*. So what happens in the great reversal? They are blessed and more … *'they will rest from their labor, for their deeds will follow them.'* Deeds follow you. This is too big to get our heads around.

There are things like this we don't even want to think about in our Christian life. It's too scary. It's the same thing the apostle Paul spoke about.

> For we [Christians] must all appear before the judgment seat of Christ, so that each of us may receive what is due us for the things done while in the body, whether good or bad (2 Cor. 5:10).

This is too much. But it doesn't need to be scary if you know the eternal gospel. There is no condemnation for those who are in Christ Jesus, so there is no fear that your sin can be brought up to judge you. It has been nailed to the cross. You can never be condemned for your sin, but you will *receive what is due for the things done in the body*. The positive thing is that as a Christian it means that all your faithful labor counts and will be appropriately rewarded! Your *deeds will follow you*. That means your suffering is working for you. It's not just a hurdle to get through ...

> For our light and momentary troubles are <u>achieving for us</u> an eternal glory that far outweighs them all (2 Cor. 4:17).

Achieving an eternal weight of glory. What is Revelation saying? ... *'they will rest from their labor, for their <u>deeds will follow them</u>'* (14:13). Nothing you ever did to fight the good fight in battling temptation, doing good, or praising God in loneliness or trial is wasted! It's amazing to think it will all be rewarded. You receive what is due for things done in the body. Isn't this what Jesus said in the Sermon on the Mount? Great is your reward in heaven if you are insulted or persecuted for Jesus (Matt. 5:11-12). The Lord even notices and rewards your giving (Matt. 6:4) and prayers (Matt. 6:6).

We get so fervent defending the truth that salvation is not by works that sometimes we think once we are saved the Lord couldn't care less about what we do, as long as we toe the line, we're all going to heaven anyway. But this says something else. Heaven will be different for each of us. The Lord cares about your faithfulness. He rewards individually! And we wouldn't want it any other way. Those who have suffered great torture throughout their life for Jesus ... we want them to receive a greater reward! It's right and fair. Just as hell has a penalty appropriately 'according to what people have done', so too heaven is blessed appropriate to the individual. *Blessed are the dead who die in the Lord from now on ... for their deeds will follow them.'*

Their deeds will follow them. *Their* money will not follow them. *Their* careers and achievements will not follow them. *Their* homes, cars and clothes will not follow them. *Their* highest ecstasies and pleasures of this world will not follow them. There is not much that will follow you. But every single act of service or faithfulness to the Lord will not be forgotten. *Their deeds* will follow them. Your reward will go on into the next life. You will experience the benefits of your labor in the next. *This calls for patient endurance on the part of the people of God who keep his commands and remain faithful to Jesus* (14:12).

Life is real and has meaning down to our daily deeds. God has a plan for you. Not that worldly 'Christian' cliché which says, 'Come to Jesus, he has a wonderful plan for your life,' which translates, 'I will get all the good stuff of this world.' No, Jesus has a *real* plan and purpose that lasts forever. Don't reject God's purpose for you. Even the suffering. Nothing is wasted. It is not just a drudge to get through, like God wants you to jump through hoops to see if you can make it. No. God is working grace even in the trials and works he has prepared in advance for you to do for your reward. Life is real all the way through. It's a win, win. Jesus wins! Sins forgiven. No condemnation. But service to the Lord rewarded. All grace in Jesus.

So what are we doing placing all our stock in this short time? Forever is forever! It has already begun and will continue forever! Store up treasures in heaven! It's the great question in Joshua 24:15. Choose this day which God you will serve. We can't expect to fully appreciate the eternal perspective because we live in this time and haven't seen that perspective yet. That's why we are given this Revelation! We are given this snippet here in the word of God. We are all going to live forever, either in heaven or hell. The great divide. Either in rest and blessedness, or in no rest day and night, forever.

'And the smoke of their torment will rise for ever and ever. There will be no rest day or night for those who worship the beast and its image, or for anyone who receives the mark of its name.' This calls for patient endurance on the part of the people of god who keep his commands and remain faithful to Jesus. Then I heard a voice from heaven say, 'Write this: Blessed are the dead who die in the Lord from now on.' 'Yes,' says the Spirit, 'they will rest from their labor, for their deeds will follow them' (14:11-13).

Study Questions

1. Can reincarnation be worked into the Christian text, and this text in particular? Give reasons.

2. What is annihilation? Defend the biblical position against it.

3. Why would so many who claim to believe in the Bible also believe in annihilation?

4. How can something as graphic as described in this text not be cruel?

5. Give reasons why this text might be speaking to all Christians.

6. Why might Christians in heaven be more blessed 'from now on'?

7. Have you ever thought of heaven and hell as appropriate to each individual? Support your answer from Scripture.

8. How does this encourage you in the meaning of your personal circumstances?

25
Blood up to the Horses' Bridles
(Revelation 14:14-20)

The God of the OT is so harsh. A judging God. People being cut down, blood and guts. A vengeful God. Wow, I am so glad we have got to the peace and calm of the NT God here in Revelation. Really? Sickles and blood flowing up to the bridles on the horses!

> I looked, and there before me was a white cloud, and seated on the cloud was one like a son of man with a crown of gold on his head and a sharp sickle in his hand (14:14).

This looks like the Day of Judgment. But the Preterist says no! Everything must happen before and leading up to the destruction of the temple in Jerusalem in AD 70. The reason this is not the final judgment, they say, is because Jesus is **seated on the cloud**. He is not said to be '*coming* on the cloud', so he doesn't come down on this occasion. I am not convinced by this argument that the **son of man** is just sitting up there on the cloud and stays there. What is he doing sitting up there? He must have a long sickle to reach down to reap from just sitting up there. But no, I think this is describing the Judgment just as Revelation opened, anticipating this ...

> 'Look, he is coming with the clouds,' and 'every eye will see him, even those who pierced him'; and all the peoples on earth 'will mourn because of him.' So shall it be! Amen (1:7).

God on clouds in the Scriptures means judgment! As it does here in 14:14 *I looked, and there before me was a white cloud, and seated on the cloud was one like a son of man* ... John recognizes this from what he saw in Rev. 1. He saw Jesus, *one like a son of man,* and of course John lived with Jesus on earth and heard Jesus refer to himself many times as 'the son of man'. John sees all this fulfilling the glorious *son of man* from Daniel 7:13. Jesus is judge *because he is the son of man*, as John recorded in his gospel (John 5:27). But here is a chilling thought. The 'time' has come.

> Then another angel came out of the temple and called in a loud voice to him who was sitting on the cloud, 'Take your sickle and reap, because the time to reap has come, for the harvest of the earth is ripe' (14:15).

There is a particular time when the measure of sin becomes full. That is the *time* when the Lord says it is **time to reap** when the **harvest of the earth is ripe**. This is like when the LORD pronounced Sodom and Gomorrah's sin had reached a point that the outcry had reached heaven (Gen. 19:20-21). Ripe for judgment! Or when the LORD told Abraham that his descendants could not go into the Promised Land until 400 years had passed. Why? Contrary to what many people think about OT wars, they did not happen arbitrarily. The Canaanites were destroyed by the Israelites only in a particular generation when the Lord determined their sin was ripe!

> In the fourth generation your descendants will come back here, for the sin of the Amorites has not yet reached its full measure (Gen. 15:16).

Wait Abraham! You can't take the Promised Land yet. There is judgment coming on the Canaanites there, but it can't happen until their sin reaches a level worthy of that judgment. It was another 400 years before that time was ripe. What were the great sins that eventually made the Canaanites ripe, when the LORD said to Israel 400 years later, 'Go and destroy them, all of them'? It's ironic that it was because of the level of idolatry, the killing of their own children and sexual immorality (Deut. 18:9-13, 2 Kings 16:3, Lev. 18:24). That is when God said they were ripe for judgment and to be *driven out*.

When will our world today be ripe for judgment? I can't say, but today we are at an unprecedented point of rampant idolatry, the killing of our own children (unborn), and sexual immorality like never before. I wonder when we will be ripe? It's hard to know just how long God will hold out. But when the time is ripe it will be like this … **'Take your sickle and reap, because the time to reap has come, for the harvest of the earth is ripe.'**

This is interesting. Why would an angel have the authority to tell Jesus when he can take up his sickle for judgment? The answer has to be because of where the angel is coming from—**out of the temple**, indicating this angel gets instruction from the Father to tell the Son when to *'take your sickle'*. But why is this message being relayed from an angel to the Son of God? This is an enigma. It's also an expression of the Son who is God and yet humble in submission to the Father, even when he is glorified. It's so gloriously unfathomable that the Lord of glory is also the humble one before his Father. It makes the problems we have with submission and authority seem so petty. We balk at gender roles, male leadership in the church and in marriage. Children balk at parent's leadership. Workers don't like the boss telling them what to do. Let's face it, human beings hate authority, full stop. We don't like the idea of submitting to anyone, and yet the eternal Son of God, fully God and *fully* equal to the Father (John 5:18), submits to him (1 Cor. 15:28). Did you get that—if you are in a leadership role? Those you lead are fully equal to you. God himself has this harmony of roles inbuilt within the relationship of God, Father, Son and Holy Spirit, without any hang-ups or conflict in their roles, and yet Jesus in all his glory is equal to the Father, and still submits to him. But now the *time* comes and Jesus is told 'take your sickle'.

> So he who was seated on the cloud swung his sickle over the earth, and the earth was harvested. Another angel came out of the temple in heaven, and he too had a sharp sickle. Still another angel, who had charge of the fire, came from the altar and called in a loud voice to him who had the sharp sickle, 'Take your sharp sickle and gather the clusters of grapes from the earth's vine, because its grapes are ripe.' The angel swung his sickle on the earth, gathered its grapes and threw them into the great winepress of God's wrath (14:16-19).

Futurists see this as the battle of Armageddon, but *not* the final judgment of the wicked, which in their view will still be 1000 years away. But what would the apostle John think as he sees this vision drawing on the OT prophet Joel prophesying final judgment …

> Swing the sickle, for the harvest is ripe. Come, trample the grapes, for the winepress is full and the vats overflow—so great is their wickedness! (Joel 3:13).

This is the rapture I believe in! Perhaps not in the way it's thought of in the popular sense. The sickle is out for reaping by the Son of God.

When Judgment Day arrives, God's people are quickly taken out of the way ... **So he who was seated on the cloud swung his sickle over the earth, and the earth was harvested.** But then the winepress squashes the grapes. **The angel swung his sickle on the earth, gathered them and threw him into the great winepress of God's wrath.**

Back in 6:10 the martyrs were crying out, *'How long o Lord before you judge the inhabitants of the earth?'* Well, this is the answer.

> They were trampled in the winepress outside the city, and blood flowed out of the press, rising as high as the horses' bridles for a distance of 1,600 stadia (14:20).

Have we forgotten where all this talk about wine came from? **They were trampled in the winepress.** What about the cup of the *wine* of God's wrath which leads us into this (14:8, 10)? The Futurist says it needs to be another 1000 years after this event before the final judgment, and what we have here is the battle of Armageddon, and the grapes being trampled outside the city is referring to Jerusalem. But I would have thought this scene is about as final a judgment on unbelievers as you get. You don't get any more final and squashed than these grapes! It's symbolic of course, but it has to be symbolic *of* something. And surely this is trying to convey in the most graphic terms the finality of the judgment. We see it's a continuation of the metaphors from 14:10—the *full strength* wine of God's wrath. There the finality of it all was described as *their torment rises forever* (14:11). And the imagery of wine and trampled in the winepress (14:19) also fits with so many of Jesus' parables which refer to that final harvest at the end.

Well, what about the city? This all happens outside the city. Jerusalem? Yes, in one sense, because this fits with the final judgment also described later in this very book, where unbelievers are judged outside the beloved heavenly city, the New Jerusalem, which is the people of God. The bride!

> Then I saw 'a new heaven and a new earth', for the first heaven and the first earth had passed away, and there was no longer any sea. I saw the Holy City, the new Jerusalem, coming down out of heaven from God, prepared as a bride beautifully dressed for her husband (21:1-2).

Remember the first readers in those churches in Asia Minor were told *they* were the 'New Jerusalem' (3:12). They were the 'bride', the Holy City. But unbelievers will be trampled *outside* the city.

> Blessed are those who wash their robes, that they may have the right to the tree of life and may go through the gates into the city. Outside are the dogs, those who practice magic arts, the sexually immoral, the murderers, the idolaters and everyone who loves and practices falsehood (22:14-15).

It's all *outside the city* for the judgment of unbelievers, just as the blood of Jesus was shed (in judgment for us) *outside the city*. So, *they were trampled in the winepress* **outside the city, and blood flowed out of the press, rising as high as the horses' bridles for a distance of 1,600 stadia.** How far is '1600 stadia'? It's about 200 miles (300km). But why 1600? Some have noted 1600 stadia is the length of Palestine, although apparently if measured properly that's quite a bit out, so it's not actually true. Revelation has consistently used numbers symbolically, but this *1600* is admittedly difficult. Some look to the number of judgment as 40 (40 years in the wilderness, 40 lashes in Deut. 25:31), so it's 40 x 40, a full judgment. The number four is the creation's number, so could it be judgment of the whole earth? It's hard to know for sure. But what about all this blood? The *blood flowed out of the press, rising as high as the horses' bridles...* (14:20).

Blood as high as the horses' bridles! That is real ancient battle language. But we are in trouble if we want to interpret these symbols literally. Even the most convinced literalists take this symbolically, which tells us that if the blood this high is a symbol, it follows that the distance is also symbolic. It would be inconsistent to have symbolic blood in a literal distance. And is there even enough blood in all the people of the earth to fill with blood that high? The point is that it symbolizes something horrific. Also, a symbol always *points* to something (but not something less), so how terrible must the reality be? So much for the idea that the God of the OT was a judging God, but the God of the NT is gentler and more peaceful ... *blood flowed out of the press, rising as high as the horses' bridles for a distance of 1,600 stadia.*

It is gruesome for us, but how much more if you lived in the first century reading this? You firmly have in mind the imagery of the old style of wine production, where the grapes were literally stomped on.

It would be all the more chilling and real for you. You picture judgment, grapes getting squashed, but as John gets a closer look at this vision, he sees it is not grape juice squeezing out, but actual blood. Human blood. What is the message? Jesus gave his lifeblood that you would not have to have your lifeblood judged. Sin flows through the blood of *your* veins. It needs to be cleansed or you must face this too! You too will be *outside the city!*

So is the OT God the only one who is the severe Judge? How much more gruesome do you want than this picture of blood gushing like this, squeezed out of the winepress of judgment? Does this make you feel sick? Does this make you feel uneasy? It's meant to! That is what it is written for. People of God persevere! It's the same call we heard in this very context …

> This calls for patient endurance on the part of the people of God who keep his commands and remain faithful to Jesus (14:12).

And if you are persevering, secure in the Lord, and you have no fear of this happening to you, then why is this *still* written to you? And the answer must be … focus! Do you want the unbelievers in your life to head straight to this without even having been warned? The seven churches that received this book were challenged about their witness for Jesus. It was one of the themes of the letters to the seven churches. Revelation starts off with Jesus identifying himself as the faithful and true witness … *and from Jesus Christ, who is the faithful witness* … (1:5). At the church at Pergamum, Antipas was the faithful witness unto death. Of the seven churches called 'lampstands' only two were faithful witnesses without rebuke. And in Rev. 11 it was only the two witnesses, the *lampstands*, who were faithful witnesses to the end. So, if this gory imagery of blood up to the horses' bridles makes you feel sick, remember, it's meant to! Unbelievers are not reading this. You are! So what are you meant to do with this?

At the very least, picture your friends and everyone who hasn't been freed by the blood of the Lamb with their own blood mixed in that sea of blood. For those who think taking Revelation as symbolic somehow weakens its reality, they might want to change their minds here and wish this *was* literal. If only this was literal. If it was literal people would just be squashed once, with nothing but their blood left over! But sadly, no one will get off that lightly. This blood symbolizes death and all that the second death brings (20:12-15). We have already seen in Rev. 14 the eternal consciousness in death of paying for your own sin. There is *no rest day or night*. Blood signifies *that* death. Jesus' blood signifies his death. So all history and the purpose of your life, meaning, and destiny come down to this text 14:20 ...

It's either Jesus' blood or your blood in that winepress. In 12:11 believers triumphed by the *blood* of the Lamb. Everything comes down to this in the end. But unbelievers aren't reading this. You are! So what should you be doing with this text? Memorize it. Repeat it every day. Pray about it. Put the names of your friends and family in there.

> The angel swung his sickle on the earth, gathered [my buddy Joe] and threw them into the great winepress of God's wrath. [Joe] was trampled in the winepress outside the city, and blood flowed out of the press, rising as high as the horses' bridles ... (14:19-20).

Does that move you? It should. What should you do with this? Well it's right before you now, what you should do with it. Remember in 12:14 where the woman (that is believers), has a place prepared for her in the wilderness? What is the wilderness? It's this world you are passing through now in your exact time and place (Acts 17:26-27). It's the place *prepared* for you. And if you have been guaranteed entrance to the Promised Land, then what is your role in this journey where you have been placed? *It's to be a witness*. It's one of the messages of Revelation to the churches. Who will follow Jesus as a *faithful and true witness?* Who are the true witnesses of Rev. 11?

But how do we go about it? You say, 'I'm not an evangelist'. Well Eph. 4:11-12 says God gave 'pastors and teachers' to equip God's people for works of ministry. If you believe in Jesus then you are one of God's people, and as a Pastor I am supposed to be equipping you for evangelizing the world—to be this witness. So here it is. Tip number 1. Memorize 14:19-20 and see the urgency of that blood. 2. Start praying urgently for people. 3. Start witnessing. Firstly, with your life. Live out the fruit of the Spirit which earns the right to share your faith in the home, in the workplace, to everyone who crosses your path. Then you have to hold forth the word of life (Phil. 2:15-16). Explain the gospel. Have a supply of your favorite evangelism tracts and books and be prepared to give them away. And in all this, look into the faces of people and know they will either triumph by the blood of the Lamb, or their blood will be mixed in that sea of blood. Have a heart for the eternal souls of people who cross your path. Think of the most spiritually weak people in your congregation. Who are they? There are probably many people within the circle of your church who unless they repent are headed for that pool of blood at the end of time. Think of one person in your circle whom you could disciple, befriend, do good deeds for and show unconditional love. Give the time of day to one person. Keep contact each week and offer to pray with them. There are a million evangelism techniques, and I'll repeat my advanced technique: Turn off the TV, phone and computer for one hour per week and give someone the time of day. Go out of your way to build a relationship with someone to earn the right to share the gospel, or invite him or her to a special church service or Bible study. Give one hour a week to a non-Christian or weak Christian who needs discipling. Read the Bible with them. Look out for them. Call them if they are missing. Maybe they are lonely. Maybe they are sick. Maybe you could be the one to bring them to the saving blood rather than the judgment blood.

Be a faithful and true witness. Join a Bible study, not for what you can get out of it, but to encourage and invite others. If you think your church is lacking in fellowship, or support, or ministry in some particular area, talk to your Pastor. But brace yourself. Guess whom he might ask to head up that new ministry? Churches don't need just ideas, they need workers—workers who have memorized this text and taken it to heart. If you have taken this to heart it will transform you. When everyone else is complaining about life, be the one who has joy. Why? Because you have joy! You are not headed for that pool of blood! You have been forgiven so you know how to forgive! Is that you? Is that how you live with difficult people in the home? In the workplace? In your church? Have you seen that blood? Are you changed by the Spirit of God? If you have you will be a faithful and true witness. Why? Because you believe this is coming ...

[Joe and Jill] *were trampled in the winepress outside the city and the <u>blood flowed out</u> of the press, <u>rising as high as the horses' bridles</u> for a distance of 1,600 stadia* (14:20).

Study Questions

1. Do you think this text is describing the final Judgment Day? Why?

2. Evaluate the Preterist and Futurist arguments for this text as other than Judgment Day.

3. Why does God have a specific 'time' to bring judgment? Support your answer from other parts of Scripture.

4. Why does humanity have difficulty with authority/roles in a way that God doesn't?

5. What role do angels play in judgment? Provide Scriptural support for your answer.

6. What connection is there with the words 'winepress' and 'outside the city' with other parts of Scripture that might help us to interpret this text?

7. If the blood up to the bridles of the horses is symbolic, what is it symbolizing?

8. Rev. 14:12 provides an ongoing theme. How is this text meant to encourage the saints to persevere?

9. Does this text motivate you in your evangelism?

10. What practical ways could you change to be a more effective witness?

26
The Song
(Revelation 15:1-3a)

Jesus, the Master film director, changes scenes again and again, holding this tension that goes back and forth. On one hand, we get scenes of terror—judgment, persecution and warnings. And yet, interspersed we have seen these shots of the victory already won. We know by now it is to remind Christians, from those first readers sitting in the pews at the churches in Ephesus, Smyrna, Pergamum Thyatira, Sardis, Philadelphia and Laodicea, to those throughout history that this book was written to you! It's for the purpose of strengthening you to keep on going. In this vision John sees judgment, even the final Judgment about to unfold …

> I saw in heaven another great and marvelous sign: seven angels with the seven last plagues—<u>last, because with them God's wrath is completed</u> (15:1).

John says this sight is **marvelous**. I would be amazed too, to see seven angels lined up. It's like John has a front row seat at the Olympic games 100 meters final. They are all lined up. Ready! These seven angels at the starters' blocks, ready to go, and are to take the very bowls containing the final plagues of God. The end!

And yet the very next verse is a picture of heaven with the people 'victorious'. Why the switch from anticipating judgment to victory already? Again, it's a message to the readers. Hold on you Christians down there in Smyrna and Philadelphia in the midst of persecution and pain. Here is your motivation to keep going. Take a look at how it all ends!

> And I saw what looked like a sea of glass glowing with fire and, standing beside the sea, those who had been victorious over the beast and its image and over the number of its name. They held harps given them by God (15:2).

John says, '**I saw** them!' And he is passing on this Revelation to those Christians going through the pain. Take a look at this! These are your brothers and sisters who fought the good fight against the Beast. They didn't submit to his mark. They persevered. They made it! Look at them now! *This calls for patient endurance on the part of God's people.* This Revelation is given to say, 'Look at what has happened to the those who persevered.' They made it to the other side of the sea! They are singing! So keep going. That is the heart of Revelation. Don't give up. Jesus wins!

The picture of this final victory is the backdrop going on to the final bowls of God's wrath. But before we go on to the bowls, we are given this introduction in 15:2 that takes us back to the Exodus with a song of Moses by the sea. There are actually two songs of Moses in the OT. One is in Deuteronomy 32, the other is in Exodus 15 (that takes place beside the Red Sea) and is similar to what is happening here after the victory over the enemy. We see the Red Sea connection in **what looked like a sea of glass mixed with fire and, standing beside the sea, those who had been victorious over the beast and its image and over the number of its name**. It's the triumph of those victorious standing by the sea! That would make John think of Exodus 15. And what follows? Seven bowls with seven plagues. Now we are really connecting to Exodus. The plagues of Egypt! And here, just as in the Exodus, when God's people made their escape and deliverance from Egypt through the Red Sea, what happened next? A victory song at the other side!

This scene shows the **sea** has been tamed and so has the Beast, as they are **victorious over the beast**. The OT often uses the sea as an image of evil and chaos, and it has already been used in that way in Rev. 13:1. But here it is no more in chaos. No more evil. No more uprising. Even the sea is calm! Though we note it is mixed with fire. Fire is a metaphor for judgment (used 21 times in Revelation), so we see the finality of the judgment against the Beast in this victory. It's like we are looking at a smoking gun. *Victorious over the Beast* is the picture we get here and the believers in the Lamb share that victory. Both the Preterist and the Futurist would say these are not all the believers in heaven joining in this victory song, but only a select group who had to tackle the Beast. In both these views the Beast is confined to a relatively short time of history. If you are of the Preterist view you confine the work of the Beast to before AD 70, and the Futurist says the Beast only comes on the scene for a short time in the future (seven years), so only those *who are victorious over the Beast* in that short time are singing this victory song. It's a select group in heaven. Most Christians from the church throughout history are also in heaven, but they are not involved in this victory song over the Beast in this view.

But I want you to note this is the same heaven we were introduced to in front of the sea of glass back in 4:5-6, and just as in that heavenly scene, the calm sea was all around the throne of God, so this is a picture of all people in heaven. We have looked at various reasons why the Beast is not confined to a short time before AD 70 or a short time way in the future. The Beast is made in the image of the Dragon. The Beast works with the Dragon, and just like the Dragon, he has been around attacking the people of God for a *long* time, including attacks on the first readers of Revelation in Asia Minor in those churches, and all the saints throughout history. They have all found comfort in the book of Revelation through their struggles with its central message that we all agree on. Jesus wins! Over the Beast!

Now what we are seeing in 15:2 is that victory. It was all worth it! Being faithful through the time that sorely tested your *patient endurance*. All those times when the world was tempting you. All those times when it would have been so much easier to go along with compromise. When the Beast made it permissible to sexually exploit women on TV, movies or the computer screen. Everyone was into it. But you held fast. You fought with patient endurance. Likewise, when the Beast made it so much easier to go along with the crowd, it even affected your economic opportunity, with just a little compromise you could have had more to buy or sell. But you stood your ground with patient endurance. The Beast made it politically incorrect for you to witness to your faith, and you were made to look like a fool. 'What! You don't believe in sexual freedom, marriage equality, abortion or euthanasia?' But despite the attacks, you stood up for the Lord with patient endurance. You showed love in the face of the Beast's enemy attacks. You displayed the fruit of the Spirit with love and joy in the middle of attack. Was it for nothing? And now you see ... *those who had been victorious over the beast and its image and over the number of its name* (15:2).

This is a picture of victory over the Beast. We know by now the Beast is not a physical creature, but a symbol taken from the beasts of Daniel 7. That is, the Beast is worldly powers. The image and his number and his number represent man and the marks of worldly ways, and all the temptations to compromise. It seemed so often that Christian people were defeated. They fought on but it looked like the Beast was winning. But here is the full-time result. The final score? Jesus' people—standing! *Those who had been victorious over the Beast ... are standing* (15:2)! The battle seemed to go on and on. Did you feel it saints? The saints are downcast by the ferocity of the Beast and its attacks, but those who are faithful will stand in this victory. There is a victory, but it is not finally in this world. There is a plan and justice and reward. There is meaning to this battle against the Beast. Your efforts serving the Lord will follow you and be rewarded (14:13).

Revelation is written to make plain that though it *seems* like the Beast is winning, though it *seems* like the Beast has the power and upper hand, though it *seems like* your efforts are unnoticed, though it *seems* like faithfulness has no reward, though it *seems* like you are losing, and your life is not all what you had hoped, all is not what is *seems!* Jesus wins! This is written to you. This calls for patient endurance of the saints and this victory is your answer as to why!

Revelation is pulling back the curtain on reality. There comes this day. And you get to learn to play the harp ... eventually. **They held harps given them by God.** For some of us it will take a lot longer than others to learn to play the harp. That might be why heaven is for eternity. But the 'victory' (overcoming the Beast) is a theme in Revelation (interspersed in between judgment scenes) which refers to not just a portion of Jews (as some with the Futurist view), not just a limited number who fought the Beast near the end of history (Futurist), not just a limited number who fought the Beast before AD 70 (Preterist), but for *all* in heaven who have victory over the Beast throughout church history. Those who were *victorious*. It is the theme that starts with the letters to the Christian churches and continues throughout the rest of Revelation. How could we miss it? To those first people who read Revelation, Jews and Gentiles, six out of seven churches were told: *To the one who is victorious*. This whole book of Revelation was written to them, and now they see what Jesus meant, and what it finally comes down to when he said *to the one who is victorious*. This is it here in Rev. 15! They can all see it now.

It stood out for the first readers, because in the original Greek language when it says *those who were victorious* (15:2), it is actually the *same* Greek root word used every time in the letters to the churches when Jesus told them, *to the one who is victorious*.... It's like a buzzword for those first readers. They heard it over and over again in their letters (Rev. 2-3). So they knew this was written to *them!* It's also written to all Christians, you who are victorious! This is written for you to persevere! This calls for the patient endurance of the saints.

Not everyone gets those harps. How do you know if you will persevere if you have been struggling? That is what Revelation is written for. It's written to backsliding churches. If you have backslidden, if you are lukewarm, or if you have lost your first love, this is the message for you! Repent and believe the gospel. It's the same message Jesus had for the churches. Whoever has ears, let them hear! Those who are victorious—get to sing.

> ... and sang the <u>song of God's servant Moses</u> and the song of the Lamb: 'Great and marvelous are your deeds, Lord God Almighty. Just and true are your ways, King of the nations' (15:3).

Here we see this picture that is pointing back to the OT victory celebration of their salvation in Exodus 15, when the Israelites crossed through the Red Sea on the way to the Promised Land, when they reached dry land and they **sang the song of God's servant Moses**! Here they are in Rev. 15 with the people of God having crossed through their own terrifying battles on *their* way to the Promised Land, and they sing the song of Moses, and the song of the Lamb. Does that mean they sang two songs?

In actual fact, the song that follows from 15:3 is not taken directly from either of Moses' songs in Exodus 15 or Deuteronomy 32. (This song is a composite from Exod. 34:10, one snippet from Moses' song in Deut. 32:4, Ps. 86:9, 98:2, 111:2, 139:14, 145:17, Isa. 2:2, Jer. 10:7, 11:20, Amos 3:13, 4:13, and Mal. 1:11.) So it's not even trying to replicate the old song of Moses at all. So why is it called a song of Moses? Also, the words are not part of any official 'song of the Lamb' either. We do have hymns in Revelation referring to the Lamb. So why is it referred to as the song of Moses and the Lamb? Well, the song relates to both Moses' song and the victory of Jesus in the sense that it is the salvation song of all God's servants which ultimately points to the one saving work. One song. One salvation. One people of God. We must sing to the Lord the new song of the

Lamb and what he has done, but it's not disconnected with what God was doing all along with the people in Moses' time.

I have been arguing against the popular idea that Revelation is largely speaking about a specific group of Jews at some future point. The gospel that we find in the OT and NT is represented here. We have seen constant references to the joining of the Gentiles to Israel in the gospel as being a fulfillment of the promises to Israel. A kingdom and priests, the New Jerusalem etc. Here the song of Moses and the song of the Lamb confirm the two become one in one victory song. This is the mystery of the gospel Paul describes in Ephesians 2:11-22, that Jesus broke down the wall of hostility ... Jew and Gentile become one, with Gentiles also receiving the blessings of the covenant of Israel. He calls it the mystery of the gospel! It is the same gospel that has been preached from the beginning.

> There is neither <u>Jew nor Gentile</u>, neither slave nor free, nor is there male and female, for you are all one in Christ Jesus (Gal. 3:28).

This gospel joins the two and makes them one! In Romans 11, Gentiles are grafted in with the natural branches of Israel. We have also looked at Eph. 2:11-14, which specifically says that in the gospel Gentiles and Jews are no longer two but one, and that formerly Gentiles were excluded from citizenship in Israel, but are now included in citizenship in Israel. We saw how the woman in Rev. 12 represented the people of the Messiah before he came and after. Again, that's why Paul called the Galatian Christians the 'Israel of God' (Gal. 6:16), and the mystery of the gospel is that the Gentiles are joined as one to Israel (Eph. 3:6). So what we have here in our text is the culmination of this great mystery. One song. Moses and the Lamb together! One people of God. One salvation. There is a sense in which the new covenant people sing the song of Moses and the old covenant people sing the song of the Lamb. It is all pointing to the one salvation of the one Lord and one people of God. This is the real point of departure I have with the idea of Jewish temples being rebuilt or Jews being saved *separately* at some future point. God will continue to bring in his ethnic people Israel to their Messiah and the whole mystery of the gospel is that it brings the two together to sing one song *together*. Moses and the Lamb. The final goal, even of the temple of God at the end of Revelation has its foundations made up of both Jew and Gentile joined *together*, with the names of the 12 tribes *and* names of the 12 apostles. As Paul says in Ephesians 2:21-22 together you, Jew and Gentile, are being built into *one* house of God. We don't have separate houses! No separate churches for Jew and Gentile to worship. All worship in Christ together. One song.

The connection is extraordinary. Moses and Jesus. Moses is pointing to Jesus as fulfillment. Moses' deliverance was celebrated with a song of Moses and was to be commemorated every year throughout history as the celebration of the Passover lamb, which reminded the people of God what the Lord had done. But the Passover lamb has massive overtones for us this side of the cross. Jesus is the Passover Lamb for Jew and Gentile who trust in him.

This connection with Exodus gets deeper the more you look at it. We have seen references throughout Revelation alluding to the OT, especially books like Daniel and Exodus, but many of these connections seem to be saying that it is more than just an analogy or metaphor. The connections speak of a richer meaning behind them. We have seen the example of the Israelites wandering through the wilderness, and then in Rev. 12 with the woman (the people of the Messiah beginning in the old covenant producing the Messiah and reaching into the new covenant after Jesus' ascension). She is said to have her own desert wilderness wandering. In other words, these things that happened long ago to the Israelites were real, and yet in the amazing sovereignty of God, they were also a forerunner of how and what the people of God would go through in the new covenant. It's kind of scary. Just how far are you willing to believe in the sovereignty of God? It's all planned. History repeating itself and showing us what *must* happen, and yet we are living it out as real. What goes around comes around. We need to read the Bible in a new light. All those things of the OT relate to what God does again. You see it in the life of Jesus and all the prophecies that preceded him. Christ is there when King David says he thirsts, and he is given vinegar for his thirst. Or when he is betrayed by those closest to him or …

> All my bones are on display; people stare and gloat over me. They divide my clothes among them and cast lots for my garment (Ps. 22:17-18).

Those things really happened to David, but we know they were also really experienced by Jesus much later in history. It was all a plan. It goes around! It comes around! This world is rigged! God is not leaving anything up to chance. This song of Moses is indeed also the song of the Lamb because the first deliverance by the sea was real in history and was looking to the other deliverance to happen in history. The ancient people of God went through the wilderness on their way to the Promised Land and along the way were nourished by the manna from heaven, but not by bread alone, but by every word that comes from the mouth of God. And now the church (including *you* individual Christian), has to go through its (your) own wilderness wandering. You are taken care of, that is, nourished by the word of God during this sojourn on your way to the ultimate Promised Land. It was all a plan. Just as Moses and the people were pursued by the enemy and were able to sing the victory song by the sea after their enemy was vanquished, so too now, the people of God pursued by their enemy finally are singing, with the Beast having been vanquished.

We are the people of God, who by faith have to walk through the frightful Red Sea with the enemy pursuing us. But we too will arrive safely on the other side and we will sing. Oh, how we will sing! The song of Moses yes. But more. The song of the Lamb!

When those Israelites of old made it to the bank of the Red Sea and burst into song—that was you … to come! You were there! Well no, you weren't literally there, but you were planned in that very history unfolding. There is nothing new under the sun. The new Exodus. The escape from the slavery. It was the Lamb who saved us! Now we know it was the cross! It was hidden in shadows in the Passover lamb they would kill. But it was Jesus who was killed for our sin in order to defeat our great enemies: sin, death and hell. It was a great substitution. It was his death and hell in exchange for yours, so you could celebrate this victory.

If you have not yet really seen the magnitude of what God has done, enter into it by faith now, because without faith you won't escape from the God who has planned everything, including your life. Either you will enter his plan or be like the Pharisees who 'rejected God's purpose for themselves' (Luke 7:30). Turn from deeds of darkness and believe in Jesus and you too will be victorious! You become part of God's plan. The wilderness has been prepared for you to go through. It's a tough journey, but it *is* a plan!

And read your OT and the book of Exodus with different eyes now. All the promises of God are, *yes and amen in Jesus!* They were all there all along. There is nothing new under the sun. God is unfolding it all just as he has done, only in more fullness. Your life and path have been planned and mapped out long ago. Now walk in it. Don't try to get around the wilderness. Be faithful until the victory song. It's an old song and yet it is a new song. Why? Because it brings the fullness of the meaning in the new covenant in the Lamb of God.

... and sang the song of God's servant Moses and the song of the Lamb: 'Great and marvelous are your deeds, Lord God Almighty. Just and true are your ways, King of the nations' (15:3).

Study Questions

1. Within two verses (15:1-2) there is both the threat of judgment and a victory song. What, if any, is the connection?

2. Give two possible connections for the scene of the 'sea' here.

3. What message was this scene meant to give to the first readers?

4. Is this only a select group of Christians singing? Give reasons.

5. Why would the word *victorious* mean so much to the first readers?

6. Where can this song of Moses be found elsewhere in Scripture and where is the song of the Lamb?

7. What are these two songs combined conveying? Support your answer from other parts of Revelation and other books of Scripture.

8. How might the connection of the two songs affect our OT reading?

9. How does God's bringing his people to victory through the wilderness help you reflect on your own pilgrimage?

27
Why They are Singing
(Revelation 15:3b-4)

Imagine you are in a church in Ephesus in the first century. You live in the city of Ephesus (in Asia Minor which is modern day Turkey), and your church is the first of the seven churches to receive this book of Revelation from your former Pastor, the apostle John. He has sent it to you from the island of Patmos where he is now imprisoned by the Roman Empire. You have been reading through this scroll in your worship services each Lord's Day. You have just read in Rev. 13-14 about the Beast and the mark of the Beast. You understand the Beast is worldly power that persecutes the church and you don't need any pre-historic rocket science to figure out that the Beast in your day has to be the Roman Empire. The same Beast you have just read about looks like he is winning because the very apostle John who is writing this to you is writing from jail, where he has been imprisoned by the Beast! So then, you start to read Rev. 15 and you are introduced to the final round of God's judgment, the bowls, but just before you get into that, you get this picture of heaven. And it's this song of Moses and of the Lamb.

> ...and [they] sang the song of God's servant Moses and the song of the Lamb: 'Great and marvelous are your deeds, Lord God Almighty. Just and true are your ways, King of the nations. Who will not fear you, Lord, and bring glory to your name? For you alone are holy. All nations will come and worship before you, for your righteous acts have been revealed' (15:3-4).

We noted in our previous chapter the words of the song are not taken from the original song of Moses sung by the sea in Exodus 15. The original song has as much to do with proclaiming God's justice upon the powers of evil as to do with rescuing his people. It points back to the injustice, the slavery that occurred in Egypt, as part of

God's motive for the rescue. And here in this song in Rev. 15 it has all praise. **Great and marvelous are your deeds, Lord God Almighty. Just and true are your ways.** That theme wouldn't be out of place in either the first song of Moses, the Exodus deliverance song, or the singing of the Lamb who was slain and the defeat of our enemies: sin, Satan, death and hell.

In one part in the Exodus song, there is a rhythm in the original Hebrew language that is difficult to capture in English. Scholar John Durham notes there is a staccato style in the original Hebrew language with the repeating of the phrase, *I will… I will…* In Exodus 15:9 that is a kind of mockery of Pharaoh's arrogance, mimicking the way Pharaoh unrelentingly hounded the Israelites.[27] In other words, 'I will get them. I will do this. I will do that.' Just as a relentless enemy that seemed unstoppable pursued the Israelites, the Devil and his Beast pursue us relentlessly! Pursuing, pursuing …

But it turns out these foes, relentless and powerful as they were, are defeated. This then is victory! So they sing this song of Moses. And all that seemingly 'neck and neck' level of struggle against Pharaoh and his magicians back in Egypt, as though they were genuine rivals to the living God, have now been literally submerged beneath the sea when the Israelites sing Moses' victory song.

That is what those first readers are meant to see when they see this Revelation version, the victory song by the sea, the song of Moses and the Lamb. In fact, this is for all believers for their strengthening. You don't have to wait until we get to the end to see *how* it ends. In the midst of this book of Revelation, of battling Beasts and Dragons, with judgment still to come, the Lord gives us snippets of heaven along the way to remind us when you are at the bottom, just when you think you can't go on, he shows you the finish line to lift you up to finish the race. There you are singing the victory song. *'Great and marvelous are your deeds, Lord God Almighty. Just and true are your ways …'* The phrase *just and true are your ways* is taken from Psalm 145.

> The LORD is righteous in all his ways and faithful in all he does (Ps. 145:17).

Other translations of Psalm 145 say *kind* or *gracious toward all he has*

---

[27] John I Durham, Word Biblical Commentary, Exodus, (Waco Texas: Word Books, 1987), p.207

made. Now that is interesting, because here in Rev. 15, the context is the people of God victorious and seeing the judgment of God poured out on their enemies. They battled the Beast and now 15:2 says it's a victory celebration *over* the Beast, just like the original song of Moses where the people see the demise of unbelievers in the Red Sea. As this Revelation context suggests, the people in heaven are rejoicing in the victory and the demise of their enemies. Interesting indeed. We see that most graphically in Isaiah 66:24, where the saints look down on those in hell. And yet here in Rev. 15, the song borrows from Psalm 145, which says the LORD is gracious or kind to all he has made. Just and true are all his ways. This alludes to that question we looked at in Rev. 14. How could redeemed saints in heaven look down upon people in hell and be rejoicing in song? Well, the answer has not changed, but in this text, we are seeing it from the point of view of the victors (whereas in 14:11, the scene was from those in hell). Hell is a terrible place to be, but there is nothing unkind, unloving, or ungracious about it. His ways are always right. *Just and true are your ways*. The Lord is kind to all he has made, so there can be nothing 'unkind' about his judgment. I have personally found Psalm 145, and now 15:3 reassuring to know one thing is certain: No one we know in hell is experiencing anything from God that is cruel or unjust, indeed nothing that is unloving or unkind, but only that which is *just and true*.

The only question saints in heaven will have is, 'How come I'm not there as well?' 'What am I doing here?' That is when the rejoicing really begins, when we can really understand the words of this song. How richly I deserve to be there, receiving what is *just and true* from God. It's only then we will see something of the cross. We really did deserve to be there. Why would God save me if I *should* be down there? And we will burst into song ... **'Great and marvelous are your deeds, Lord God Almighty. Just and true are your ways, King of the nations. Who will not fear you, Lord, and bring glory to your name? For you alone are holy. All nations will come and worship before you, for your righteous acts have been revealed.'**

All nations will come! Everyone. Do you see the song of the Lamb in there too? Every tribe, nation and tongue. *All nations will come and worship before you*. All those who worshiped the Beast now see who the true God is. The idolatry of man is exposed, judgment is seen to be right and fair, and *your righteous acts have been revealed*. People who claim they are not religious are now shown up for their inner selves. They *were* religious! Don't say you didn't worship other gods. You did worship—the Beast! You worshiped things, people, idols, even yourself! But always to the exclusion of the true God, never submitting your life to the one who gave you, life, breath and everything in it. The lie will *not* go on any longer. And we are given the reason why the Lord is to be worshiped. He alone is holy.

> Who will not fear you, O Lord, and bring glory to your name? <u>For you alone are holy</u> (15:4).

God alone! Set apart and pure. God alone is the one who has the authority to determine right from wrong. Humans tried to usurp that power, and the result was the fall of this world. Yet God withheld his righteous judgment on that rebellion and evil. But not anymore. Why did he hold back? He gave a day of grace for those who would repent, but few took up the pardon. The Lamb came and was slain, but it mattered little to most. They didn't want forgiveness. They didn't think they needed it. They didn't like what the Lamb said. They rejected the Lord. They said of the LORD and his anointed, *Let us break their chains and throw off their shackles* (Ps. 2:3). They didn't want his restrictions, so they worshiped the Beast and his image, the counterfeit. Now the true God is shown up as God. He alone was right. He *alone is holy*.

So this is the song of Moses and the song of the Lamb, and the believers who have been victorious sing it. This is the song we need to sing each week—the song of Moses and the song of the Lamb. (It's a wonder the church has not had more music put to these literal words.) But it's more than just these specific words; it's the truth they convey. The point is it's a worship celebration. It's a song we will sing when we look back on the enemies cast down: the Beast, the Devil, sin, death and hell. For now, we gather together to worship God each week with the foretaste of this future. A reminder of what has been accomplished as we sing, *great and marvelous are your deeds*, and look forward to that final victory, when *all nations will come and worship*.

This is what this book of Revelation is doing by putting this song right in the middle, between judgment visions. We are about to see the seven bowls poured out straight after this (the completion of

God's wrath). This is what those Christians were reading in the first century while enduring attacks from the Beast. Judgment is coming, and this is how it ends. Jesus wins. So resist the Beast and keep persevering.

That's why the church worships together. You've heard friends or family, nominal believers who don't know Christ tell you 'I believe, but I just don't need to go to church.' We could respond by saying, 'Well you don't obey God's command to not give up meeting together' (Heb. 10:25). But that ends up sounding a bit like law, as if coming to church makes you a Christian. So we could talk about the need for fellowship and teaching, but they might just say, 'I can manage on my own thanks. I have Jesus in my heart.' But the real issue for people who claim to believe but don't come to worship with God's people is that they don't have faith. Many will say, 'But I do have faith in Jesus.' So how can I say they don't have faith?

Well picture the saints of old who sang the song of Moses at the other side of the Red Sea at the Exodus. Just before that event, the Israelites believed they were truly doomed. They had come to a halt at the edge of the sea. Pharaoh's army appeared on the horizon. They could hear the sound of horses' hooves, the sound of chariots with armed and dangerous men, with a bloodlust, riding fiercely towards them. The Israelites were certain they would all be slaughtered ... men, women and children, because they were backed against the Red Sea. 'Now what are you gonna do Moses? We always said you brought us out here to kill us. Pharaoh and the Egyptians figure if they can't keep us as slaves, they will kill us.' This is the OT version of the Beast—the earthly power that oppresses and persecutes God's people. And just like the Beast, we know the devil is behind it. We noted the original Hebrew in Exodus 15 has this staccato style in the song which mocks the Egyptians boasting of their thirst for blood. It's a staccato rhythmic style that can't really be captured in an English translation, but if you can picture the heavy breathing as they bear down on the Israelites backed on to the Red sea. In Exodus 15:9 there is this repeating. 'I will, I will.'

> The enemy boasted, '<u>I will</u> pursue, <u>I will</u> overtake them. <u>I will</u> divide the spoils; <u>I will</u> gorge myself on them. <u>I will</u> draw my sword and my hand <u>will</u> destroy them' (Exod. 15:9).

Picture them driving, driving, driving with murderous intent, with deep, smelly, panting breaths in rhythm with their lurching forward. This was the enemy pursuing them. And this is when the Israelites must have thought, 'We're dead, our families, our children are going to be slaughtered. We are caught between the devil and the deep blue sea. And the sea is not even blue … it's red!'

Then God did the impossible! Moses raises his staff and the sea parts for them to go through! But who is going to go first? It's parted, but for how long? Who said it's going to stay like that? Moses looks at the two walls of water and when they said, 'You go first Moses.' Moses takes up his staff and says, 'Not me, I gotta hold this thing up. You go first.' 'No, I insist you go first.' But there was no choice. 'If we stay, the Egyptians are sure to kill us.' So they set off on this frightening trek.

It must have been the most terrifying path through the bottom of the sea. It's bigger than the greatest seismic sea wave held up in midair. On both sides! Will it hold? They take one terrifying step after another with their enemies bearing down on them to kill them. Breathing down their necks. On each side of them, there are two walls of the sea. Could they see the sharks and stingrays swimming beside them like in an aquarium? Or was it too raging to see anything on the other side of the wall of water? Finally, they get to the other side! And they turn to see their enemies are still in hot pursuit, breathing, bearing down. But at God's direction, Moses releases the sea and it caves in on the attackers. The enemies are vanquished!

What do you do with that? What did *they* do? If you really lived through that, what would you do? I'll tell you what they did. We read about it in the first song of Moses in Exodus 15. They worshiped God! They worshiped! They sang the song of Moses.

If you know the living God who brought about this event in history, you will know he now tells us he has given us an even greater deliverance. You too were in slavery—slavery to your enemies who pursued you. The devil, the Beast, sin, death and hell. But Jesus cast down those enemies! He triumphed over them by the cross. We can sing this song of Moses *and* the song of the Lamb! We have more this side of the cross! We come together each week to worship God for our rescue and seek to do his will on earth as we see it done here in heaven. That is, we worship together.

Of course, phony 'believers' will never get that. When those

Israelites made it to the other side do you think they sang that song with an attitude, 'We must come together and sing a song to God so we can be good enough to get to the Promised Land?' Of course not! You have already been saved! Do you think they were worshiping God in Moses' song so that they could feel good? 'Oh yes, we should join Moses and the crew in the worship service to help us get through next week as well.' Would those Israelites worship with that song because they felt guilty or duty-bound, or because it's what Pastor Moses told them? None of these!

When you *really know* God has rescued you, you don't question why you should come together to worship God. You know! It's not just because God has commanded you, even though he did. It's not just whether you get something out of it, even if you do. It's not just because it helps. In fact, it's not about you at all! It comes out of a heart that overflows with gratitude to God. It comes from *faith!* Only a heart that has really *believed* in the rescue can respond in worship for the sake of God. Can you answer these questions: Have you really seen it by faith? Do you believe? Do you desire to worship? Are you really standing this side of the Red Sea having seen the rescue? Or are you still to be rescued? Have you really seen what God has done? Have you really seen the cross? The song of Moses *and* the Lamb?

Those Israelites must have learned that song and practiced it on the bank after their rescue. They sing like they have never sung before. We don't sing the exact same old song of Moses by the Red Sea. Why not? We haven't been there! You can't sing the song as they did. You haven't been there with chariots, Egyptians and the Red Sea.

Why does the unbeliever or phony 'believer' see no importance to worshiping at church? Because they haven't been there! They don't know the cross of Jesus! They have never seen themselves on the cliff about to drop into a hell that would be so *just and true*. They haven't seen the Savior plunge into that hell for them. They can't respond with unconditional worship. They have no *faith!* Only God's true people can sing it!

What about those Christian readers who know the Lord in those churches under pressure in Smyrna and Pergamum? Or those reading it in the churches in the Middle East right now, or in China, or in Frankston North in Australia? God has planned to have you all sing this song in the future together. It's the song of victory of Moses and the Lamb. But he gives you this sneak preview into the future.

Even before he tells you of the judgment coming on the earth. Why? So you will hang on. So you won't give up. So you will sing the song of Moses and the Lamb now in anticipation, knowing that you have a sure and certain victory to sing it in the future. Can you see yourself singing? That's why we gather at church services. To worship! This is a foretaste of the future in Rev. 15. This song is for you. The victory song. The song of Moses and the Lamb. Two eras, but one song. One God of deliverance. And as you read those words you can see the Exodus deliverance and the cross fitting perfectly.

… and sang the song of God's servant Moses and the song of the Lamb: 'Great and marvelous are your deeds, Lord God Almighty. Just and true are your ways, King of the nations. Who will not fear you, Lord, and bring glory to your name? For you alone are holy. All nations will come and worship before you, for your righteous acts have been revealed' (15:3-4).

Study Questions

1. What elements of the song in Rev. 15 could apply just as easily to those singing the original song of Moses in Exod. 15?

2. What is there in the song in Exodus with the enemies bearing down that could apply in the new covenant?

3. How does the context of the song in Rev. 15 minister to us when we think of those who have died without being saved?

4. Make a list of ways this song is truly a song of the Lamb.

5. What are some excuses nominal believers make as to why they don't attend church, and how do you usually respond?

6. How does this text cut through to the heart of why we should attend church services?

7. Why is being a regular part of a church a matter of faith?

28
The Ten Commandments
(Revelation 15:5-8)

I hope you love to sing because we keep getting these pictures of heaven in Revelation and they often seem to involve singing. So it turns out the contemporary style of worship got it right after all. Endless singing! Maybe the contemporary style services are preparing saints for the discipline you will require in heaven—to just keep on singing, another chorus, and another, forever and ever. Well, not really. In fact, we have seen heaven already and will see more of it as we go through Revelation, and there is a whole lot more to heaven than just singing. In fact, the section in Rev. 15 has only a single song (not endlessly repeated). You also notice when Jesus and his disciples sang, it was a single hymn (Matt. 26:30), so maybe we should only have one song per worship service? But I don't think any of that is meant to be prescriptive. The real point about this song is that it comes as the interlude, the triumphant vision of heaven before the judgment. It's the victory song of Moses and of the Lamb.

So if this is the victory song then why is it that John has yet *another* vision which goes back to more judgment? How can we go back to judgment if we have been in heaven? And it's not just any judgment, but the most complete and terrifying judgment. The famous seven bowls of God's wrath which 15:1 says are the *last* of God's judgments. By now we understand these visions of heaven are interludes to remind the struggling, persecuted Christians to keep their eyes on the finish line.

But this also brings into focus the question of how we understand Revelation with the seven seals, seven trumpets and now the seven bowls. Many have understood them to be occurring one after the other. But if that is the case, how do we have this great victory celebration with a song of Moses and the Lamb occurring *before* the pouring out of the final seven bowls of God's wrath? Answer: We have seen that the seven seals, trumpets and bowls are *parallel*.

They are different camera angles of the same time period, but each one revealing more of what *leads up* to the final judgment. If you remember my analogy of when my son gave me a present, a large package. I opened it up and inside was another package. Open it up and inside was another package. That is what is happening in Revelation. Each package reveals more inside rather than packages given separately one after another. So when we got to the end of the seventh seal, we looked inside that seal and we found seven trumpets. And the whole process of building up to the end begins again. So too, at the end of the trumpets. We look inside and the bowls are poured out. So the seals, trumpets and bowls are happening alongside each other. Several packages, but inside one another, all given at the same time.

But that doesn't tell the whole story either. We must not forget that Revelation is always progressing. As we move through the seals, trumpets and then bowls, there is also a progression. Each package reveals more and more and builds up in intensity, all leading to the final judgment. The seals affected one-fourth on the earth, the trumpets increased to one-third and we will see the bowls are completely poured out. After the seven bowls, there are no more packages inside. There is no more after the bowls! Because this is the last—where God's wrath is completed.

> I saw in heaven another great and marvelous sign: seven angels with the seven <u>last</u> plagues—<u>last</u>, because with them God's wrath is <u>completed</u> (15:1).

So while they are parallel, they are different camera angles revealing different details. The first four trumpets affect nature, whereas the first four bowls affect evildoers. Even though they might occur alongside each other. Many of the effects on nature, especially things like famine, affect both nature and man, and when the natural world is affected so are humans. But what the bowls are giving us is revealing more of the intensity and progression towards the final judgment.

Look at the parallels in both the trumpet's plagues and the bowl's plagues …

Trumpets: 1st Earth; 2nd Sea; 3rd Rivers; 4th Sun; 5th Darkness for the evil; 6th the Euphrates and demonic influence on evildoers; and 7th Final judgment: lightning, sounds, thunders.

Bowls: 1st Earth; 2nd Sea; 3rd Rivers; 4th Sun; 5th Darkness for the evil; 6th the Euphrates and demonic influence on evildoers; and 7th Final judgment: lightning, sounds, thunders.

They are also similar in that they are both drawing on the plagues from the Exodus. We will get more into that in the individual bowls. But the parallels are not meant to be exact. They are different camera angles so there are differences as they reveal more. But they all lead up to the end. So while we don't get into the specifics of the bowls being poured out in Rev. 15, we are introduced to the angels at the starters' blocks about to burst out to deliver them.

> After this I looked, and I saw in heaven the temple—that is, the tabernacle of the covenant law—and it was opened. Out of the temple came the seven angels with the seven plagues (15:5-6a).

Before he even sees the angels, the first thing John noticed was the temple. There are two main words in the original Greek language that are used for the word *temple*. One refers to the entire temple complex. The other refers only to the sanctuary, that is, the holy place and holy of holies, where only the priests were allowed to enter. The Greek word John uses here to describe the temple is the second. But wait. 'Look at this,' says John as he sees the vision! The holy sanctuary is **opened** and visible! To John this is the vision form of what happened after Jesus went to the cross and the curtain of the temple was torn in two. Jesus' death provided access into the temple, into the presence of the Lord. We, ordinary sinners, can now see into where we could not see before. **After this I looked and in heaven the temple—that is, the tabernacle of the covenant law** ... And just when you thought we had seen the connection with the Exodus and wilderness wanderings, he sees *the tabernacle of the covenant law*, as Stephen the disciple said in Acts …

> 'Our ancestors had the tabernacle of the covenant law with them in the wilderness. It had been made as God directed Moses, according to the pattern he had seen' (Acts 7:44).

John is describing the heavenly temple in its Exodus recognized form, the tabernacle. But this is even more interesting. It's *the tabernacle of the covenant law*. Why does John see the tabernacle of covenant law and not the 'tent of meeting'? There is a significant reason. In Exodus, Moses placed the two tablets of the covenant law in the ark of the tabernacle (Exod. 31:18). What are the two tablets of the covenant law? The Ten Commandments. Most commentators point out when 15:5 highlights *the tabernacle of the covenant law*, it's highlighting the Ten Commandments (TC), the written testimony of God. The 'two tablets of *covenant'* are the TC.

Along with the *tabernacle of the covenant law*, the tabernacle was also the location of the mercy seat, but here we are being introduced to the bowls of God's wrath, a time when the day of mercy is over and judgment comes. How will God judge this world? By what standard? The rich young ruler asked the question: 'What must I do to inherit eternal life?' (Mark 10:17). And Jesus replied with the TC. What standard will God judge people by? The tablets of the covenant law. The TC which humanity has trampled upon will be the standard the Lord will judge by—his holy law. The tablets of the covenant law contained in *the tabernacle* are the criterion God will use as judgment that is about to follow in the pouring out of the bowls. But what if you have never heard of the TC? How can they judge you? Well, the Lord even has that covered. He says in Romans 2:14-15 that the law is written on the heart of every human being and God will judge the conscience of men and women according to that law which is written on their hearts. How did God see Cain's murder of Abel as wrong when Cain had not yet received the TC? Because the law is written on the human heart. Yes, our own rebellion causes us to suppress, ignore or sear our own conscience, but it's in there.

So, in our text this tabernacle of the covenant law **was opened** ... What's inside? The TC, but this *tabernacle of the covenant law* has another reference point in the book of Revelation. The word in the original Greek translated 'covenant law' is the same word that is usually translated *testimony* or *witness*. It's that same word we have seen before and is where we get our English word *martyr*. That is why most other translations call it the tabernacle of *testimony* or tabernacle of *witness*. This verse does not occur in a vacuum. Revelation is revealing things about Jesus. This same word *testimony* is used another 17 times in Revelation, always referring to the testimony of Jesus himself. Jesus is the prototype who gives the faithful *witness* or *testimony*. He is the faithful and true *witness* (3:14). We have seen before that Jesus is also the true tabernacle in John's other writings.

> The Word became flesh and made his dwelling among us. We have seen his glory, the glory of the one and only Son, who came from the Father, full of grace and truth (John 1:14).

Remember the Greek word for *dwelling* is literally *tabernacled* amongst us. It's a strange playing with grammar that highlights *God with us*. God was with his people in the tabernacle in the OT, which was always pointing to Jesus. Jesus is God with us in the flesh. All the promises of God are 'Yes' and 'Amen' in Christ Jesus. Or in John 2:20-22 they spoke about the earthly temple, but the temple Jesus was talking about was his body. Jesus is the true temple, not the shadow. Jesus is the true tabernacle. So by what standard will God judge the world? His holy law in the TC (the *testimony* of the covenant law), *and* the *testimony* of Jesus! God will judge by and through the Son of God.

What has this introductory vision in 15:5 got to do with the bowls of God's wrath about to be poured out? Two things. The wrath that follows is due to humanity's rejection of God's holy law, the TC, *and* the rejection of his Son. This testimony is coming from heaven itself and heaven will require it of you, if you have rejected this testimony. So John sees the angels coming up the runway out of the temple for this judgment ...

> Out of the temple came the seven angels with the seven plagues. They were dressed in clean, shining linen and wore golden sashes around their chests. Then one of the four living creatures gave to the seven angels seven golden bowls filled with the wrath of God, who lives for ever and ever (15:6-7).

What do angels look like? What do they wear? Remarkably similar clothing to what Jesus wore in 1:13, which suggests these angels are carrying out the work of their master. Also note the golden bowls are filled. Back in 5:8 there were golden bowls filled with the prayers of God's people. In 6:9-11 God's people prayed *how long before you judge the evildoers of the earth?* How long will evil reign? Well, now this seems to be more of God's answer to those prayers. The Lord had not forgotten those prayers in the golden bowls. He returns the golden bowls filled with his wrath against evildoers.

We also note that 15:7 highlights that God is the one **who lives forever and ever**. All the things we put our hopes in, rather than God, are idols. Idolatry is one of the primary sins highlighted in Revelation, and of course is forbidden in the second commandment in the tabernacle of covenant law. All idols will die, but the Lord is the only one who lasts *forever and ever*.

His justice also lasts forever. Doesn't it send chills down your spine when you hear people talk about someone who just died saying, 'Oh, they are in heaven now.' Really? I hope they are. And maybe they are. But how do you know? 'He was a good person.' But what standard will *God* judge humans by? The TC and his Son. If you thought that by ignoring him God would go away, it won't work. You might die, but God doesn't. He is the one *who is forever and ever!* You can't escape his wrath even in death. I like the way Michael Wilcox puts it. It's like a horror movie where you try to escape the thing you fear by locking yourself inside a dark refuge, only to find that you have locked yourself inside with the thing you were fleeing from.[28] Dying just locks you into the presence of God. The Lord and his wrath are forever and ever…

> And the temple was filled with smoke from the glory of God and from his power, and <u>no one could enter the temple</u> until the seven plagues of the seven angels were completed (15:8).

No one can get inside the temple for the glory of God. This helps to remind us that this is about the glory of God. Even the wrath of God is about the glory of God. And the plagues are not just coming from angels or the living creatures but from the Lord himself.

For John, this is familiar Exodus imagery with the glory cloud, but also for John the real reminder is Ezekiel 10:2-4 and especially Isaiah 6:1,4, because Isaiah is the only other place where it is said the *smoke* filled the temple. John is actually seeing this vision and it's so mind-blowing that even these mighty angels and heavenly beings can't come into the presence of the Lord because the glory of the Lord *fills* the temple. It was the same situation in the OT when Moses

---

[28] Michael Wilcock, The Message of Revelation, BST (London: Intervarsity Press, 1989), p.143

couldn't come into the presence of the LORD (Exod. 40:34-35).

How awesome must be the presence of the LORD? Who can stand in his presence? Isaiah couldn't. And there was that smoke ...

> In the year that King Uzziah died, I saw the Lord, high and exalted, seated on a throne; and the train of his robe filled the temple. Above him were seraphim, each with six wings: With two wings they covered their faces, with two they covered their feet, and with two they were flying. And they were calling to one another: 'Holy, holy, holy is the LORD Almighty; the whole earth is full of his glory.' At the sound of their voices the doorposts and thresholds shook and the temple was filled with <u>smoke</u>. 'Woe to me!' I cried. 'I am ruined! For I am a man of unclean lips, and I live among a people of unclean lips, and my eyes have seen the King, the LORD Almighty' (Isa. 6:1-5).

Woe to me, I am ruined, a man of unclean lips! It is the same awesome scene John sees in Revelation where even the sinless angels can't come into his presence. **And the temple was filled with smoke from the glory of God and from his power, and <u>no one could enter the temple</u> until the seven plagues of the seven angels were completed.** No one could enter the temple until the wrath of God was completed. The time for praying to God has passed! He is answering the prayers of his people who called out for justice with the ultimate answer. But now you can't get into the temple, not even with a prayer, until this is completed. God has held back his anger through the ages. Held back, held back. But when he lets it go, the time for prayers of intercession is finished. Not even prayers can get in now. *No one could enter the temple.* The Lord has set the course and he will not stop.

This symbol is no longer that of shadows of the OT. The Lord said in Hebrews the earthly temple that was *made with human hands* was *not* the true temple. This heavenly temple is the *true* temple. This is the undiluted, pure presence of the Lord himself. Yes, symbolized with all these familiar OT trappings, but symbolizing the fact that the true temple is the presence of the Lord.

So now the angels are released to judge—to pour out the bowls of God's wrath. And what standard does God judge by? The testimony of the tabernacle of the covenant law! What testimony? Do you know the TC? It's written on your heart. Just in case you haven't seen what's written on your heart lately, I have it written down here for you:

THE TEN COMMANDMENTS

1. You shall have no other gods before me. *Love the Lord your God with all your heart and with all your soul and with all your mind and with all your strength* (Mark 12:30).

2. You shall not make for yourself an idol in the form of anything in heaven above or on the earth beneath or in the waters below... *They worshiped and served created things rather than the creator...* (Rom. 1:25).

3. You shall not misuse the name of the Lord your God... *But I tell you that men will have to give account on the day of judgement for every careless word they have spoken* (Matt. 12:36).

4. Remember the Sabbath day by keeping it holy. Six days you shall labor and do all your work but the seventh day is a Sabbath to the Lord your God. ... *Let us not give up our meeting together as some are in the habit of doing* (Heb. 10:25).

5. Honor your father and your mother... *Children obey your parents in the Lord for this is right* (Eph. 6:1).

6. You shall not murder. *You have heard it said, 'Anyone who murders will be subject to judgment, but I tell you that anyone who is angry with his brother will be subject to judgement'* (Matt. 5:21-22).

7. You shall not commit adultery. *But I tell you that anyone who looks at a woman lustfully has already committed adultery with her in his heart* (Matt. 5:28).

8. You shall not steal. *Do not be deceived: ...thieves... will not inherit the kingdom of God* (1 Cor. 6:9-10).

9. You shall not give false testimony [lie]... *...and all liars — their place will be in the fiery lake of burning sulfur* (Rev. 21:8).

10. You shall not covet...anything that belongs to your neighbor ... *you covet and cannot have what you want* (Jas. 4:2).

This is the criteria with which God judges the world. God's standard. What did Jesus say earlier in Revelation? *...I am he who searches hearts and minds, and I will repay each of you according to your deeds* (2:23).

Man set up his own standard and decided he would determine right and wrong when he rebelled against God in the first place, but God's standard will not change *forever and ever.* This is the wrath of God we are about to see unleashed against the idolatry of man setting up his own gods. *The tabernacle of the <u>covenant law</u> was <u>opened</u>!* (15:5). The TCs were there to be seen. Who can stand? Look at God's standard that was kept in the tabernacle of the covenant law. How are you doing with God's standard? If you are honest you should be undone in the sight of the TC. But there is another testimony God has given through whom he will judge this world. The true tabernacle. The one who tabernacled amongst us. God will judge through his Son. The apostle Paul said, *For he has set a day when he will judge the world with justice <u>by the man</u> he has appointed ...* (Acts 17:31). He will judge by Jesus. And everything will come down to this question. What did you do with Jesus? God came down. The offer was there. But what if like the Pharisees who *refused to come to [Jesus] to have life* (John 5:40), you have clung to those idols and trampled on those TC?

If we are to be judged by the TC, we have as much hope as the rich young ruler who walked away sad. But God's testimony is not completed with only the Law. God sent his Son to be punished for all the times you have broken the commandments *and* to free you from your sin. But it's only for those who repent and humble themselves before the true Lord, trusting in what he has done at the cross to take away their sin as far as east is from the west. It's for those who are no longer following idols of their own making but are following the true Lord. It's for those who no longer make up their own right and wrong, who no longer trample on the TC deliberately, and who hate the sin that nailed Jesus to the cross. It's for those who throw themselves on the mercy of the Savior, obeying as the Lord enables, with joy, knowing the one who took away their hell for every time they fall short. So, obeying, but in freedom! Freedom to serve and obey knowing you have a Savior. That is how you are characterized, as ... *those who obey God's commandments and hold to <u>the testimony</u> about Jesus* (12:17). If you are a true believer, the wrath of God was poured out already! Not on you, but on the cross of Jesus. Hallelujah! What a Savior!

And the temple was filled with smoke from the glory of God and from his power, and no one could enter the temple until the seven plagues of the seven angels were completed (15:8).

Study Questions

1. How do we reconcile the finality of judgment after the seals and trumpets, and yet a new description of heaven comes in Rev. 15 and then the bowls of judgment begin?

2. Give examples of partial judgments that show the trumpets and bowls could be parallel.

3. If there are parallels between the seals, trumpets and bowls, then how do you explain the differences?

4. What part of the temple is John looking into and why is that significant?

5. Why is seeing the tabernacle of the covenant law important in relation to judgment coming?

6. What would come to John's mind when he sees the glory of the Lord and what is the significance of that?

7. How does viewing the Ten Commandments make you respond?

8. God also judges by his Son. Does that mean we no longer need to concern ourselves with obedience to the TC?

29
The First Two Bowls
(Revelation 16:1-3)

The apostle John is shaking in his sandals again at the visions he is receiving. Awesome sights and this time—awesome sound. A voice from inside the temple. A *loud* voice. In 15:5-8 it was the Lord God who was in his temple and no one could enter for his glory, so surely this is God himself whose voice thunders when he says it's time for the wrath of God to be poured out. So here it is ...

> Then I heard a loud voice from the temple saying to the seven angels, 'Go, pour out the seven bowls of God's wrath on the earth' (16:1).

The angels have been on the starting blocks since 15:1. Now the starter's gun is blasted. Trumpets warn. But now we are up to the bowls. No more warnings.

Notice the timing is down to the second. The angels have been ready since early Rev. 15, but they ain't movin' until the *second* they are called by that loud voice in the temple. **Go!** The voice of God. God is in control! The judgments that come upon this world, including those partial judgments that happen in our time, are timed down to the millisecond. They will not happen one second before, or one second after. And now the time has arrived.

Just as Jesus drank the cup of God's wrath (metaphor for God's judgment), so these bowls of judgment are to be poured out ...

> The first angel went and poured out his bowl on the land, and ugly, festering sores broke out on the people who had the mark of the beast and worshiped its image (16:2).

Sores on your skin! Ugly and festering! What might the people in those seven churches who first received Revelation have thought of this? In fact, not only them, but what about any Christian over the past 2000 years who knows their Bible? Does the sight of these plagues bring to mind anything? Something the Lord has done in judgment before? The plagues of Egypt! Here the plague in 16:2 is said to be <u>*ugly and festering sores*</u>. Sound familiar? It would if you know this ...

> Then the LORD said to Moses and Aaron, 'Take handfuls of soot from a furnace and have Moses toss it into the air in the presence of Pharaoh. It will become fine dust over the whole land of Egypt, and <u>festering boils will break out on people and animals</u> throughout the land' (Exod. 9:8-9).

But they break out on particular people ...

> The first angel went and poured out his bowl on the land, and <u>ugly, festering sores</u> broke out on the people who had the <u>mark of the beast</u> and worshiped his image (16:2).

By now we know the mark of the Beast is deeper than just a visible outward tattoo, and we noted if all unbelievers had a tattoo on their foreheads it would make evangelism easy. 'Don't bother telling him the good news, he has the mark.' Or is it a mark you can wash off if you are converted? No. We have already considered the mark of the Beast as a distinguishing mark that is borne out in the way people live as they worship the Beast. Either in what they put their hand to (mark of the hand), or what they believe in their mind (mark of the forehead). *By their fruit you will recognize them.*

We've noted before that all the views of Revelation take the Beast as *symbolic* of worldly power of some sort. If we all agree the Beast is symbolic, should that help us interpret this verse? If the Beast is symbolic, and the mark of the Beast is symbolic of something deeper and more significant than just an outward sign on the skin, could it be that the mark of pain on the unbelievers might also be deeper than just a bad case of shingles? We don't have to rule out literal **ugly, festering sores,** cancers or diseases that break out on people, but this could be *worse* than physical boils. It may be symbolic of other painful afflictions.

When the fifth trumpet sounded tormenting people, we looked at the possibility of the psychological torment, so this bowl could be either psychological *or* physical torment in the body of unbelievers, who would not give up their idolatry, as later verses explain. Idols always cause pain. They promise so much, but it's not just that they don't deliver the satisfaction they promise, but they leave people hollow and tormented. Mick Jagger's girlfriend, L'wren Scott, a famous fashion designer and well ... Mick Jagger's girlfriend! She has it all, right? But she committed suicide. Depressed. Robin Williams, great comedian and actor. Suicide by hanging. Depressed. Charlotte Dawson, Sydney TV presenter and famous model who had everything going for her. A glamorous lifestyle and a career in TV. She hanged herself. Depressed. Annalise Braakensiek, international model and supporter of those suffering depression also committed suicide. The Beast is a cruel master. The list of people who 'had it all' but end up like this just goes on and on. They kill themselves either deliberately or end up destroying themselves with drugs or alcohol. Every time it happens, the press and social media light up and everyone wants to know how someone who 'has it all' could be so depressed to want to commit suicide.[29]

There were hints all was not right with L'Wren Scott when on one of her final postings on Instagram she said: *Fashion is the armor to survive the reality of life.* Fashion? Fashion obviously doesn't make good armor.

Then the second bowl is poured out ...

> The second angel poured out his bowl on the sea, and it turned into blood like that of a dead person, and every living thing in the sea died (16:3).

Again, the first readers of Revelation along with any careful reader of the Bible would think of the judgment on Egypt ...

> This is what the LORD says: 'By this you will know that I am the LORD: With the staff that is in my hand I will strike the water of the Nile, and it will be changed into blood. The fish in the Nile will die, and the river will stink; the Egyptians will not be able to drink its water' (Ex. 7:17-18).

Remember the parallel between the trumpets and the bowls. We are up to the second bowl, and the second trumpet was also associated

---

[29] https://www.telegraph.co.uk/women/womens-life/10705706/LWren-Scott-deserves-to-be-remembered-in-her-own-right-not-just-Mick-Jaggers-girlfriend.html

with the sea. A third of the sea turned to blood. But we are learning something new here. This is not a third, but total. What is going on? The whole sea turned to blood. The great advantage if you hold to the Futurist view of Revelation is that no matter how difficult it looks, if it is happening in the future, God can do anything! But Futurists, including some of the most conservative literalist scholars, recognize the difficulty here and allow for symbolism on this verse. Biederwolf sees the death of people here in the sea as the death of nations, but in the sense of morally and spiritually.[30] Even John Walvoord has room for symbolism on this one, saying the sea does not become literally human blood and the sea may be limited to the Mediterranean.[31] No doubt Walvoord and others like him see the difficulties of having enough literal human blood to fill the sea. The other reason even many literalist scholars may have seen this as symbolic is that when it says **every living thing in the sea died**, the Greek word in the original language for 'living thing' is literally every 'soul'. Soul is used about 100 times in the NT and every time it refers to humans. If that is the case, then having literally every single soul in the sea, die half-way through the tribulation would not fit with any view, not the Preterist, Historicist, Futurist or the Idealist. This one is difficult. The question becomes not *if* it is symbolic, but *what* does it symbolize? And we are still no closer to understanding what all this is, or when it all happens.

Some have suggested the sea itself is symbolic of people who die. That is not as farfetched as it might first seem. Remember the Beast comes up out of where in 13:1? The Sea. We know the Beast is symbolic of worldly kingdoms. So what would governments be doing coming up out of the sea? Remember the sea is a well-used metaphor in the OT for evil, but also specifically for unbelieving nations (Isa. 17:12-13). Now in 16:3 the sea (unbelievers) experiences death, symbolized by blood. This is not such a great leap as you might think, to take waters symbolizing unbelieving nations, because in the very next chapter Revelation specifically says the 'many waters' the prostitute sits by are actually a symbol for unbelieving nations …

---

[30] cited in *Revelation Four views,* Ed. Steve Gregg, (Nashville: Thomas Nelson Publishers, 1997), p.361
[31] Ibid

> Then the angel said to me, 'The waters you saw, where the prostitute sits, are <u>peoples, multitudes, nations and languages</u>' (17:15).

Unbelieving nations! In fact, it's possible the waters mentioned in 16:4 represent unbelievers, as 16:6 says *they* (the waters) *shed the blood of your people*. Literal waters don't usually persecute saints, people do. So with the sea turning to blood at the second trumpet, we saw blood is a great metaphor for death. It could be referring to the death of sea creatures, but this could also be talking about the death of humans.

As in all of Revelation, I am approaching this with some caution and trying to have some humility. What is even more difficult is that there seems to be no agreement between scholars who would otherwise agree with each other on their overall view. So even if I can convince you of a particular interpretation, or you have your favorite view, or that of your favorite scholar, ultimately, we are all wrong because what good is a word from God that the whole body of Christ has not been able to benefit from? If it's only select theologians who have been able to get this right, then how can this be a blessing for all who read it and take it to heart?

Is there a big picture God is teaching us here which transcends and even uses the different views that might speak to everyone? We know the big picture of the whole of Revelation that all Christians can take away. Jesus wins! So is there a 'big picture' way of looking at Rev. 16? All the views of Revelation agree that for the bowls, the forerunner or influence or inspiration are the great plagues in Egypt. What is the big picture that we get from the bowls that follows on from the seals and the trumpets? It's the same thing as the judgment that fell on Egypt. When judgment fell on Egypt, it didn't all happen at once. God's judgment came in warnings. It built up in intensity—up and up until the full and final judgment came. God reveals his holy character. A God of grace warning and a God of justice in full and final judgment. The Egyptians had no excuse with all those warnings. That is also the big picture of Rev. 16. It follows the progression of the plagues of Egypt! Warning after warning until finally, no more warnings. God is revealing himself from heaven now. This is what the apostle Paul taught in the text we keep referring back to …

> The wrath of God is <u>being revealed</u> from heaven against all the godlessness and wickedness of people, who suppress the truth by their wickedness, ... (Rom. 1:18).

The apostle Paul says in his day God was *already* revealing his wrath from heaven. So Revelation is revealing more of what Paul said. God is slowly revealing himself and his judgments through the church age. The wrath of God *is* being revealed. In Romans, Paul talks about men being given up to themselves and suffering the penalty, which can include physical illness and death, or it could be the emotional torment of life for those who rebel against God. But partial judgments are being revealed which lead up to the final judgment. The warnings along the way culminate in the completeness of the bowls.

No matter what our interpretive framework of Revelation, we can agree on this much. If we use the plagues of Egypt as our guide, they are warning plagues. They increased in severity and intensity. Warning after warning after warning. But the warnings were not heeded. The people of Egypt from Pharaoh down treated them as though 'it was just bad luck, we will always bounce back.' But there came a time when there were no more warnings. The final judgment was completely poured out. Was it a harsh judgment on Egypt? The death of their firstborn and then drowning in the Red Sea! That's harsh. But is it really so harsh in light of the *constant warnings* and the stubborn refusal to heed all that had gone before it? They were without excuse. Without excuse? Sound familiar? In the same Romans passage where the apostle Paul said God is revealing his wrath to humanity, he also said God made himself plain to humans through the things he made so that man is what... *without excuse!* (Rom. 1:18-20). God doesn't leave us without warning.

The one thing we can *all* take away from Rev. 16 is this. The absolute *certainty* history *will* repeat itself. Just as it did in Egypt. Warning after warning, but they will run out and the full bowls of wrath *will* be poured out. Death is happening before our eyes.

The seals were opened. One fourth. The trumpets warned. One third. People die. Land, vegetation, animals and humans afflicted and still no one sees this world is under judgment. The bowls seem so extreme, but are they really? The warnings came repeatedly just as they did for Egypt, they didn't listen. And one day—no more warnings. Jesus said people would be eating, drinking, marrying and giving in marriage right up to the day. People go on doing ordinary things, as if the warnings were of no consequence. 'It must be bad luck!' But like a thief it will come!

We might not be able to agree on when this is happening, but I think it's important to remember Jesus' words, that his second coming will be *like a thief*, that is, unexpectedly. Read Rev. 16 again and read it through the lens of those words of Jesus in the gospels, that he will come like a thief. After all, if unbelievers are walking around with a literal tattoo on their foreheads saying 'Beast' and the sea literally all turns to blood and everyone in it dies, if it is all so obvious then Jesus will *not* be coming like a thief! Thieves don't advertise their arrival so blatantly. It won't happen so we can say, 'It's okay Jesus. We've read Revelation and we know when you are coming!'

As if to underline the importance of this, what do we see pop up in Rev. 16? Jesus quoting himself from the gospels, *Look, I come like a thief!* Whichever way we interpret the bowls, it can't contradict Jesus' words. He will come unexpectedly. The end will not come with your careful observation. This is another reason why even though I am holding loosely to the details and am open to correction on the finer points, I am staying with the idea these bowls occur during the church age, parallel to seals and trumpets, though showing the progression of greater intensity to the end. You just won't be able to plot Jesus' return! It could be unfolding right under our eyes.

William Hendriksen says if you think of the seals, trumpets and bowls as parallel, they can serve two purposes concurrently. A warning from a trumpet for one might be a final judgment for another. Hendriksen uses the example of how Herod's disease ended in death for him. But what was final and fatal for Herod (a bowl) served as a warning (a trumpet) and moved others to fear the Lord.[32] We can trace it through history. What is for one person a trumpet, that is, a warning, for another is the full bowl poured out, death. For some they already had their trumpet warnings, so death comes and it's all too late. Straight to hell and no more warnings. So God works out his great purposes with the seals, trumpets and bowls in parallel,

---

[32] William Hendriksen, *More Than Conquerors*, (Grand Rapids Michigan: Baker Book House), 1967, p. 194

but always intensifying to the end. We see it in horrible ways with shocking things going on in some countries where people are brutalized,[33] and yet for some of those it causes them to cry out and heed the warning, so for them it leads to eternal life. *Oh, the depth of the riches of the wisdom and knowledge of God! How unsearchable his judgments,* ... (Rom. 11:33).

The reason this could all be happening now is that even though death is not the final judgment, it seals the fate eternally of those who die unrepentant. For many the full bowl is poured out on them. Their fate is sealed forever. We take death for granted. People actually say it is part of life. How oxy is that moron? How is death part of life? See how Jesus was so deeply troubled at the death of Lazarus that he wept. He knew he would raise Lazarus up, but Jesus grieved at death as the ultimate intrusion into God's world. It's not normal. Unbelievers die. Everyone dies! But for every soul in that sea that dies (if the sea represents unbelieving nations), there is no escape once they die. The whole bowl is poured out on them. Death comes as a judgment. It stands out as a great warning and turning point for others. A trumpet blast! The wrath of God *is* being revealed from heaven.

But how do we explain the fact that these things don't just happen to *un*believers. *Believer*s can receive painful sores (cancers and diseases) or can suffer economic devastation and other torments. *Believers die* just as often as unbelievers. How could this whole thing of disease (painful sores) and death be a bowl of judgment only to unbelievers?

There is a massive difference. Don't miss it. Do we really believe the Scripture that tells us God works all things together for good for those who love him? That promise in Romans 8:28 (and most people miss it), is in the context of suffering. *Our present sufferings are not worth comparing with the glory that will be revealed* ... (Rom. 8:18). Sufferings are working in the life of the believer to produce an eternal glory that far outweighs them all (2 Cor. 4:17). They are working out a *refining* in our lives. Faith. Suffering *produces* (Rom. 5:3-4)! Do you believe this? There is no believer who has suffered physically or financially or even died who has not had the Lord working it for his or her good. You

---

[33] See Tom Doyle, Killing Christians, (Nashville, Tennessee: W. Publishing Group, 2015)

might not see the immediate good while you are going through your particular difficulty, but who are you going to believe? God, or your current feelings? All believers will look back and see God was doing good. This is one of the great themes of Revelation and where it finally heads. Unbelievers suffer in this life and die to their great loss and destruction due to the warnings and judgment being revealed from heaven on this world. But believers experience suffering and even death to their great gain! Better by far!

We need to get this into our heads. It's no use calling yourself a Christian if you don't *believe*. Revelation and the gospel are about a bigger picture of the whole of life. The promise from God for his people is that all things work together for good. But not just that. What does the very next verse say? You were predestined to be conformed to the likeness of God's Son (Rom. 8:29). That is the plan. You are to become more like Jesus before you get to heaven. And what did the Son go through? Suffering! The testimony of so many Christians who have been struck by different illnesses is that they saw the Lord work great good through it. This is Revelation. Re-read those first seven letters and see all that the Lord is promising in the midst of their *suffering*. For those who are faithful a crown awaits. Hidden manna. Heavenly reward for suffering. While in this life the Lord is refining his people ('those I love I rebuke'), he is blessing and transforming them into the likeness of God's Son with every increasing glory (2 Cor. 3:18). The promise to the church at Philadelphia was that he would keep you through the trials (3:10). Jesus died to take judgment for you, and that love will continue for all who repent and believe. For those who reject that love ...

Then I heard a loud voice from the temple saying to the seven angels, 'Go, pour out the seven bowls of God's wrath on the earth.' The first angel went and poured out his bowl on the land, and ugly, festering sores broke out on the people who had the mark of the beast and worshiped its image. The second angel poured out his bowl on the sea, and it turned into blood like that of a dead person, and every living thing in the sea died (16:1-3).

Study Questions

1. What OT imagery are the bowls modeled on, and in particular, the first bowl?

2. What are some of the ways those *painful sores* can be seen in our world today?

3. Why is it that the rich and famous are just as prone to suicide?

4. Why do those even among the most ardent literalist scholars allow for symbolism for the sea turning to blood?

5. Is interpreting the sea as 'unbelievers' a realistic option?

6. If we can never figure out how to interpret the details of this text, is there an overall lesson in it that most people could take away?

7. How does Jesus' warning that he will come like 'a thief' help us put a perspective on this text?

8. How can the trumpets and bowls be working in parallel when they may be the same event?

9. How can these bowls only affect unbelievers when believers also experience disease and death?

30
The Third and Fourth Bowls
(Revelation 16:4-9)

Ever heard this one? 'I would repent if I just had more evidence.' Hold that thought.

The bowls of God's wrath are being poured out. We have seen the warnings intensifying on earth with the seven trumpets. But now the bowls signal the end is nigh. And we are seeing that instead of people heeding the warning they are unrepentant. The world is under judgment and it is unbelievers, particularly those who persecute God's people, who are receiving this judgment.

But when is this happening? The Preterist has some good arguments here for their pre-AD 70 timeframe. The Jewish leadership had persecuted the saints (16:6) and the 'prophets' throughout the ages, and when judgment came with Rome surrounding Jerusalem, the water supplies were contaminated, but worse, it became somewhat literal with the bloodshed that followed. So this is one way we could understand this verse...

> The third angel poured out his bowl on the rivers and springs of water, and they became blood (16:4).

When we were looking at the trumpets we looked at all the ways 'blood', as a metaphor for death, can occur from water, that is, from contamination. It was not hard to conceive of one third of the world's water supplies, including in third world countries, carrying diseases that could cause sickness and death. But remember in our previous chapter we noted Revelation later uses *waters* as a symbol for unbelieving nations, even spelling that out in 17:15. The waters there are actually the unbelieving nations! So could this explain these waters here?

That would mean the bowl poured out on the rivers and waters is a judgment poured out on unbelievers causing death ('blood'). In our previous chapter, we also looked at the fact that death comes to unbelievers as a judgment, while for the believer the same death is deliverance to 'better by far'. But like the rest of this most difficult chapter, it's hard to be certain of the meaning of the details, and even if you think your interpretation is correct, it's hard to find anyone to agree with you! There is little consensus even amongst scholars who hold the same *overall* view.

Some say the waters are referring to economic devastation, famines etc., based on other references in Rev. 18, and that could be. So, what is the answer? Remember our big picture that transcends our different interpretations. These bowls are drawn from the Egyptian plagues. The warnings came and came, but Pharaoh and most Egyptians would not listen. They took the warnings in their stride and after each judgment warning they returned to their lives without change. But the full and final judgment did arrive. This is what the bowls teach us. The wrath of God comes partially, one-fourth in the seals and one-third in the trumpets. But there comes a time when there is no more warning. The bowls are poured out. Notice the angel does not see the striking of the waters with death as cruel or harsh. You were warned! So it is declared just!

> Then I heard the angel in charge of the waters say: 'You are just in these judgments, O Holy One, you who are and who were, …' (16:5).

But what about the innocent believers? They suffer and die too. Where is the justice? But they were not forgotten.

> '…for they have shed the blood of your holy people and your prophets, and you have given them blood to drink as they deserve' (16:6).

People have said this verse is the classic 'the punishment fits the crime'. Those who persecuted Christians, including shedding the blood of the saints, receive what penalty? **Blood to drink as they deserve.** This might have been familiar to John, a student of the OT Scriptures from his boyhood. He would recognize this from …

> I will make your oppressors eat their own flesh; they will be drunk on their own blood, as with wine. Then all mankind will know that I, the LORD, am your Savior, your Redeemer, the Mighty One of Jacob (Isa. 49:26).

In that Isaiah context, drinking your own blood was figurative language. It does not mean every single oppressor literally drinks their own blood, but that severe judgment will definitely come upon them. It's the same figurative language in Psalm 79:3, 10, 12. So even though it's symbolic, it is symbolic of a just judgment that only the Lord can give …

> And I heard the altar respond: 'Yes, Lord God Almighty, <u>true and just are your judgments</u>' (16:7).

The main point being made here is exact justice, a *punishment that fits the crime*. Spill blood. Drink blood. God is just. We remember that from …

> Show no pity: life for life, eye for eye, tooth for tooth, hand for hand, foot for foot (Deut. 19:21).

People use 'eye for eye' to criticize the Bible as though it teaches personal vengeance. But the opposite is true. The OT context is *civil justice*. How was Moses to carry out justice as the civil ruler and judge for his people? Answer: Justly. If someone kills your ox, pay back an ox. If someone steals your goods, they have to pay back exactly that plus interest. Our current justice system could learn from this. It's the principle of appropriate punishment to fit the crime. So eye for eye, tooth for tooth is the principle on which Moses and his magistrates were to carry out justice. There is no record of any Israelite ever literally having his or her eye gouged out or losing any tooth as the result of a court decision, but that was the guiding principle for implementing justice. The punishment should fit the crime! And that is the principle here. Blood for blood. You shed blood. You will drink it. It's a metaphor and the point is that these persecutors are getting exactly what they deserve. And when that happens this is the response.

> And I heard the altar respond: 'Yes, Lord God Almighty, true and just are your judgments' (16:7).

A voice from the altar responds. This is the classic connection back to 6:9-10. In Rev. 6 the souls who had been slain were under the 'altar'. The altar is the protection of Jesus who was slain for them, but this **altar** reminds us of *their* prayer from under the altar, 'How long O Lord?' When will justice come? Again, this is their answer. But when does this *next* bowl happen?

> The fourth angel poured out his bowl on the sun, and the sun was allowed to scorch people with fire (16:8).

Here we get another hint this is symbolic language. The angel pours out his bowl on the sun. It must be a mighty big bowl! It's the same kind of language which follows in the rest of Revelation. Even Futurist scholars generally see some sort of symbolism here. Some say the sun represents a supreme governing authority. But even if it is symbolic, it doesn't rule out symbolizing different effects the sun can literally have. The sun burns. One skin cancer website says ...

> Over the past three decades, more people have had skin cancer than all other cancers combined.[34]

One person dies of melanoma every 57 minutes. Today we have all the troubles of ozone layer depletion and we see a rise in the incidence of skin cancer. **The sun was given power to scorch people with fire.** The trumpets had fire symbolizing the land in famine. Could this include the same thing? Christians also get skin cancers, but their trials work for their good because whatever this is symbolizing, the judgment coming on the unbeliever is in *complete contrast* to the picture of what happens to the believer, as they are delivered through death as we already saw ...

> Never again will they hunger; never again will they thirst. <u>The sun will not beat upon them, nor any scorching heat</u> (7:16).

Believers are delivered in death and even fire that comes upon them in this life (illnesses from the sun), will be used for their good. But by the time we get to this stage the warning factor in these judgments appears to be almost totally useless. The unbelievers are not interested in repentance at all.

> They were seared by the intense heat and they cursed the name of God, who had control over these plagues, <u>but they refused to repent and glorify him</u> (16:9).

---

[34] https://www.skincancer.org/skin-cancer-information/skin-cancer-facts

I know of people dying of skin cancer who have cursed God, and it's not unusual that the worse their illness gets, the more they dig their heels in. Pride is an amazing thing. People say they want evidence, but do they really? Years ago, I had regular discussion with a man who showed interest in the gospel. We would meet every week, but it didn't matter how many questions I answered, he would quickly move on to the next one without skipping a beat, as if the last one was now irrelevant. On one occasion I asked him, 'What if I could answer all your questions to your satisfaction, would you fall at the feet of Jesus and repent of your sin? Would I see you in church next week and every week, as a Bible carrying Christian?' He just smirked. We continued but didn't get anywhere, and eventually we lost touch. Many years later he showed up at my church and said he had become a Christian. I asked what happened and he said, 'Remember when you asked me if I got every answer I wanted, would I repent? And I thought to myself, no I wouldn't. I don't want to repent. So it always bothered me that evidence was not really the issue. I just refused to repent.' That story had a happy ending because the man came to his senses as to what the real problem was. And that is a good question to try next time someone says to you they just want 'evidence'. But by the time we get to the bowls it is too late ... *They refused to repent and glorify him.'*

Of course, we can and should give answers to people about genuine faith questions (1 Pet. 3:15), but 'answers' and 'evidence' are not the underlying issue. I remember hearing a story years ago of an atheist from the Skeptics Society telling someone from Creation Ministries, 'I wouldn't care if you discovered Noah's ark and wheeled it down Bourke St. I still wouldn't believe.' And that is why we read ... *'Yes, Lord God Almighty, true and just are your judgments'* (16:7). The judgment is deserved. It's *true and just.* They were unrepentant. But surely you would humble yourself before God if you knew he was judging you?

They cursed the name of God, who had control over these plagues. Can you believe people would do that even while judgment is falling? When could a time come when people who are under judgment actually curse the name of God? Do they even know they are under judgment? The hint is in that verse. They cursed the one *who had control over these plagues* ... It's an almost redundant phrase. Of course the *one who had control over these plagues* is God. In other words, they cursed the God whom they knew *had control over these plagues*. Isn't that what people do? They get angry at the things 'God is doing'. They know somewhere deep down it is the hand of God. They know it's him who is bringing judgment! If they didn't know God exists, why are they angry with him?

But when is this all happening? The Preterist says it's in the first century. The Historicist says it's also in the past. The Futurist in the future. The Idealist says it's now and throughout the last 2000 years. Perhaps we will never be able to settle it. But consider this. There is no debate that elsewhere in the NT the apostle Paul says what you see in this world now is God bringing judgment and people remain unrepentant! I know I keep bringing us back to this text, but it speaks volumes in interpreting Revelation. Here it is in more fullness …

> The wrath of God <u>is being</u> revealed from heaven against all the godlessness and wickedness of people, who suppress the truth by their wickedness, since <u>what may be known</u> about God is plain to them, because God has made it plain to them. For since the creation of the world God's invisible qualities—his eternal power and divine nature—have been clearly seen, being understood from what has been made, so that people are without excuse. For <u>although they knew God</u>, they neither glorified him as God nor gave thanks to him, but their thinking became futile and their foolish hearts were darkened (Rom. 1:18-21).

Judgment has been coming from heaven on people who know God since Paul's day. They obviously don't know God in a relationship sense, but they *know* he is there. It's the same thing in Rev. 16. They suppress the truth even though the wrath of God *is* being revealed! So in the verses about the waters in 16:4, or sun judgments in 16:8, whether the 'blood' is death and people are dying, or even literally people are getting skin cancer, they all add up to the same thing. The details might be disputable, but one thing is not, this is a world under judgment! The wrath of God *is being* revealed from heaven. It's right before our eyes. Everyone is dying. Death is not normal, but we keep acting as though it is! Cancers and a world in chaos. In our previous chapter, we saw the painful sores upon people. Is that normal? Even unbelievers know it's not normal. That is why they complain and curse God! They say God is evil for doing this! People *curse God* all the time!

You probably know people who think God is harsh and that's *why* they won't repent. It's like the parable of the talents when the master effectively says, 'Well if you thought I was harsh, then all the more reason you should have not buried what I gave you' (Matt. 25:24-25). Even if you really believe God is harsh, then shouldn't that wake you up? It's no excuse to not repent. Of course God is not harsh, but that attitude shows how just and true are God's judgments.

Do the partial judgments of God intensify more before the end? How much more? That we don't know. This could be it! We are oblivious to how most of the world lives (and dies!) because the Western world simply doesn't experience the same level of persecution, starvation and disease as other countries. We are living in Pontypandy with Postman Pat! But if you see death, cancer, disaster and famine coming upon the world and wonder if there is a God, surely at the very least you can deduce that he is not happy with what we are doing. But instead people curse God. Who curses God? People do it every day! They reject God for allowing all this to happen! They *expose* they know it's coming from God! After a huge tsunami wiped out many lives an unbelieving friend said to me, 'We shouldn't be surprised God brings these things considering what we do.' I was impressed that an unbeliever had that insight, but she still didn't repent! And still hasn't to this day. And that is the scariest part of all. They don't even have the excuse that they don't know God is there. Did you notice that? They *refused to glorify him*. Similar to that same Romans passage where Paul says the wrath of God is being revealed from heaven, then he says, although they *knew God they neither glorified him as God*. Deep down in their hearts they knew it was God. They just refused to glorify him.

This puts a whole new perspective on the excuses people make when they say, 'I can't believe. God can't blame me for that. Not enough evidence.' The word of God says you lie. Deep down in your heart you suppress the truth by your wickedness. Anti-Christian sentiment and cursing God is at a level we have never seen before. The God people reject is blamed for everything! The new atheism is illogical. Whatever happened to, 'I don't care what you believe, as long as you don't push it on me'? Now with the likes of Richard Dawkins it's as though he *hates* the God he doesn't believe in. And they remain unrepentant to the end, even when the bowls are being poured out. History is being repeated. The Scriptures are not a random disparate group of events. They teach us.

When Israel rebelled against God, God determined to punish them using Babylon to exile them, removing them from God's city and temple in Jerusalem. There were no more chances. It was too late. The judgment had fallen. But God still said if they submitted to their punishment and went with the Babylonians, they would live and God would bless them in their exile. That's like a microcosm of this world. This world is gone. Judgment is already underway, and a day of full judgment is still to come. It could be any day. But all is not lost. Submit to the God of judgment. When you see the judgments coming on the world, when you see death, disaster, disease, and evil men committing evil, given up to themselves, instead of rebelling more, know that there is still hope. God will judge the evil and he will judge you if you don't repent. But what then? Your repentance won't stop the judgment. The city is lost. This world is lost. You might say, 'What is the point of submitting if we have lost it anyway?' Answer: Everything. This was what God said to Israel with the same situation. Judgment is underway and certain judgment is coming …

> Furthermore, tell the people, 'This is what the LORD says: See, I am setting before you the way of <u>life</u> and the way of <u>death</u>. Whoever stays in <u>this city</u> will die by the sword, famine or plague. But whoever goes out and surrenders to the Babylonians who are besieging you will live; they will escape with their lives' (Jer. 21:8-9).

He said judgment had already begun on Jerusalem and would be completed. So get out of that city and submit and you will be kept. It is the same for us. We can't stop the judgment this world is under either, but you can submit to God. Don't pull a Lot's wife and look back at what you're losing in this material city. God said to the Israelites, 'I'm setting before you life or death! Choose life!' It's too late to make this home! Did you get that? It's the same for us. It's too late to make this world home! But God says he will bring those who *do* submit to restoration and joy. But only for those who repent! God has been making it clear that this world is doomed by dropping bombs of judgment upon it. It's intensifying. Death comes! There are deadly plagues. A barrage of plagues has hit this world. One after another. What world are you living in? How could you miss it? And blood! Death. Everywhere death. The world is cursed. We are so used to it we think it's normal, but death is the result of a cursed world. And death happens to everyone! And all these things coming upon the earth are intensifying during the church age as the seals, trumpets and bowls are released. But still they refuse to repent. Still they curse the name of God!

What would you do if you were God in this situation? You have the power to judge, but people just curse you! The unrepentant commit even greater evil. The very people (sinners) who caused this world to be the way it is curse *you!* What would you do? We know what we would do if anyone treated us that way. Bring it on! Fair judgment is what they deserve. Pound them! That's what we would do!

But what does God do? He sends his Son into this enemy territory, into the enemy war zone, into this cursed world. This evil rebellious world is the world God came into to save it. Jesus went to the cross to pay the judgment in advance. For whom? Not for those who remain unrepentant. But for those who will repent and believe in Jesus.

And if you do repent you still have to go through the wilderness! That is why we have this theme in Revelation: *This calls for patient endurance and faithfulness on the part God's people* (1:9, 13:10, 14:12). Jesus' bride suffers. Suffering and death also come upon *believers*, the innocent and righteous, but for their good, for the kingdom and for their transformation. And death is a wonderful transport to glory. Now you suffer grief in many trials. These have come for your refining. Suffering produces! But for the unbeliever suffering is just suffering. And death is an express chute into hell. Judgment. The bowls are being poured out! In this world now he sets before us the evidence of judgment. And he calls on us as he did to the Israelites long ago. I set before you, life and death. Now will you repent and choose life? Or remain as the many...

They were seared by the intense heat and they cursed the name of God, who had control over these plagues, but they refused to repent and glorify him (16:9).

Study Questions

1. What is the central theme of the bowls that we can take from the Exodus plagues on Egypt?

2. Why is the drinking of blood unlikely to be literal in this passage?

3. What principle is being taught in this 'drinking of blood' that could help us understand 'eye for eye'?

4. How do you interpret the sun given power to scorch?

5. Can you think of examples of people cursing God when affected by these bowls?

6. What can you say to the person who says, 'I would believe if there was more evidence'?

7. How does Rom.1:18-21 open up possible interpretations of Rev. 16?

8. What is a lesson from Israel's exile we can take into our world, and how does it affect your view of this world and your part in it?

9. How do these partial judgments speak about God's character?

31
The Fifth Bowl
(Revelation 16:10-11)

The Lord judges justly. The seven bowls of God's wrath are being poured out and we come to the fifth bowl and this is even uglier than before …

> The fifth angel poured out his bowl on the throne of the beast, and its kingdom was plunged into darkness. People gnawed their tongues in agony (16:10).

People are gnawing their own tongues! Personally, I have never been able to stomach eating cow tongue let alone my own tongue. And this bowl is different. The first four bowls were poured out upon nature, men, sea, rivers and the sun, but this fifth bowl is poured out on the Beast. Remember the Beast is state power that persecutes God's people. Notice it's poured out on the *throne* of the Beast. That would connect with those first readers in the seven churches. The church at Pergamum was told they live where *Satan has his throne* (2:13). The Beast is the image of the Dragon, who is Satan. The Roman Empire and Emperor worship was at the center in Pergamum, the throne of Satan.

But what we are seeing here in the pouring out of the fifth bowl is that this state power is brought down. *Plunged into darkness!* And people who had put their hopes in the Beast to provide for them are in agony. They gnawed their tongues. When could all this happen? State power that persecutes God's people being brought down? I would suggest all throughout history from the first century. The Roman Empire was eventually brought down, and on through every other manifestation of the Beast until recent history, such as the communist superpower Soviet Russia which killed multitudes for the faith—brought down. But also, what an apt description of what we have seen in Western countries in recent years when the Beast (state powers) came down throughout the world when the Global Financial Crisis hit. Those who worship the Beast and were looking to the Beast to provide and give them security gnawed at their own tongues, not only in the GFC, but every time there is any stock market crash. I know people who had put all their money into superannuation and made big money with the government incentives. They stored up all their money and planned a nice early retirement to live off this great nest egg the Beast was providing. But when the Beast has his throne taken away, when the GFC hit, the Beast couldn't control the financial world and they lost everything. No more early retirement. They stored their hopes in all that the Beast had promised in superannuation and then they lost the lot. Plenty of tongue gnawing went on. There were violent protests in European countries where the throne of the Beast was destroyed. Even the United States was in chaos with people selling their houses for $300 and looking to the government in despair, but it was tottering. Greece and other countries were simply going broke and tried austerity measures to survive, which drove those looking to the government to bail them out to protest even more violently. When the Beast was brought down, truly **people gnawed their tongues in agony.**

Whenever there is a significant stock market crash we hear of high flying businessmen taking their own lives. But even if they lost most of their stocks they would hardly be as destitute as most poor people. But to them there is something even more humiliating than just the loss of money.[35]

When Mick Jagger's girlfriend took her own life, it was reportedly because her failed business was $6 million in debt. The Beast couldn't help her (and I don't mean Mick Jagger). The Beast promotes financial prosperity as an end in itself. So when the idol comes crashing down, life is not worth living. But is this darkness into which the Beast is plunged only financial ruin? Remember these bowls draw on imagery from the plagues in Egypt …

> Then the LORD said to Moses, 'Stretch out your hand toward the sky so that darkness will spread over Egypt—<u>darkness that can be felt</u>.' So Moses stretched out his hand toward the sky, and total darkness

---

[35] http://www.smh.com.au/lifestyle/celebrity/lwren-scott-more-than-just-mick-jaggers-girlfriend-20140319-3511c.html#ixzz2wNhRx5aF

> covered all Egypt for three days. No one could see anyone else or move about for three days. Yet all the Israelites had light in the places where they lived (Exod. 10:21-23).

The darkness is so thick that people were separated. This is not the only place in Scripture where the darkness is great and separates. In 2 Pet. 2:17 and Jude 13 *blackest darkness has been reserved forever.* The darkness in Jude is referring to hell. Separation. Contrary to popular opinion there is no party in hell. It won't be, 'I'll be there with all my mates.' No. Just separation. Blackest darkness. You didn't want God in this life? You get what you want—separation from all light and the God who is light. It's one of the themes of the Bible. Darkness vs. light! Jesus is the light of the world. 'Let there be light.' God created a good world. But as people harden their hearts against the Lord, when the Beast plunges into darkness it is not only an overthrowing of a government financially, but also a moral decay. A deeper darkness. The pouring out of this bowl is the society plunging into deeper moral darkness.

Gnawing tongues is another indication we are not talking about darkness as just a physical lack of light. People don't normally gnaw at their tongues just because the lights go out. The parallel with the trumpets helps us. The darkness of the fifth trumpet caused psychological as much as physical torment. People realize the meaninglessness of this life. All their pursuits add up to nothing and then they are going to die. It might take a lifetime of denial before they realize it was all meaningless. Some can go on in life thinking they have it all, until the end, then it ends in darkness. But most people feel the darkness, the meaninglessness of life, long before the end. Gnawing their tongues. But they won't let it go. Rev. 16:11 will tell us they refused to repent. They love darkness. As Jesus said …

> This is the verdict: Light has come into the world, but people <u>loved darkness</u> instead of light because their deeds were evil. Everyone who does evil hates the light, and will not come into the light for fear that their deeds will be exposed (John 3:19-20).

Here is the irony. Men love their spiritual darkness, so God gives them up to themselves and that spiritual darkness turns into a physical reality. Blackest darkness in hell. As this fifth bowl is poured out, the Beast **and <u>its kingdom</u> was plunged into darkness** …

We can see our world sinking into a moral darkness we could never have imagined only a short time ago. It's the celebration of evil as good and good as evil (Isa. 5:20). The Beast promotes prosperity as the end itself, which leaves the poor starving. We call it self-assertion, ambition, or fulfilling potential. We kill our unborn and call it choice. A woman's right! Right to kill! We outlaw disciplining our children by calling it child abuse. We covet status and our neighbors' possessions and call it being highly motivated. We are filled with profanity and pornography and call it freedom of expression. We ridicule the values of the past and call it progression. So dark is the darkness. These moral failures have always been around, but today like never before it is happening in nations that have had the blessing of the gospel.

In defiance of God we want the choice to end the lives of the elderly when they have no *quality of life*. But God says every life has quality and dignity because the most disabled or debilitated human is made in the image of God. But we don't want God telling us anything. Man must have his right to choose his own right and wrong. When ABC's *Four Corners* program reported on the gay men who brought up a little boy from babyhood, only to abuse him throughout the world in their pedophile syndicate (on a previous interview the same couple had been portrayed as model gay parents to promote same-sex marriage), presenter Kerry O'Brien rushed to put the disclaimer to exonerate gay marriage, saying gay marriage between men doesn't necessarily mean abuse for children. Of course it doesn't! Neither does celibacy of the priesthood automatically mean that priests will be pedophiles, but both of those situations are a rejection of God's word *and* his natural order which creates a platform for those evils. Darkness. Man is given up to himself and when things go wrong, man is unrepentant.

The world has gone crazy in its lust for darkness. The fifth bowl plunges them further into darkness. And as the apostle Paul says, God judges in this lifetime. How? By giving people up to what they want, and the result is they not only store up more judgment for eternity, but receive the penalty in this life, though they might think they are getting away with it for a time.

> In the same way the men also abandoned natural relations with women and were inflamed with lust for one another. Men committed shameful

acts with other men, and <u>received in themselves the due penalty</u> for their error. Furthermore, just as they did not think it worthwhile to retain the knowledge of God, so God <u>gave them over</u> to a depraved mind, so that they do what ought not to be done. [Before you start judging homosexuals as being the only problem, see if you find yourself in here.] They have become filled with every kind of wickedness, evil, <u>greed</u> and depravity. They are full of envy, murder, strife, deceit and malice. They are gossips, slanderers, God-haters, insolent, arrogant and boastful; they invent ways of doing evil; they disobey their parents; they have no understanding, no fidelity, no love, no mercy. Although they know God's righteous decree that those who do such things deserve death, they not only continue to do these very things but also approve of those who practice them (Rom. 1:27-32).

Calling evil good. How dark is the darkness! They had put their hope in the Beast to give them what they wanted. The Beast made their choices of lifestyle legal. Life without discipline or self-control. But it turns to darkness. Agony.

A young Christian man who had repented of his former gay lifestyle told me how he was walking along an alley in his gay neighborhood in the early hours one morning and a young gay man who was visibly upset came up alongside him and put his arm around him in tears and said (expletive excluded), 'The gay lifestyle is a ****.' Many will confess in their most transparent moments that it's not a *gay* lifestyle at all. It's darkness. It's sanctioned and promoted by the Beast. It's supposed freedom, but it just causes agony. Here we are not just talking about AIDS and other STDs, but agony of soul. They **cursed the God of heaven because of their pains and their sores, but they <u>refused</u> to repent of what they had done.**

They refused the one thing that could save them. To turn and repent. 'But they can't repent without the grace of God.' But one thing they have full volition and power to do is to 'refuse' God. This they do with full freedom and choice. To *refuse* to repent! Again, as Jesus said, 'You *refuse* to come to me to have life' (John 5:40).

So much for the idea that people would just quickly repent upon the verge of death. These people know God is there. They see everything going under. They see it is hopeless and even painful, *the pain and their sores*, the diseases and cancers that humans contract. But would they turn to God at this last agony? No. *They refused to repent.* One common criticism people have against Christianity is, 'People could just live an evil life, knowing they can just repent at the end.'

My response to that is, 'Show me! Show me where someone has done that!' Yes, there are such things as genuine deathbed conversions, and I am grateful for the very few I have seen, but it's usually just the opposite. Rather than repent, people become more hardened. 'If God is there why doesn't God do something to help me and let me live?' They curse God! Why? Because God is not mocked. If there is willful rejection throughout one's life, it is very rare that people soften and change at the last minute. It does happen, but it's rare.

Notice the bowls could be occurring at the same time as each other because the effects of the first bowl are still around from 16:2. Those *painful sores* that broke out are still bothering people at this fifth bowl. The painful sores from the first bowl won't go away. This at least suggests it's not a literal darkness but a spiritual darkness, because if these bowls are occurring concurrently, how can the sun be scorching with heat in the fourth bowl (16:8-9) at the same time as darkness comes. But it does make sense if it's a moral darkness they are plunged into and *they <u>refused</u> to repent of what they had done.*

It's that refusal to repent that progresses things to final judgment. So the fifth bowl really is introducing the finality. Another hint we are dealing with something spiritual here is the parallel in the fifth trumpet involving those scorpions. We know from Jesus' words that scorpions can be a metaphor for the demonic (Luke 10:19). And if the trumpets are parallel to the bowls, maybe it's the scorpions inflicting the pain. That is, demonic forces. The bowl that follows is also all about the demonic. Spiritual darkness increases!

Therefore, it doesn't matter that deep-down people realize it is God who has brought judgment on this world, because they still actually *cursed the God of heaven*. It's like that great contradiction when people say God doesn't exist because of suffering and evil. Many who claim to be atheists speak with such venom against God. God is evil. Wait a minute! If you don't believe in God, why are you so angry with God? And why are you angry at all? Why should suffering and evil be a problem if atheism is true? Isn't life just about survival of the fittest? There can be no definition of suffering and evil if there is no God who determines absolute morals. If evil exists, then God must exist to have decided what is good vs. evil. If there is no God, there is no evil or good. So rejecting God because of suffering and evil makes no logical sense. It's like me saying I don't believe in UFOs because all the aliens I've seen are all too ugly!

But the truth is people know there is such a thing as evil and good and with that admission they are testifying there must be an absolute moral authority which put in our hearts a moral right and wrong. The hurt in our hearts testifies there must be a greater meaning and a greater being. Where did that sense of right and wrong come from? It has no 'survival of the fittest' value. Even the professing atheist seems to know this truth deep down. They are not simply disbelieving in God. They are upset with God. They are *cursing God!*

So instead of the **pains** causing people to turn to God and **repent,** they defy God more, and in that defiance, they receive the full bowl of God's wrath. They are not at rest. They are not at peace. Gnawing at their tongues, cursing God. It is all meaningless. But they keep on doing **what they had done.** When AIDS began, it wiped out multitudes, spread mostly through sexual immorality and drug use, and then it progressed to killing innocent parties. But instead of repentance, they *refused* to change their behavior. Why do people curse God? They want to blame God for *what they had done.* We are shareholders in Adam's sin. We all sinned in Adam (Rom. 5:12), so the evil of this world is both collectively and individually man's fault, but people want to blame God for *what they had done!* And it doesn't stop there. Like the Exodus plagues the heart gets hardened. Pharaoh knows it's God, but that doesn't stop him. What is being taught in these bowls then?

There comes a point when people, just like Pharaoh, will have their hearts hardened. How scary is that? If you are unrepentant in sin in your life now, you could be hardening your heart! How can you know if you are not one of those whose heart is hardening? That's what Revelation is for. It is a call. It is warning that there comes a time when you won't even want to repent. Evil will increase and be called good. Darkness overtakes. What if you have been letting darkness overtake you? This is why Revelation is written! *Whoever has ears, let them hear!* If you hear the call to repent, then that is God calling. He has not given up on you. And if God is calling you, it would be a good idea to listen to him!

Insurance companies won't give young men insurance on fast cars until they are 25 years old. So the companies forgo millions of dollars on premiums, gambling on young men to kill themselves or at least wreck their cars. The insurance companies figure it is such a sure bet they would end up losing, having to payout on dead, young men's wrecked cars. If you are under 25 you are not worth the risk, say astute businesspeople. They actually bet on you smashing your car. So does that slow down young drivers? Does that stop young guys wanting to win the bet and get the powerful cars? Drive too fast. Drink and drive. What more evidence do they want? The insurance companies are betting millions on them! But they still don't get it. And we shake our heads at all this knowingly saying, 'How foolish young people are.' But this is the human condition being taught in Rev. 16. Even in the face of the greatest warnings they are still unrepentant! If you are playing with sin and are unrepentant, then you are like those young guys driving too fast thinking life just goes on.

The bowls also tell us God doesn't just keep warning. There comes a day when it's too late and no one will be able to say, 'Why didn't you warn me?' We have had constant warnings in this fallen world. Disease. Disaster. Darkness. Wake up! But still the world is unrepentant. Oh, how just are God's judgments. How right he is to judge. What is so amazing is that God sent his Son into this world of evil and darkness so that *he* would go into that darkness on the cross. *He* became darkness for us. *He* became sin for us. For whom? It's inconceivable! For those who sinned against him! This is love. When we were still sinners, when we were God's enemies, Christ died for us (Rom. 5:6-10). Even for those who have been caught up in those sins, Christ will take the judgment away, take the record away and replace it with his perfect record ... for those who repent and believe in him. Today if you hear his voice do not harden your heart.

Study Questions

1. How might the Beast be plunged into darkness?

2. What does it mean to convey when it says *men gnaw their tongues?*

3. To what is the darkness referring? Provide support from Scripture for your answer.

4. How do we see darkness manifest today?

5. How might this kind of darkness cause agony?

6. How could people be judged when they are doing what they want?

7. Give more than one reason why is it dangerous to plan to repent at the end of your life.

8. Are there any reasons to suggest the bowls could be poured out concurrently?

9. Do you find you are more or less sensitive to sin? Are you in danger of a hardening heart?

10. What is the overall message of this text?

32
The Sixth Bowl
(Revelation 16:12-14)

Armageddon has finally arrived. This is World War 3. This is the war that leaves all others in its wake. And here it is described in Revelation. We know there are different views among Christians on Revelation, but whatever your view, this is exciting. We have a real live war to end all wars, then Jesus comes to the rescue. Here is the climax of the central theme of Revelation that all Christians believe. Jesus wins!

If you follow the most popular Christian view on this, then the timeline for the Futurist rapture view goes something like this (with a few variations, just as all views including mine have variations). Sometime in the future there will be a short seven-year tribulation, but either just before that tribulation or half-way through it, all Christians are raptured from the earth, leaving behind unbelievers to go through that tribulation. Towards the end of those seven years, the different kings of the earth gather their armies together at a place in Palestine at a mountain near a place called Megiddo, in Hebrew it's called Harmageddon ('Har' is mountain in Hebrew, Megiddo is the place. Mountain of Megiddo, thus Armageddon). After the armies have assembled at this mountain they prepare for war against Christ, but Jesus comes and defeats them and sets up his kingly rule in Jerusalem and reigns for 1000 years on earth. After the 1000 years comes the Day of Judgment for unbelievers. There will be many unbelievers converted during that seven-year tribulation. They will be largely Jewish people and will worship Jesus in the newly constructed temple in Jerusalem. So what we have here in Rev. 16 is the world war that occurs just *before* Jesus sets up his earthly kingdom. We are up to the sixth bowl of God's wrath just before this war …

The sixth angel poured out his bowl on the great river Euphrates, and its water was dried up to prepare the way for the kings from the East (16:12).

I have been advancing the idea that the trumpets and bowls are parallel. The sixth trumpet, like this sixth bowl, not only mentions the Euphrates river, but the trumpet also mentions 200 million troops ready for battle, which fits the battle we are about to see. Some Futurists say these are Chinese troops, that is, *kings of the East*. This is drawing on the sixth trumpet ... *The number of the mounted troops was twice ten thousand times ten thousand* (which is 200 million). *I heard their number* (9:16). Other Futurists say the *kings of the East* are actually Japanese, because in the original Greek language it does not literally say *kings of the East*, but says 'kings of the sun rise' (hence East). And Japan is called the land of the rising sun. All this is happening **because the great river Euphrates was dried up to prepare the way for the kings of the East.**

John the apostle, knowing his OT, might have thought of the *kings of the East* as the symbol of evil power. The Assyrians and Babylonians came from the East to attack Israel. Even the Persians came from the East to overthrow the Babylonians. So John might be thinking of those kings of the East. But John knew the OT promised that the drying up of the Euphrates would happen to enable men to cross ...

> The LORD will dry up the gulf of the Egyptian sea; with a scorching wind he will sweep his hand over the Euphrates River. He will break it up into seven streams so that anyone can cross over in sandals (Isa. 11:15).

This prophecy is important and is one of the reasons why I am not going with a literal drying up of the Euphrates sometime in the future, because this promise that the Euphrates River would be dried up for men from the East to cross has *already* literally been fulfilled. King Cyrus the Persian blocked off the river and dried it in 539BC so he could advance his army to attack Babylon. So there has already been a literal fulfillment in the OT. God raised up kings from the East. God delivered judgment upon Babylon using King Cyrus from the East, the area of the Euphrates.

> 'Who has stirred up one from the east, calling him in righteousness to

his service? He hands nations over to him and subdues kings before him. He turns them to dust with his sword, to windblown chaff with his bow' (Isa. 41:2).

This is one of the amazing prophecies fulfilled in the OT. Isaiah, writing nearly 200 years before this event happens, even names, names. He names King Cyrus two centuries before the man existed! And sure enough, King Cyrus diverted the river till it ran dry, enabling his army to get into Babylon and take it by surprise. That was the historical fall of Babylon at the hands of the Medes and Persians over which King Cyrus reigned. We even have that event (of the water drying up) recorded in historical sources *outside* the Bible (Herodotus 1:190-191 Xeonphon, Cyropedia). This is how Isaiah described it a couple of centuries before it occurred.

> ...who says to the watery deep, 'Be dry, and I will dry up your streams,' who says of Cyrus, 'He is my shepherd and will accomplish all that I please;' he will say of Jerusalem, 'Let it be rebuilt,' and of the temple, 'Let its foundations be laid' (Isa. 44:27-28).

About 200 years after Isaiah wrote this, along comes a king named Cyrus who diverted the river to dry it up so his army could pass through to attack and overthrow the superpower, the Babylonians, who had oppressed God's people. Cyrus subsequently enabled the exiled Jews to return to Jerusalem and rebuild as predicted! This is the fulfilment that has already happened in the past.

So what should we be doing with this text here in Rev. 16? The Futurist says why not another literal fulfillment? That would be strange to say the least, but of course anything is possible in the future. But what has Revelation consistently been teaching us all the way through? It uses OT historical events, times and places to describe what is to happen in a far wider reaching way. We have seen this with all the references to the Exodus. Not least of all the plagues as we have seen them alluded to in the bowls and trumpets, where we saw locusts which represent demonic powers (not literal locusts), water turning to blood, and hail and frogs, but again with an explicit spiritual fulfillment. We have also seen references to the tabernacle, the twelve tribes of Israel and John eating scrolls like Ezekiel. Rev. 11 talks about a city, but explicitly says the great city is *figuratively* called Sodom and Egypt. He spells out that he is figuratively applying

OT places or events to apply spiritually to even greater things in these later times. We have seen this all the way through Revelation. A song of Moses is also a song of the Lamb. Indeed, the Lamb himself is not literally a lamb but that image is drawn on from the OT Passover lamb. We have seen great connections with historical places and events of the OT, but in Revelation we are now given a far more profound, worldwide fulfillment. Not the small historical one by comparison. Look at this text. The Euphrates is not the only significant OT geographic name used in Rev. 16. Babylon (16:19) is not referring to the literal historical Babylon, the ancient long-ceased-to-exist city, but draws on the OT image. The details of Rev. 16 have been dealing with deliberate symbolic language consistent with the rest of Revelation. The enemies are given blood to drink (16:6), but we know from the OT (Isa. 49:26, Ps. 79:3, 10, 12) that is metaphor for just judgment meted out. You shed blood and so blood you shall drink. By the time we get to 16:15, *he who keeps his clothes with him* is an obvious metaphor for spiritual clothing, like the white robes washed in blood of the Lamb.

So when we come to waters of the Euphrates in Rev. 16, are they literal or figurative? Revelation interprets waters figuratively in its very next chapter …

> Then the angel said to me, 'The <u>waters</u> you saw, where the prostitute sits, are peoples, multitudes, nations and languages' (17:15).

The waters are actually people. If that is the case for the Euphrates then it is saying 'whatever waters (people) might have stood in the way of those opposing the cause of Christ before, they are no longer an obstacle'. The waters (people or nations) that *would* have been barriers are now 'dried up'!

A literal fulfillment of the Euphrates drying up was of great significance in King Cyrus' day. In the ancient world, the Euphrates was a boundary dividing the East from West, but that barrier no longer exists today. It no longer has any military significance, nor does it divide East from West anymore. Even if it did, the crossing of that river with today's military transport and technology makes the whole thing mundane and no longer the issue it was in the ancient world. But for John, when Cyrus dried up and crossed the river Euphrates, it was a major historical event which would eventually lead to Jerusalem's restoration. It really meant something. Now it means even more if the spiritual metaphor is taken into account, because at the very least 16:12 is saying that these forces come to a point where there is a clear passage for them to march forward to this attack in this battle. And any hindrance there was before has now been dried up. Look out.

Just as Revelation has been doing all along, I'm suggesting this verse is using OT events and places to describe even greater realities to come. The real point is that these forces can now advance unhindered.

As we get further into this passage we see that the forces coming are mentioned as demonic and deceiving! Just as we have seen the references to the Exodus plagues coming again in this greater spiritual reality, what goes around comes around. And sure enough, one of those plagues we will be dealing with is the plague of the frogs. Is it the same kind of literal frogs that attacked Pharaoh? No. We are told they are demons. The physical OT history becomes the metaphor for what is a *greater spiritual reality*.

> Then I saw three <u>impure spirits</u> that looked like frogs; they came out of <u>the mouth</u> of the dragon, out of the <u>mouth</u> of the beast and out of the <u>mouth</u> of the false prophet (16:13).

There is the unholy trinity in all its infamy. Not Father, Son and Holy Spirit, but the mockery, the counterfeit—the Dragon, the Beast and the False Prophet. But notice it's that **mouth** again. Deception (see 12:15) sending forth demonic lies. And frogs? Not a literal replica of the Exodus plague. The term *impure spirits* in the original Greek language is literally *unclean*. Frogs are unclean creatures according to Leviticus 11:10, so it is the ugliest kind of creature coming out of the mouth of the unholy Trinity. But it's the *mouth* repeated three times that is significant. We are dealing with deception. Slimy like frogs, slimy in deception. So the warfare we are dealing with, is primarily to do with the demonic mouth. Deception.

The Historicists, looking to single events or persons from history say *out of the mouth of the false prophet* is referring to Muhammad, the founder of Islam. Sounds interesting. But while false prophets are part of it, in Rev. 16 we are seeing the demonic power that is *behind* them. What was worked out with physical frogs in the Exodus before is now exposed as spiritual fulfillment. Its demon driven. It's interesting that the plague of frogs was one of only two plagues that the Egyptian magicians were able to replicate with their evil powers! Revelation uses the OT historical, literal physical (frogs) as analogy to the spiritual. This is the argument I have been using for the plagues brought on by the bowls, the Euphrates etc. But here it is actually spelt out. The frogs …

> They are demonic spirits that perform signs, and they go out to the kings of the whole world, to gather them for the battle on the great day of God Almighty (16:14).

Is this where the 200 million Chinese troops fight Jesus? As always, the strength of the Futurist argument is that anything can happen in the future. But we mentioned the logical difficulty with that back in 9:16, when we noted an army of 200 million was a problem even for the Chinese (previous figures have the Chinese army at 1.6 million). But when we were back at the sixth trumpet blast, we saw the number of 200 million can be easily accounted for as spiritual warriors. Isn't that what this text is on about? Evil spirits. The frogs are evil spirits. And there are 200 million of them!

Now before we delve into when this battle happens, let's pause and recap. We have this sixth bowl poured out which dries up or removes any hindrance to the advance of these forces to prepare for these kings. But behind them are evil spirits from the Dragon, the Beast and the False Prophet. **They go out to the kings of the whole world, to gather them for the battle on the great day of God Almighty.** Did you notice that? Now we see this was so much more than just some guys from the East. Before the great day, this is a gathering together of no longer just the kings of the East, but now the *whole world* is in it together. The whole world! Spiritually deceived into a united attack.

When will this happen? Isn't it interesting how even in the so-called Christian West so much has changed in such a short space of time? There is a uniting together like we've never seen before. Within the last decade national political US and Australian leaders like Barack Obama, Hilary Clinton, Kevin Rudd and Julia Gillard all went from believing marriage was between a man and a woman to uniting together with the Western world to push for same-sex marriage. The speed with which it all turned around is extraordinary. And this is despite same-sex marriage being unheard of in all of history. It's as though something changed and the push to legalize it was unhindered!

Who could have predicted that God having created us male and female would be challenged by the mainstream within only the last few years? Only a short time ago, the charge was made (unfairly) that because Christians believe in creation, they deny the science of biology. Now with gender fluidity it is the secular world that is willing to openly deny biology. A generation or two ago there were certain social and cultural norms that gave respect or rights to the Christian faith, but now this has disappeared, whether in art, films, music, media and entertainment. Then there is the open aggressive push of atheists who are no longer content to have the right to their point of view. Now they aggressively demand the *removal* of religion as evil, even calling it child abuse to teach your children the way of Jesus. Also look at the speed at which the public has accepted and even embraced the name of Jesus Christ as a swear word on our airwaves, which would only a few years back not be tolerated. But now there is what? *No hindrance!* Any former barrier has dried up! And this is just in the so-called Christian countries. But what of the real persecution of Christians? Remember when I pointed out the article from the Melbourne *Age Newspaper*, saying the persecution of Christians in 139 nations has become the great human rights issue of our time and possibly worse than at any time in history, including under the Roman Empire.[36] That was a rare article, because despite the escalation of this worldwide persecution of Christians, secular newspapers just don't normally report about *a war on Christianity*. It doesn't rate a mention. It's unhindered! There is a united front against the faith. It's not just the 'East', but also all the authorities of the world are joining … *they go out to the kings of the <u>whole world</u>, to gather them for the battle on the great day of God Almighty.*

The kings or government powers of the *whole world* join together. You cannot blaspheme any other religion or religious leader. But the aggressive push to remove the teaching of Christianity in schools before would have been considered outrageous. Now it is as though

---

[36] Barney Zwartz, The Age Newspaper, Fairfax Media, Melbourne, Australia, November 2nd, 2013.

Christian religious education teachers are the ones breaking laws. No more barriers! And this is just in a Christian country. What about those persecuted 139 countries?

So these evil spirits start at the top of society. The kings of the world. Governments. If you have laws from governments that work against Christ, his ethics and gospel, then the multitudes will follow. Those with the mark of the Beast will go along with, even support the deception, albeit unknown to them, because 'the mouth' is so deceptive.

I have already recommended *The Third Choice* by Mark Durie. It documents the historical doctrine of Dhimma as 'the third choice'. Christians are given the choice to convert to Islam, die, or pay Jizya (extra tax) for being Christian, limiting their ability to buy or sell. It's been part of the history of Islam and it's coming alive again today. But what has that got to do with uniting of the world? Notice the *unity* in these verses! The devil musters support. He gathers the governments of the world into action. They are *joined* in their effort. They might not even realize they are united. That is the spiritual deception. What do persecuting Muslim countries and persecuting communist countries have in common? They would say, 'Nothing!' But they *join together* in the persecuting of Christians! Atheists and so-called liberal Christians might not think they have anything in common, but they *join together* to undermine the cause of Jesus. Anti-creation atheists and progressive clergymen write *forewords* in each other's books because they have a common enemy. The cause of Jesus! They *join* forces. What do openly persecuting countries have to do with Western governments that legalize the very things that blaspheme Jesus and his ethics? They *join together* to undermine the advance of Jesus and his cause.

They are deceived firstly into thinking they are on the side of good by opposing Christ, and secondly into thinking that by joining forces with each other they will win. It is back to Revelation's favorite Psalm.

> Why do the <u>nations conspire</u> and the peoples plot in vain? The <u>kings</u> of the earth rise up and the <u>rulers band together against the LORD and against his anointed</u>, saying, 'Let us break their chains and throw off their shackles' (Ps. 2:1-3).

Christ and his word will not shackle the kings, those rulers of the earth, anymore. 'We will not be restricted. Dry up that river. We want to advance unhindered.' The world's powers, cultures and institutions which might *hate* each other on other fronts, and have no conscious union with each other, unite practically on this one thing. They want to remove Christ *and* his followers. Jesus summed it up.

> Whoever is not with me is against me, ... (Matt. 12:30).

THERE IS NO NEUTRAL GROUND! If we look at the world through the lens of a spiritual battle for one side or the other, then it makes sense how the nations are coming together in this cause. Every government institution, every part of culture, the media, arts, commerce, entertainment, ideology and every individual human being is either on the side of the Beast ... or of Christ. It puts a whole new light on society and history and the workings of this world if you simply divide people into one of two kingdoms. Christ or Satan. No in-between. You are either with him or against him. Don't say, 'I may not have fully submitted all of my life, but I am not against him.' Deceived by the *mouth!* There is no such thing as half with Jesus. *Whoever is not with me is against me*. Everyone who has not handed over their life to Jesus, everyone who said, 'I just try to be a good person. I am not against Jesus, but I don't need the cross,' or, 'I am Lord of my own life,' is joined together *against him*. We saw the end described in Rev. 11 when the inhabitants of the earth gloated over the demise of the witnesses (which were the lampstands, the churches). The whole world was united against the church. And just like in Rev. 11, the world is against the church, gathering forces so certain they can kill off Christ and his cause completely. *They are demonic spirits that perform signs, and they go out to the kings of the whole world, to gather them for the battle on the great day of God Almighty.*

Demons are behind the powers of the world with a *new* intensity. No more hindrance! The whole point of these demonic forces deceiving the kings is ... *to gather them for the battle on the great day of God Almighty*. All of Satan's trickery and deceit over history builds up and finally comes down to this. THIS IS *THE* BATTLE OF ARMAGGEDON! When, what, and how does it finally come about? Well pray it doesn't happen before we get to our next chapter to find out.

Study Questions

1. What does the name Armageddon mean?

2. What might John have thought of from the OT when he saw the prophecy of the Euphrates River drying up?

3. Give reasons why the drying up of the Euphrates River might not be literal in this text.

4. Give examples of how Revelation has used OT events, places and people to teach wider truth.

5. If the river is not literally dried up, what is being taught about the king's advancement?

6. What parts of this text show this is speaking about spiritual realities drawn from OT historical events?

7. How could this speak into today when the text says the *whole world* is united in this battle?

8. How could the *whole world* be united in one cause when many of them are against each other?

9. How do Jesus' words, *'Whoever is not with me is against me'* shed light on this text and does it enable you to see the world differently?

33
Like a Thief
(Revelation 16:15)

It's finally here. The Battle of Armageddon. How does it all work? Are we even supposed to know, because our text opens with ... *Look, I come like a thief* (16:15)!

When Jesus says he is coming like a thief, does it mean he is going to steal something? No. Jesus means unexpectedly! And this verse is in red ink in your Bible! (That is if you have a Bible with Jesus' words in red letters.) Then you can know it really must be true! Well of course that doesn't make it any more inspired. All Scripture is God-breathed. We can only note these are words specifically said by Jesus himself. So when is Jesus saying this? To whom is he saying it? And for what purpose?

The answer to that depends on which of the main views of Revelation you hold. The Preterist says Jesus is warning of the destruction of Jerusalem in AD 70. The Futurist has two main variations. One where the rapture occurs before (or in the middle of) the tribulation; the other Futurist view (without pre-tribulation rapture) says this is Jesus' warning of his return to set up his 1000-year millennial reign, but not to bring final judgment to the wicked, as that only happens after the 1000-year reign. The Historicist and Idealist views say Jesus is warning about the Day of Judgment. The final Day.

Well, what difference does it make? Do we need to get bogged down in secondary theological views? Not really when it comes to our unity in Christ. When you break it down, all Christians actually stand together on end times. That might sound weird in light of all this, but it's true. We are actually radically united on end times, in contrast to unbelievers. All Bible believing Christians believe in the *physical* return of Jesus! All Christians believe he will judge the world in his resurrected glorified body. All Christians agree it is through faith in Christ alone that anyone can survive this Judgment. We all believe in the future reign of Christ, including on the earth. None of the essentials of the Christian faith are compromised, nor is our unity in Christ affected, even though we differ on the unfolding of the details. We *all* believe Jesus wins! On the essentials of end times, we Christians are a united force.

Perhaps we need to pause to acknowledge this unity every now and then, because it should be a 'can't lose' situation as we dig into the details. Our Christian unity is not compromised at all, so we don't have to be afraid if we come out on different sides on the details. If you have a different view from mine (Idealist) and have gotten this far, congratulations! You win the longsuffering *unity in essentials* prize! The finer points of eschatology are not in the same ballpark as those things of first importance on which we are unified. So then why bother with it at all?

Well, all Scripture is God-breathed and is useful, and depending on the meaning of the words of our text, *Look, I come like a thief*, it could be helpful in building you up, giving you inspiration for evangelism and your sense of urgency to be ready for the judgment. So how *do* we understand Jesus' words *Look, I come like a thief!* When Jesus said these words who was he speaking to, and how seriously does he mean his return will be a surprise?

Many with the rapture view simply say Jesus is warning that he comes like a thief *before* the tribulation (or in the middle), so this is his warning about the rapture to come. Be ready. But if you look closely at these words of Jesus we are in trouble. When does Jesus say this? Jesus is interjecting with these words right near the climactic *end* of the tribulation, right in between the sixth bowl from ... *The sixth angel poured out his bowl on the great river Euphrates...* (16:12), and the seventh bowl ... *The seventh angel poured out his bowl into the air...* (16:17). In between those sixth and seventh's bowls Jesus says... *Look, I come like a thief* (16:15)!

Jesus is warning towards the *end* of the tribulation that he is *yet to come* like a thief. Now if Jesus is warning of the rapture *before* or in the *middle* of the seven years, why is Jesus saying, '*Look, I come like a thief!*' near the *end* of the tribulation? *After* six plagues are already poured out, he is supposed to have already come like a thief in the rapture before the bowls, or half-way through the seven-year tribulation.

I couldn't help but notice that the Schofield reference Bible[37] (which has had a major influence on people over the last 100 years in the Dispensation Futurist rapture view), and other dispensational commentators on Revelation like Warren Wiersbe,[38] conspicuously leave out any comment altogether on Jesus' words in 16:15, *Look, I come like a thief!* Is it because this verse is in the wrong place for that view?

John MacArthur believes in the rapture, but to his credit he takes seriously the location of this verse. Jesus can't be warning people *before* the rapture if the rapture has *already* occurred by the sixth bowl! This is well into the tribulation, so MacArthur would not say Jesus is warning about the rapture, but rather is giving comfort to believers so they know they will be remembered when Jesus *physically* returns to set up his millennial kingdom.[39]

While it's good that MacArthur takes seriously where this verse is placed *after* the sixth bowl, that actually makes this even more difficult. Jesus' words that he 'will come like a thief' means *unexpectedly*. No one knows the hour or day. But not according MacArthur's rapture view. You can set your watch as to when Jesus is coming back. Everyone on the whole earth will know the exact day. Jesus will give a warning as to when you can begin counting down to the day with the most amazing public spectacular supernatural event in history, greater than Moses parting the Red Sea. A far greater public magnitude than the resurrection of Jesus, because millions of Christians throughout the earth will one day suddenly all disappear in the rapture. If you are left behind, take note of that date! And no doubt there would be multitudes left behind who would. They would be saying to themselves, 'Those rapturists were right after all. Write down that date!' Then simply count down the seven years (or 3½ years for mid-tribulation rapture) to Jesus' return to set up his millennial kingdom.

One argument to counter this is that the Antichrist will bring a strong delusion to many, so they won't wake up as to why there are all these missing millions and empty graves. The problem with this theory is that it is also said there will be a great many who are *converted*

---

[37] https://www.biblestudytools.com/commentaries/scofield-reference-notes/
[38] www.preceptaustin.org/pdf/61242
[39] John MacArthur, *Because the Time is Near,* Moody Publishers, Chicago, 2007, p.255

during this seven-year tribulation. John MacArthur says the tribulation will be a time when the number of those being saved will be like never before.[40] So the unprecedented many who are born again *during* the tribulation can't be deluded, so at least *they* can calculate Jesus' return down to the exact day. No thief there. Think of the mega millions who sat in Dispensational Bible studies but were *left behind*, or those who read the Scofield Bible or John MacArthur's works, or the 63 million who read the *Left Behind Series*. Now they all know the jig is up when suddenly all the real Christians disappear. Now they all know it's true and it has all unfolded just as all those crazy Christians said it would. No more debates. Christianity is proven right (in particular, the rapture view), and Jesus' return is just around the corner. No wonder MacArthur says there will be so many conversions. Who wouldn't believe with a sign like that! And bonus, you get to know exactly when Jesus is coming back! Those who are left behind who convert can set their watches by the date of the disappearance of the Christians, and exactly seven years from then they can say, 'We have an exact date of Jesus' return!' None of this, *I come like a thief!*

In fact, it is even worse if this rapture happens halfway through the seven years because all the way up to the 3½-year mark *Christians* (pre-rapture), would be able to predict the exact time the *rapture* is to occur as well. Remember the Futurist view claims to take the symbols and signs of Revelation literally, so following each event, for example, a third of the sea literally turns to blood, a literal third of the sun, moon and stars are turned dark, counting down to the rapture at the 3½ year mark, when all Christians will suddenly disappear! We can predict the date of the rapture! What's more, those left behind will be able to predict Jesus' physical return. Christians have been going around telling everyone for the first 3½ years of the tribulation, 'Look at all these things, sea turning to blood. Get ready for the rapture.' And then the rapture happens! (By the way, if everything starts literally happening as the Futurist says, I'll be one of those Christians saying 'I was wrong about Revelation! I told you it was just a disputable matter and I could be wrong!') All the Christians disappear and come out of the graves exactly when they

---

[40] John MacArthur, *The MacArthur Study Bible*, (Nashville: Word Publishing, 1997), p. 2002

said. And so sure enough, the mega millions left behind (especially all those converted during that time), set their watches for exactly another 3½ years for when Jesus returns physically. No thief. No surprise.

The other Futurist view (no rapture before the tribulation), has both Christians *and* non-Christians going through a short, sharp, seven-year tribulation before Jesus returns. The *non-*rapture Futurist at least has only one second coming of Jesus. It's before his millennial reign on earth. Trouble is, it has the same problem of Jesus not actually coming *like a thief!* This second Futurist view can also narrow it down closely as to when Jesus returns. Once the seven-year tribulation begins and all these events literally unfold, when you see the seals, trumpets, locusts, the sea literally turning to blood, the moon, the sun and stars turning dark, then Christians would be able to track the beginning of the seven years from when Jesus is coming back. In other words, Jesus will *not come like a thief!* At least that would explain how the literal armies know when to prepare in advance for the upcoming battle of Armageddon against Jesus before he has even arrived. They all know when he is coming!

But does Jesus come like a thief or not? If all the events of Revelation are going to literally happen with hail and fire mixed with blood falling to earth, and not least, the armies of the world gathering in Palestine—this doesn't sound like Jesus is going to come unexpectedly like a thief. That is more like coming as the king of Moomba. Lots of warning, noise and preparation! Because of this ...

> Then they gathered the kings together to the place that in Hebrew is called Armageddon (16:16).

So the armies of the world prepare in advance to fight against Jesus. When he returns he overthrows them to set up his millennial reign. But how does he come like a thief? The two Futurist views are the most popular views among Bible-believing Christians today, and we can still affirm that those essentials of Jesus' return are not compromised. But these words of Jesus (in red letters) in 16:15 are meant to be taken seriously. Jesus really means he will come *unexpectedly*. I don't think these words are irrelevant to Christians, as though it is only speaking to those left behind in some future seven years. I think it speaks to all Christians now. And whatever you think about the tribulation, it should not undermine these words …

> 'Look, I come like a thief! Blessed is the one who stays awake and remains clothed, so as to not go naked and be shamefully exposed' (16:15).

Surely we were already familiar with these words. The first readers of Revelation in the seven churches recognize Jesus' words about their clothes and about coming like a thief. *He who is victorious will be dressed in white*, he told the church at Sardis. What else?

> Remember, therefore, what you have received and heard; hold it fast, and repent. But if you do not wake up, I will come like a thief, and you will not know at what time I will come to you (3:3).

Why the same warning as in 16:15? Because he is speaking to the same people! The churches! The whole of Revelation is addressed to them (1:4). This is a message to all Christians from as far back as the first century. I don't think it is a word only to a few in some future seven-year pocket when you can set your watch as to Jesus' return. Jesus really means it when he says *Look, I come like a thief!*

Isn't this the same warning Jesus gave on earth to his people when he likened his return to judge the world as coming like a thief? This is important because the Futurist view has Jesus coming like a thief, but not for Judgment, because according to the Futurist view, final Judgment of the wicked does not occur until *after* another 1000 years from Jesus' return (which comes *after* the tribulation). But what does Jesus say about coming like a thief? It's always in relation to the Judgment of the wicked! Not first to a rapture or tribulation, then a 1000-year reign, and only then Judgment. Rather he warns that when he comes back like a thief, he is returning to judge!

> 'But about that day or hour no one knows, not even the angels in heaven, nor the Son, but only the Father. As it was in the days of Noah, so it will be at the coming of the Son of Man. [What are the days of Noah? Leading up to Judgment.] For in the days before the flood, people were eating and drinking, marrying and giving in marriage, up to the day Noah entered the ark; and they knew nothing about what would happen until the flood came and took them all away. [Judgment.] That is how it will be at the coming of the Son of Man. Two men will be in the field; one will be taken and the other left. Two women will be grinding with a hand mill; one will be taken and the

other left. [The context is Judgment, like Noah's flood.] Therefore keep watch, because you do not know on what day your Lord will come. But understand this: If the owner of the house had known at what time of <u>night the thief</u> was coming, he would have kept watch and would not have let his house be broken into. So you also must be ready, because the Son of Man will come at an hour when you do not expect him' (Matt. 24:36-44).

There it is! The same 'coming like a thief' analogy that Jesus uses in relation to his return in Judgment! The apostle Peter said the same thing …

But the <u>day of the Lord</u> will come <u>like a thief</u>. The heavens will disappear with a roar; the elements will be destroyed by fire, and the earth and everything in it will be laid bare (2 Pet. 3:10).

The Day of the Lord, 'like a thief', is the cosmic end of the world! It's not a secret rapture. Nor is it an introduction to 1000 years of relative peace *before* the judgment of the wicked. It's the most public judgment you could ever imagine, like the one described several times in Revelation. Heavens disappearing with a roar, elements destroyed by fire, everything laid bare. New heaven and new earth. No one left behind, no reign of peace alongside unbelievers. Just terrible judgment. And 'like a thief' means it will be *unexpected!* Judgment is the context virtually *every* time our text 'like a thief' is brought up. It's the Day of the Lord! This phrase is in the verse just before our text …

They are demonic spirits that perform signs, and they go out to the kings of the whole world, to gather them for the battle <u>on the great day of God Almighty</u> (16:14).

How many *Great days of God Almighty* are there? This leads into our text **'Look, I come like a thief! Blessed is the one who stays awake and remains clothed, so as to not go <u>naked</u> and be <u>shamefully exposed</u>.'** What does he mean by *not go naked and be shamefully exposed?* That is what it's like getting caught out at Judgment. It sounds a whole lot worse than just being left behind and having seven (or 3½) more years to change your mind, or even another 1000 years on top of that to change your mind. I remember when I was an unbeliever, whenever religious people would talk about a seven-year tribulation or a 1000-year reign after Jesus comes back, I would say, 'So what's the urgency then? We unbelievers can just sit on the fence and if it turns out the way you said, I'll have seven years (or 1000 years) to change my mind.' No urgency. No thief. But Jesus' words in 16:15 are saying no more chances. You will be *naked* on the Judgment Day and be *shame*fully exposed. What does that remind you of?

> Multitudes who sleep in the dust of the earth will awake: some to everlasting life, others to shame and everlasting contempt (Dan. 12:2).

'Shame' again. It's all over. It's the Day of the Lord. Exposed shamefully (16:15)! It's Judgment! The Great Day of God Almighty (16:14). This leads into 16:15 which says Jesus is coming like a thief unexpectedly ... *to judge*. All in such a loud manner you can't miss it! No secrets here. Being caught up with the Lord and Jesus' loud return is the same day! The whole secret rapture view is built on this following text. (There are a couple of others that are used such as 1 Cor. 15:52 and John 14:2-3, but they don't provide any distinct rapture theology that couldn't just as easily be explained as Judgment Day or just dying and going to be with the Lord.) The rapture really hinges on the following text. So let's look at this one and ask if it really teaches a *secret* rapture ...

> According to the Lord's own word, we tell you that we who are still alive, who are left till the coming of the Lord, will certainly not precede those who have fallen asleep. For the Lord himself will come down from heaven, with a loud command [It's not just a command, it's a loud command.], with the voice of the archangel [angels typically announce judgment in Scriptures] and with the trumpet call of God [Trumpet calls. It's *very* loud!], and the dead in Christ will rise first. [People coming out of graves! Daniel 12 says it's all for judgment.] After that, we who are still alive and are left will be caught up together with them in the clouds to meet the Lord in the air. And so we will be with the Lord forever... [It's public and loud! It's final. Jesus returning publicly and then people are caught up to be with the Lord *forever*. This is the rapture I believe in! If you had never heard of a secret rapture, would this text really read 'secret rapture' or very public Day of Judgment? Paul settles the argument in the next verses.] Now, brothers and sisters, about times and dates we do not need to write to you, for you know very well that the day of the Lord will come like a thief in the night. [Same as our

text 16:15. What happens when he comes like a thief?] While people are saying, 'Peace and safety,' <u>destruction</u> will come on them suddenly, as labor pains on a pregnant woman, and they will not escape (1 Thess. 4:15-5:3).

Destruction! Suddenly! No escape! Judgment! No one left behind for more chances. Paul spells out that Jesus' return to gather his people is not secret but the Day of Judgment! It's all over. There is no inserting either a seven-year tribulation or 1000-years before the Judgment of the wicked arrives. It has arrived. *Destruction!* It will be like the days of Noah. No secret coming. You won't miss it! There will be trumpets blasting and a *loud* command. It's loud and it's public. It's exactly where Revelation started out.

> Look, he is coming with the clouds, and <u>every eye will see him</u> … (1:7).

No one will miss it! But they won't be counting down to it. It will be unexpected. Like a thief. 1 Thessalonians 4 (the so-called rapture text) has people being taken up, and others actually coming up out of the graves! All over the world, holes in the graves—to be raptured up secretly? No! That doesn't fit with the way Jesus describes it when people come out of the grave at that time.

> 'Do not be amazed at this, for a time is coming when <u>all</u> who are in their graves will hear his voice and come out—those who have done good will rise to live, and those who have done evil will rise to be condemned' (John 5:28-29).

Everyone rises together. Judgment has arrived! There is no room to insert 1000 years between the judgment of good and evil. When Jesus comes back that is it! So come back to our text where Jesus says he will *come like a thief!* The main thing to note about Jesus' words is the urgency, with no second chance. How do the parables of Jesus read in regard to his return? The parable of the virgins or the sheep and the goats? When the bridegroom returns, when the king returns, it's all over. Depart you who are cursed.

I started out affirming that all Christians agree on the main elements of end times. Jesus returns and wins. I stick with that.

But I find that I can't agree with all of the details of the Futurist view for four reasons in particular that I want to recap.

First, because of the overall text of Revelation, how it's written, who its written to and for what purpose.

Secondly, I believe the Scriptures teach one gospel for Jew and Gentile and all the promises of the OT are fulfilled (Yes and Amen) in Christ, in what Paul calls the mystery of the gospel where Gentiles are joined to Jews to become one (Eph. 3:6). Gentiles are grafted into the one vine so there is no need for a *separate* future salvation for Jews. That means today is the day to evangelize the Jews! Praise God many of his ethnic chosen are coming to faith today. His true remnant as promised. We need an urgency to evangelize them now, not leaving it to some future time.

Thirdly, I admit I am suspicious because of the origins of the Futurist view. Yes, it is the most popular view of the last 100 years, but the Futurist view began in the 1500s and was invented by a RC Jesuit priest, Francisco Ribera, for the sole purpose of trying to exonerate the Pope because the Reformers said the Pope was the Antichrist. With the Futurist concept, Ribera and other RCs could say to the Reformers, 'Haha, if it's all future you can no longer call the Pope the Antichrist because Revelation is all happening in the future.' And so no Protestant would touch futurism in Revelation for another 250 years until Samuel Maitland took it up in 1826 and then John N. Darby, the founder of the exclusive Brethren, began Dispensationalism in 1830. It's said the rapture idea popped into Darby's head one day. None of this proves it is wrong, but it makes me want to test the Scriptures even more cautiously to make sure I am driven only by the text of Scripture and not by man's ideas.

The fourth reason I have difficulty with the Futurist view is because of the importance of our text. Jesus will come not with your careful observation. He will not tell you the time, and most importantly when he comes it will be for judgment. He will *come like a thief* for the great Day of Judgment. And our text is a call to stay awake. '*Blessed is the one who <u>stays awake</u> and <u>remains clothed</u>, so as to not go naked and be <u>shamefully exposed</u>.*' Keep your clothes on. Stay alert! So you will not be exposed on that day. *Look, he is coming like a thief!* Who is coming like a thief? He is not sending the US military or even a myriad of angels. God incarnate is coming in person to judge. He is the same one who came first to deal with sin. If Jesus' death on the cross to take away your sin means so little to you that you can still dabble with sin and excuse it as in, 'We are all sinners,' then you *are* *not* ready. If your heart is not changed, if it means so little to you that God came down to be nailed up to receive God's eternal wrath on the cross, then you will be shamefully exposed. If you don't know him and have not been saved, you need to repent now! Why?

He comes like a thief. No one knows the hour. You have to be alert! Who is he saying this to? The same people he said it to back in Rev. 3. He is speaking to the churches. He is speaking to you! Jesus knows if you have been lukewarm. He knows if you are the one who has lost your first love. He knows if you have compromised with sexual immorality and followed Jezebel. (See 16:15, gotta keep your clothes on!) He knows if you have compromised with work or business (for the sake of what you can buy or sell). In fact, as we have gone through Revelation, there is no part of the tribulation that can't be said in some way to have unfolded before our eyes already.

When Jesus came the first time it had been prophesied in Scripture, and yet it unfolded before their eyes and they missed their Messiah! Can you believe it? They were looking for a literal fulfillment. They expected a Messiah who would come and defeat their enemies. They thought Jesus was going to come and literally kill the Romans. Even believers thought that, even the apostles had to be corrected. They missed it! But Jesus' coming was bigger than their *literal* earthly interpretation! The Messiah came to defeat their true enemies of sin, death, hell and Satan. Jesus came. The prophecies unfolded before their eyes and they missed it. All because it wasn't how they expected it to *literally* unfold. The same thing will happen again. People will miss it. Even believers will miscalculate. How do I know that? Because Jesus *said* to believers he will come like a thief. He will come when you don't expect it. We are 2000 years closer to the certainty of Jesus' return than when he said this. So what is the real point of this text? It's this ...

Jesus could come back any time. Not with your careful observation, but like a thief! And when he does, there will be no second chances, none left behind to rethink. Today is the day to repent. Today is the day to evangelize. On that day, it will be too late. Shamefully exposed. ...

'Look, I come like a thief! Blessed is the one who <u>stays awake</u> and remains clothed, so as to not go naked and be shamefully exposed' (16:15).

Study Questions

1. What does Jesus essentially mean by saying he will come like a thief?

2. How are these words understood in the four major views of Revelation?

3. Make a list of points all Christians are united on in their eschatology.

4. Why is this text problematic if Jesus is warning about a coming rapture?

5. Why is this an even greater problem for the rapture view if Jesus is warning of his return to judge and/or set up his millennial reign?

6. Does the Futurist view without the rapture fully alleviate this problem?

7. Where else is Jesus' coming like a thief mentioned in Revelation and how can that help us understand the meaning of this text?

8. Where else is this theme mentioned in the rest of the NT and how does it help us understand the meaning of this text?

9. Evaluate 1 Thess. 4:15-5:3. What does it teach about a rapture and about Rev. 16:15?

10. How did the Futurist view begin?

11. When Jesus came the first time it caught most people out and did not unfold as they expected. In what way might that make us see the gravity of Jesus' words in 16:15?

34

Armageddon
(Revelation 16:16)

We almost got to the battle of Armageddon last time, but it got delayed due to Defense Force budget cuts. We left off last time with Jesus saying he would come like a thief, *unexpectedly*. How will that fit with this enormous gathering of the world's armies for the battle of Armageddon? It's exactly the same problem we looked at in our previous chapter. If the world's armies gather in one place, won't that be the sign everyone will be able to use to calculate *exactly* when Jesus is coming back? It says right here in our text that before he comes there is a gathering for a war.

> Then they gathered the kings together to the place that in Hebrew is called Armageddon (16:16).

As we noted before, Har is Hebrew for mountain, and there is a place called Megiddo in Northern Israel. Har Megiddo (mountain of Megiddo), thus Armageddon. But those who know the geography say there is *no* mountain near Megiddo! It *has been* a battlefield of Canaan. This is the location where the good king Josiah was killed by Pharaoh Necho, king of Egypt (2 Kings 23:29-30). But there is no literal mountain of Megiddo. And to confuse us even further, if we line up other descriptions of this same battle in Revelation it is saying 'Armageddon' is 'the city God loves'. But the city God loves is Jerusalem or Mount Zion, not Megiddo as we read later in Revelation.

> ... and will go out to deceive the nations in the four corners of the earth—Gog and Magog—to gather <u>them for battle</u>. In number they are like the sand on the seashore. They marched across the breadth of the earth and surrounded the camp of God's people, <u>the city he loves</u>, ... (20:8-9).

The climax of the battle is at Jerusalem! In fact, OT prophecies of the final battle are always said to be at the city of Jerusalem and Mount Zion or the mountains that surround it. The literal area of Megiddo is about two days walk north of Jerusalem with *no mountain*. Did God get it wrong? Or did *we* get God wrong when God has been speaking to us all through Revelation using OT landmarks, events and cities to speak metaphorically into our lives and the future. In this very same chapter (Rev. 16) the Euphrates river and Babylon are used as reference points, though very few expositors suggest this is a reference to a literal Babylon or the literal Euphrates River, because Jeremiah predicted Babylon would never rise again. But we have seen OT physical locations that have much to teach us by way of *analogy* to describe even greater happenings for future events and places. What might Megiddo signal for the apostle John who saw this vision? It may not immediately jump out at us. Why? We don't know our OT as well as John. And we are far less familiar than he was with the landscape being described there in Israel. John knew there was no mountain at Megiddo, but *mountain* is the great OT metaphor (and Revelation metaphor) for kingdoms. OT Babylon is used in Rev. 16 as a metaphor for worldly cities that entice God's people. OT Euphrates River is used as a metaphor for a dividing boundary line that is hard to cross unless it dries up. So what might the mountain in Megiddo or Armageddon bring to the apostle John's mind?

While there is no 'mountain' of Megiddo and never has been, there *were* battles at Megiddo (see Judges 5:8, 19, 21). Megiddo was the place where Israel had literal battles, when God delivered his people. So Megiddo would symbolize for John the kind of battle where the LORD delivers his oppressed people, as he did at Megiddo in times of old.

So what is the battle of Armageddon? Is Jesus going to return to earth to 'duke it out' literally with human armies at the mountain of Megiddo in Israel, where there is no mountain anyway?

There are two things that seem to be contradicting each other with this view. The verse before our text, 16:15, says Jesus comes like a thief. That should set a framework for our understanding of Jesus' return. He will come unexpectedly. But the rest of the text talks about a concerted, conscious effort of earthly powers *gathering* together. How do you put these two together? If the Battle of Armageddon is so obvious, and the armies of all nations of the world line up in Megiddo in Israel before Jesus returns, then once again we have to say Jesus will not be coming like a thief! Fanfare and lots of announcement! If indeed all the armies of the world gathered like that, we would all know he is returning. We are told many things in Rev.16 of what leads up to this battle and it is *not* a physical military blood and guts battle. It's the frogs you need to worry about!

> Then I saw three <u>impure spirits</u> that <u>looked like</u> frogs; they came out of the <u>mouth</u> of the dragon, out of the <u>mouth</u> of the beast and out of the <u>mouth</u> of the false prophet. <u>They are demonic spirits</u> that perform signs, and <u>they</u> go out to the kings of the whole world, to gather them for the battle on the great day of God Almighty (16:13-14).

It is the demons that go out! *They go out.* It is the *demons* that gather the kings. Not physical frogs, but the ones that come out of the mouths of the Dragon, Beast and False Prophet. It's the mouth again (16:13)! All along we have seen that the main weapon of the Dragon has been his *mouth* (Rev. 12). He is the father of all lies. He was a liar from the beginning and has continued using that weapon of his mouth throughout history. That alone suggests the primary means of warfare will be lies and deception. Here it is again in the lead up to this battle in 16:13, *the mouth*. Demonic deception coming from the mouth of the father of all lies and his two cohorts, the Beast (worldly governing powers) and the False Prophet (false religion), as well as Babylon, the city connected with the two Beasts.

If we take the spiritual nature of this battle seriously, we are told outright it is demonic power that is driving the whole world to unite against Christ. Read the lead up to our text again in 16:13-14 and you will see it's a Dragon-powered, demon-powered, spiritual warfare!

The mouths of deception are the weapons of this war. The battle of Armageddon is both big enough to be worldwide, including all the powers of the earthly kings, *and yet* still not so obvious that everyone can plot Jesus' return and undermine Jesus' words that he will come like a thief. How? It is all about deception. Spiritual deception.

This can account for great armies joined even now! Remember our 200 million Chinese troops back in 9:16? Except they couldn't have been Chinese troops! The context was spiritual forces, that is, demonic powers. Now they are joining the powers of the world together in one concerted assault. Principalities and powers, the Dragon's minions, and there are myriads and myriads of them. Our struggle is not against flesh and blood! This means the demons are very conscious of the war they are making against Christ. They could be doing it before your very eyes now! They enlist the Beast (worldly governments) and the False Prophet (false religion) who are united in one thing—to make war against Jesus. But how could this all happen without it being so obvious that Jesus does *not* come like a thief? We looked at this before. You can bring all spiritual warfare down to one line from Jesus.

Whoever is not with me, is against me. Whose side are you on and whom are you uniting with? Those who are united with Jesus ... or those who are united against him? There is no in between!

Is this happening now? There is certainly an intensifying and unifying of the world's powers against the cause of Christ. How much more intense can it get before Jesus comes back? I don't know. Maybe a lot more can happen. Even if it can be said we are living in the greatest time of anti-Christian attacks in the world ever, even more than during the Roman Empire. Even if four out of five acts of persecution in the world are against Christians, can it get worse? Of course it could. Anything can happen! But don't forget this warning ... *Look, I come like a thief* (16:15)!

It won't come when you expect it. It won't come when it is so obvious that you will be able to watch the news and see all the world's armies gathering in Israel and know just when the Lord is returning. No. It will be a shock! A terrible, terrible shock. He will come like a thief!

The people of the world are not aware they are gathering for this battle. Why? They are *deceived* by the mouth! If you think of Revelation describing things in worldly terms and worldly events, then you have got this problem of worldly armies gathering in Israel to *surprise* Jesus who is supposed to be coming like a thief. Then Jesus arrives, donning his army fatigues and manning the army tank and shooting it out, albeit, he will have bigger and more powerful bullets because he will win (Rev. 19 says he actually rides a white horse). But if the battle is not against flesh and blood but against principalities and powers ... if this is a real war of wars ... not with little hobbits and their pea-shooters against Jesus, but a real war of eternity in the heavenly realms ... if it's like the one Revelation has been describing up to this point, with the real opponents of Jesus being the Dragon and his locusts from the Abyss ... principalities and powers of evil in the heavenly realms ... then Revelation has been pulling back the curtain on the real war which has been building up. All we have learned about the Dragon, the Beast and the False Prophet, who are unseen to the naked eye, has been exposed and revealed in Revelation. And it has revealed to us that the battle in life is not about human powers, armies or the Illuminati, or the Freemasons plotting. It's not the hobbits fighting Jesus! It's about this ... Satan!

Satan vs. Jesus. The Dragon, the Beast and the False Prophet. *They go out to fight! They gather the kings of the earth in their plot. They unite them.* All of life revolves around that one statement of Jesus as to how this war is fought ... *Whoever is not with me, is against me.* Those who are not for Jesus are strangely united in the cause of Satan against Christ. We noted previously how the atheist and the nice, ecumenical 'liberal Christian', the Buddhist and the radical Muslim all see themselves as so different. The average Aussie who blasphemes Jesus' name is so different from the preacher of prosperity or the pedophile priest. They are all so different. No, they're not! What does the hypocrite sitting in church each week holding on to his/her favorite addictions, and the guy who never darkens the door of church have in common? And even you, if you have not committed your life to Jesus, what do you have in common with rank, antagonistic, anti-Christian unbelievers? Aren't you all so different? No. You are all joined together for the Battle ... *Whoever is not with me, is against me.*

It's Jesus vs. Satan. All are on one side or the other. The Beast (governments) who has democracy and freedom but downgrades the values of Christ's ethics, joins with the False Prophet who puts it in religious garb. What do they have to do with the closed Muslim state which kills Christians? Everything, in the spiritual realm. Non-Christian religions, the passive Buddhist and extreme religious terrorist all join together against the Lord and his anointed. They all say you can be right with God without needing the Savior. Together they cry, 'You don't need Jesus!' They are against the need for a Savior. Anti-Savior. Anti-Christ! United! It's all about the fight over Jesus.

The frogs deceive people into joining forces against Christians in the home, at work, or in open persecution or marginalization (in other countries), unbeknown to them the *kings of the whole world* are *deceived* into the plan of the Beast to *stop* the message of Jesus. They make *war* against him—as though somehow, they really had a chance. People are fooled now to thinking they have a chance against Jesus. 'If Jesus is real and I have to face him, I will have a few things to say to him about how he runs this world. He won't call me to account. And he will have to let me into heaven because I have not been a bad person. I am as good as any Christian. And those Christians deserve to be put down. We don't want to get rid of Jesus, just his followers.' But Jesus said to Saul on the road to Damascus that when he was persecuting the church it was actually Jesus he persecuted. (Acts 9:5). Jesus also said *whatever you did to the least of these brothers and sisters of mine you did it to me* (Matt. 25:40). They united together in the war *against Jesus*.

So what is the actual battle of Armageddon? Remember the parallels that occur between the seals, trumpets and bowls. We are at the sixth bowl. What was going on at the same point with the sixth seal that might give us some idea of what is happening at the sixth bowl? The same *kings of the earth* are gathered together for what? What sort of battle?

> Then the <u>kings of the earth</u>, the princes, the generals, the rich, the mighty, and everyone else, both slave and free, hid in caves and among the rocks of the mountains ... For the great day of their wrath has come, and who can withstand it? (6:15,17).

It's the great day of wrath! This battle is the war to end all wars all right. The *kings of the earth* are there, and so is everyone else. The same battle is described in more detail later in Revelation where the Beast and the False Prophet are thrown into the fiery lake never to return. It's all over. No more time for the devil or people to oppose the Lord. The same kings of the earth are gathering ...

> Then I saw the beast and the '<u>kings of the earth' and their armies gathered together to wage war</u> against the rider on the horse and his army. [That is Jesus. It's the same scene as here in Rev. 16.] But the beast was captured, and with it the false prophet who had performed the miraculous signs on its behalf. With these signs he had

> deluded those who had received the mark of the beast and worshiped its image. The two of them were thrown alive into the fiery lake of burning sulfur (19:19-20).

It's the Day of Judgment! Does it get any more final than the Beast and False Prophet thrown into the fiery lake? But we knew that. We were already told what this battle was from the straightforward statement at 16:14. This is the great Day of the Lord Almighty! How many great days of the Lord are there? It's the day Jesus spoke about many times. It's the day when Jesus comes like a thief! It's the day that ends all days of this world. So I will disagree with the Futurist who says there is more than one Great Day and more than one Judgment. This is it!

So what is the actual battle of Armageddon? It's when Jesus comes to judge and rescue his people just as God did at Megiddo so long ago. Only this time he does it finally and fully. It is the great Day of Judgment and there will be no other. There will be no division of judgment for the good and wicked, separated by 1000 years. This battle is describing the battle of all battles that Jesus wins ... the Day of Judgment. See how our text fits with what went before it ...

> 'Look, I come like a thief! Blessed is the one who stays awake and remains clothed, so as to not go naked and be shamefully exposed.' [Isn't that a warning about judgment? And here it is.] ... Then they gathered the kings together to the place that in Hebrew is called Armageddon (16:15-16).

Armageddon is when Jesus comes to rescue his people, just as they had cried out in 6:10 ... *'How long, Sovereign Lord, holy and true, until you judge the inhabitants of the earth and avenge our blood?'* When the whole world thinks it has trounced Christ and his people, when even governments approve and legalize the ridicule and blasphemy of God's word and call evil good, and good evil; when all the kings and powers of politics, media, entertainment, and culture gather together in that sense ... that's when God's patience runs out! That's when Jesus returns to fight for his people. That is the great day. When the Lord's people hurt, he says 'when you persecute my people you are persecuting me'. When the secular world and false religion join together, tightening in closer and closer, and more and more nations are united in the one cause, anti-Christ, that is when the Lord finally says, 'Enough!' Then the Lord will begin the Battle *for his people* against those who opposed him. How? Judgment!

Rev. 16 is another camera angle of Rev. 11, when the church, the two witnesses that were lampstands (churches 1:20), were so devastated and beaten down, by whom? All the inhabitants of the *world* gathered, united… *every people, tribe, language and nation.* Remember they gloated over their victory in the battle! But remember in Rev. 11 that is when the voice of their Lord Jesus calls them up to heaven and says, 'let me take this over now'. The champion of the battle comes, and the enemies are in shock and horror. The witnesses were killed, but they are raised and taken up to be with the Lord, and what happens then in Rev. 11? Judgment! Followed by the seventh trumpet with that familiar judgment language of *flashes of lightning, rumblings, peals of thunder, an earthquake and a great hailstorm.* This is the kind of description and Scriptural judgment language that goes beyond just earthly human armies fighting it out.

So the nations gather together spiritually in their cause against Christ, but don't the nations physically gather together in this battle? Absolutely! Hasn't Scripture told us many times? *EVERY people, tribe, language and nation. Every knee will bow* and *every* tongue confesses. They gather all right! *All the nations!* Not one will be missing. And it turns out to be a shock for them that will reverberate through eternity.

The battle of Armageddon is one that Jesus wins. I don't believe he *provisionally* wins over *some* evil or partially wins with further battles to take place later, or you have to wait for another 1000 years before the wicked are judged. He comes back to judge with the sword of his mouth, and when Jesus comes back to fight for his oppressed people it *won't be a fair fight.* It won't be human armies having a sword or fistfight or with army tanks and Jesus manages to outfight them. It won't even be the best nuclear weapons man can make. It will not even be a contest. If it takes only one angel to kill 185,000 Assyrians (2 Kings 19:35), do you really think human armies could have a real contest against Jesus? This will be the war that ends all wars and all time of this world. But let's be clear. Jesus will *crush* his enemies!

Surely the main point of this passage is not how well we can picture a human WW3, but what *is* being taught is a pulling back of the curtain of the spiritual warfare that is *going on now* behind the kings or governments and peoples of the world *which leads* to the intensifying of the battle *up to* the day of Christ.

In our previous chapter, we noted that despite all the prophecies, people missed the first coming of Christ. Why? They expected him to come as a king who literally fought wars like King David. That's how they missed it. This misunderstanding will happen again. People are already falling for the same mistake. When Jesus returns, it won't be a military fight against humans on their level. For humans, it will be a totally devastating, *losing* battle. It will be what 16:14 calls the 'Great Day'. Who can stand? Only those who are truly *with* Christ. If it is a spiritual battle of intensity, then it doesn't have to be some science fiction-type future. The lead up to the battle of Armageddon can be happening right now in this world. Principalities and powers behind worldly governments are either directly or indirectly pitting themselves against Christ to put down the church. It's done overtly in most of the world, or subtly in the West with the pushing out the Christian faith. How intense does it become before Jesus returns? How could we possibly know? He comes like a thief! That means it will be unexpected. It won't come with your careful observation. It won't come in such an obvious way that you can figure it out! That is the point!

'Look, I come like a thief! Blessed is the one who stays awake and remains clothed, so as to not go naked and be shamefully exposed.' Then they gathered the kings together to the place that in Hebrew is called Armageddon (16:15-16).

Study Questions

1. How does 16:16 at first glance appear to be in conflict with 16:15?

2. Where does the name Armageddon come from?

3. If there are problems with a literal mountain in Megiddo, what might John have drawn on to understand its meaning in this context?

4. How can this text make sense of a world gathering, yet with Jesus still coming back unexpectedly?

5. How are the kings being gathered and in what way are they united?

6. What examples of this could we see happening now?

7. How do the parallels of Revelation in seals, trumpets and bowls help us to understand the nature and result of this battle?

8. Do all nations gather physically in this battle against Jesus? What is the result?

9. How does the spiritual perspective of this 'battle' affect your view of the world and end times?

35
The Seventh Bowl
(Revelation 16:17-21)

The battle of Armageddon arrived in our previous chapter and there wasn't an earthly military army in sight, let alone all the nations coming together in Megiddo in Palestine for WW3 to physically fight it out against Jesus. Those who take that view say we must interpret Revelation literally. But if that is the case, we are in trouble with what happens next, because that would mean Jesus returns to set up his 1000-year reign of peace and the islands roll up and mountains are fleeing. Why would all that be happening when the judgment of the wicked is not supposed to occur until the end of another 1000 years? Some who hold to that view seem to flee from a literal interpretation here, because it doesn't fit with the chronology of Jesus' 1000-year reign following immediately after his return, because the islands and mountains are disappearing!

But this is apocalyptic literature and it makes sense if is describing the Day of Judgment. I think this is about as big and final as the end can get. *It is done!*

> The seventh angel poured out his bowl into the air, and out of the temple came a loud voice from the throne, saying, 'It is done!' (16:17).

The battle of Armageddon arrived with the sixth bowl, and just as the sixth seal and the sixth trumpet introduced the Day of Judgment, which was then completed by the seventh seal and seventh trumpet, so too the seventh bowl *completes* the description of Judgment saying **It is done!**

Notice the seventh bowl is poured into the air. This might indicate judgment upon the forces of evil in the heavenly realms. We know that Satan is the prince of the *air* (Eph. 2:2). So again, we see those familiar images of the final judgment ...

> Then there came flashes of lightning, rumblings, peals of thunder and a severe earthquake … (16:18).

This has become familiar to us now. We have seen the same judgment at the end of the seals and trumpets. Remember at the seventh seal …

> Then the angel took the censer, filled it with fire from the altar, and hurled it on the earth; and there came peals of thunder, rumblings, flashes of lightning and an earthquake (8:5).

And at the end of the seventh trumpet…

> Then God's temple in heaven was opened, and within his temple was seen the ark of his covenant. And there came flashes of lightning, rumblings, peals of thunder, an earthquake and a great hailstorm (11:19).

Now we can see how clearly the seals, trumpets and bowls are parallel, giving different details and providing different camera angles of the same thing culminating in this same final judgment. As with this seventh bowl …

> Then there came flashes of lightning, rumblings, peals of thunder and a severe earthquake. No earthquake like it has <u>ever occurred since mankind has been on earth</u>, so tremendous was the quake (16:18).

Nothing like this **ever occurred since mankind has been on earth**. This might have sounded familiar to the apostle John from his favorite book of the Bible from his childhood Saturday school classes, the book of Daniel (the favorite of Revelation).

> 'At that time Michael, the great prince who protects your people, will arise. There will be a time <u>of distress such as has not happened from the beginning of nations until then</u>. [Same sort of prophecy.] But at that time your people—everyone whose name is found written in the book—will be delivered. Multitudes who sleep in the dust of the earth will awake: some to everlasting life, others to shame and everlasting contempt' (Dan. 12:1-2).

Again, it seems to be clearly dealing with the final Day of Judgment, rather than an introduction to 1000 years of relative peace …

> The great city split into three parts, and the cities of the nations collapsed. God remembered Babylon the Great and gave her the cup filled with the wine of the fury of his wrath (16:19).

The effect of this earthquake *like never before* is to destroy the great city, Babylon. What is the great city? Some say it is a revived ancient Babylon, but we have already noted God promised in Jeremiah that Babylon would never rise again. But consistent with what we have looked at in Revelation and Rev. 16 in particular, OT places are used as metaphors for God's future dealings. So, what is Babylon representing here? The OT Babylon was that great city which stood for everything that defied God in its pride, values, lifestyle, idolatry and oppression of God's people. The Lord brought the historical Babylon down for good. And he will do it to her latter-day likeness as well. We see even in this verse that Babylon represents more than just a single city. **The great city split into three parts, and the cities of the nations collapsed ...** *Cities*, plural, so at the very least, Babylon is connected with great cities throughout the nations.

This becomes a problem for the Preterist who understands the great city as Jerusalem being destroyed in AD 70. Our text says the *cities of the nations* are *also* collapsing, but we know that didn't happen in AD 70. However, if we take Babylon as a metaphor representing the great cities and their powers, be they economic, social and cultural powers driven by the Beast, then Babylon represents all these things—legalizing and promoting pleasures, luxuries and values which oppose Christ in the city where you live! These are the idols the people worshiped and in which they put their hopes and satisfaction. They said they're 'never gonna die', but they did die...**God remembered Babylon the Great and gave her the cup filled with the wine of the fury of his wrath.**

God remembered Babylon. The great complaint against God was that he doesn't care about evil. Why does he allow it? But God hasn't allowed it. People thought they were getting away with it, but God has not forgotten, not even one little detail. *God remembered!* ... And gave her the cup filled with ... his wrath! The full measure of God's anger poured out. Babylon is destroyed. It's full justice.

The Futurist (rapture) view says this seventh bowl is something that only comes on a portion of the population who are 'left behind' in a seven-year tribulation, to be followed by another 1000 years before judgment of the wicked. But I am suggesting this is the Day of Judgment of the wicked and it's a complete judgment. There is no fuller *cup of God's wrath* than this. He *gave her the cup filled with the wine of the fury of his wrath.* It is the full cup! This is it! *It is done* (16:17)! If this is not giving us a picture of the end, what is?

> Every island fled away and the mountains could not be found (16:20).

Surely this is the final day. The cosmos is being rolled up like a scroll. We encountered this back in the parallel of the seals ...

> The heavens receded like a scroll being rolled up, and every mountain and island was removed from its place (6:14).

As if to underline this is the end, it also happens to fit with the later description that everyone agrees is the end ...

> Then I saw a great white throne and him who was seated on it. Earth and sky fled from his presence, and there was no place for them (20:11).

It's the same scene. So I suggest this is the same final Day of Judgment, a cosmic cleanout being described in 16:20 ... **Every island fled away and the mountains could not be found.** Rather than some in-between event where Jesus returns to bring in 1000 years of peace, this is a cosmic and literally earth-shattering judgment bringing in the new heaven and new earth. It's describing the end with the same kind of language as elsewhere in the NT...

> At that time his voice shook the earth, but now he has promised, 'Once more I will shake not only the earth but also the heavens.' The words 'once more' indicate the removing of what can be shaken—that is, created things—so that what cannot be shaken may remain (Heb. 12:26-27).

This is the same end being described, and it gets worse ...

> From the sky huge hailstones, each weighing about a hundred pounds, fell on people. And they cursed God on account of the plague of hail, because the plague was so terrible (16:21).

Another reason this is a scene of finality of judgment is that the seventh bowl is said to bring to completion God's wrath. We were told this when we were first introduced to the seven bowls …

> I saw in heaven another great and marvelous sign: seven angels with <u>the seven last plagues</u>—last, because with them <u>God's wrath is completed</u> (15:1).

It doesn't get any more 'end' and *completed* than the seventh bowl. So I am disagreeing with the view that this is not the end, and God's wrath upon the wicked will not take place for another 1000 years after this. I'm taking these words seriously: *with them God's wrath is completed!* Completed literally means completed.

But at this judgment something extraordinary happens. Even though the complete wrath and judgment is being poured out, what do the people who are receiving this experience do? … **<u>They cursed God</u> on account of the plague of hail, because the plague was so terrible.**

If this massive judgment is coming and you knew it was God, wouldn't you kind of plead for mercy? But they actually cursed God! This fits with what we have seen before in Revelation, when unbelievers are receiving judgment and we are told: *but they would not repent of their sin.* What is exposed here is that men loved their sin even to the point that when facing judgment, they would rather curse God than acknowledge him. They are not even looking for forgiveness. That day has gone.

Here again is another confirmation of how believers could enjoy heaven, knowing people who are receiving judgment. The Day will expose how much people *hated* God and loved the sin that attacked God, rejecting forgiveness. Even when God brings a judgment upon sin, their hearts harden even more. Even *cursing God*. When this happens, you will see how rich their just desserts are. Just like God's judgment on Jerusalem of old, when the Lord assured his people they would be consoled (Ezek. 14:22-23) with the knowledge that the LORD'S judgment was right. So too, when you see men cursing God even to his face, you will be consoled that God did the right thing. Humans claim they hate evil. They shake their fist at God for not doing enough about it. But they never hated the very root of evil — human rebellion against God! They hate the consequences of sin, but they *love* rebellion against God. They are a part of it. They blame God for the very thing they do themselves. They say, 'Why doesn't God do something about it?' And when God does, they curse him. What we have in this picture of judgment is what God thinks of evil and what he will do about it. He drops 100lb (45kg) hailstones on men. Is it metaphor? On that day, people will wish it was only literal! At least then they would be squashed out of having to face the completion of God's wrath. The largest ever recorded hailstone is 2lb (1kg), 8" (20cm) in diameter. So 100lb might be 3-4 yards/meters in diameter. It's hard to imagine there would be anything left after getting hit by one of those for people to even be able to curse God.

Most people don't curse God outwardly. Most cursing of God is not even done consciously. When people use God's name as an expletive or curse word (OMG), most of them don't even think of it as cursing God, even though it is clearly breaking the third commandment. Perhaps that is the worst cursing of all. Cursing someone who means so little to you that you are unaware of it.

Perhaps the most insidious cursing of God is the inner attitude of the heart. Here is one for self-examination. Are you a secret curser of God? 'Never,' you say. But when you inwardly resent God's providence in your life or complain about your lot as though 'bad luck' brought it about, that grumbling is against God. Or do you inwardly resent God's commands or see them as restrictive? 'God's commands keep me from the doing the good stuff.' You want to be free from judgment, so you love the idea of Jesus the Savior. You would never outwardly grumble against God's commands, you would never dream of *outwardly* cursing God, but inwardly you would rather be free from the commands of God. You see them as a shackle and a burden. You might have outward obedience to God, but inwardly you resent the restriction. That is inward cursing and it will fully come out on this day described here. You have even deceived yourself, but on that day the heart is exposed. *Then* you will *openly* curse God! And his judgment will fall upon you ... *and they cursed God.* If that is you, then you must be born again! When you are born again you *believe* in Jesus and what he did on the cross for *your* sin. It affects your heart. Then you come to hate what caused Jesus to be nailed to the cross. You no longer see it as the 'good stuff' that God is keeping you from.

I still vividly recall the testimony of one of our church members making her profession of faith coming into our church membership.

There was not a dry eye in the place the way she described that after a lifetime living in the lesbian lifestyle how she turned to Christ. But it was her *motive* to turn from sin that was so powerful when she said; 'I can no longer live in a way that put pain on my Savior on the cross.' Implication: I don't care if I have to remain single the rest of my life. I love Jesus more. That is someone who is born again. They have a whole new attitude to sin. Sin is no longer the good stuff you can't have. When you really believe, the commands of God are no longer restrictions. You will hate sin and what Jesus had to go through to free you from it.

Years ago, I was mentoring a heroin addict, and the way he described his addiction was analogous. He said, 'I was able to give it up for *two years,* but in all of that time I never really came to hate it. Even while I was running from it, I had a secret desire for it. I just hated the consequences of it, but I never hated it.' So he resumed his habit.

If that is your relationship with sin, then you haven't seen the Savior by faith. You are not a believer. You must be born again. You are still one of those who curse God. Ask yourself, 'Do I love my addictions or the Savior?' What about those temptations? I didn't say they weren't tempting. There is money (or better still, all the good stuff it buys), coveting the better life, car, house, clothes, or addiction to pornography, lust of the eyes, or gambling, swearing, smoking, alcohol or drugs. But there are also the subtler secret addictions such as an unforgiving heart, pride, jealousy, envy and lying. I am not asking if you have ever fallen for them. I'm not asking if you sin or even if the temptation pounds you severely at times. But do you hate sin? Or do you wish those restrictions were not there. Do you unknowingly curse God?

Wives, do you secretly hate the idea of submission to your husbands? 'Well if he loved me as he ought, I wouldn't.' And husbands do you resent having to give yourself up for your wife? 'Well I would if she just did her bit.' It's God you are resenting.

What is exposed on this day when people openly curse God is that many of them are legalists. A legalist is someone who tries to be saved by the law. We think of legalists as those who make great demands with strict adherence to their view of the law to prove you are really Christian. It's a 'salvation by works' mentality. But that is not the only form of legalism. Legalists can be among the laziest people of all who obey next to none of God's commands. They don't care about holiness; they perhaps don't even attend church regularly. They don't bother with basic disciplines of a gospel call and yet they are just as much legalists. They still have a salvation by works. It's just that they have a much *lower standard* of how many works they need to be right with God. They respond to a rebuke from the word of God with, 'It doesn't matter. God knows my heart.' In other words, they still think they are right with God because of who *they* are, not who Jesus is. They still have a standard of works for a 'real Christian'. It's only that their standard of legalism is much *lower* than other legalists. But it's the same principle. The bottom line is they don't hate sin and they haven't truly believed in the Savior. They are satisfied to 'do enough' or 'believe enough'. Their phony love of Jesus does not produce hatred for sin … only hatred for having to obey. And without knowing it, they curse God. That is why there will be shocks on this day. Cursing will come from the mouths of some who outwardly looked like Christians, but on this day… *they cursed God* …

You hear it said, 'Oh, he loves the Lord.' But if he lives carnally or doesn't hate the sin that Jesus died for, that is not love for Jesus. Christians might debate the finer points of how we carry out the Christian life and not all agree on the detail, but the question is, 'Do you hate sin and love Jesus?' What happens when you run that Ephesians 4:17-5:20 test by your television shows or movies, your music or computer games? (No unwholesome talk, no course joking or obscenity and not even a hint of sexual immorality.) Do you rejoice that the Savior gave you Ephesians to help you to find out what pleases the Lord? Or do you curse God for putting restrictions on your entertainment or the way you speak? The legalist says, 'Why do I have to bother with all that, I'm not hurting anyone!' The legalist is still trying to justify himself by his works and leaves out the fact that it is not just about 'hurting anyone', but it is God we sin against first and foremost.

What about all those illegal downloads? Do you hate even the clothing stained by sin? Or does the forbidden free fruit taste sweet? Do you resent having to pay for stuff you can get for free? Curse those goody two-shoes who would restrict me. No, it's God you curse. The unconverted soul sees the Christian faith as just a bunch of oppressive rules. And they curse God by complaining that some

Christians are just too strict. Why *does* the Christian life seem so strict? Because you must be born again. If you don't hate sin, if you hate denying yourself and you don't rejoice in following the Savior and being counted worthy to suffer for his name, you curse God. This text shows that some people will do that all the way to the Day of Judgment.

You can keep yourself outwardly clean. You don't smoke or swear or steal or cheat on your spouse, and you tithe and go to church. All the outward things real Christians do. Good works! But if, like the heroin addict, you never really hated your sin, you have never really *believed* in the cross! You must be born again!

If this describes you, you've never seen how much *God* hated sin! So much so that he drops 100lb hailstones on sinners on the Day of Judgment. That's how evil God sees sin! And if you don't hate what God hates, you are not converted! Most of all, you've never seen the love of God. You've never seen the earthquake and the 100lb hailstones. Because if you did believe, you would see it was *Jesus* who was pounded from above! The eternal wrath of God pounded and crushed *Jesus!* If 100lb hailstones are a description of the kind of judgment a man receives on that day, multiply it by the world! Jesus took the sins of the *world* upon him. What is the cry here on the Day of Judgment when this terror is completed? *It is done!* (16:17).

That is like the cry of Jesus from the cross. *It is finished!* The full wrath of God poured out on *him!* Judgment completed. It came upon Jesus for all who truly believe in him. If you are not at the point where you hate the sin that put Jesus on the cross, then you need a new heart. And only the Lord can give it to you. Call upon the name of the Lord! Seek him with all your heart.

A young woman I met years ago said she didn't believe in God but knew that if Christianity was true, she needed to know. So she asked me what should she do? I told her pray every day and read the Bible and ask the Lord to convert her heart. For nearly a year she read her Bible and prayed and would meet me every two weeks saying, 'Nothing happening, not working'. I told her to keep seeking because the Lord promises everyone who seeks will find. So she kept on calling upon him every day and then one day she came to me jumping for joy! 'It happened. I found him!' She was thoroughly converted and went on to do missionary work in China. All who call on the name of the Lord will be saved!

If you don't hate sin, pray for a new heart. Seek and go on seeking. Don't give up. Pray for God to show you what he really thinks of sin. Look at this text and see those hailstones falling. Pray to trust only in the Savior to take the weight of those hailstones in your place. Right now, your sin is either taken away on that cross 2000 years ago, or it is still attached to your body, and if you stay that way you will stand before God with it. But the promise is everyone who seeks will find (Matt. 7:8), and when you find God, you won't find the God who will bring on you the earthquake to end all earthquakes, or pound you with 100lb hail stones. What you will find is the most amazing love, that he would give his only Son to become sin for us, to take that great weight of wrath. How deep the Father's love for us…

Study Questions

1. What elements of this text make it difficult to accommodate this event followed by a 1000-year reign before Judgment of the wicked?

2. How does the parallel of seals and trumpets help us interpret this text?

3. Why can't the great city Babylon be literal Babylon?

4. What does Babylon represent?

5. What difficulty does this text provide for the Preterist view?

6. What are different ways people curse God?

7. What does this text tell us about how God feels about sin?

8. Why is your attitude to sin related to whether you believe?

9. Give different ways legalism can be expressed.

10. As far as you know your own heart, do you hate sin?

ABOUT THE AUTHOR

Bill Medley spent 15 years in the entertainment industry working as a comedian and actor. He was not brought up in a religious home and had no desire to ever become part of any 'organized religion'. In fact, he actually believed "Religion is for fools" and occasionally used religion as the butt of his jokes in his stand-up comedy.

No one shared the gospel with Bill, but he always thought one day he would investigate the religions of the world as an academic exercise. However, by age 32 and some life experience, he was ready to investigate in a deeper way. He set about reading the Scriptures of the five major world religions including the Bible, the Buddhist Scriptures, the Hindu Scriptures and the Koran. The uniqueness of Christ and his claims brought him to faith.

He has been the Pastor of Frankston Presbyterian Church in outer Melbourne Australia since 2006. He is married to Diana and they have three sons, Rick, Luke and Joshua.

OTHER BOOKS BY BILL MEDLEY